THE **SMASHING** BOOK #4

NEW PERSPECTIVES ON
WEB DESIGN

THANK YOU!

To all the members of the Smashing Magazine community:
We truly appreciate your support. It means the world to us.
YOU mean the world to us.

Published 2013 by Smashing Magazine GmbH, Freiburg, Germany.
Printed in the EU.

Cover Design and Illustrations created by Anna Shuvalova.
Proofreading: Owen Gregory, Iris Lješnjanin.
Editing and Quality Control: Vitaly Friedman.
eBook Production: Cosima Mielke.
Layout: Markus Seyfferth.
Typefaces used: Elena by Nicole Dotin (Process Foundry),
Ideal Sans by Hoefler & Frere-Jones.

The Smashing Book #4: New Perspectives on Web Design was written by Vitaly Friedman,
Harry Roberts, Nicholas Zakas, Christian Heilmann, Tim Kadlec, Mat Marquis,
Addy Osmani, Aaron Gustafson, Paul Tero, Marko Dugonjić, Corey Vilhauer,
Rachel Andrew, Nishant Kothary and Christopher Murphy.

The reviewers are: Sindre Sorhus, Addy Osmani, Brian Arnold, Sean Coates,
Sergey Chikuyonok, Ben Dowling, Inayaili de León, Jonathan Snook,
Andy Davies, Nicholas C. Zakas, Dan Ariely and Tim Brown.

Idea and concept: Vitaly Friedman, Sven Lennartz.

All links featured in this book can be found at smashed.by/links.

Smashing Book #4. Crafted by the Smashing Magazine's team and well-respected
members of the design community with care and love. http://smashed.by/sb4

TABLE OF CONTENTS

TABLE OF CONTENTS

BY VITALY FRIEDMAN

PREFACE

THE BEAUTY OF THE WEB lies in its longevity and flexibility. Time never stands still in Web development, and the more time you spend on the Web, the more frantic the pace seems to become. Some of you might have started developing websites a while back, others have jumped into Web design just recently; but all of you have probably seen techniques and practices coming and going, tools and libraries praised and neglected, trends appearing and falling over the cliff.

The Web is dynamic and versatile—coding techniques aren't black or white, and our decisions always emerge from those shady gray areas. There are no perfect solutions, and usually it's a matter of reaching a sound compromise within given constraints. Web design today requires pragmatic, open-minded approaches.

This book will not change everything you know about Web design and development. Neither will it revolutionize your workflow or your tools. But hopefully it *will* challenge you to think a bit differently about how you approach design problems and how to meaningfully solve them in real life.

Smashing Book #4 is a practical book for professional designers and Web developers. It doesn't discuss flat design or skeuomorphism, and it isn't concerned with visual styles or trends.

With *New Perspectives on Web Design*, we want to explore handy techniques and smart strategies derived from actual projects. Covering both technical and design aspects of UX design, this book provides insights into scalable front-end architecture, obscure back-end tricks, responsible responsive Web design and performance optimization, but also adaptive interfaces, Web typography, content strategy, customer support, the creative process, and the psychology of human behavior on the Web.

We can't foresee what is coming up next. But we can look closely at the state of the art today, and keep improving our workflow with small, gradual enhancements—learning from our colleagues and from our own experiences. And this is exactly why this book exists—to keep up with, enrich and improve the wonderful, flexible, unpredictable Web that has become an integral part of our lives over all these years.

Chapter

01

Modern CSS Architecture and Front-End Development

Written by Harry Roberts

CHAPTER ONE · BY HARRY ROBERTS

MODERN CSS ARCHITECTURE AND FRONT-END DEVELOPMENT

I N THIS CHAPTER WE ARE GOING TO TAKE A WHIRLWIND TOUR of a new approach to building more powerful front-ends for the Web today. After the somewhat erratic introduction (there's a lot to cover, and so little time!), we'll look at the nitty-gritty of structuring CSS for modern, powerful websites. Our journey starts, somewhat unexpectedly, in England, in the 1700s...

The Luddites

The Industrial Revolution, which occurred loosely between the mid-1700s to mid-1800s, signalled a major shift in the world's commercial manufacturing techniques; traditional hand-working and craftsmanship made way for newer processes involving machines and automation. In early 19th-century England, increasing mechanization gave rise to a group known as the Luddites, a formation of artisanal textile workers — craftsmen and skilled labourers — whose jobs were slowly but surely being made obsolete by the new wave of machine-led manufacturing[1]. The Luddites were an unfor-

---

1 Inayaili de León gave a fantastic talk at DIBI Conference entitled "The Mechanical Revolution" back in 2011. This talk speaks in much greater detail about the plight of the Luddites, as well as likening their agenda to that of Web developers. I urge you to look it up: https://vimeo.com/27487587.

tunate, though, in hindsight, probably not unexpected byproduct of the Industrial Revolution.

The machines being introduced could do the work of ten skilled workers, and at ten times the pace. Their slow, handcrafted work was being replaced with the desire for more powerful and profitable means of production. This shift, naturally, didn't sit so well with the workers, who increasingly found themselves ousted from roles they had held for decades. The Luddites are a shining example of people resisting change, and paying dearly for it. Change is good, change is difficult, change is necessary, and change will happen — it's how we deal with it that counts.

The Web is changing. Are you keeping up?

The Web Then

There was a time (not so long ago, really) when websites were built using tables for structure, and markup like <font color="red">Foo</font> was used to apply purely visual features. These techniques stayed around for quite a long time.

I started to get into Web development quite recently, around 2007 or so. I was incredibly lucky that the days of tables for layout were long gone, and I strode straight into an arena where technologies like CSS were considered the standard. Each article I read spoke of semantics, clean HTML, and using as few IDs and classes as possible.

CSS made its entrance years before my interest in building websites. Tables were phased out and replaced with a far more powerful and suitable language. For many this was a huge change from what they were used to; for me it was just how things were done when I arrived on the scene. The transition from table-based to CSS-based layouts seemed, on the whole, a welcome change. It took a while for some developers to make the move because, as is always the case with front-end development, people were largely at the mercy of the browsers their audiences were using.

I remember one tale from an older developer, who built a site in a mixture of tables and CSS in the hope of making the transition more gradual.

Despite how long the transition did (or didn't) take, people by and large seemed to love CSS. This was a huge change in development and production workflows that almost everyone — certainly everyone I know personally — welcomed with open arms. CSS could let us do so much more than we were used to: we could build things faster, smarter, bigger and better. We embraced the change and things were better for it.

Despite these shifts in technology, though, websites were still typically quite small affairs. A dozen years ago, websites were often just a few pages used to show off pictures of your cat and auto-play your favourite Rush song; now websites are often hundreds, if not thousands of pages in size and generate tens of billions of dollars a year.

The move from tables to CSS was a change of technology, but there was very little change in landscape; sites fifteen years ago were typically all relatively similar in size and purpose, regardless of what they were built upon. The Web then was a much humbler little place, and the advice we were given regarding Web standards and CSS and semantics and clean code and avoiding extra markup and classes held true. But that was then; the Web has changed — and it is still changing — but I worry that we've stopped changing with it. Our best practices were overhauled around a decade ago but we don't seem to have taken another look at them since.

The Web Now

Today's Web is quite a different beast: websites are typically far larger, far more complex, far more important (they are often comprise people's sole means of income), and make a lot more money.

With companies like Amazon posting a 2012 revenue of over $60 billion[2], Twitter boasting 200 million active users[3], Google employing almost

---

2 http://smashed.by/amzn-stock
3 https://blog.twitter.com/2013/celebrating-twitter7

54,000 people[4], and even the company I work for — Sky Bet — making over a hundred million pounds a year[5] and employing 450 people solely from money made online, it would be naive to think we can treat websites today as we did ten or even five years ago. However, a lot of us still do.

With websites getting bigger, their dev teams growing larger, and their goals becoming more tightly defined and, I dare say, more important, we need to take another look at how we actually build them. It's no longer practical to hand-craft code, and pursue semantic purity and clean markup; a much more rapid, powerful and pragmatic approach is needed. We need to change *again*.

The books, articles and blog posts written on Web standards over the last decade or so all contained relevant, sound advice — there is no denying that — but the Web has changed at a much faster rate than our best practices have. We've outgrown the methods of years gone by and it's now up to us to update the unwritten rules of Web development to fit the new landscape. Bigger, app-like sites that serve millions of users a day and generate billions of dollars of income require an approach that early-2000s advice simply cannot offer us. We need to embrace another change in attitude, one that takes into account the different nature of the Web today, and also that of the people involved in it: your stakeholders.

Note: Nicolas Gallagher recently gave a great talk at W3Conf about "Questioning Best Practices"[6]. It is well worth a watch.

The Three Stakeholders

By and large, with any Web project, there are three main stakeholders, the three groups of people to whom the site matters the most. This is, of course, a massive generalization, but I find that, for the most part, it holds true:

---

4 http://investor.google.com/financial/tables.html
5 http://smashed.by/skybet
6 http://smashed.by/best-pract

1. *The client:* The person paying you to build the site, the person paying your bills.
2. *The users:* The people who will be using the site that the client is paying you to build.
3. *You:* The developer, who has to work with, scale and maintain the site.

You need to remember these stakeholders and make sure you do the right things for the right people for the right reasons.

THE CLIENT

The client doesn't care about semantics. The client doesn't care about how many IDs and classes you have or haven't used. They don't want to know that you can't quickly duplicate a piece of content because you used an ID and IDs aren't reusable. It's not their problem to worry about things like that, and it's your responsibility to shield them from these things.

The client cares about how quickly and efficiently (and therefore cheaply) you can update their site, they care about how reliable and robust it is, how nicely it works on a wide variety of browsers and devices.

THE USER

Users don't care about code: we all use sites day in, day out, that use terrible-looking code (though not necessarily terrible code in itself). Even as developers we have no concern over how well-written Facebook's or Google's markup is; we care that the sites and services we want to use are fast and reliable. Code is to a website what bricks and mortar are to a building: very important, but not really what people turn up to see.

YOU, THE DEVELOPER

You care about how well-documented the codebase is, how nice it is to work with, how naturally it can scale, how easily it can be maintained, how quickly you can make changes, how effectively you can fulfill clients' requests.

The client doesn't care if you managed to avoid using any classes and wrote no extraneous markup, but if using two classes and an extra div makes your job easier, and makes the site easier to maintain, you should opt for the extra code every time. There is no use making your life more difficult because you think that avoiding an extra few characters of HTML is the right way to go. Be kind to yourself and your team.

KEEP THE RIGHT PEOPLE HAPPY

By keeping all of these three stakeholders in mind, we can begin to make more informed decisions about how we write our front-end code: users don't care if we've written semantic classes; clients don't care how many IDs we've used; and only we care about how nice our code is to work with.

In reality, developers are the only people who really care about code. Write it for yourself, but write it to be fast (for the users) and robust (for the client). Everyone benefits in some way from good code, but users and clients only benefit from its results. Developers benefit directly from the quality of the actual code itself (sensible naming conventions, plenty of comments, and so on).

Takeaway: The code we write has to serve more people than just ourselves, and in different ways. We need to write fast, robust code for clients and users, and maintainable, sane code for ourselves.

Some Misconceptions About CSS

There are still some greatly misunderstood aspects of CSS (and HTML) that — at a fundamental level — will affect the way you approach building websites. These misconceptions need acknowledging and fixing. In so doing, we will free ourselves from years-old dogma and feel a lot more liberated and empowered to build bigger, faster, more powerful front-ends.

I honestly believe it was realizing, understanding and subsequently ditching these misconceptions that took me from being able to merely write CSS to being able to scale CSS for massive websites.

SEMANTICS

Our first misconception involves semantics. Semantics — at least where front-end development is concerned — is a greatly misunderstood and overdefended area. Semantics in front-end developments concerns whether to use a div or a header, or if some text should be a paragraph or a heading, or whether a list is to be ordered or unordered, and so on.

Semantics in front-end development is about elements and not attributes. It's about machines (screen readers, browsers, assistive technologies, bots) gleaning meaning from the elements we use to mark up our documents. Semantics is not about how we name our classes or IDs; the only things to gather meaning from classes and IDs are humans. Anything else that reads or accesses a class or an ID merely matches it; it does not derive any meaning from them at all. This, straight from the HTML(5) spec:

Particular meanings should not be derived from the value of the ID attribute.

Take the two following snippets:

```
<div class="heading-one">My page title</div>
```

and:

```
<h1 class="red">My page title</h1>
```

The first is an improper semantic implementation: the author should be using an h1 element to mark up their page's title, not a div. Even though the class used is highly descriptive, this is not where the semantics lie. A machine will gain nothing at all from that snippet of markup.

The second snippet is far more semantic: a machine reading this will know that it's a top-level heading. The fact that the author used a class of red is entirely irrelevant to any machine. If there is a corresponding .red{} rule set in the CSS then the browser will style this heading no matter what.

Machines do not discriminate at all against the classes you use because they do not understand them; it is merely their job to match them.

SEMANTICS VS. SENSIBLENESS

When most people talk about semantics, what they're really referring to is *sensibleness*. As we have ascertained, classes and IDs have no bearing on semantics whatsoever. A class of red is neither semantic nor not semantic, because classes are not found on the semantic spectrum. A class of red, however, is probably quite ill-advised.

When choosing names for your classes, forget about the idea of semantics and look more at their longevity. How long will this name continue to make sense? How long will it stay relevant? How much sense will it make in six months?

Taking the .red example further, it is clear to see why this is an unwise name for a class. Imagine you're working on an e-commerce site and you need to style a price differently because it is a special offer, like so:

```
<strong class="red">$99.99</strong>

.red {
    color: red;
}
```

If that style just happens to involve the color red then a class and selector of red might be used, perhaps inadvisably. If, for whatever reason, you want to change all special offer prices to be blue then you'd end up with something like this:

```
<strong class="red">$99.99</strong>

.red {
    color: blue;
}
```

A machine would not struggle with this at all — a machine's only duty is to match and style the classes. What does get awkward, however, is when humans (that is, developers) start working with this code. It is confusing to see a class of red which actually makes something blue. This is not a sensible class, one that has little longevity and that won't always make sense.

A far better option would be:

```
<strong class="special-offer">$99.99</strong>

.special-offer {
    color: blue;
}
```

It doesn't matter if the special offer is red, green, blue or purple — that selector will always make sense to a human. It is a sensible, though not semantic, class.

Sensibleness is about ease of maintenance, longevity and how much sense something makes to a human being, because humans are the only things to take any amount of meaning from class names.

THE SEPARATION OF CONTENT AND STYLE

Traditionally, the separation of content and style refers to splitting the markup and styling of content into distinct languages. It does not refer to keeping the two languages *physically* separate.

Way back when, we wrote HTML like `<font color="red">Foo</font>`. The issue here is that HTML both marks up and styles this content, when we should use a distinct language for each. This is why CSS was born: to separate these concerns. The separation of content and style refers purely to using separate and independent technologies for each role, *not* to avoiding presentational classes in your markup.

The previous example displays a lack of separate content and style; the following example has its content and style separated perfectly:

```
<a href="#" class="big-red-button-with-white-text">Foo</a>
```

It's just pretty poorly named. *The separation of content and style is about separating content and styling languages, not their locations.*

By understanding this, you begin to see that this misconception has led to a blanket and dogmatic hatred of any form of presentational classes. Just because classes might read as presentational does not equate to mixing content and style; in fact it comes back around to our points above: it's all about how sensibly you're doing things.

A snippet of HTML like `<div class="red">` ... `</div>` has perfectly decoupled content and style, it's just not very sensible.

Takeaway: We've still got a couple of misconceptions surrounding CSS. Recognizing and dropping them is very liberating and opens up the possibilities to build better front-ends.

A Change in Attitude

By now, we should find ourselves in a frame of mind better equipped for building more powerful, pragmatic front-ends.

If we accept that the Web is a much more serious environment than it was ten years ago, and if we accept that the code we write has to serve a number of different people in a number of different ways, then I don't think it's too much to assume that we also accept that we need a change in attitude.

As Nicole Sullivan once said, "Our (CSS) best practices are killing us[7]"; our desire to write markup that doesn't use any classes serves no one, and often causes ourselves problems.

The pursuit of clean markup and semantic classes and all that came with it was well-intentioned but helped no one. It led to verbose, difficult to maintain, tangled style sheets. The price of omitting a few classes

---

7 Nicole Sullivan, "Our (CSS) Best Practices Are Killing Us", (April 28, 2011).
   http://www.stubbornella.org/content/2011/04/28/ our-best-practices-are-killing-us/

was having to write giant, convoluted selectors to target these orphaned, unnamed DOM elements. As the saying goes, we robbed Peter to pay Paul. We were writing clean markup at the cost of writing verbose, messy and convoluted CSS. We just moved the mess somewhere else.

Today's Web requires a more informed and less dogmatic view of things like semantics. We need to realize that our actual code benefits no one other than other developers, so we need to write it for them. We need to realize that users and clients just want fast, reliable, robust websites. The Web is growing bigger and bigger, faster and faster. Code is no longer a craft, it's a power tool.

I believe that the sooner we drop these well-intentioned but misguided ideals of yesteryear, then we can be more liberated and able to build bigger, better quality sites in a more timely and responsive manner. As I mentioned before, it was recognizing and dropping these old-fashioned ideals that made me the developer I am today.

LISTEN TO DEVELOPERS

One of the biggest changes in attitude I made was moving from being a design-led front-end developer to being an *engineering*-led front-end developer. Just a few years ago, I used to be a hardline semantics guy. I believed that my markup should be handcrafted and clean and perfect, and that avoiding classes and using clever selectors was awesome, and the sure sign of a great developer!

Then I started my job as senior UI developer at BSkyB, where I was the only front-end developer in a company full of incredibly talented software engineers. I'd moved from an agency-like company where other front-end developers shared the same ideals — the yearn for lean markup and semantics — and now I was in a company with no one who thought like that at all, and I was working on sites that I would have to scale and maintain for years to come. Being in this environment, surrounded by engineers, really opened my eyes.

I picked up so much from these guys, things like abstraction, DRY-ness, object-oriented development, performance, extensibility. I learned firsthand from some of the cleverest people I've ever met that code isn't about prettiness, or being expressive, or avoiding something just because. I learned that you don't get points for being pretty, you get points for being powerful. This shift in approach, for me, was what started the ball rolling. I started asking about concepts like the single responsibility principle, abstraction, the high-level thinking behind object orientation, and lots, lots more. Then I started to wonder how to apply these tried-and-tested programming principles to front-end code: namely CSS.

I still maintain that CSS was left in the hands of the wrong people. Sure, designers like myself often make the most use of CSS, but CSS is still code. Granted, it might not have any logic behind it, it's not a programming language, but code is code is code, and it's still subject to all the same things that programming languages are: things like speed, efficiency, reuse, maintainability, scalability. I took what I'd learned about certain CSS misconceptions and then rolled that up with what I gleaned from my colleagues and started putting CSS on steroids. I totally changed my outlook on CSS and the benefits were tangible.

Takeaway: It's time we looked at our code with a fresh pair of eyes to embrace and manage the shift in focus, size and nature of front-end projects.

Object-Oriented CSS

In my opinion, one of the biggest, single shifts in writing and scaling CSS was the advent of *object-oriented* CSS[8], or OOCSS.

OOCSS — a term and methodology coined by Nicole Sullivan[9] — borrows a lot from the world of software development and programming. OO programming is a paradigm which aims to separate code into discrete,

---

8 https://github.com/stubbornella/oocss/wiki
9 http://stubbornella.org

logical chunks which can then interact with each other. Instead of one monolithic piece of code to complete tasks ABC, you'd end up with each of A, B and C abstracted into its own object. Now we'd have A which we can combine with either B or C in any order we choose.

This idea, brought to CSS, allows us to do away with cumbersome rule sets that do one specific thing, so we can use several smaller, simpler rule sets that can be combined to achieve the same result.

As well as abstraction, OOCSS also introduces the principle of structure and skin: what makes up the structure of a component should exist separately from what makes up its visual features. The same, underlying skeleton can be repeated over and over on a website, but skinned to look totally different in each case. This is the advantage of abstracting repeatable objects: the ability to manipulate and repurpose them in many different scenarios.

Takeaway: Spot repeated design patterns, abstract them, reuse them. Separate components into structure and skin and embrace tried-and-tested programming paradigms. For more information about OOCSS I would recommend reading Nicole Sullivan's GitHub Wiki[10].

Code Structure

When writing large amounts of CSS, it is important to plan how you're going to organize it. As the old saying goes, failing to plan is planning to fail, and it is vital that you spend a lot of time thinking about your architecture before you dive straight in and start coding.

BREAKING THINGS DOWN

If you have a mortgage or student debt, or have ever done any spring cleaning, you will be familiar with breaking these things down into smaller, more manageable chunks. You might have a mortgage of $200,000, but

---

10 github.com/stubbornella/oocss/wiki

you're unlikely to ever pay that back all at once; you pay several hundred dollars a month in order to make that huge total more manageable. When you're spring cleaning your house, you break it into smaller tasks: clean the bathroom, vacuum the carpets, wash the paintwork. Breaking things down is just a common-sense approach to tackling larger obstacles one step at a time, and the same applies to building websites.

When faced with building a large-scale front-end, it is important to not look at the bigger picture. Zoom in and spot smaller tasks that, as you're completing them, chip away at the project as a whole. To borrow yet another saying, take care of the pennies and the pounds will take care of themselves. Or, as my good friend Jamie Mason[11] likes to say, "take care of the bits and the bytes will take care of themselves."[12]

LEGO

One of my favourite analogies for breaking code down is from Nicole Sullivan. She said that you should treat code like Lego; many smaller, simpler chunks can be combined and arranged to make a huge variety of structures. With a box of assorted Lego pieces you could build a car, or an airplane, or the Eiffel Tower, or Big Ben, or anything! All by combining the same little tiny pieces in different quantities, in a different way, and in a different order.

So, instead of looking at your project and preparing to build a monolithic contact page, think about combining a series of inputs and buttons inside a content area, which is next to a subcontent area, which in turn is surrounded by a header and a footer. Stop thinking in terms of pages and start thinking in terms of components. If you need to build a search form, you can probably reuse and repurpose the same inputs from the contact form. Breaking your code down into Lego-like chunks gives you the ability to do a lot more with it.

---

11 https://twitter.com/GotNoSugarBaby
12 https://twitter.com/csswizardry/status/334962253029838849

Another analogy that I have used before is the *Subway analogy*. If you have ever ordered at a Subway sandwich store you will be familiar with the way they offer food. They break everything into separate ingredients, so you can combine your chosen meat with your favourite salad and top it all with your favourite sauce.

Breaking things down to this level affords an enormous number of combinations of the same basic ingredients, and it allows customers to pick and choose the bits they do and don't want. One day you could have tuna and cucumber with sweetcorn and mayo; the next day you could have cured meats with mayo, onion, lettuce and cucumber. There are some ingredients shared across both, but because each is distinct, you can simply swap ingredients and make entirely new sandwiches. So, instead of coding up a sandwich, code up all the ingredients and make your sandwich from those.

By thinking of your code in the same way as you do Lego and sandwich ingredients, you should be able to start looking at the smaller pictures and focus on easier, micro-tasks. The result of these tasks is a whole load of combinable chunks of code.

WHERE TO BREAK IT UP

It's all well and good saying we need to break code down into smaller pieces, but where do we break it all down?

Unfortunately, there is no right or wrong answer. But! I do feel there are some helpful analogies and pointers. I mentioned earlier that breaking things down is just common sense, so think now about how you, as a Web developer who's probably never worked in construction, would go about building a house. I imagine we'd all build a house in roughly the following order:

1. *Foundations* upon which to build everything else.
2. *Structure* such as walls, to keep the building up.
3. *Fixtures* like doors, windows and staircases.
4. *Decoration* like wallpaper or paint, carpets or wood flooring.
5. *Ornaments* such as paintings, canvases and posters.

This is a sensible order in which to build a house; we can't hang photos before we have walls, and we can't erect walls without foundations, so we have to assemble things in a certain order. That is not to say we have to make the individual parts in a certain order, certainly not. Our ornaments might be antiques made hundreds of years ago, but they can't become part of the house until we have our shelves in place.

Let's carry this analogy over to our websites, then. Our foundations are our CSS reset; our grid systems are structure; components and widgets are our fixtures and fittings; our design is the decoration; and, finally, any skinning or theming (for example, a special offer badge on a product, or a Christmas-themed logo) are our ornaments.

Again, we could design our components and widgets long before they are dropped into a page, but when it comes to assembly order there needs to be a page there to drop that component into. We need to build things in a certain order, so why not start breaking our code up there?

So now we should be in a position to start breaking our build up into logical chunks, for example:

1. I want to use *normalize.css*, so that needs to go in first.
2. This is what grid system I will be using.
3. This is what I want an unclassed h2 to look like.
4. This is what the store locator widget will look like.
5. This is what the store locator widget will look like if there are no stores in your area.

We can keep all of these things nice and separate, so we should. We have convenient, natural points at which to start breaking our code up into pieces.

These little pieces leave us with code which adheres to what, in the computer science field, is known as the single responsibility principle. My diluted and very high-level definition of the single responsibility principle is basically: code that does one job, one job only, and one job *very well*.

Think back to our Subway ingredients: carrot is excellent at being carrot, because that is all it is intended to do. Carrot absolutely sucks at being chicken, but that's fine because it's not meant to have anything to do with chicken. The idea is that we have lots of tiny pieces of code that have one single responsibility each. These responsibilities should never merge or leak into each other, but they should play very well alongside each other when combined.

ORGANIZING IT ALL

Now we have these lovely, Subwayesque, Lego-like, SRP chunks of code, we have to start thinking about how to get them all playing well together. Luckily, the way we outlined our house build is pretty much the ideal order in which to form our style sheets.

A few years ago, before I started thinking about the SRP and granular CSS, I often laid out my style sheets to roughly mirror the structure of a typical page. It may have looked something like this:

1. Reset
2. High-level styles (body backgrounds, etc.)
3. Header styles
4. Page styles (content, subcontent, etc.)
5. Content (forms, typography, images, tables)
6. Footer styles

This is obviously a vast simplification, but I really did order style sheets with no appreciation of how the CSS was structured, and with no real regard for the cascade or inheritance. Since starting to work on larger sites, I found that the most effective way to order rule sets was in inheritance order. That is to say, *every rule set should inherit from and add to the previous ones.* You start with your very basic stuff, your foundations, and you add structure, then components, then visual design. Your rule sets should be ordered from most to least generic. Not only does this mean your style sheets are saner, it probably means they are also far smaller and more efficient. If every rule set simply adds to and extends the ones defined previously then there is far less chance of having to undo styling, far less chance of hitting any specificity problems, and far less chance of tripping yourself up.

Jonathan Snook writes about this kind of thing — in a far better manner than I could ever hope to — in his book *SMACSS*: Scalable and Modular Architecture for CSS[13]. If you haven't yet read *SMACSS* then stop listening to me right now (I won't be offended, I promise) and go get yourself a copy. I firmly believe it is one of the best publications that modern CSS development has seen.

So, now my project's CSS might look a little more like this:

1. Reset/normalize.css
2. Grid system
3. Element-level styling: elements without classes, like headings, lists, and html and body elements
4. Components and classed elements: navigational elements, image galleries, buttons, forms
5. Style trumps: things like error states, seasonal themes, etc.

These things all layer one on top of one another, providing a logical and planned scalability. Everything should fall into one of those categories and sensibly slot into place, able to extend anything that came previously, and pave the way for anything that might come next.

MANAGING IT ALL

Now you have the skeleton of a big ol', well-structured project, how are you actually going to manage it? Well, my simple advice would be to use a lot files in a lot of directories, plus a preprocessor.

---

13   http://smacss.com

I know a lot of people are still on the fence about the value of preprocessors, but the beauty of them is that you can use as much or as little as you need. Where managing big projects is concerned, I think preprocessors' concatenation (`@import`) is invaluable. You don't have to make use of mixins, or variables, or anything else, but the ability to split your codebase into a lot of little includes is really, really handy when working on big projects.

I use Sass, so by having files like `normalize.scss`, `grids.scss`, `forms.scss` and so on, I can import everything I need to as and when and, most importantly, where I want. Because we now have these granular chunks of SRP CSS, we can simply move our includes up and down our master Sass file to really quickly reorder our entire style sheet. For example, let's imagine this is our main Sass file that imports the entire project's CSS:

```
@import "generic/normalize",
        "base/grids",
        "base/headings",
        "base/forms",
        "gui/page-head",
        "gui/page-foot",
        "gui/image-gallery",
        "gui/date-picker",
        "gui/blog-posts";
```

All we need to do is nudge a few lines up or down accordingly and we can completely rearchitect our compiled output. This ability to manage whole components as single lines rather than in their entirety makes it really easy to quickly make huge changes to the structure of your CSS should you need to. It also means you can remove chunks of CSS you no longer require just by commenting out one of the included files. Don't need the image gallery any more? Simple:

```
@import "gui/page-foot",
     // "gui/image-gallery",
        "gui/date-picker";
```

Organizing the Files

The directory structure will probably mirror the house-build splits in your code. This is what a CSS directory structure looks like at BSkyB, for example:

```
vars.scss
generic/
    *.scss
base/
    *.scss
objects/
    *.scss
gui/
    *.scss
style.scss
```

Please be aware that the above is written out in *implementation order*, rather than alphabetical order, as you might be used to seeing. That order means that:

1. We have a variables file which holds things like brand colors and font sizes.
2. Then we have a generic directory with our reset, clearfix and so on.
3. Next up is our base directory, which holds our unclassed elements like h2s, tables, etc.
4. Then we have a series of objects and abstractions, like the media object.
5. On top of that we sit our GUI layer: carousels, accordions, headers, footers and the like.
6. That all then gets compiled into the product-specific CSS file, made from our master style.scss Sass file.

So now we are left with a very organized directory of Sass files, each containing small, discrete chunks of CSS. It is these chunks, organized in this manner, that will allow us to combine — and ultimately scale — our CSS indefinitely.

Takeaway: Break your code down into smaller, more discrete parts which can then be added, removed, combined and layered in a common-sense order.

CSS Selectors

One of the simplest ways to make your CSS more scalable and suitable for bigger, modern front-ends is to simply pay more attention to your CSS selectors. It really is a surprisingly quick win. The bite-sized guideline for decent CSS selectors is basically: keep them well-named, as short as possible, and keep specificity low at all costs.

CSS selectors, such as IDs and classes and so on, are one of the first things you learn when entering the world of front-end development. The ability to match something like <div id="foo"> with #foo {} is Web development 101. Simple stuff, I'm sure we'd all agree.

However, CSS selectors, as humble as they are, hold one of the biggest keys to writing scalable, modular, extensible and fast UIs. CSS selectors all impact, in some way:

- Location dependency
- Code portability
- Robustness
- Specificity
- Selector intent
- ...and even efficiency

ANATOMY OF A CSS SELECTOR

Before we continue, we should familiarize ourselves with the anatomy of a CSS rule set. I won't go into loads of detail, but let's take the following:

```
.foo .bar .baz {
    float: left;
}
```

Lines 1–3 — the whole block — is called a *rule set*. Line 1 is our (compound) selector. The whole of line 2 is a declaration, made up of float, which is a property, and left, which is a value. .baz, the final selector before the { is our key selector. If selectors represent much of the key to scalable CSS, the key selector definitely holds the key to selectors in general.

WHICH SELECTOR(S) SHOULD YOU USE?

The answer to this is actually fairly straightforward: the short version is *classes*. They offer granularity, low specificity and reusability, they can be combined, they're (obviously) very well supported and they're great!

If you split code into smaller, single-responsibility-principle-adhering, Lego-like, modular chunks, then it only makes sense that your style sheets will be made up, predominantly, of classes. I can't think of a selector that lends itself better to the ideals of low specificity, reusability, portability and explicitness better than the humble class. As the acronym goes: "keep it simple, stupid." Classes are a straightforward, simple, tried-and-tested selector that fit the needs of a CSS architect perfectly.

IDs

Anyone who's seen me speak — or read any of my articles — will immediately be able to guess what I'm about to say next: do *not* use IDs in CSS.

The problems with IDs are manifold. First, they cannot be reused. Only one instance of an ID should exist on any given HTML page: to do otherwise is invalid. Interestingly, however, your CSS will still match and style all occurrences of a repeated ID, but JavaScript will only match the first element it finds, and then stop. This is why IDs in JavaScript are nice and fast.

Now, it may well be that you never want anything more than once on a page, and that you don't need a reusable selector at all. This is all well and good, so an ID might be appropriate here, but as we'll see, there are far greater downsides.

The second — and far biggest — problem with IDs is their specificity. If you aim to write a more painless, more extensible, often larger front-end, then you will always want to keep your specificity as low as possible. Specificity, after all, is the reason we have !important.

IDs have a much higher specificity that any other type of selector (save for inline styles). They are, in fact, infinitely more specific than classes. No amount of chained classes will ever be as specific as just one ID.

This hike in specificity can have some pretty unexpected, and certainly undesirable, side effects. Take for example:

```
#sidebar {
    background-color: #09f;
}

#sidebar,
    #sidebar a {
        color: #fff;
    }

.twitter-widget {
    background-color: #fff;
}

.twitter-widget,
    .twitter-widget a {
        color: #09f;
    }
```

Here we simply have a sidebar (#sidebar {}) which has a blue (#09f) background and whose text and any links inside it are white. We also have a reusable Twitter widget (.twitter {}) which has a white background and whose text and links are blue, the inverse of the sidebar.

What do you suppose would happen if we were to put the Twitter widget in the sidebar? Yep, its links would become white on the widget's white background. Certainly not what we wanted. This happened because the #sidebar a {} selector is *infinitely* more specific than the .twitter a {} selector, thus trumping it. This is where IDs can become a huge pain.

Anything you can do with an ID, you can do with a class, and more. If you want to use a component once on a page, you can do that with a class. If you want to use it a thousand times on a page you can do that with a class. Classes have all the same benefits of an ID but none of the drawbacks.

KEEP YOUR SELECTORS SHORT

When I say keep your selectors short, I do not mean the names themselves, I mean the size of the *compound selector*. A compound CSS selector is a selector made up of smaller selectors, for example:

```
.a-css-selector {}
#a .compound .css [selector] {}
```

Avoid compound selectors wherever possible. There are a number of reasons why this makes sense.

Location Dependency

Nested or compound selectors most likely use a lot of descendant selectors, selecting a thing that lives inside another thing. For example:

```
.sidebar .button {}
```

One problem here is that the `.button` style can now only be used in your sidebar. There may come a time when a client wants to use the same button elsewhere, but they can't. To do that you would need to write some more CSS:

```
.sidebar .button,
.footer .button {}
```

This might not seem too bad initally, but it's clearly not a very maintainable, scalable or future-proof solution; you will have to keep adding more and more CSS to achieve your goal. This is far from ideal. Tying selectors to a location reduces their scope for reuse.

A far better selector would have been:

```
.button--secondary {}
```

This can now live anywhere without us having to touch (and bloat) our CSS. All selectors should be as free to move as possible. You might never want to move them, but there is no benefit in tying them down unnecessarily.

Portability

We just covered how we can move our DOM elements about more freely without descendant selectors, but we can also increase what DOM elements we can apply selectors to. Take, for example:

```
input.button {}
```

This looks like a fairly inconspicuous bit of CSS, right? Wrong! We shouldn't qualify our selectors with elements.

Imagine we wanted to apply the .button styling to a link. It wouldn't work because we have tied our selector to an input element.

By omitting this leading qualifying selector, we instantly open up the possibility of applying the class to a wider array of HTML elements. Any time you see anything like the following:

```
ul.nav {}
div.header {}
p.comment {}
a.button {}
```

...and so on, aim to rewrite them as:

```
.nav {}
.header {}
.comment {}
.button {}
```

Robustness

If you have long selectors with tons of stuff going on in them then it only stands to reason that there is, statistically, a higher chance of something going wrong. Let's look at an example:

```
section.content p:first-child {
    font-size: 1.333em;
}
```

Here we have four smaller selectors in one compound selector. That means there are potentially four places for this code to break. If we change the `section` to an `article`, the selector will break. If we change the class of `.content` to `.page`, the selector will break. If we introduce an element before that paragraph, the selector will break. Basically, there is a lot to go wrong because of the size of — and number of parts in — this selector.

A far more robust replacement would be to simply use:

```
.intro {
    font-size: 1.333em;
}
```

Nothing can go wrong here. The only way we can prevent this selector from working is to remove it entirely from our markup, and if we do that then we *intend* to break it. Keeping selectors shorter keeps them far more robust, purely by lowering the statistical chance that they can break.

Decrease Specificity

As I mentioned before, specificity is an absolute nightmare. Specificity is what causes CSS to spiral out of control. Specificity is why we have `!important`. Thankfully, by keeping selectors short, you inherently keep your specificity low. This is a good place to be!

As well as avoiding IDs, we need to avoid adding anything unnecessary to our selectors. Anything that can be removed from a selector should be.

As well as decreasing portability and robustness, increasing selector length increases specificity — this is the worst of all worlds.

The Single Responsibility Principle

We're back to the SRP again! Now that we have these tiny, class-based short selectors, we can combine them far more easily with each other. This is yet another benefit of keeping our selectors short. Their small, one-job-and-one-job-only nature makes them really easy to combine, add to and subtract from each other.

Takeaway: Keep your selectors as short as possible, keep their specificity low at all costs, keep them as combinable as possible, keep them on the SRP and make sure they have sound selector intent.

Naming Conventions

With all these dozens of abstracted, SRP classes, we need a decent, consistent and workable way of naming them. You'd be surprised just how troublesome poorly named classes can be, but I wouldn't advise finding out the hard way. As Phil Karlton once said:

> There are only two hard things in Computer Science: cache invalidation and naming things.

For the longest time, we've been told that our class names should be semantic. As we covered previously, this is all a bit of fool's gold: only humans make any sense of classes, so write them for people.

Giving a list a class of `.blog-posts` is redundant. We can tell from the content that this is a list of blog posts so there is no need to state that in your class, which is merely a style hook. Instead of restricting yourself to only using this class to style a list of blog posts, why not name it more neutrally? You could then apply it to any list at all: a list of products, a list of latest news items, a list of usernames, anything.

Keep your class names relevant but neutral, sensible but portable. Instead of writing class names that describe the content, try to write names that can be applied to any type of content, and that describe the visual treatment that the class will add. Writing classes that describe content is redundant and serves to help no one.

What is useful is knowing a class isn't tied to a particular type of content, and that it is abstracted enough to be reused elsewhere. Nicole Sullivan's media object[14] is a perfect example of this way of thinking. Class names that don't allude at all to the type of content are highly reusable.

To quote Nicolas Gallagher:

Class names should communicate useful information to developers. [...] Tying your class name semantics tightly to the nature of the content has already reduced the ability of your architecture to scale or be easily put to use by other developers.[15]

Of course, some names won't need this level of reusability; your page header, for example, can happily take a class of .page-head. The above rules apply mainly to abstracted design patterns that could be reused anywhere, rather than to specific components. It's a fine balance to strike, but one that makes itself quite apparent.

WHAT'S IN A NAME?

So, we've discussed how our classes should be written for developers, and describe the styling's purpose rather than the content, and how they should be named as neutrally as possible — but how do we actually name them?

---

14 Nicole Sullivan, "The media object saves hundreds of lines of code"
http://smashed.by/media-object, June 25, 2010
15 Nicolas Gallagher, About HTML semantics and front-end architecture
http://nicolasgallagher.com/about-html-semantics-front-end-architecture/, March 15, 2012

To quote Google developer, Jens O. Meiert: "Use names that are as short as possible but as long as necessary"[16].

A class like `.content` is preferable to a class like `.cntnt` or `.the-area-of-the-page-that-will-hold-the-main-content`.

Classes that deal with general design patterns and abstractions should be vague, abstract and neutral. The media object, again, is a perfect example of this. I came up with the idea of the island object: a design pattern whose only job is to create a padded box. The reason I chose "island" is because it can be applied to all manner of elements. An island is something separated from its surroundings on all sides; the island object boxes off some content.

For very high-level abstractions and design patterns, use abstract names that lend themselves well to reuse, and don't align themselves too tightly to a specific type of content. This vague and abstract relationship allows for greater portability and reuse of your classes.

For specific components (like carousels, or headers or accordions) you need to use specific, unambiguous names which tell developers a lot about the component from the classes in the markup alone. Let's use a quick example:

```
<div class="widget  foobar-widget">
    <h2 class="widget-title"></h2>
    <div class="widget-body">
        <img src="" alt="" class="widget-thumbnail">
    </div>
</div>
```

Here we can see how all of our classes are well named, very explicit and clear. Looking at these classes tells us a lot about the component already: that it is designed to have a heading and an image, for example. But wait, there's more...

---

16 Jens O. Meiert, Best Practice for ID and Class Names, http://smashed.by/ids-classes, August 12, 2008

BEM: BLOCK, ELEMENT, MODIFIER

Taking explicit naming even further, let's take a look at BEM.

BEM — meaning *block, element, modifier* — is a front-end naming methodology thought up by the guys at Yandex, based in Russia. It is a smart way of naming your CSS classes to give them more transparency and meaning to other developers. They are far more strict and informative, which makes the BEM naming convention ideal for teams of developers on larger projects that might last a while.

The flavor of BEM that I use is actually a modification thought up by Nicolas Gallagher, and follows this pattern:

```
.block {}
.block__element {}
.block--modifier {}
```

- `.block` represents the higher level of an abstraction or component.
- `.block__element` represents a descendent of `.block` that helps form `.block` as a whole.
- `.block--modifier` represents a different state or version of `.block`.

Let's rewrite the previous example with BEM:

```
<div class="widget widget--foobar">
   <h2 class="widget__title"></h2>
   <div class="widget__body">
      <img src="" alt="" class="widget__thumbnail">
   </div>
</div>
```

Here we can see that block is `.widget`; `.widget--foobar` is a modification of that widget; and `.widget__title`, `.widget__body` and `.widget__thumbnail` are all elements of the widget.

The advantages here might not be immediately apparent, but now take this similar example:

```html
<div class="widget foobar-widget">
    <div class="media">
        <img src alt class="img  thumbnail">
        <div class="body">
            <h1 class="heading"></h1>
                <p></p>
        </div>
    </div>
</div>
```

How do the classes .img and .widget relate to each other? Do they
relate to each other at all? How about .media and .thumbnail? Well, if we
were to rewrite it with BEM:

```html
<div class="widget widget--foobar">
    <div class="media">
    <img src alt class="media__img  widget__thumbnail">
        <div class="media__body">
            <h1 class="widget__heading">    </h1>
            <p>    </p>
        </div>
    </div>
</div>
```

Here we can instantly see how all these classes relate to one another.
If we wanted to remove all the styling associated with the widget, we can
quickly spot the related classes. BEM gives developers a really detailed
overview of an entire chunk of markup purely by taking a quick glance
over its classes.

BEM looks ugly, sure, and it is verbose, but the power it gives far outweighs any of the superficial cons. If you strive for pretty code over powerful code, I dare say you're focusing on entirely the wrong things.

LOOSE CLASSES

We've covered two real types of class here. First, we looked at really abstract, highly reusable classes with really abstract names that don't align themselves to anything in particular. Second, on the flip side, we looked at classes that do specific jobs and thus receive explicit, verbose, namespaced names. Combining the two is a very bad idea. Giving a specific component a very loose class is extremely unwise.

A loose class name is one that isn't named explicitly enough for its intended purpose. Imagine you work on a huge site with loads of developers and you see a class of .card. What does this do? Such a class name is very loose, and loose class names are very bad for two main reasons.

First, you can't necessarily glean its purpose from the class alone (is it a user's profile card, an e-card, a field in a form that accepts credit card numbers?). Second, it's so vague that it could very easily be redefined accidentally by another developer. Loose classes are like global variables: hard to keep track of, easy to (accidentally) override, and readily able to sneak into your work where you least expect them.

A loose class name is to CSS what global scope is to JavaScript. A variable in global scope could accidentally be reassigned by or accidentally introduced into unrelated parts of the program. This is why developers shy away from global scope where possible.

By paying attention to our class names, and avoiding using loose selectors for specific jobs, we can better control our selectors' scope.

RECAP

So, let's review. Very high-level abstractions should have very abstract names. They should not align themselves to any particular content, and the meaning they convey should allude to visual patterns rather than describing the affected content.

Specific components should have very explicit naming conventions, and making use of things like BEM can really help out with this. Such classes, because they usually work in conjunction with other classes, should give developers a helpful and insightful overview of the code they're working with.

Finally, you should never combine the two. If a class does a specific job, it should have an equally explicit name (e.g. `.user-profile__name` rather than `.name`).

Takeaway: Make sure the names you use for selectors are appropriate, and that they expose as much information as they can. Do not worry about being long-winded with classes (I recently wrote a class of `.accordion__trigger--closed`), and name them so that other developers will find them practical and sensible to work with.

Verbosity in HTML

Let's talk about the elephant in the room. All this talk of granularity and abstractions and objects surely means more classes in our markup, and more verbose HTML, right? Right. Many people shy away from using more classes in their HTML because of misconceptions around semantics and clean markup. As we've discussed, this is understandable but a little misguided. The main reason to avoid using too many classes is maintainability. This is important, but there needs to be a degree of pragmatism and a balance.

In relation to the maintenance overhead of more classes, we often think about the cost of having to change classes in many HTML files or views or templates. Avoiding adding more classes, therefore, means that we have less to change across HTML files should we ever need to. This, of course, is very true. More classes does mean more HTML to potentially maintain.

However, avoiding classes means you're probably writing less granular CSS, so your CSS isn't separated out and it will be harder to maintain. You've simply moved the maintenance overhead from your HTML to your

CSS, and changing a few classes in your markup is far easier than refactoring tangled style sheets.

In preparation for a talk I gave in mid-2013, I decided to conduct a very lo-fi and unscientific experiment. At work I'd built a fairly large site over the previous six months, containing loads of view files using lots of classes. I had to make a far-reaching change which involved editing a class which appeared in many places across many of those files. I decided to time this process to see just how much effort was involved in changing a few classes in markup used across a whole site. It took twelve minutes. That was it. I have lost entire days fixing mangled CSS. Whole, full days. By using these extra classes I had totally granular CSS which was a joy to work with, and making changes across this entire project took less than a quarter of an hour.

The reason it was so fast was simple: automation. You can automate find and replace but you cannot automate CSS refactoring. My process was simple. I just ran:

```
$ git grep "$CLASS_I_WANTED_TO_FIND"
```

This gave me a list of all the files containing that class in my project. I then opened all these files in my text editor and ran a global find and replace. Easy.

The overhead of these extra classes is nothing compared to the effort involved in reworking CSS. Take the easy route of adding more classes and use automation (grep, ack, sed) when you need to change them.

The other thing I often tend to say in this situation is this: you are a Web developer, it is your job to maintain code. Instead of complaining about having to change some code you wrote, begin to embrace ways of doing it faster.

So if classes don't impact semantics, and no one cares about how clean your markup is, and more classes aren't that much harder to maintain, I think it's time we embraced them a little more.

Now, I do advocate the use of more classes but, of course, it can be taken too far:

```
<div class="red-text brand-face rounded margin-bottom">
```

This level of granularity will soon balloon and become a total nightmare to maintain. Your CSS will be too granular and incoherent. Both your CSS and your HTML will become much harder to look after.

WHERE TO DRAW THE LINE

Unfortunately, it is very difficult to identify the points at which to start using more or to stop using so many classes in our HTML. My own little litmus test is that if something has to do N things, it should have N hooks applied to it. As with the single responsibility principle, you can take away different aspects of a component just by removing the corresponding classes. Let's take an example:

```
<a href="" class="btn  btn--purchase  btn--full  js-button"
id="js-purchase-button" data-user-id="2893348">Purchase</a>
```

We can really quickly and clearly see this markup does a few things. First, it's a link (<a>) and it's styled like a button (.btn), specifically a full-width (.btn--full) purchase (.btn--purchase) button.

Second, we can also see that we're binding to it via JavaScript because it's a button (.js-button), and also because it's specifically the purchase button (#js-purchase-button). Finally, we can see that the button has a data attribute (data-user-id="2893348") which holds some data about the user. This markup does look very verbose, but it's only as verbose as it needs to be.

We could probably have written that markup like this:

```
<a href="" id="purchase-button" data-user-id="2893348">Purchase</a>
```

We could attach all our styles and bind all our JavaScript to that one ID, and still access the data attribute as normal. This would work, and it is far more concise, but it's incredibly unreusable. We have attached far too many functions to one overly specific selector which means our CSS is not very DRY (don't repeat yourself) and we won't easily be able to make discrete changes to that HTML (like removing JavaScript binding, for example).

The single responsibility principle is tried and tested, and keeping your code's tasks granular and discrete makes your application far more flexible, as well as much faster to work with.

Takeaway: HTML is easier to update than CSS is to refactor. If a piece of markup has to do five jobs, it needs five hooks, be they classes, data attributes or anything else.

In Closing

In this whirlwind look at more modern approaches to front-end development, you have hopefully picked up a thing or two, as well as realized that, despite their intentions, the things we've been doing for years need constant re-evaluation. Our valiant pursuit of clean markup and semantic classes and IDs has served to help no one, and often hindered us. To summarize this all-too-brief chapter:

- *Change can be good, it's going to happen and you should learn to embrace it*, and even forge your own methods to stay ahead of the curve and lead the next wave of Web standards.

- *Code needs to serve different people in different ways*, so make sure you write it with each stakeholder in mind. No one but developers cares about your actual code, so write it for them. Users and clients just want fast, robust, reliable and scalable websites.

- *Our old ideals have been holding us back*, and we need to leave some of these misconceptions behind in order to be able to deliver today's Web, which is a vastly different beast from what it was during the first wave of Web standards.

- *We need to take a more pragmatic and engineering-led approach to code.* Code is not art; it is not meant to be pretty. It is a powerful tool that we need to manipulate to create bigger, faster, more robust websites. Borrowing paradigms from developers and engineers can help us no end.

ABOUT THE AUTHOR

Harry Roberts works as Consultant Front-end Architect. He specialises in authoring and scaling massive front-ends. He is the lead and sole developer of inuit.css, a powerful, scalable, Sass-based, BEM, OOCSS framework. Harry writes on the subjects of maintainability, architecture, performance, OOCSS and more at csswizardry.com and tweets at @csswizardry.

ABOUT THE REVIEWER

Inayaili de León is Lead Web Designer at Canonical — the company behind Ubuntu — where she focuses on establishing and evangelizing the brands' visual direction online. She has established herself as an advocate of clean, semantic HTML and CSS. She blogs at webdesignernotebook.com and tweets at @yaili.

ABOUT THE REVIEWER

Jonathan Snook (@snookca) writes about Web design and development. He speaks at conferences and blogs on snook.ca.

Chapter

02

Writing Maintainable, Future-Friendly Code

Written by Nicholas Zakas

CHAPTER TWO · BY NICHOLAS ZAKAS

WRITING MAINTAINABLE, FUTURE-FRIENDLY CODE

W HETHER YOU LEARNED HOW TO WRITE CODE in school or on your own, it's unlikely that you learned one of the strange truths of computer programming: most code is a mess. I remember thinking when I was young that massive websites must have the most unbelievably clean yet complex code running them. When I joined Yahoo!, I found that the code running some of the world's most popular websites looked strikingly similar to the code running my personal blog. The truth is, code is code no matter where you go, and code has a tendency to get messy as it gets large and old.

Unfortunately, developers are rarely taught how to deal with messy code. The most common response is to rewrite everything from scratch. Yet doing so gives you only a moment of peace as this code very quickly starts to become messy as well. Things start to break, you find it hard to figure out why bugs are occurring, and there are parts of the codebase that seem to be "magic" (a term I use when nobody understands how a piece of code works).

This tends to happen because writing code is more fun than planning to write code. Most of us are so anxious to get coding that we don't stop to think about what we are doing and how it might be used in the future. What if you need to make changes? What if you didn't anticipate the additional features that would be required? What if the project ends up going in a different direction? Can your code adapt?

When we write code to implement features, we may not think much about the future. We have deadlines to meet and so we write enough code to successfully meet that deadline. However, someone is going to have to maintain that code. That someone might be you next month or it might be someone else next year, but someone eventually will need to maintain that code. On a large project with many developers, the problem is magnified. How can everyone work in the same codebase in such a way that making changes in the future are easy? That's what this chapter is about.

What's that Smell?

We will all have to work with someone else's code at some point. Not all code written by others is bad, even though our natural inclination is to think so. How can you tell that the code you're dealing with is a problem? Here are a few signs:

- Missing or incomplete documentation: there's some part of the code for which there isn't a good reference to understand why it exists and what it does.
- Missing or incomplete tests: you can't be sure that a change you've made hasn't broken expected behavior.
- Fear of change: you genuinely feel fear when touching the code because you're not sure what the end result will be.
- Fragile code: changing one seemingly isolated piece of code has ripple effects throughout the software that are hard to predict.

- Works temporarily: the code works only so long as some unrelated factor remains true (such as browser version).
- Each change requires touching multiple files: whenever you want to make a change, you need to touch multiple files, which increases the likelihood of introducing errors.

Each of these has a 'code smell', something that makes the code you're working with quite unpleasant and is an indicator that something is wrong. Fortunately, you can start making such code easier to deal with by applying some good practices as you continue working with it.

Code Conventions

When I was studying computer science in college, I had one extremely tough professor. His name was Dr. Maxey and he taught the more complicated courses like data structures and computer architecture. He was a wonderful teacher with a talent for articulating difficult concepts, but also an extremely tough grader. Not only would he look over your code to make sure that it worked, he would subtract points for stylistic issues. If your code lacked appropriate comments, or even if comments contained a misspelled word or two, he would deduct points. If your code was messy (by his standards), he would deduct points. The message was clear: the quality of your code is not just in its execution but also in its appearance. That was my first experience with coding style.

WHAT'S A STYLE ANYWAY?

Coding style is how your code looks, plain and simple. And by "your" I actually mean the code written by you, the person reading this chapter. Coding style is extremely personal and everyone has their own preferred approach. You can discover your own personal style by looking back over code that you've written when you didn't have a style guide to adhere to. Everyone has their own style because of the way they learned to code. If you used an IDE like Visual Studio to learn coding, your style probably matches the one enforced by the editor. If you learned using a plain text editor, your style likely evolved from what you thought was more readable. You may even notice that your style changes from language to language. The decisions that you made in JavaScript might not carry over to your CSS. For instance, you might decide JavaScript strings should use double quotes while in CSS strings should use single quotes. This isn't uncommon as we tend to switch context when we move back and forth between languages. Still, it's an interesting exercise in self-observation.

Coding style is made up of numerous small decisions based on the language:

- How and when to use comments,
- Tabs or spaces for indentation (and how many spaces),
- Appropriate use of white space,
- Proper naming of variables and functions,
- Code grouping an organization,
- Patterns to be used and patterns to be avoided.

This is by no means an exhaustive list, as coding style can be both extremely fine-grained, such as the Google JavaScript Style Guide[1], or more general, such as the jQuery Core Style Guidelines[2].

IT'S PERSONAL

The personal nature of coding style is a challenge in a team atmosphere. Often, seeking to avoid lengthy arguments, teams defer creating style guides under the guise of not wanting to discourage innovation and expression. Some see team-defined style guides as a way of forcing all developers to be the same.

---

1 http://smashed.by/javascriptguide
2 http://smashed.by/jqueryguide

Some developers rebel when presented with style guides, believing that they can't properly do their job if someone is telling them how to write their code.

I liken the situation to a group of musicians trying to form a band. Each one comes in believing that their way of doing things is best (their method or process). The band will struggle so long as everyone is trying to do their own thing. It's impossible to create good music unless everyone in the band agrees on the tempo, the style, and who should take the lead during a song. Anyone who has ever heard a high school band perform knows this to be true. Unless everyone is on the same page, you aren't going to accomplish much. That's why I strongly recommend style guides for software development teams. Getting everyone on the same page is difficult, and the style guide is a great place to start. By having everyone write code that looks the same you can avoid a lot of problems down the road.

COMMUNICATION IS KEY

Programs are meant to be read by humans
and only incidentally for computers to execute.

— Harold Abelson and Gerald Jay Sussman,
Structure and Interpretation of Computer Programs, 1984

The most important thing when working in a team is communication. People need to be able to work together effectively and the only way to do that is by communicating. As developers, we communicate primarily through code. We communicate with other parts of the software through code and we communicate with other developers through code.

While the software your code communicates with doesn't care how the code looks, the other developers on your team certainly do. The way code looks adds to our understanding of it. How many times have you opened up a piece of code that somebody else wrote and, before doing anything else, re-indented it the way you like? That's your brain not being able to figure out the code because of how it looks. When everyone writes code that looks different, everyone is constantly trying to parse the code before being able to understand it. When everyone writes code that looks the same, your brain can relax a bit as the understanding comes faster.

When you start thinking of code as communication with other developers, you start to realize that you're not simply writing code, you're crafting code. You put extra thought into each keystroke because the code is no longer just for a computer to execute, but for another person to understand. Your code should clearly communicate its purpose to the casual observer. Keep in mind, your code is destined to be maintained by somebody other than you. Not only are you communicating with other members of your team in the present, you're also communicating with members of your team in the future.

I recently received an email from someone working on code I wrote 10 years ago. Apparently, much to my shock and horror, my code is still being used in the product. He felt compelled to email me to say that he enjoyed working with my code. I smiled. My future teammate actually did appreciate the coding style I followed.

LEAVE YOURSELF CLUES WITH COMMENTS

If you know your enemies and know yourself,
you will not be imperiled in a hundred battles.

—Sun Tzu, *The Art of War*

Knowing yourself is important in life as well as coding. However, you'll never know yourself well enough to remember exactly what you were thinking when you wrote each line of code. Most developers have experienced looking at a very old piece of code that they wrote and not having any idea why they wrote it. It's not that your memories are bad, it's just that you make so many little decisions while writing code that it's impossible to keep track of them all.

Writing code to a style guide transfers that information into the code itself. When you decide when and where to use comments, as well as which patterns should and shouldn't be used, you leave a breadcrumb trail for your future self to find your way back to the purpose of the code. It's incredibly refreshing to open up an old piece of code and have it look like a new piece of code. You're able to acclimate quickly, sidestepping the tedious process of relearning what the code does before you can start investigating the real issue.

Any good style guide prescribes when and how to leave comments in code. Most developers have an aversion to comments because it seems a lot like writing documentation — and developers tend to hate writing documentation. This is usually because writing documentation is seen as time not writing code. However, it's the documentation that allows you to come back to code you wrote in the past and quickly get back up to speed.

Another common argument against using comments is that code should be self-documenting. In reality, there is no such thing as self-documenting code. Self-documenting code is a myth perpetuated by people who hate to write documentation. A common argument against writing comments is, "if you can't understand my code, then you're not smart enough." In reality, understanding code has nothing to do with how smart a developer is, but rather providing enough context so the code make sense. Without comments, or a direct discussion with the code author, it's very hard to get enough context.

The best-understood code is littered with comments explaining key sections. You certainly don't want a comment for every line of code, and comments must provide additional context and information that cannot otherwise be gleaned from reading the code. Here's an example of a bad comment:

```
// set initial count to 0
var count = 0;
```

This comment provides no additional context or information to the line of code it describes. Comments of this type should be avoided at all costs. A good comment includes information such as:

- A description of what the code is doing,
- Why the code is doing it in this way (as opposed to an alternative),
- A reference to any related bug or issue in an issue tracker.

For example, here is an excellent comment from the jQuery codebase:

```
// #8138, IE may throw an exception when accessing
// a field from window.location if document.domain has been set

try {
    ajaxLocation = location.href;
        } catch( e ) {

// Use the href attribute of an A element
// since IE will modify it given document.location

    ajaxLocation = document.createElement( "a" );
    ajaxLocation.href = "";
    ajaxLocation = ajaxLocation.href;
}
```

The comment references an issue number and provides a description of the original bug. The second comment describes the approach that fixes the issue. It's very easy for anyone reading over the code to understand why this code was included and where to go if more information is required. Here's another good example from the YUI CSS library:

```
h1 {
/*18px via YUI Fonts CSS foundation*/
    font-size:138.5%;
}
```

Without the comment, you might wonder why 138.5% is a significant number. With the comment, you know two important pieces of information. First, this file requires the YUI Fonts CSS foundation to work properly. Second, 138.5% is equal to 18px based on that requirement. What could easily have been a source of confusion is now a source of information and understanding.

How do you know if code needs a comment? Think of comments as Post-it notes in your code. Anytime you're afraid you may forget what the code is doing or how it's doing it, add a comment. Anytime you come across something that might trip up another developer, such as a browser-specific hack, leave a comment. If you're implementing a specific algorithm, leave a comment. Leave a comment whenever you feel like you'd be missing some important information if you went away for six months and then needed to work on the code again.

Good developers make judicious use of comments and don't expect the code to speak for itself. You shouldn't need to read through all of the code just to make sense of what's going on. Comments short-circuit that need by providing narrative that more succinctly describes what the code actually does. And that is incredibly valuable for the long-term hygiene of your code.

MAKE ERRORS OBVIOUS

One of the most important reasons to have a coherent style guide is to help make errors more obvious. Style guides do this by familiarizing developers with certain patterns. Once you're acclimated, unfamiliar patterns jump out of the code when you look at it. Such patterns aren't always errors, but they definitely require a closer look to make sure that nothing is amiss.

For example, consider the JavaScript `switch` statement. It's a very common error to mistakenly allow one `case` to fall through into another, such as this:

```
switch(value) {
    case 1:
        doSomething();
    case 2:
        doSomethingElse();
    break;
    default:
    doDefaultThing();
}
```

The first case falls through into the second case so if value is 1, then both doSomething() and doSomethingElse() are executed. And here's the question: is there an error here? It's possible that the developer forgot to include a break in the first case, but it's also equally possible that the developer intended for the first case to fall through to the second case. There's no way to tell just from looking at the code.

Now suppose you have a JavaScript style guide that says something like this:

> *All switch statement cases must end with* break, throw, return, *or a comment indicating a fall-through.*

Judging by this guideline, there is definitely a stylistic error and that means there could be a logic error. If the first case was supposed to fall through to the second case, then it should look like this:

```
switch(value) {
    case 1:
        doSomething();
        // falls through
    case 2:
        doSomethingElse();
        break;
    default:
        doDefaultThing();
}
```

If the first `case` wasn't supposed to fall through, then it should end with a statement such as `break`. In either case, the original code doesn't match the style guide and that means you need to double-check the intended functionality. In doing so, you might very well find a bug.

As another example, members of one of my teams decided that they did not like using three values for `padding` or `margin` in CSS, such as:

```
.box {
    padding: 5px 10px 6px;
}
```

The consensus was that three values didn't clearly indicate the intent of the author. Is it obvious that the fourth value was left off on purpose? Is it an accident? While you may not think of this as a likely error condition, my team did, and so we made a rule that you could have one, two or four values for `padding` and `margin` but not three. That way, if we ever saw just three values, we would know that it was a mistake of leaving off the fourth.

When you have a style guide, code that otherwise seems innocuous immediately raises a flag because the style isn't followed. This is one of the most overlooked aspects of style guides: by defining what correct code looks like, you are more easily able to identify incorrect code and therefore avoid potential bugs before they happen.

Coding style takes care of what code looks like, which is an important first step. The next step is to take care of how the code is organized, and that's where a good architecture comes into play.

Architecture

There is an interesting tension between developers and architects in most software engineering organizations. Developers see architects as theoreticians who like to draw diagrams and make proclamations about how software should be built, without taking into account that the world isn't perfect. Architects are frequently looked at as those who are incapable of implementing their own designs due to a lack of on-the-ground, in-the-trenches perspective.

Truth be told, there are architects who fit that description, but good architects are priceless commodities who increase the value of an entire organization through their high-level vision and perspective. Such vision and perspective transform an architecture.

The role of architecture is overlooked in many places when it may be the most important part of software. A robust architecture:

- Provides easy ways to complete common tasks.
- Ensures everything has a place and a purpose.
- Allows us to quickly add or augment functionality.
- Encourages good software design.

Most of the horribly unmaintainable code I've come across in my career could be traced back to a lack of good architecture. Without such structure, we get confused about where and when to make certain changes. When that happens, we end up hacking solutions where they don't belong and that starts a downward spiral of code quality. Anytime someone can't answer the question "Where does this go?", it means that code ends up in an unexpected location and that, in turn, perpetuates the problem.

Code has a habit of multiplying when you're not looking. If there is when the component was recently one way of doing something in the codebase then there will quickly be two instances of that same pattern. Two leads to four, and it continues until that pattern has permeated the entire system. This happens when developers look for examples of how others have achieved certain functionality. When they find an example, it gets copied into another place for a similar purpose. If the pattern is good, then you're getting a desired result; if the pattern is bad, then your code becomes less maintainable as you go.

That's why the best architectures have a place for everything.

Whenever you need to make a change or addition, you know exactly where to do so. YUI, for example, has several different types of objects available for extending the library.

If you want to add completely new functionality, then you create a module. If you want to add more methods to DOM elements, then you create a node plugin. There is always an answer to "How do I do this?" in YUI, and that makes it easy to work with and extend.

Keep in mind that YUI's system works well for a JavaScript library, but you need different approaches depending on what you're trying to create. There are library architectures (such as YUI and jQuery's plugin system), framework architectures (Node.js module system) and application architectures (Model-View-Controller or MVC). There are architectures for every type of software and choosing one isn't always easy. On the other hand, not choosing one is the best way to ensure your code will become unmanageable in short order.

Web developers traditionally don't think about architecture very much but that is starting to change. More and more, libraries and frameworks with defined architectures are making their way into projects. JavaScript and CSS for large applications, in particular, have benefited from a lot of research into how code should be structured. Today, there are a number of approaches and prebuilt solutions to help you create applications in a logical way.

Backbone.js

Backbone.js[3] is credited with starting the MV architectural movement in JavaScript. Not a traditional MVC framework for its lack of a controller, Backbone.js provides common patterns for manipulating views (HTML) with structured data. A view can be automatically updated when the data represented in the view changes. Backbone.js itself is pretty small and doesn't represent an entire architecture, but it can be a good building block for a larger design.

3 http://backbonejs.org

Scalable JavaScript

An approach that I devised for a complete JavaScript application architecture that scales and grows as your application does. The primary approach is to separate an application into a series of small pieces, each with specific responsibilities and constraints. The architecture can be built on top of any JavaScript library and extended through the addition of plugins at each level. There is no single JavaScript library for this approach, as it was presented as a high-level architectural design (though there are many implementations to be found online). See my slides and transcript on SlideShare[4] for more information.

Ember.js

Ember.js[5] is a complete application framework that includes everything you need to build a JavaScript application. It provides an MVC framework plus routing capabilities. These are all mixed in with Handlebars[6], a templating language. Ember.js is opinionated — there's a way to do everything: the Ember.js way. Doing so allows you to focus on building your application rather than worrying about the design of the surrounding architecture.

Object-Oriented CSS

OOCSS is an approach created by Nicole Sullivan to make CSS more maintainable. The general idea is to create small, reusable objects (a combination of markup and CSS classes) that represent common patterns. With enough of these small pieces, you can create an infinite number of pages that look different even though they use the same underlying patterns.

---

4 http://smashed.by/js-architecture
5 http://emberjs.com
6 http://handlebarsjs.com

Arranging CSS styles into structure, skins, content and other groupings brings order to CSS. See Louis Lazarus's "An Introduction to Object-Oriented CSS"[7] for a good primer. Nicole also offers a library based on these principles[8].

Scalable and Modular Architecture for CSS

SMACSS[9] was devised by Jonathan Snook to clearly outline the responsibilities of each piece of CSS. He categorizes rules into base, layout, module, state and theme, and each category provides a guideline as to which properties may be used and for what purpose. There is no library that goes along with this approach as SMACSS is a description of a high-level architecture rather than a specific implementation.

These are just a sampling of the available architectures for JavaScript and CSS. Do some research to figure out which architecture works best for you. Don't make the mistake of worrying about architecture too late — that's a recipe for technical debt from the start. Choosing an architecture is a lot like laying a foundation for a house. If the foundation is strong, you can build anything on top of it; if the foundation is weak or absent, then the quality of the entire house is at risk.

Even if you are unable to find the perfect architecture for your project, just pick one. Having some organization is much better than having no organization. When you've decided how to structure the code, you've taken an important step toward creating a sustainable codebase. Anytime such an important decision is made, it's a good idea to write down how it works and why it's designed in this way. Documenting all of this makes it easier for new developers to come on board.

---

7 http://smashed.by/oocss
8 http://github.com/stubbornella/oocss
9 http://smacss.com

Documentation

Documentation is the part of the job that developers like the least, yet it is frequently just as important as the code itself. If you look at the success of any major open-source software, you can usually draw a straight line between that success and the presence of excellent documentation. jQuery owes much of its success to the excellent documentation that surrounds the library[10], a large amount contributed by a passionate community. Furthermore, other jQuery users set up their own blogs with tips and tricks, and tutorials abound. That was even before jQuery books started popping up. These days you can do a quick search for anything related to jQuery and find hundreds of examples and tutorials.

Twitter Bootstrap[11] is another library that benefits from excellent documentation. When you arrive at the site, you're met with a lot of information about how to get started. All of the patterns are documented with code and live examples so you can see exactly what you'd get by applying certain classes to HTML. The popularity of Bootstrap is owed in part to the simplicity of getting started, and that is because of the high-quality documentation.

There's a reason why popular open-source software asks for and spends time on contributions to its documentation: if software is hard to use or too opaque, then people won't bother with it. Yet the same developers who regularly complain about some software's lack of documentation are the same people who look for excuses to not write documentation for their own software. Good software is well-documented software, and bad software has little documentation. There is no such thing as maintainable code that isn't also documented.

Even the most horribly written software becomes more manageable when there's documentation. The documentation lifts the veil of magic around the code and allows developers to work more effectively with it.

---

10 http://docs.jquery.com
11 http://twitter.github.io/bootstrap/

That's why no piece of software should be considered complete without accompanying documentation. Writing good documentation isn't hard, it's just a matter of transferring your thoughts into text and images. Depending on the type of software you're building, it may make sense to structure your documentation in different ways. However, there are some common approaches to documentation that everyone should be aware of.

Getting Started

A quick start guide describes how to get up and running. This is the traditional "Hello world" example that many libraries have. A good quick start guide describes how to obtain and set up the library, and how to start using the functionality immediately. Twitter Bootstrap has a great getting started guide[12].

Tutorials

There are common use cases that library users frequently need and so it's important to show them how to complete those tasks. The tutorials should be in narrative form, describing each step of the process and resulting in a functional prototype at the end. jQuery has a large amount of tutorials[13] that are very well written.

API Documentation

If you offer an API for others to use, then API documentation is very important. This describes every public interface of the API in very fine detail, including the names of functions, the types of arguments the functions expect, return values, available classes, and more. The YUI library has an excellent and fully searchable set of API documentation[14].

---

12 http://twitter.github.io/bootstrap/getting-started.html
13 http://docs.jquery.com/Tutorials
14 http://yuilibrary.com/yui/docs/api/

Design Document

Design documents describe the architecture and options available within some piece of software. It is frequently written before coding begins and updated once coding is complete. Design documents answer the question, "How does this work?" It's quite common to see diagrams as well as discussions around design philosophy, design patterns used, and assumptions the software makes. Chromium, the open-source project on which Google Chrome and Opera are based, has an excellent set of design documents[15]. When you inherit some code that you must begin to maintain, the design document for that code should be the first place you go to get a good understanding of the code.

In general, getting started guides and tutorials are necessary when you're creating a library for others to use. API documentation and design documents are good regardless of the software you're writing. The exact structure of these documents necessarily varies based on the software you're creating and the intended audience.

API documentation is the minimum that a project should have for documentation. Most languages, including JavaScript and CSS, have tools for generating documentation from the source code. These documentation generators use comments embedded within the code to create standalone documentation (typically in HTML format) describing the code. The exact comment style depends on the tool being used. Here are some tools worth investigating:

- JSDoc[16]: the original JavaScript documentation generator. It uses JavaDoc-style comments to create API documentation.
- YUIDoc[17]: a JavaScript documentation generator from the YUI team. It also uses JavaDoc-style comments to create API documentation.

---

15 http://www.chromium.org/developers/design-documents
16 http://usejsdoc.org
17 http://yuilibrary.com/projects/yuidoc

- Docco[18]: a JavaScript narrative documentation generator. Instead of creating API documentation, this tool creates a narrative where the description of the code shows up on the left and the actual code shows up on the right.
- KSS[19]: a CSS style guide generator. Extracts comments inside of CSS, SCSS or LESS files and generates a style guide with example output.

There are documentation generators for almost any language you would use to build a Web application. Research them, learn them and use them. The best way to ensure good comments in code is knowing they'll end up in actual documentation. I've seen this happen several times: as soon as documentation starts getting generated and the result is available for all to see, more time is spent crafting the comments that show up.

There is no such thing as too much documentation for code, but there is such a thing as too little. The best way to encourage documentation writing is to make it part of the feature deliverable. A feature should not be considered complete until adequate documentation is written and placed in the appropriate location. Requiring a design document before coding starts also helps keep documentation at the front of everyone's minds. Regardless of how you decide to set it up, documentation needs to be part of the deliverable whenever code is written. The exact type of documentation will depend on the type of code, but all code needs documentation, even if it's just the addition of one sentence to an existing document.

Having some good coding style guides, a well-defined architecture, and generous amounts of documentation sets up any project for success. The truly challenging part comes when you want to include code that wasn't written by your team, and having guidelines for how to do that is important for the overall health of your application.

---

18   http://jashkenas.github.io/docco/
19   http://warpspire.com/kss/styleguides

Managing Third-Party Components

Unless you're working on a personal project, chances are your Web application will rely on one or more third-party components to function properly. Even the best, most experienced developers turn to third-party components when there are aspects of the Web application that they don't want to own or maintain. It doesn't make sense for everyone to create their own way of doing everything and so third-party components help get Web applications up and running faster while outsourcing maintenance to someone else.

For example, when a new browser comes out you can be sure that jQuery will be updated to support it. All you need to do is drop in the latest version and your Web application continues to work fine. If you had created your own browser abstraction library, it would be up to you to keep it up to date whenever a new browser is released. Since that happens every six weeks for Chrome and Firefox, updating your code would be an onerous and repetitive task that keeps you from doing more important things.

You aren't adding value to your business or application by constantly rewriting low-level utilities. Using third-party components frees you up to focus on the true value you can provide to your users.

HOW TO CHOOSE THIRD-PARTY COMPONENTS

There are many different kinds of third-party components. There are JavaScript libraries for almost everything, CSS frameworks and toolkits, images and fonts, and other types of components that will continue to evolve along with Web technologies. Choosing these third-party components is a very important decision because they represent the materials and tools with which your Web application will be built. Just like building a house, you want to make sure that the materials are solid and the tools are trustworthy.

Web development has a vibrant open source community with very many third-party components available free of charge. That's the good news. The bad news is that sifting through the large sea of open-source components makes it hard to find quality. Even component catalogs, such as the jQuery Plugin Registry[20] and the NPM Registry[21], make it difficult to find quality components. Each component is placed on an equal footing with the others, and sometimes arbitrary rating systems, such as stars or popularity, or when the component was recently updated, don't tell the full story.

What you are looking for is a third-party component you can trust. The whole point of using a third-party component is to free yourself from maintaining some code. To do that, you need a reasonable degree of certainty that the code hasn't been abandoned. If you end up including a third-party component that is no longer updated then, eventually, you will end up maintaining it for yourself. Likewise, if the component is being maintained but it takes a long time for the developer to respond to your queries, then you will ultimately modify it yourself because you can't wait for an official release.

So how can you tell that a third-party component is trustworthy? Here are some things to evaluate.

When was it last updated? If the component was recently updated, there is a greater chance that it will continue to be updated in the future. If the component hasn't been recently updated, then it might be abandoned. In general, look for things that have been changed in the past month. That's a pretty good indicator that they're still under active development.

Who is the developer? If the component is provided by a company or organization, it is a safer bet than a component supported by a single person. There are lots of open-source projects that are released by their authors and then discarded. Avoid those components whenever you can.

---

20 http://plugins.jquery.com/
21 http://npmjs.org

If a component is updated by a single person and that person is backed by a company or organization (that is, this developer is paid to maintain the component), then it's also probably safe to use. Any component that looks like it's somebody's hobby should be avoided, even if it appears to do everything you want. Unless you are willing to nurture that project in the future, it's a good idea to steer clear.

How responsive is the developer? At some point, you will find an error in the component that you're using. That error might be causing a functionality issue in your Web application and so you want to get it fixed as quickly as possible. The speed with which the developer can address your concern is important. You can get a good sense of this by browsing public issue trackers to see how long certain issues were open before being resolved. Keep in mind that being resolved doesn't necessarily mean there has to be an official release, it could mean that the maintainer checked in a fix so that the reporter can patch their own copy while waiting for the release. A good turnaround time for a significant issue is measured in days rather than weeks. If you can't rely on fast turnaround from a third-party component developer then the component probably shouldn't be used.

How stable is the API? You might be tempted to use a third-party component that is considered to be up-and-coming. Be wary of relying on anything that hasn't yet reached version 1.0. Prior to a 1.0 release, components have a tendency to change quite dramatically. APIs are typically not locked down until version 1.0 and that creates a challenge when you try to upgrade the component. Relying on an ever-changing API footprint means you will constantly be changing your code so that it will work with the component. Do yourself a favor and wait until the component has reached maturity before relying on it.

Who else is using it? Do your research to figure out who else is using this component. Ideally you want something that is being used by two or more large Web applications.

When large companies or organizations rely on the component, there is more incentive for its developer to keep updating the component and fixing bugs.

That doesn't mean you shouldn't deploy anything unless it's being used by Facebook or Google, it just means that your Web application shouldn't be the first to rely on that component. There is safety in numbers and the more users of any component, the more likely it will continue to evolve and issues will be resolved.

So make sure to keep in mind that not all jQuery plugins are the built the same. Not all NPM modules are built the same. And certainly not all open-source projects are built the same. Anyone can create an open-source component but not everyone is dedicated to continuing it. Make sure to do your due diligence on any third-party component before including it in your product. One bad decision could create cracks in your foundation that may be hard to fix later.

Part of your due diligence should be to look at the third-party code itself. You need to be sure there's nothing malicious buried inside before deploying it. Failing to do some cursory examination of the code could lead to trouble. In 2011, a now-defunct website disappeared from Google search results overnight[22]. After some lengthy exploration, it was determined that a WordPress plugin was to blame. Whenever the Googlebot visited the site, the plugin would redirect elsewhere. The person who wrote the plugin had made a mistake in the code as he intended only to block the Googlebot from the plugins directory (see his explanation[23]). Unfortunately, the damage was done and caused a lot of inconvenience for those using the plugin.

Intentional or not, the potential damage third-party components can cause to your application is significant. Don't assume that all third-party components are made the same. Spend time investigating before including them in your application.

---

22 http://smashed.by/wp-plugins-traffic
23 http://smashed.by/apologies

FORKING THIRD-PARTY COMPONENTS

After you've selected some third-party components for your Web application you may find that they don't quite do everything that you need. At that point, you have a decision to make. You can either start your search again for a new component or you can try to make this component work the way you need it to. Unfortunately, many developers tend to take the latter approach which means forking the original code. Forking is any activity where the third-party component is modified by someone other than the maintainer. It doesn't matter if you are adding a new function, removing an existing function, or changing existing functionality, all of these are considered forking.

Forking a third-party component is a bad idea. By doing so, you ensure a non-linear upgrade path for that component. Upgrading the component should be as simple as removing your current file and dropping in a new file. Sometimes the component API will change slightly and so you will need to adjust your code accordingly. Good components, however, minimize this type of occurrence. A drop-in upgrade is considered linear.

A non-linear upgrade path is one where dropping in the new version is only the start of the upgrade. You then have to trawl your code and make appropriate fixes for the new version. If you have forked the component, then you dramatically increase the likelihood of a non-linear upgrade path. There are all kinds of different issues that can arise. For example, you might have added a new method on the component only to find that the next official version of the component has a function with that name that does something different. That means not only do you need to change the name of your function, but you also have to change all the places where it's used in your code.

When you decide to use a third-party component, it's best to avoid forking it in any way. Preserving a linear upgrade path is very important for these components. Remember, the whole point of using a third-party component is to eliminate maintenance overhead.

As soon as you fork a component, you condemn yourself to maintenance issues in the future.

To make the separation between your code and third-party code clear, be sure to store them in separate directories. For example, if you have a /js directory in which all JavaScript code lives, then place all third-party JavaScript code in /js/external or /js/3rdparty. The same can be said for CSS as well. Keeping third-party code separate is a good reminder that it's not appropriate to edit these files in any way.

It's likely that a third-party component won't do everything that you need it to do. At that point, it gets increasingly tempting to edit the component. Resist this urge as it destroys the linear upgrade path for the component. Instead, look for ways to add additional functionality that don't require you to edit the third-party code directly.

Well-designed components typically have plugin or extension systems. These are provided so that developers can augment the existing functionality in a predictable and controllable way. jQuery, YUI and Dojo all have plugin systems that allow you to add new functionality without editing the main files. If you find that the third-party component doesn't provide all the functionality that you need, you should first try to write a plugin or extension for that component.

When doing this, your code should not be in the same file as the component code. To preserve a linear upgrade path, you want to be sure you can drop in a new version of the component file without needing to modify it in any way. Need more jQuery functionality? Create a jQuery plugin and put it in /js/plugins (not in /js/external or /js/3rdparty).

If the component you rely on does not have a plugin system, then the best approach is to create a wrapper component that abstracts away the third-party code. The wrapper component is one that you create and manage, so you can provide whatever functionality you want. You can create functions that pass through directly to the third-party component, as well as new functions where you have implemented custom pieces of functionality.

Forking third-party components is always a bad idea, so make sure that you keep third-party component code and your code as separate as possible. Preserve linear upgrade paths for third-party components by keeping them in a separate directory from code that you write yourself.

BETTING THE HOUSE

Bringing third-party components into your Web application is a great way to get up and running quickly. However, by doing so you place a very significant bet on those components. You bet that the time saved by using these components outweighs the time you would spend creating similar components on your own and looking after them. That's why choosing the right third-party components and managing them appropriately is so important. Once a component is in use in the Web application, it's very hard to extract that component and replace it with another one.

That's the most important thing to keep in mind when using third-party components: once you commit, it's hard to change your mind. The third-party code starts to get referenced in multiple places in your codebase, and so changing to a different component means going through your entire codebase and making changes. That's something that you typically don't have the luxury of doing on a continual basis. There are new features to build and bugs to fix, and the last thing you want to do is replace a shaky foundation when you could be providing more value to your users.

Having everything in place for a maintainable codebase can only really be guaranteed when starting from scratch. But what happens when you're not able to do that? How do you start to work with code that isn't very well organized or has other glaring problems?

Dealing with Legacy Code

The definition of legacy code depends on whom you ask. Some describe legacy code as code relating to functionality that's no longer supported. Others describe it as code written by somebody who no longer maintains it. I describe legacy code as any code that you inherit from someone else without a formal hand-off. This frequently happens because the code was written by somebody who no longer works on the project and so managing the code becomes an expedition through unfamiliar territory. You're expected to be able to fix bugs and extend the previous work without fully understanding what it does or why it was built a certain way. In short, I describe legacy code as code that someone else wrote and that you have to maintain.

I have yet to meet a developer who enjoys working with legacy code. It's a frustrating experience to have to keep somebody else's code running without fully understanding it. There's a natural inclination to believe that everything in the legacy code was done incorrectly and therefore should be completely thrown away to start anew. Practically, you will rarely get the opportunity to start a project completely from scratch, and so it becomes important to understand how to deal with this old code.

But before you can learn how to effectively work with legacy code, you must come to grips with one simple fact: the code you write today is tomorrow's legacy code. Every line of code you write will eventually be maintained by somebody else. Keeping that in mind helps guide the decisions that you make today about any code that you are working on. Ask yourself, what will a person who maintains this file need to know in order to work effectively?

WRITE IT DOWN

I often describe working with legacy code as being similar to spelunking, the hobby of exploring caves. In spelunking, you don't always know what's around the corner. Caves are dark, wet and not always very stable. Delving into legacy code has similar pitfalls in that you may not entirely be sure what each piece of code does. In effect, you are an explorer trying to make sure that the cave doesn't fall in on you. Making it further into the code is an achievement, and to make it easier for others it helps to draw a map.

One of the primary tasks of the code maintainer is to eliminate magic from the codebase. As you work with the code, fixing bugs or adding new functionality, make sure that you document what you do. Every time you touch legacy code, seek to get a better understanding of what it's doing. When you make a discovery, write it down. Writing it down is as simple as leaving a comment or two in the code so that the next person who looks at it won't have to wonder why something was done.

It's best to leave a trail of comments such as this so that you slowly start to build up a base of knowledge around how the code works. This comes in handy not just for others, but for you if you find yourself working on this code again months or years down the line.

ADD TESTS

Michael C. Feathers, author of *Working Effectively with Legacy Code* (Pearson, 2004), describes legacy code as any code that doesn't have tests. In practice, the pain of legacy code is often associated with a lack of tests, which is why the code begins to seem like magic. Without anything documenting expected behavior, either in the way of comments, formal documentation or good tests, it's very hard to feel confident when making changes to legacy code. Once again, it's unlikely that you'll ever have enough time to stop and write tests for all the legacy code at once. That doesn't mean that you should give up on tests altogether.

The approach for adding tests to legacy code is very similar to adding comments in legacy code. Whenever you work with the code, make it a point to add at least one test. If you're fixing a bug, write a test that reproduces the issue before attempting to fix it. This is called *test-driven development*. You start by writing a test that fails (because of the bug) and then write code that makes the test pass. After fixing the bug, you can add comments to the code and check in the new test. That's now one less part of the code that seems to be magic.

The combination of code comments and tests helps to bring legacy code under control. Even though progress will seem slow by adding one test at a time, having one test is better than having no tests. Having two tests is better than having one. As you continue to work with the code and continue to add tests, you'll expose more and more functionality to the light of day. Parts of the legacy code will start to make sense because you have simple ways of determining if the code is functioning properly. It's important to think of running a marathon rather than a sprint. You can't write all the tests at once, but as long as you continue down the path of writing tests, you'll eventually reach a much better understanding of the legacy code.

REFACTORING AND REWRITING

If you are lucky, you may actually get some time to refactor or rewrite legacy code. Refactoring involves leaving the public interface of an API unchanged while changing the underlying implementation. This is where effective unit tests are extremely important. Good unit tests exercise the public interface without regard for implementation details. In short, unit tests are designed to test interfaces by asserting that certain inputs result in certain outputs. Outputs can be return values, changes to existing objects, errors that are thrown, or any other visible effect of executing some code. It is impossible to effectively refactor code unless you have unit tests in place to verify that your changes result in the same outcomes as the old code.

Rewriting code is when you make significant changes to both the public interface and the implementation. This is a developer's dream: you have free reign to start from scratch and make something better than what you've been working with. When rewriting code, it doesn't matter what you replace because you are creating something new. Unfortunately, this is usually the time when the least future-friendly code gets written.

Something interesting happens in a developer's mind when given a blank slate. It feels like there are no rules, as you are no longer constrained by previous work. You start dreaming about how wonderful things could be and how your work is so much better than what came before it. What you fail to realize is that creating something from scratch means that you're writing future legacy code. Your code will be given to someone else to look after, and so it's now on you to prevent the creation of yet more horrible code.

One of my mentors told me that there are very few developers who can effectively start from scratch and build up a project. In the exuberance of creation you are far more likely to forget the basics and take shortcuts to get the job done. In fact, many rewrites represent the beginning of the familiar legacy code spiral:

1. Code is rewritten.
2. Authors of the rewritten code are present to answer questions.
3. Team works more effectively with new code.
4. Authors of the new code begin to leave.
5. Questions emerge as to how parts of the code work.
6. More and more parts of the code become magic.
7. Development slowed by lack of understanding.
8. Developers become frustrated and declare they can't work with this code for much longer.
9. Go to #1.

Even though rewriting is something that developers love to do, refactoring often achieves positive results more quickly and without thrusting the team back into the legacy code rewrite loop.

You can, of course, effectively rewrite code if you come at it with the proper perspective. Whenever you write new code you should think five years into the future and of how someone else is going to pick up where you left off. Think about the trouble you've had while working with legacy code: not enough tests, too little documentation, patterns that make no sense. Then, solve those problems as you write the new code.

Conclusion

This entire chapter covers the specific steps you can take to make sure code you write is as maintainable and future-friendly as possible. The best way to avoid spaghetti code is to put the work in up front to organize things. Code conventions ensure that everyone speaks the same language. An architecture lays a solid foundation on which to build. Good documentation is important so others can extend your code later. Choosing and managing third-party components appropriately makes sure you have a linear upgrade path as fixes become available.

Of course, it's not every day that you start out with a blank slate. You'll deal with someone else's code quite frequently. If that code falls into the category of legacy code, then your path forward is to make small pieces of that code easier to understand every day. Add documentation. Add tests. Don't believe in magic.

A codebase takes on a life of its own over time. Some grow to be elegant and beautiful while others grow to be gnarly and stinky. Exactly how your codebase grows depends on how you nurture it, the structure you give it, and how comfortable people are with making modifications.

ABOUT THE AUTHOR

Nicholas C. Zakas is a Staff Software Engineer at Box. He worked at Yahoo! for almost five years, where he was front-end tech lead for the Yahoo! homepage and a contributor to the YUI library. He is the author of *Maintainable JavaScript, Professional JavaScript for Web Developers, High Performance JavaScript* and *Professional Ajax*. Nicholas is a strong advocate for development best practices including progressive enhancement, accessibility, performance, scalability and maintainability. Nicholas blogs regularly at http://www.nczonline.net/ and can be found on Twitter at @slicknet.

ABOUT THE REVIEWER

Addy Osmani is working on the Chrome team at Google, building and advocating for tools to help improve developer productivity and satisfaction. His personal projects include TodoMVC, which helps developers compare JavaScript MVC frameworks and AuraJS. He's also written *Developing Backbone.js Applications* and *Learning JavaScript Design Patterns*.

Chapter

03

The Vanilla Web Diet

Written by Christian Heilmann

CHAPTER THREE · BY CHRISTIAN HEILMANN

THE VANILLA WEB DIET

T HERE'S NO QUESTION ABOUT IT: a lot of the content on the Web these days is consumed on mobile devices and tablets. In some new and emerging markets, mobile devices will be the first thing people use to go online as the infrastructure for desktop devices isn't available and mobile masts are easier to put up than putting fiber optics in the ground.

We should be ready for that challenge — Web technology is flexible enough after all — but when you look at the things we put on the Web and how many companies opt for native apps or mobile-optimized versions in parallel to their main website, there seems to be a worrying disconnect.

The hype about HTML5 and its perceived victory over Flash is receding slightly and now is a good time to analyze what we do and change our approach to be ready for a new bunch of people coming to the Web.

With Moore's Law[1] in full effect, we all work on very powerful, high-resolution devices with fast connections when we develop, and a lot

---

1 http://en.wikipedia.org/wiki/Moore%27s_law

of our clients have the same. That leads to beautiful and impressive web-sites and showcases that clock up hundreds of server requests and several megabytes of data.

When we go out and use our mobile devices, or the wireless connections available in cafés and hotels, things look different, though. A large part of our time is spent watching spinning animations show us something is loading, and often we are told that the connection is wonky and that we should try again. The same issue will come up for the next generation of online users. Remember how frustrating dial-up was? We must not repeat the same mistake of adding lots of slick-looking content and functionality while we develop just because we can. We must get leaner and lose some of the fat.

As with any weight loss, just flexing our muscles and going to the gym is not enough — we also need to analyze and change what we put into our bodies. Our gym time right now concentrates on generating a new, more professional workflow for the Web. Instead of writing CSS, HTML and JavaScript, we use build processes and scripts like Grunt, we preprocess our CSS with Sass and LESS, and we automatically generate image sprites from many images in a folder. Many people also proclaim the only way we'll ever be flexible enough to build 'real apps' is to move to other, new languages like Dart and TypeScript and apply more software engineering, computer science and pattern-driven approaches to the Web. This reminds me of the time when JavaScript libraries were all the rage and made browsers behave predictably. Of the hundreds of libraries created back then, only a few remain now and we can easily predict that many of the so-called "essential tools" we create and rely on now will become unfashionable and outdated.

Maybe we should also take a break in our drive to be cool and new and innovative the whole time, simply for the sake of being so, and check what we are doing — analyze our eating habits, so to say. I call this the *Vanilla Web Diet*, much like people have started to call using JavaScript without libraries vanilla JavaScript. I want to share some ideas and thoughts you can bear in mind to help slim down an existing website or your next app.

None of the parts that make up the vanilla Web diet are new but they very much warrant repeating. Here's what we'll cover:

- Build on what works
- Lack of support is an opportunity
- Browser-specific code cannot be trusted
- Use a mix of technologies, each for what it does best
- Ask questions
- Write as much as needed, not the least possible
- It is not about what you can add: it is about what we can't take away
- Usefulness beats consistency across browsers
- Load only what is needed
- Analyzing effects beats adding FX
- Strong foundations beat a possible future addition

The first rule of the vanilla Web diet is to start from a clean slate. It's tempting to start with many of the existing HTML5 boilerplates or CSS reset solutions out there, but let's not do that right away.

The promise of an HTML boilerplate or CSS framework is to flatten the differences between browsers and to allow you to start at a baseline that apparently works across them. In many cases this really means a few desktop browsers — many of which aren't even in use any longer or will never be available in a mobile environment. That's why performance experts started advocating against boilerplates: they're considered too heavy. Making them more lightweight is one way of dealing with that issue, but it also means we effectively create a code fork that needs maintaining and upgrading should there be necessary changes in the original. There is one true boilerplate — it's called *HTML5* and it is supported in a predictable manner by all current browsers and, especially, mobile browsers. The whole idea behind HTML5 was to have a parser that is the same in every browser, so let's concentrate on using that, rather than extraneous padding for browsing environments that are extinct.

Without further ado, let's dive into the first part of a healthy Web product: a sensible starting point.

Build on What Works

Our base layer should be plain and simple HTML that does what the product is meant to do.

Something that looks like a button but doesn't do anything does not help our users. When everything else fails, HTML is what users get: let's not deprive them of that. Mistakes happen, errors can arise from lots of sources, many of which might not be under our control. As Jake Archibald put it: "All of our users have JavaScript disabled until your first script loads and is executed." That's why time spent thinking about the base layer of what we do is never time wasted.

This should be the main principle behind what we build — and it is nothing new. We've called it "semantic layering, progressive enhancement"; we even came up with cute acronyms like POSH (for plain old semantic HTML). Yet we keep forgetting this principle again and again. It seems that the pursuit of crafting sensible HTML that explains itself confuses people who come from an object-oriented programming world, where everything needs to be instantiated and changed before it's applied. In HTML, not so much. It makes sense to see HTML as a foundation to build on. You can't build something heavy and large on a rickety foundation, so let's use as much HTML as needed — but not more — and when we use HTML, let's use what works.

Say, for example, you want to have a tab control. It is not uncommon for JavaScript widgets to come up with something like the following, either as the HTML you have to create for them to work, or generated by JavaScript:

```
<div class="tabcontrol">
  <div class="tab">One</div>
  <div class="tab">Two</div>
  <div class="tab">Three</div>
```

```
  <div class="panel">Panel One</div>
  <div class="panel">Panel Two</div>
  <div class="panel">Panel Three</div>
</div>
```

The structural meaning of this is exactly zero. No, semantic class names don't cut it — they don't mean a thing for the browser and they don't trigger any of the rendering or interaction functionality browsers are so good at. So why not use what we have — and have had at our disposal since the first browsers?

```
<section class="tabcontrol">
  <nav id="nav">
    <ul>
      <li><a href="#one">One</a></li>
      <li><a href="#two">Two</a></li>
      <li><a href="#three">Three</a></li>
    </ul>
  </nav>
  <article id="one">
    <header><h1>One</h1></header>
    <section>
      <!-- fill me with content -->
    </section>
    <footer>
      <p class="back"><a href="#nav">Back to menu</a></p>
    </footer>
  </article>
  <article id="two">
    <header><h1>Two</h1></header>
    <section><!-- fill me with content --></section>
    <footer>
      <p class="back"><a href="#nav">Back to menu</a></p>
    </footer>
  </article>
  <article id="three">
    <header><h1>Three</h1></header>
    <section>
      <!-- fill me with content -->
    </section>
</section>
```

```
    <footer>
      <p class="back"><a href="#nav">Back to menu</a></p>
    </footer>
  </article>
</section>
```

Granted, this is a lot more HTML, but here's the thing: you get a boatload of benefits from this structure.

- It works without any JavaScript or CSS. Visitors get a list of links that point to parts of the document, a tried and true way to skip to the interesting bits in a large document. The links back to the menu allow you to easily return.

- By using real targets in the document in the shape of IDs on elements (the days of named anchors really are over by now), our panel can be bookmarked automatically and seed the history of the browser without having to use pushState or the horrible hack of hashbangs.

- We have a lot of hooks in there for styles and JavaScript. We could even use the `:target` selector in CSS and not need JavaScript at all.

- When browsers eventually do something useful with the outline algorithm of `sections`, `articles` and `nav` (for example, they could create an automatic table of contents, like Word does, or make them discoverable in screen readers like headings and lists and links are now), we'll already have the right HTML in place — we can build for things to come instead of simulating them.

- Assistive technology loves this. Users are informed that the navigation consists of a list of six items, or they could circumvent the whole thing and jump from heading to heading.

Of course, there are drawbacks. Using more than one of these tab controls means you need to create unique IDs for all the different targets. Let's face it, though — someone who does not understand that an ID is unique will have trouble coding at all. In the documentation of the widget, you'd explain that each ID also becomes a part of the URL and thus create readable URLs as a bonus.

Ideas about HTML should form our main thinking before we go nuts on extra features and special effects. When everything else breaks, this is what our users get. Browsers are incredibly forgiving these days; the HTML5 parser has been built to be backwards compatible. It has to be, because of the awful markup sins we and our tools committed in the past in attempts to support terrible browsers that needed hack after hack to render usable interfaces. This backwards compatibility, however, should not give us *carte blanche* to do whatever we want and rely on the browser to fix it for us. Clean HTML is like good grammar. It is not absolutely essential but it makes what you do much easier to understand and simpler to translate.

Writing semantic, clean and understandable HTML has fallen out of fashion. This is sad as it is the *lingua franca* of the Web and we seem to have lost a lot of vocabulary when we got all excited about widget libraries and CMS solutions. Now that browsers have moved on and a lot of the rendering problems of "the browser which shall not be named any longer" are no longer an issue, we should take a look at all the amazing things HTML gives us and stop using random constructs because they can be easily styled.

The most common example of HTML abuse is adding links that point nowhere. A # as the href attribute or, even worse, javascript:void(0), means you end up writing HTML for a script, and not for the browser to render or the user to interact with. If you need to call a script, use a button element. They can be beautifully styled, have in-built keyboard support and various states, and they can even be disabled using an attribute. By using attribute selectors in your CSS you can style them. Links are so much more than initiators of script functionality: they allow users to right-click them to get a context menu full of useful functionality like "Bookmark", "Save as" or "Open in a new tab". None of these make sense if the URL is #, do they?

Forms have come a long way, too. A simple `required` attribute on an `input` element means the user cannot submit the form until that data has been entered. Adding a `pattern` attribute allows you to define a rule in the form of a regular expression. In the past, all of this required a lot of JavaScript — now it is in browsers by default.

We'll discuss more examples like this as the chapter progresses. For now, keep your eyes open and look at what HTML5 has to offer you, without the knee-jerk reaction of saying a particular feature doesn't work in your favorite browser. We are building for a new set of conditions and for people who do not share our developer pain. Having a rich vocabulary is a wonderful thing. We should not only be Web-literate, we should be mark-up poets.

Lack of Support is an Opportunity

If an old browser cannot do something, we have the chance to test for it and not provide that functionality. In most cases, the functionality is merely nice to have and isn't needed.

One big mistake we made in the past, and which we keep carrying forward, is giving standardized and highly demanding code to non-standard and outdated technology. Yes, this is about *OldIE*, as we like to call it, but also concerns the new problem child browsers: stock browsers of older versions of Android and iOS.

As creators of the Web we have two duties. First, we have to deliver a working interface which should be exciting and a joy to use. Enjoyment is a worthwhile goal, but the most important part is the working bit. Our second duty is to use what browser makers give us to make the results of fulfilling the first duty as amazing as possible, and as maintainable as possible for the people we hand our code over to.

What do we do to achieve that? Every time a new technology comes out we polyfill and patch and add libraries to give that technology to browsers that should not be used any longer. We base this on the misconception that the premise of the Web is to give everybody the same experience. Most of the time, this is not our idea but one our managers, clients or project plan dictate. We try to make the experience of those using outdated technology as amazing as possible, because we consider it wrong to leave them with less than those users who have up-to-date environments that keep getting updated. This is not what the Web is about. No one forces us to support outdated technology with features readily available in newer technology.

The premise of the Web is to deliver content to everybody regardless of ability, technical capabilities and knowledge, or geographical location. Web technologies allow us to do that, but only when we use them wisely and don't try to give everyone the same experience, leaving us all disappointed as we race to cater to the lowest common denominator.

We seem to be obsessed with the question, "Will this work in browser X?" and use all kinds of tricks and workarounds to make it work. We waste a lot of effort on unsatisfying results and this increases our frustration. If we give functionality to a browser by means of a hack or workaround, we also take it on ourselves to keep supporting and testing in this browser. More rewarding would be to ask, "What does *not* work in this browser?" and then use the answer to define which supported technologies we'll apply.

When you include a style sheet these days, you don't worry at all about browsers that don't support CSS — you know that browsers will only apply what they understand, so there is no chance of it causing any trouble. A compass needle pointing south is as useful as one that points in the right direction — you just need to use it correctly.

A great example of this is the Smashing Magazine website. It uses responsive design using CSS media queries. These aren't supported by OldIE which is why, originally, the website employed a JavaScript patch called `respond.js` to make older versions of IE also switch designs around when the screen size changed.

However, this turned out to be overkill, as all that was needed was a fixed-width design for older IE, letting the browser decide if responsive design was within its powers or not.

How about we leave nobody out but build for the next generation of technology? Give outdated browsers only what they can stomach: a bit of CSS and HTML that really does the job. Semantic HTML that has meaning and triggers functionality every browser offered from the start; links that point somewhere; URLs that can be bookmarked; navigation that seeds the history of the browser; forms that are validated and processed on the server and sent back to the browser.

Only then should we add layers and layers of awesomeness for those browsers which can deal with them. For example, take the wonderful and standardized `addEventListener()`. OldIE doesn't understand that, so we wrote a filler to overwrite `attachEvent()`. Bad plan. This is software ballast we'll carry with us for years to come and it caters to a tiny sub-group of users that will get smaller and smaller. Why not just wrap all of our JavaScript in `if (window.addEventListener) {}` and never pester OldIE with the demanding JavaScript we write these days?

The same logic applies to CSS. If we wrap the amazing and beautiful parts of our CSS in a media query, OldIE and stock browsers will be none the wiser and won't try to parse what we give them.

Outdated browsers are retired; we shouldn't pester them with more and more demands to execute code that wasn't meant for them and will never run smoothly. If you use a filler library to support old browsers, you also burden yourself with testing in them to make sure the users of those browsers receive a smooth and beautiful experience. Testing outdated browsers in the development environments we have today is a chore, and only adds lots and lots of unhappy hours to our workload. Why do that?

Start with basic code that works in all browsers, then add to it and make sure that browsers that should not be in use at all do not get code they might choke on — you'll leave everybody happy.

Things I've never seen, I cannot miss. Things I can see that don't work, frustrate me. A lack of support is a great opportunity to not promise things you cannot and should not try to offer.

BROWSER-SPECIFIC CODE CANNOT BE TRUSTED

Each line of code you write with browser prefixes simply adds to the mass of code that will break very, very soon.

The release of the iPhone and the subsequent stir in the developer community made the hair on the back of my neck prickle. I was vividly reminded of the times when people told me that everything that only works in IE6 and no other browser is what every developer should follow, as there will be no other browsers in the future. That turned out to be rubbish, and so is all the code on the Web now that only works on the first generation iPhone, or even blocks other browsers from accessing the content of the page at all.

If you ever encounter a white button with white text there is a distinct possibility that the developer used `-webkit-linear-gradient` and nothing else on the button's CSS background definition. This is neither clever, modern nor pragmatic. It is broken code that only worked for a very short time in a fleeting environment. Writing browser-specific code is much like releasing movies only on VHS. It seems like a cheap and quick solution at the time and gets the job done, but it leaves you with thousands of unsold copies that nobody can watch because the hardware is obsolete.

If you use prefixed code, at least wrap it in a test condition. The best way, however, is to precede it with a fallback that works everywhere and follow that with the standardized code. In the example of the button with white text on a white background, all would be fine if the developer defined a background first and a browser-specific linear gradient afterwards.

Browser-specific code is a to-do. If you cannot revisit and fix the code once the functionality has been standardized then you write broken, unreliable code. Environments change. That is why we have standards.

Use a Mix of Technologies, Each for What it Does Best

It is very tempting to do everything in JavaScript, but you shouldn't.

When you have a shiny new hammer, everything looks like a nail — and turns out to be a thumb once you start hammering. We have incredibly powerful technologies in the Web stack, the most powerful probably being JavaScript. CSS is a strong second, considering the recent additions. In general, it is possible to do everything to and in a browser with JavaScript. You can create whole applications with just a body tag in your HTML. You can make outdated browsers behave like their modern versions, you can interact with windows and the DOM, and move data to and from the server. Retaining control makes it tempting to do everything with JavaScript. Whole frameworks have been built on that premise (qooxdoo[2], for example) with amazing performance and great programming principles. Sooner or later, though, they become outdated and do things in JavaScript that no longer need to be done at the cost of processor computation.

Remember when we created lots of small images to add rounded corners to things? And how cool it is now to have CSS border radius and background gradients to change the look and feel, without needing to recreate all of them or ensure our users don't have the old ones cached?

The same thing is happening to JavaScript right now. A lot of what we use JavaScript (and especially libraries like jQuery) for is now handled by CSS: transitions, animations, media queries. This allows us to create amazingly smooth experiences and benefit from the browser working to ensure they stay smooth. If we use JavaScript, we get more control but our larger responsibility is to ensure things are smooth. And this responsibility very much depends on the browser and the technological contexts — contexts that change from month to month.

One thing that massively slows down apps and websites is DOM access. Yet the simplicity of jQuery's DOM access API bred a whole generation of developers whose first lesson learned was how to write a loop

---

2 http://qooxdoo.org/

(hidden in a `$()` selector chained to a method) to access elements in the document to change their look and feel. In a lot of cases, that is just not needed. You could use event handling instead, or condition checking in JavaScript and add a class to the body or the parent element of what you want to change and let CSS do the rest. It's something the browser does on reflows and rendering anyway, so why not piggyback on that?

If you check what you need to achieve before getting excited about the simplicity of chaining and selecting elements in JavaScript, you will find that most of what you need to do now involves adding and removing classes, and loading content. JavaScript is good for on-the-fly changes triggered by interaction; CSS is great for making the changes appear.

Browser makers do a great job of allowing us, in developer tools, to tap into the rendering by the browser and see what happens.

A `requestAnimationFrame()` lets you change things and only display them when the result can end up onscreen. Furthermore, when the browser tab your script runs in is inactive (when the user is in another tab or window), the animation doesn't run, thereby not wasting computation time and shortening battery life. In contrast, a `setTimeout()` hopes that the browser is ready to draw and runs whether the user is viewing your animation or not.

Animations and transitions in CSS are hardware-accelerated; JavaScript animations are not. So are transformations in CSS, which means that a `transform: translate(x,y)` beats a `position: absolute; top: x; left: y;` when it comes to performance.

I urge anyone working on the Web to keep up to date with browser technology and standards support. Only when developers use what browsers offer can we make the Web better. If functionality defined in the standards is not used, browser makers are less inclined to support it. Why support `input type="range"` when most developers use a `div` and a jQuery plugin to turn it into a slider? You probably won't have the time to constantly update your code, so be lazy about this — use what is fit for the job and enhance as needed with JavaScript. We can only resolve the chicken and egg problem of standards support by demanding that browser makers add the support when we can show our products are ready for it.

Every good Web solution works by leaving the right tasks to the right technology. We often get too excited about our specialisms and want everything to be possible in the one we favor. A band creates music when its members play the instruments that they want to play. Very few people can play the drums, guitar and trombone, and sing — none can at the same time. Pick and choose, don't try to replace.

ASK THE "IF" QUESTION

Whatever you do should be wrapped in an "if", so only environments that can apply what you want do so.

Using "if" is a powerful tool, both in conversations and coding. Good coding is defensive — it tests the depth of the water before diving in. Our solutions should not just assume that a certain user has what's needed to consume the content we give them.

Wrapping the loading of content in test cases is an incredibly powerful way to achieve the most enjoyable experience for different users — we'll come back to that later.

However, "if" can be used for much more. You can ask the current environment about its capabilities before applying a certain functionality. You can stop the browser from trying to run whole blocks of JavaScript by first asking if it can do even the simplest things required. The less code we force our browsers to parse, the better their performance will be. Why read a whole book in Icelandic to a friend without asking if they understand the language in the first place?

Sometimes it is necessary to apply some trickery to avoid very bad experiences. HTML5 video is one of those examples. You might have seen the following demo code in a few places.

```
<video src="kittens.mp4" controls>
  Your browser cannot play HTML5 video.</video>
```

First, this sentence is not fallback content for browsers that cannot play HTML5 video: this is making your problem the user's problem, which is especially frustrating if they are not tech savvy. Imagine trying to do something and people keep telling you, "Your phleems cannot work with boodiloo." OK, what does that mean? A much better way is to give the user a link to the video as the fallback:

```
<video src="kittens.mp4" controls>
  <a href="kittens.mp4">Check the video of kittens</a>.</video>
```

That way, users of old browsers can watch the video in the media player of their operating systems simply by following the link. You can make that even better by adding a screenshot. Not only does this provide a visual aid but it allows social media sites like Facebook to show a thumbnail preview — everybody wins. Well, almost.

Browsers that understand the HTML5 video element but do not understand the MP4 file format (as it is not an open format) will not show the fallback content. Instead, they show a gray box with a message about a video not being able to be played, and do not offer a link to follow.

This is annoying, but accords with the standards definitions. Reading up on those, there is a way to check if a video can be played.

Say we have this HTML:

```
<video controls>
  <source src="dynamicsearch.mp4" type="video/mp4"></source>
  <a href="dynamicsearch.mp4">
    <img src="dynamicsearch.jpg"
         alt="Dynamic app search in Firefox OS">
  </a>
  <p>Click image to play a video demo of
     dynamic app search</p>
</video>
```

The following JavaScript shows the way to make a browser (one that supports the `video` element but is unable to play it) show the fallback content instead:

```
if (window.addEventListener && document.querySelector) {
  var v = document.querySelector('video'),
      sources = v.querySelectorAll('source'),
      lastsource = sources[sources.length-1];
  lastsource.addEventListener('error', function(ev) {
    var d = document.createElement('div');
    d.innerHTML = v.innerHTML;
    v.parentNode.replaceChild(d, v);
  }, false);
}
```

What's going on here? When a browser fails to play a video, it fires an error handler on the last source element in the `video` element. So, we test that the browser understands `addEventListener()` and `querySelector()` (which is the standard way of jQuery's `$()`, really) and then get the last source element in the `video` element. If there is an error event being fired, we create a `div` element and replace the `video` with that one.

By asking the browser what it can do, we can fix an unsatisfactory fallback experience and make this work for everybody. Not the same experience, but still one that works. Such action needs thought and research (I believed, for example, that the video element fires an error event instead of the last `source`), but it is worthwhile as we don't pass on our problems to our users. "If" is a mighty construct and it makes your code better and independent of its environment.

WRITE AS MUCH AS NEEDED, NOT THE LEAST POSSIBLE

Let's think about what we write before we write it, instead of adding lots of small, quick solutions.

The rise of jQuery started something of a fetish in the Web developer community: the less code you write, the more effective you are considered to be; and the more code you write that does something in a short period of time, the more awesome you get. This is not necessarily true.

Yes, typing less means we can do other things, but if it comes at the cost of abstracting what we do into libraries and plugins it can get tricky. What we never know on the Web is what our users do or have at their disposal. So relying on an abstraction that we don't control and whose processes we don't understand seems dangerous. We feel this already. A lot of small solutions dependent on jQuery or other libraries perform incredibly badly on mobile devices.

Impressive plugins that tell us they are only a few KB or take just three lines of code to implement tend to end up sending a much larger number of bytes to our users, wrapped up in many HTTP requests and adding to the overall amount of JavaScript in our apps. It is not uncommon to see people use several libraries at once because they like widgets built in each of them. This is not the purpose of browser libraries. They should solve problems and make our work easier, not harder. It is especially dangerous when libraries stop being maintained or updated and turn out to cause performance problems. Of course, a good build or deployment script deals with these issues — yet another thing to learn and to maintain. Why add more to undo what was done before, when we should avoid overloading our solutions with small, seemingly useful helpers in the first place?

As shown earlier, using a bit more semantic HTML can trigger the benefits of built-in browser functionality. The same applies to all of our code. It is much more important to build a solid base into our products, an easy to read and understandable core that can be added to. We do this by writing clean, easy-to-understand code that has sensible variable and method names that does one thing well. Not by writing abstraction APIs for others to use to achieve a lot quickly without knowing what they're doing and hiding the complexities away from them.

The advocacy for short code is at times just an excuse to be lazy. This can lead to ridiculous threads on forums and message boards where people use <b> and <i> elements instead of <span> with a sensible class name to save time, or they omit quotes around attributes to save yet another keystroke from adding to the workload in long documents. Either practice means you save some time now but both lead to confusion later on when you need to extend your code. Omitting the quotes around attributes, for example, only works until you need to add another value that is space separated (for example with the class attribute), so why not add them right now to allow for more to be added?

Using unreadable, terse and rushed code to get things out the door quickly doesn't mean you are more effective. It means you will get into trouble later on. The maintainability of your code is the most important part to think about and you can only do that while you write it. "Get this out now, we can clean it up later" is as much of a lie as agreeing that "I have read the full terms and conditions." Build for the person who takes over from you, not for the current state of the browser and you'll be a great person to work with.

IT'S NOT ABOUT WHAT YOU CAN ADD, IT'S ABOUT WHAT WE CAN'T TAKE AWAY

Basic functionality should always be there.
A curious thing about software is that it is fallible.

We, who are excited about it, are prone to forget that. Using a fancy MVC (Model-View-Controller) framework to build a single-page app with incredibly clean separation of back-end tasks is a tempting thing to do. After all, this is what the cool kids do and what Google and others, who have to scale to infinity and beyond, use.

We get very excited about adding new features to our products because we see them used elsewhere and we are bored with building the same solutions year after year. It can feel like we're not progressing and, more importantly, it feels weird that almost nothing we learn in computer science courses at university can be applied once we take a job in Web development.

Something must be wrong and Web development must just not be evolved enough for proper programming tasks, right? Wrong.

There really is nothing in computing comparable to Web development, as we do not compile what we write into bytecode optimized for one or another environment. Our code goes out and is transformed on the computers and handheld devices and cars and fridges and watches and whatever else users will have in the future that is Web-enabled (glasses perhaps?). That is why a lot of best practices from the past become shoehorned into the Web, and while they are good ideas they don't necessarily yield the desired results.

In the end, we need to always offer basic functionality to users or we'll create lots of small walled environments on the Web. No, you can't expect a user to have a certain browser. No, people cannot increase the resolution of their mobile to fit your needs. No, the connection speed you have on your development machine is not what every user experiences — not by a long shot.

What does basic functionality entail? Put simply, it allows the user to do what they came for regardless of any technology failure. A textbook example of this happened recently to one of the largest Web companies out there: Google. For a whole half-day, on February 4, 2013, the download page for Chrome was unavailable. You could click the download button but nothing would happen.

Opening the Chrome developer tools revealed two things: first, the HTML of the button was the following:

```
<a class="button eula-download-button"
   href="javascript:void(0)"
   data-g-label="download chrome"
   data-g-event="cta"> … </a>
```

Second, the error console greeted you with "TypeError: chrm.download is undefined."

What happened? Well, something in the JavaScript went wrong and took the button with it. `javascript:void(0)` is not a valid URL and has no business being in an `href` attribute. It is a blinking warning sign that somewhere in the development process Google threw in the towel and created everything in JavaScript. On investigation, I found out that the purpose of the code is to show an end user license agreement before download (as hinted in the class name), and the JavaScript automatically detects the operating system to provide the appropriate install package for Chrome. Both very good uses for this page, but the way they were implemented meant Google lost half a day of Chrome downloads.

The remedy is straightforward: instead of pointing the link to a small inline JavaScript that does nothing at all, it should point to a download page that lists all the downloadable versions of Chrome. This could be a great resource in any case, as sometimes I might want to download a version not for my OS (for example, if I am on a fast connection somewhere). You can still add an event handler to the link to do all the other necessary things done in the JavaScript that was never called.

Redirecting to a EULA page on the server is easy and so is sending through the information about which OS installer is needed. This was a classic case of using the wrong tool simply because the developer could.

In essence, it is important to not break the Web with what we do: forms should be sent to a server-side control; links should point to real resources; media should be linked to *and* embedded, instead of just embedded in the hope that the browser does everything right.

Once we have this, we can add whatever we want. But seriously, trying to replace the basic transport mechanisms of the Web with our own constructs may seem faster but it will always be very prone to error. We have a working infrastructure — we should use it.

USEFULNESS BEATS CONSISTENCY ACROSS BROWSERS

Instead of attempting to give everyone the same experience, we should always find the best way to ensure people can use what we build.

Something that adds to the obesity of the Web to a very large degree is the misguided notion of giving every browser and every environment the same experience. Again, as creators of the Web we know this is foolish, but many a time we are asked to bow to this pressure by our project plans or our managers. We need to take a stand. It's an outdated and infuriatingly shortsighted idea that just refuses to die. When Web development began, we were often given print designs and asked to make them work on the Web by any means necessary. This is how we ended up with text as graphics and, later on, Flash being used for everything that needed "to meet design specifications."

Nowadays, we try to create beautiful, interactive and immersive multimedia experiences with the tools HTML5 offers, and then make them backwards compatible with environments lacking even the basic means to display a video. And we create massive, Flash-like sites and hide elements that can't be shown on a mobile screen. We still load all the content, though, and move from large to small. When high-resolution displays came out, we started to send over the wire huge, high-resolution images that could never be displayed on the low-res hardware receiving them.

This does not make sense. If we want the Web to succeed — and as it is the simplest worldwide distribution platform, we have this as a good cause — then we have to rethink our approach and build interfaces that are not just resized but also tailored to the context they will be displayed in. We need to start seeing design and UX as context-dependent tasks, and not take a one-size-fits-all approach. Instead of showing only part of the design on small-screen devices and more on larger screens, we need to think about what people want to do and what they can do best in a certain environment.

For example, I skim and triage my news feeds on my phone and book-mark to read later. When I get to my laptop, I read in detail what I book-marked and share it with the world. Yet, I have to use more or less the same interface on both devices and I'd love to have a simpler one on the phone, tailored to my need to triage, and one that makes sharing easier on the laptop.

With new ways of interacting with our content being devised all the time — gestures, touch, glasses, buttons in the steering wheels of cars — we need to be ready to build bespoke experiences quickly and with ease. We cannot do that if we try to discover the holy grail of one design that works everywhere, or start with a framework that promises us that. It doesn't exist, unless you stay incredibly simple and leave untouched a lot of the opportunities modern browsers and hardware offer.

We need to let go and leave some decisions to our users. Look at eBook readers. I love how Google Play Books changes from landscape to portrait, and how the Kindle allows me to change from black on white to gray on black when I want to read in the dark. Let's think about what our users do in different contexts, rather than throwing the kitchen sink at them and hoping that hiding parts of it is enough. We're not doing enough right now, which is why mobile browsers have "Reader" modes or allow users to force a "Desktop version" on to their small screen as the mobile interface is disappointing and frustrating.

LOAD ONLY WHAT IS NEEDED

Why should a browser get a library or a data file if it cannot do anything with it?

One of the most exciting techniques we discovered in the wake of the DHTML days and now powered by AJAX is that of lazy loading. In essence, this means that we only load resources when we need them. Why should a user on a small device get a massive image that can never be displayed in a satisfying way? Why would you include a JavaScript library targeted at iOS on an Android device or even the desktop?

JavaScript is good at testing for support and then loading resources on demand. We just don't use it enough for that. Right now, we find ourselves with more and more solutions that first load large amounts of high-end resources because caching will improve the experience as the user moves through the site. This is wasteful as it doesn't help the users who will never benefit from that high-end experience. It might not seem to be a problem at all for us, with fast connections, big screens and powerful processors. But this is not what we build for (unless you're creating developer tools) and we should ensure that our work is tested on low-power machines and mobiles and flaky connections. The more we can delay loading unnecessary content or subsequently storing it on the user's device, instead of repeatedly loading it, the better our solutions will be.

Personally, I find progress bars and animations to be admissions of failure. No one enjoyed them in Flash intros and they drive us nuts on YouTube, so why should I have to wait a few minutes because you want to preload everything, instead of analyze how I interact with your code?

So let's think before adding the 12 unnecessary fonts on the first page, the CSS framework that we use to create a two-column layout, and the kitchen sink JavaScript library we use to add a single event handler to a button.

Let's check the available screen space before loading content that will only need to be hidden because there is no room for it. Let's not load images before the user actually scrolls them into view (to avoid causing unsightly shifting of content, keep a box with the same size in place, then replace it with the image). Let's not add background music just because we think users will want it — let's wait till they are really happy to hear it.

There is natural downtime in the interaction with our apps. For example, people will spend some time entering data into forms. So why not use that time to load additional resources? A focus handler on the first text field could trigger a nice-to-have resources download. If the user never enters the form, nothing needs to happen.

This is a world where connectivity is narrower than it is on the desktop. Let's not clog up the pipes with things nobody will ever consume.

ANALYZING EFFECTS BEATS ADDING FX

If you want to add shiny things, make sure they can perform in a shiny fashion. Nobody likes their browser to slow down for an effect that lags.

All in all, we seem to be far too focused on visual effects in our designs. You can see this in the procession of design fads that come and go. The current fascination with scroll-to-parallax websites will soon look as dated and annoying as rainbow dividers or Flash tunnel pages look now.

The question we have to ask ourselves is how many effects we can add to a certain environment before we overload our users. Are the drop-shadow, rounded corners and gradient really necessary on everything, or does it make sense to create them with CSS only for those environments which support them, instead of simulating them with images and increasing load times? Moving from skeuomorphic to flat design would mean just changing the CSS — no need to find and delete orphaned images on the server or, more likely, abandon them there to add to the overall weight of the project.

Does it make sense to have two states of a widget fade into one another if it means adding another JavaScript library and calculating the fade in JavaScript? A CSS transition is done by the browser, and browser makers can tweak and improve its behavior. The video hardware can calculate it, rather than the main processor. If you do the transition by hand in JavaScript it is up to you to make it behave smoothly everywhere and you cannot rely on the browser to do the dirty work for you. Will users really love the subtle drop-shadow when their battery empties much quicker than it would without it?

Just because something works well in native apps doesn't mean it will be appropriate in Web apps or websites. We'd only be simulating an environment we could never match in terms of performance, creating unhappy, disappointed users. Nobody wants to get a lovely piece of cake only to realize at the first bite that it has no taste whatsoever. Effects are nice to have but should not be our end goal. They are great to impress Web developers and other interested parties, but we should spend far more time asking real users what their objectives are when visiting our sites or using our apps. Sometimes the simplest solutions are the most beautiful.

STRONG FOUNDATIONS BEAT A POSSIBLE FUTURE ADDITION

Often we add a lot of code or interfaces to allow for a future that we think will need them. This future hardly ever comes about. Let's build for the now.

Probably the biggest cause of bloated solutions is that we overshoot the mark when it comes to planning the architecture of our Web solutions. The Web is hot right now and there are not enough Web developers to meet the demand for products to be built. A lot of developers are needed and many of them come from more traditional software environments where systems are built in one way and one way only to scale and be robust. Often we now shoehorn these approaches into the Web, and claim cultishly that anything not built on OO (Object-Oriented) principles and with an MVC approach will never scale and be operable.

Years of Web-built products show, however, that this is not the case. Of course, a cleaner approach bears the fruit of better, maintainable code, but not when it comes at the cost of generated front-end interfaces that rely on JavaScript to work, and create distinct code for different browsers — in many cases, for different versions of the same browser. What many development approaches forget is that a single-page application requires you to not only write your app, but also replace a lot of functionality done for the Web by HTTP and the browser, like history-keeping and undo functionality. In essence, you run a thick-client app in a thin-client environment you cannot control.

A good idea is to think about what you want to achieve before you reach for the silver bullet of MVC frameworks and switch to what's touted as a better language than JavaScript merely to generate JavaScript.

Things on the Web change a lot. And in many cases it means replacing the whole code base but duplicating the functionality. Many of the apps and websites we produce are there, first and foremost, to get people to put content into them and make that content available to others. The code of the app itself should play a secondary role to that.

Every time a Web company was bought by a larger one and needed to scale to millions of users, its whole code base was replaced or altered to fit an existing framework that had already proved itself. You don't need to build Google Mail or Facebook. You should think about creating what you need to at the time, and prepare yourself to replace the lot in the near future.

This seems to counterpoint our dictum of old: that separation of concerns into HTML, JavaScript and CSS means you can redo a whole project by just changing the CSS. The Web has become much more of a commodity than it was in the past, so we need to be agile. If you build to burn down using Bootstrap and do everything with it, that's fine. But don't use lots of libraries, frameworks and server-side back-ends that generate whole apps while claiming that they'll scale. They won't just magically do that: you still need to know them really well to play them to their strengths, rather than just add a lot of code to be used later — a later that never comes.

Summary

Nothing here should really be new, but it seems that we keep forgetting the tricks and practices that first made the Web a success. Flexibility defines the Web and we keep carving out niches for all the things the Web can do and promote this quality to be the main goal for every developer out there. It's not about building thick clients or native apps on the Web, it's about using the Web and its technologies to deliver content and media, allowing people to simply add new things to this wonderful series of tubes.

I think it's time to stop looking for solutions that try to tame the Web and make it more like other environments. Instead, we should embrace the idea that the future will only bring more diverse playgrounds, and that we cannot cater to them by being restrictive. So, rather than abstracting the task of communicating with browsers into a seemingly shorter but ultimately more complex world of libraries and quick stopgap solutions, I hope you found some ideas here of how to write a few lines of code tailored to what browsers already possess.

ABOUT THE AUTHOR

Christian Heilmann is Principal Developer Evangelist of the Mozilla Developer Network and lives currently in North London, a mixing pot of people from many cool places. He works to bring technology to people and people to technology, and when he's not busy working, films are his diversion of choice. Christian has a diploma in German, English, history and astronomy. His motto is, "Start something and play with it; if you don't want to play with it, stop doing it." His message to readers is to stay hungry and stay inquisitive; something new is always around the corner.

Chapter

04

Culture of
Performance

Written by Tim Kadlec

CHAPTER FOUR · BY TIM KADLEC

CULTURE OF PERFORMANCE

M Y PARENTS WERE BIG FANS OF FAMILY TIME. They loved to get me and my four siblings together to do things. We went on a lot of family trips. Every Sunday was family movie night. They took any chance they could get to have the family doing something together.

A good example of this was choosing a Christmas tree. Now, some parents would be OK with grabbing a tree from a tree lot nearby. But not my parents. To them, this was another opportunity to do something as a family — to create some family memories. So every December, we would pile together in the van and drive to a quiet, thickly wooded part of the forest that was full of prime candidates for the perfect Christmas tree.

We took our time — picking out a Christmas tree was not something to rush. We walked around for hours in the deep snow trying to find a tree that was just right. We never worried about taking precautions to ensure we would find our way back to the van — that was something that just happened. My dad was great with directions and always seemed to know just which way to go.

Except for one year.

We found the perfect tree after what must have been three or four hours. After my dad cut it down, we started back in what we thought was the direction of the van. We walked a long time, saw a lot of forest we didn't recognize, and realized that we were lost. My dad's seemingly unfallible sense of direction had failed him.

This, of course, made everyone kind of grumpy. My dad took pride in his ability to find his way back, but it had failed him this time. My mother wasn't exactly thrilled about her five children being lost in the middle of a snow-filled forest. And we kids weren't the most patient bunch.

In my head, I had already decided that we certainly weren't getting out of the forest that night. Thinking my teenage self to be something of a rugged outdoorsman, I started coming up with the contingency plan. We could build a little shelter, start a fire with some rocks (they did it in the movies — how hard could it be?) and find some food. It would be cold, but we'd figure it out.

Thankfully for all of us, we never had to test my survival skills. When the night was so dark we could see only a foot or so in front of us, we finally stumbled on the road. From there, my dad was easily able to guide us back to the car.

The next year, we planned better. We tied strings around trees as we went, carried a compass, and frequently stopped to check our bearings. Getting lost wasn't something we felt like doing again. Instead of viewing getting back to the van as something that just happened after everything else was accomplished, we were going to be deliberate about making sure our outing was a success.

Getting Deliberate About Performance

This same sort of struggle is hurting our websites today. Websites are getting fatter and fatter at an alarming rate. From March 2012 to March 2013, the average page weight jumped by a staggering 24% according to data from the HTTP Archive[1]. We're heading the wrong way fast. Usually, we don't even notice it as it happens — and if we do, it's often too late.

I was talking to a developer about a new website that he had been working on. The website was certainly well crafted. It was a little on the heavy side though. Not much, but enough that he felt the need to explain the situation a bit. What he said highlighted the issue with Web performance in general. "I doubt anyone really wants to release a site that doesn't perform well," he explained. "It's just a product of not being afforded the luxury of time and top-down pressure."

Feel like you've been there before? Most of us, I'm sure, can easily relate to this. I know I can.

I was working on a project where I was collaborating with a team of internal developers. From the very beginning, everyone stated that, among other things, they wanted the site to be very fast. The developers I was working with were very good at their jobs, and given the seemingly high level of importance being placed on performance there was good reason to believe this was going to go well. But then it didn't.

Early mock-ups were shown to upper management before being shown to developers. By the time the developers saw the mock-ups, they had already been approved by the powers that be. There was no opportunity to try to alter them based on any potential performance risks (and there were several).

Then an internal deadline was set based on business requirements that significantly altered the aggressiveness of the timeline. The combination of tight timescales and ambitious mock-ups approved too early led to yet another issue. "Make it fast" quickly turned into "Make it work. We can always make it faster later." Of course, later never came.

And so, after a lot of very hard work, we were closing in on launch and the performance of the site was a disaster. It was slow, sluggish — everything none of us wanted it to be.

---

1 http://httparchive.org/

But this was a quality team, and one that took a lot of pride in its work.

So for the remainder of the home stretch, we all kicked it into high gear. We worked ridiculously late nights. We worked over the weekends. Things got stressful for everyone — there were short tempers and tears mixed in with an absolute dedication to improving the situation.

When the site launched, it was better. Not great, but no longer quite the monster it had been. However, it had taken a lot of incredibly hard work to get there. Even with the improvement, we had to revisit the primary landing page of the site a few months later, ditching all the work we had done and starting from scratch.

Just like when my family got lost in the woods before Christmas, the long, late (and ultimately wasted) hours on this project could have been avoided had we been more deliberate. Had performance been baked into the process of creating the site, instead of something that gets added on, the result would have been a faster site and a lot happier team.

The issue was not the competence of the developers. As I said, this was an incredibly talented team. The issue was also not just technological: a lot of smart optimizations were implemented to get the weight down. Instead, the issue was the lack of a well-established *culture of performance* — a total commitment to performance from the entire team that would drive and influence decisions during the project cycle.

To put it more succinctly, we weren't being deliberate about making sure our site performed well. It was treated as something that would happen at the end. There were no strings being tied, no checking our bearings to make sure we weren't steering off course. As a result, when things got hairy, performance was one of the first things to get swept under the rug.

Given the incredibly important role performance plays in the user experience, this is a disastrous mistake to make.

The Impact of Performance

Name something your business cares about and I'll bet good money that its performance has been an important factor. Study after study has shown that how your site performs directly impacts how users will interact with it.

- Amazon found that for every 100ms of improved page load time, it saw a 1% increase in revenue[2].
- Bing tried an experiment where it deliberately made search queries take two seconds longer. The result was a 4.3% decrease in revenue per user[3].
- Mozilla improved the performance of its landing page[4] by 2.2 seconds and saw a 15.4% increase in download conversions. This roughly translates into 60 million more downloads annually.
- Shopzilla cut its page load time[5] from 6 seconds to 1.2 seconds. In addition to a 12% increase in revenue, page traffic increased by 25%.

We could go on, but I think the picture is starting to become pretty clear: improving performance affects page views, traffic — and the bottom line. Performance is about respecting your visitors, and they notice if you don't.

- 39% of users[6] say that performance is more important to them than the functionality of a site.
- 57% of users[7] will abandon a site after waiting three seconds for the page to load.

---

2 http://smashed.by/amzn-found
3 http://smashed.by/msft-performance
4 http://smashed.by/mozilla
5 http://smashed.by/shopzilla
6 http://smashed.by/slow-websites
7 http://smashed.by/3-secs

Not only does performance affect existing users, but it can actually help you reach new audiences as well. Consider the experience YouTube had when it improved performance (see Mat Marquis' chapter). New markets, increased revenue, improved business metrics, better user satisfaction — the impact of improved Web performance is no minor detail.

None of this should be a surprise. The Web is an interactive medium. Click a button, scroll down a page, submit a form: interactions are at the heart of what it means to use a website. Performance is a fundamental component of the user experience.

We can correct the course, and we must if we want to truly capitalize on the ubiquity and interactive nature of the Web. To do so, we need to stop treating performance as nice to have, or a developer task, and start to ingrain it into our workflow.

Before this can happen, we need to get buy-in from management.

Getting Support

No matter how valuable you know performance to be, you need to get support. If the people dealing directly with budgets and timelines don't care, you'll have a hard time making sure performance is prioritized throughout the process.

MAKE IT PERSONAL

It's easy to get excited about reducing metrics like load time and page weight, but they're probably not what matters to the people you need to get support from. They want to hear about what it will do for the things they care about. Some people will want to see how it affects the bottom line. Others may care more about what it means for page views and bounce rates. Learn what others care about and focus on emphasizing how performance improves those factors. You'll have a lot more success convincing them of the importance of performance if you connect it to something that matters directly to them.

MAKE IT VISUAL

If you're trying to persuade a client or boss of the importance of performance, augment the metrics with a visual.

One very effective method is to show them their site loading next to a faster competitor site. If your client is McDonald's and Burger King's site loads faster, first show them what they stand to gain by improving performance, and then show them how Burger King beats them out. Nobody likes to lose to a competitor.

You can easily do this with WebPageTest.org[8] using one of two methods. The first is to run a test for each site individually, selecting "Capture Video" under the advanced settings. Save the two videos and queue them up side by side.

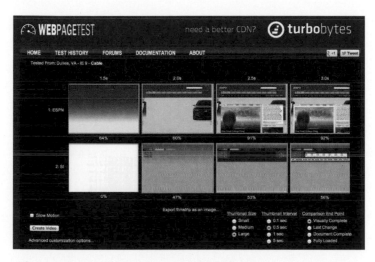

The visual comparison option on WebPageTest.org lets you easily see how quickly sites load when compared to each other.

WebPageTest also provides a "Visual Comparison" option. With this method, you add the URLs for each page to compare and then run the test. WebPageTest will capture screenshot of static images throughout the

8 http://www.webpagetest.org/

loading process so you can see exactly when things start to load on each page, and when the page completes. Sometimes this can even be a little more dramatic than a video.

Baking Performance into the Process

When I was in my early twenties, I took a job at RadioShack. This wasn't a great gig for me. Sure, RadioShack had a lot of gadgets to play with — that part was fun. But I was never a great sales person, and this was a role where I needed to be. I worked with someone who was good at it. Made for it, even. He would literally push me aside at times to get to someone eyeing up a cellphone — easily the quickest way to earn a few extra bucks on our checks.

You see, we got a minimum wage, but the only way you made any money was through commission and what they called *SPIFs* (special performance incentive fund). SPIFs were incentives you received for selling certain items. Sell a cellphone, you got a SPIF. You also got SPIFs for selling service plans. In my opinion, our service plans were frequently good value — particularly for certain items.

Service plans were also the one thing I could sell and sell well. I was consistently in the top five or six in the district for service plan sales. The reason was simple. I thought it was important, and as a result, I made it part of the process.

Most people wouldn't mention the service plan. They would focus on the phone itself — what features it had and, more importantly, what it didn't have that would make you buy the next model up. They'd come up to the cash register and after scanning the item, the point-of-sale system would pop up a little alert asking if the customer wanted the service plan.

They'd look up from the screen and ask "Do you want to buy a service plan for that? It's $8 for two years and covers any issues."

The customer wouldn't buy. Why would they? This plan hadn't been mentioned at all during the sales conversation and most customers recognized that the salesperson was asking merely because of a prompt from the register. To the customer, this was clearly not an important thing to worry about. By not discussing the plan throughout, the salespeople downplayed its importance.

My process was different. A customer would walk in asking for a cordless phone. I would say, "Sure, we have plenty of cordless phones and we also offer really good service plans to protect them. Let's go look at them and see if we can find one that works for you."

While showing them the phones and discussing the features, I would again mention the plan. "The phone itself should last for a while, but the batteries typically wear out after about a year and half. The service plan does include a free battery each year though, so you'll be safe there."

At the counter, as I scanned the phone they had picked out — and before the system got a chance to alert me — I would ask if they wanted to get the service plan. This worked for 85–90% of the people who bought phones from me.

There was no magic trick involved, no subterfuge, no attempt to fool anyone. I believed the service plan was a good idea and thought it offered value. I made sure that the customer knew I felt that way, before they bought the item. The result was that they understood this. They believed I was suggesting the plan not because some system prompted me or because I was told to do this by someone else — I was doing it because I felt it was important.

When we leave our discussion of performance to the end of the conversation, when we mention it in passing, we underplay its importance to the project. By not bringing it up throughout the process, we are saying that we don't think it is important enough to discuss further. We're saying it's something that hasn't much value.

If we want to start correcting the course of performance on the Web, we must make performance part of the discussion from the very start of the process, and we must be concrete about it. One of the best ways to do that is to set a performance budget.

Setting a Performance Budget

Brad Frost wrote a blog post about *the importance of discussing performance early on in a projects life cycle*[9] and he suggested mentioning performance in project documents:

> *Statements of work, project proposals and design briefs should explicitly and repeatedly call out performance as a primary goal. "The goal of this project is to create a stunning, flexible, lightning-fast experience..."*

He is, of course, correct.

Often, though, phrases like "lightning-fast" will prove not to be concrete enough. I've heard many people in the early stages of a project say they want their site to be fast, only to see it turn into another one of those things that would be nice to fix eventually.

One thing that I've found works well is setting a performance budget. A performance budget is exactly what it sounds like. You set a budget for your page and do not allow the page to exceed that number.

It's a good idea to *start* with a load time, but the budget you set and refer to will hold more weight if you can specify the actual page weight or request count. Referencing a particular page weight or number of requests instead of just a specific load time makes the conversation easier.

For example, if your budget states that the site must load in less than five seconds on a 3G network and you're trying to decide whether or not to add a carousel to the page, you must first translate those five seconds into a weight or request count to be able to make that determination up front.

Request count and page weight is also a relatively easy thing to reinforce in your build process, allowing you to rigidly enforce the budget if you so choose.

---

9 http://bradfrostweb.com/blog/post/performance-as-design/

Arriving at a Budget

Knowing that performance affects just about every important business metric, the ideal scenario is to make your site as fast as possible. The most well-known response time targets have been around since 1968, and were popularized by Jakob Neilsen in 1993[10]:

- *0.1 seconds*: The limit for users to feel that the system reacts instantaneously.
- *1.0 second*: The limit for uninterrupted flow of thought. The users notice the delay, but they still feel direct interaction.
- *10 seconds*: The limit for keeping user attention. Anything longer than this and the users will either give up or go off to do something else while they wait.

Ideally, your site breaks that one second time barrier. Sometimes, though, that's not realistic — whether because of the type of site you're building, the budget or other external constraints. Armed with knowledge of the importance of performance, there are two additional criteria to consider when arriving at your ideal budget:

1. *Current performance of your site*
   First, audit your existing site to see how it currently performs under different network conditions. Record load times for these benchmarks, as well as the number of HTTP requests and overall page weight.

2. *Current performance of your competitors sites*
   Next, take a look at how other sites in your industry perform. For particularly important competitors, do the same sort of analysis that you did for your own site. You can also get a good overview of how sites

---

10 http://smashed.by/limits

within your industry perform by referring to the Keynote performance indices[11] which break down analysis by industry type.

Now that you know how your site performs, as well as how your competitors fare, you can make an informed decision about what budget to settle on using Weber's law and the 20% rule.

The 20% Rule

German physician E.H. Weber observed that the noticeable difference between two properties varies in proportion to the size of the properties. For example, it's easier to tell the difference between one hour and two hours than it is to tell the difference between one minute and two minutes.

Applying this to computer interaction, Steven C. Seow came up with the 20% rule in his book, *Designing and Engineering Time: The Psychology of Time Perception*[12]. Put simply, to create a noticeable improvement in performance as perceived by your visitors, you need to improve performance by at least 20%.

If you apply this rule to the metrics you've found for your current site, you can come up with the bare minimum of improvement. If your page loads in 10 seconds, making it load in 8 seconds or less would provide a noticeable improvement; 9 seconds, much less so.

Applying the 20% rule to the metrics from your competitors can help you determine at what point you would provide a large enough improvement in performance to truly distinguish your site as faster.

For example, if your competitor's site loads in 5 seconds, you want to get your site under 4 seconds at the very least.

The ultimate goal is to make the experience as fast as possible for your visitors, but the 20% rule can provide a good starting point.

---

11 http://www.keynote.com/keynote_competitive_research/index.html
12 http://www.engineeringtime.com

IMPACT OF A PERFORMANCE BUDGET

Let's take a look at the impact on your decision making of having a performance budget in place.

Your team is debating whether it makes sense to add a content slider to display more products on the home page, or to display five items by default and provide a link to browse for more. The cases for each direction could easily be made, but you've already decided your home page can weigh no more than 400KB and its already at 350KB. The script and extra content would push the weight well above that number. At this point, because you have a performance budget to refer to, you have three options.

1. You could choose to optimize an existing feature or asset on the page. If you can decrease the weight of another feature (say an image that hasn't yet been compressed or a script that could be simplified) enough to allow the slider to be added without exceeding the budget, your team can choose to add it to the page.

2. You can remove an existing feature or asset on the page. Maybe you really want that content slider, but you can ditch the big promotional image. If you can do that and stay under budget, the content slider gets the go-ahead.

3. You can choose not to add the slider. If nothing can be optimized to a high enough degree, and you decide that the slider isn't important enough to push out another feature from the home page, then you don't add it.

Without the budget in place, you would have no framework for this discussion. Since no performance base has been set, making the case that the content slider adds too much weight to the page is difficult. When you have this baseline set, it simplifies the discussion.

Clearleft, a Web design agency in Brighton, UK, wrote about their experience using a performance budget[13] and came to this same conclusion:

> The important point is to look at every decision, right through the design/build process, as something that has consequence. Having a pre-defined 'budget' is a clear, tangible way to frame decisions about what can and can't be included, and at a suitably early stage in the project. It can also potentially provide some justification to the client about why certain things have been omitted (or rather, swapped out for something else).

Setting a budget provides this justification and framework for discussion, and continues to do so throughout the life cycle of the site. Keep enforcing the budget after launch as a way of avoiding the slow creep of bloat that tends to manifest itself.

Be Realistic

The entire point of the performance budget is to provide a very tangible point of comparison, so be explicit about it. Something like "a maximum of 500KB in size and no more than 15 HTTP requests" is what you're aiming for.

And be realistic about it. Setting a budget that is either unhelpfully high ("No more than 5MB!") or unrealistically low ("No more than 10KB!") does you absolutely no good. Be strict, but understanding of reality.

It's also worth noting that third-party services like ads, while essential for businesses, can single-handedly destroy a performance budget.

For those scenarios, it makes sense to categorize the assets on the page. Developers at the *Guardian* newspaper came up with three categories[14]:

---

13 http://smashed.by/responsive-budget
14 http://smashed.by/re-page-load

- Content
- Enhancement
- Leftovers

Content is the meat and potatoes: it's why the user visits your site. The enhancements are the dressing: the JavaScript and styling that make the experience nicer. And the leftovers, well, that's the scraps you give to the dog underneath the table, the stuff the user doesn't care about. Those are the things that should come last in the load process; give the user what they want first, and then load in the excess after the fact.

Until ad networks and other services get with the program and start creating faster services, you may need to have your budget apply to the content and enhancements only. Of course that doesn't mean you can't be diligent about limiting those third-party performance drains. It simply means we sometimes have to concede that certain pieces of the page remain out of our control.

A FEW WORDS OF CAUTION

Performance budgets are an excellent way to ensure performance remains part of the discussion. But, as we saw earlier, the budget must be set early on. If you get halfway through a project before setting a budget, you are going to have a difficult time convincing anyone it is important enough to pay attention to. Not to mention that by then, there may already be approved visuals or features that immediately crush whatever budget you may have needed to set.

The other important thing to note: when you set the budget, and as you enforce it, you should already know what content *needs* to be on the page. A performance budget is meant to help you decide how to display your content, not what content to display. Removing important content from a page is not a performance strategy.

EMBRACE THE PAIN

They say you can't understand someone until you've walked a mile in their shoes. Until you've experienced what they've experienced — the highs and the lows — it can be hard to truly empathize. This is especially the case with performance.

Recently, a big company launched a re-designed site. It was beautiful. Lovely imagery, slick interactions, excellent typography; no doubt about it, this was a beautiful site. But, like many websites, it was hiding a secret. Underneath that beautiful, glossy finish was a horribly bloated site.

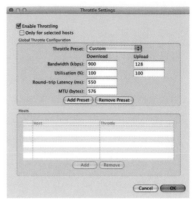

Tools like Charles offer the ability to throttle your connection to see how it feels to navigate your site over a poor network.

Firing up the site over a fast, wired connection, it seemed fine. It loaded pretty quickly, certainly not slow enough to cause any worry. But the same site, loaded on a 3G network suddenly took over 90 seconds to load. A minute and a half of staring at a white screen and a loading bar. There is no way this site would've made it live if the people designing and building it had experienced this during testing.

In addition to getting into real code as soon as possible, we need to embrace the pain of slow networks during our testing. There are a number of excellent tools available to help simulate different networks with different latency and bandwidth constraints. If you're on a Mac running OS X 10.7 or later, you can use the Network Conditioner. There is also Slowy[15], a dirt cheap app that sits in your task bar, making it easy to switch between different network simulations.

---

15 http://slowyapp.com/

You could also opt for a full-blown Web debugging proxy tool, like Charles[16] or Fiddler[17]. Both are available for Mac OS X and Windows and offer a wide range of additional features beyond network simulation.

FREQUENT PAIN

I mentioned network simulation to an engineer at a company that takes performance very seriously, and he joked that he might go back and force his team to write code for the next week over a poor connection.

A full week is probably a little excessive, but consider making network simulation part of your weekly, or even daily, process. For a couple of hours one day a week, have everyone on your team use a simulated network connection. It won't take too long before everyone will become painfully aware of any performance bottlenecks and start working to fix them.

Get Real

I'm not about to write a lengthy entreaty about how flawed designing websites in software like Photoshop is. I think the more it gets discussed, the more we realize that, as with any tool, Photoshop has things it does well and things it does poorly. We'll never fully get rid of image manipulation software in the design process and, frankly, that shouldn't be the goal. But it's important to consider what shortcomings it has so that our process can take them into account.

One valid concern with spending too much time in Photoshop versus the browser is you see a picture of a website under ideal situations and at a specific, controlled size. This is frequently cited as a problem for responsive design, but it is also a performance issue. As Brad Frost has said, *"You can't mock up performance in Photoshop."*[18]

---

16 http://www.charlesproxy.com/
17 http://fiddler2.com/
18 http://smashed.by/bf-tweet

Getting into the browser early on can help you catch potential performance bumps before they have a chance to get completely out of control. That mock-up where every element has a semi-transparent shadow may look beautiful, but fire it up on a mobile device and you may notice scrolling is an arduous task. Catching that early allows you to consider other solutions.

To be clear, those other solutions needn't be devoid of those kinds of embellishments altogether. Performant sites needn't be visually plain or boring. There's a series of trade-offs to be made by weighing the benefits and the costs. Performance and visual aesthetics are both important — your site needs to balance the two. Getting real — real code on real devices — as early as possible will help you to maintain that balance.

One of the best ways to allow you to get into the browser early is to think about your site in terms of reusable components. Have a question about how that fancy navigation embellishment is going to perform on different devices? Jump into the browser, develop that component and take it for a test run.

There are a number of ways to do this. My current favorite is Brad Frost's *Atomic Web Design approach*[19], which breaks website components down into their smallest forms allowing you to build, say, a footnote, without committing to building the rest of the page as well. This allows you to quickly see how different pieces may work at different resolutions and with different input methods.

The specific tool you use is less important than the end result: being able to quickly test bits and pieces to catch performance issues before you're too far down the road to turn back.

MAKE IT APPARENT

Another way to encourage thinking about performance optimization throughout a project is to make key performance metrics of the site (such

---

19 http://bradfrostweb.com/blog/post/atomic-web-design/

as load time) visible on every page load. Etsy, long known for its incredible dedication to performance, uses this approach, an idea originally discussed by Jeff Atwood[20].

Etsy displays the render time (calculated by the server) on the page, but with the introduction of the navigation timing API, you can easily include page load time with a couple lines of simple JavaScript. The snippet below would output the perceived load time to the console, but you could easily modify it to output to an element in your document to make it easily visible.

```
function getLoadTime() {
        var now = new Date().getTime();

        // Get the performance object
        window.performance = window.performance || window.mozPerformance
|| window.msPerformance || window.webkitPerformance || {};
        var timing = performance.timing || {};
        if (timing) {
                var load_time = now - timing.navigationStart;
                console.log('Load time: ' + load_time + 'ms');
        }
}

window.onload = function() {
        getLoadTime();
}
```

It may seem like a minor thing, but displaying the load time for every page in the top-right corner can have a big impact on how your team views performance optimization. Load time becomes a point of comparison and conversation — and if a page loads slowly, that fact will be staring them straight in the face each time they work on it.

---

20 http://smashed.by/perf-feature

A LIGHT BASE

"Be prepared." That's the Boy Scout motto. When I was growing up, I took that to heart. Whenever I was going on a trip, I would pack everything I could. My default state was to make sure I had everything with me, in case I needed it.

We often take a similar approach online. Before anything is even built, many projects will include a JavaScript framework, just in case. Before any analysis is done to determine whether one is needed, a CSS framework might get loaded. Boilerplates, meant to provide a starting point from which you can trim down, are left as is. Image carousels are added at random as a way to get more stuff onto a page. These projects are like the proverbial pocketknife — everything is there, just in case we need it.

The opposite should be true: everything that gets added to a page — each script, each image, every line of code — must be justified. It needs to serve a purpose. We know this from a visual design perspective; any designer worth their salt will tell you why the decision was made to include this image or that icon.

Performance should inform that discussion as well. Not only should an image serve a purpose, but its value should outweigh its cost. No free lunch and all that.

As for frameworks and boilerplates: there's nothing wrong with them. They're incredibly valuable tools when applied with care and used appropriately. But they are not without their own faults and there is cause for concern when they are the base from which we start, instead of tools we carefully add when needed.

If we want to reverse the troublesome trend of increasingly bloated websites we need to start with better defaults and be judicious about everything we put on our sites.

It's been shown time and time again that people love to stick with the default options. One frequently cited study deals with default options for organ donors[21] (PDF). In the United States, where the default option is *not* to be an organ donor, 28% of people consent to be organ donors. Compare that with Belgium, where the default option is to consent to being an organ donor. There, 98% of people are organ donors.

Bringing it closer to home, Jared Spool conducted an experiment[22] to see how many people changed any of the 150+ (at the time) settings available to them in Microsoft Word.

> *What we found was really interesting. Less than 5% of the users we surveyed had changed any settings at all. More than 95% had kept the settings in the exact configuration that the program installed in.*

Perhaps even more interesting, was the reason they didn't change these settings. One setting turned off by default was Word's autosaving functionality. So in the default settings, the option to save a document as a person was working on it was disabled. When people were asked why they didn't change the setting, they revealed that they assumed there was a reason it was off.

> *Of course, this mean[t] that 95% of the users were running with autosave turned off. When we interviewed a sample of them, they all told us the same thing: They assumed Microsoft had delivered it turned off for a reason, therefore who were they to set it otherwise. "Microsoft must know what they are doing," several of the participants told us.*

This thinking about defaults creeps its way into how we use our development tools as well. Much of the weight of these tools is there as a result of solving very specific issues that you may or may not run into. As Spool and many before him have discovered, when they're baked in by default

---

21 http://www.dangoldstein.com/papers/DefaultsScience.pdf
22 http://www.uie.com/brainsparks/2011/09/14/do-users-change-their-settings/

it's unlikely most developers take any time to justify the options' existence based on project needs — even when customization tools are available. Instead, we load this additional baggage into our sites by default. Just in case.

The Filament Group's responsive carousel[23] is one small example of a tool that takes the exact opposite approach. Modular, with smart defaults. They have a default script that gets the job done, and then separate scripts that extend the behavior of the carousel in different ways. Your default option is to include only what is absolutely necessary — you determine what else, if anything, needs to be included. Christian Heilmann covers this very well in the previous chapter, "The Vanilla Web Diet."

ImageOptim and ImageAlpha can team up to bring the size of your images down.

We need to apply this thinking to the way we approach projects in general. Have your base template be as lean and mean as possible. Have go-to options for certain behaviors or fixes — things you know are well-tested and lightweight. But don't make them part of your default. Roll them in only as needed, if needed.

---

23   https://github.com/filamentgroup/responsive-carousel

Usual and Unusual Suspects

For any item included on your page, do whatever you can to minimize its impact on page weight and load time. Among the greatest offenders are uncompressed images. Thankfully, they're also one of the easiest to fix. Image optimization can be automated into a build process, using excellent tools such as the ImageOptim Command Line Interface[24]. If you don't have a formal build process, or the mere sight of a terminal window sends shivers down your spine, you can just as easily use GUI-based tools such as ImageOptim[25] and ImageAlpha[26] to drastically reduce the size of your image files simply by dragging and dropping.

Social network sharing buttons are another common source of bloat. To avoid their excessive heft by default, you can lazy-load the code for the buttons only after the user makes it clear they want to make use of them. The Filament Group's SocialCount[27] is an excellent example of this technique. By default, the buttons are simply CSS with a small image. When the user takes action (for example, hovers over a button) the actual sharing script for that network is dynamically loaded and added to the button. While jQuery-based, the functionality it performs is simple enough that you could easily adopt it for your own framework, or even for vanilla JavaScript.

You can apply that same sort of thinking to other components on your page that may not be as obvious to you at first glance. In his excellent article, *Deploying JavaScript Applications*[28], Alex Sexton talked about delaying the load of entire sections of code until the user has taken an action that requires that code.

The example he provided was the Hugo Boss site. If a customer clicks on the "Write a Review" button, a modal box appears for them to rate the

---

24 http://jamiemason.github.io/ImageOptim-CLI/
25 http://imageoptim.com/
26 http://pngmini.com/
27 http://filamentgroup.com/lab/socialcount/
28 http://smashed.by/javascript-apps

The review button on the Hugo Boss site is far down the page,
and probably not frequently used.

product. This button is not only far down the page, but most likely not
used very frequently. By not loading the code and assets necessary for that
modal box until some time after page load — perhaps even waiting until
the cursor is within a few hundred pixels or the button has been clicked —
there's a nice little boost to initial page load time.

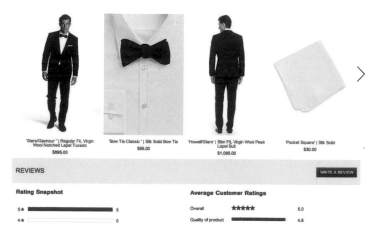

Delaying the load of the code related to that modal box until the after
initial page load could have a noticeable impact on load time.

For more specific techniques, be sure to read the chapters by Aaron Gustafson and Mat Marquis (in addition to the previously mentioned chapter by Christian Heilmann). The point being: there is a lot you can do to quickly and easily avoid excess bloat.

IF YOU CAN'T MAKE IT, FAKE IT

Executives at the Houston airport had a problem: they were getting an extremely high number of complaints about how long it took for passengers to collect their bags at the baggage claims.[29] Naturally, the first thing they decided to do was hire more baggage handlers. The wait time fell to just eight minutes, but the complaints persisted.

Digging deeper, as it so often does, revealed something far more interesting. It turns out, the walk from the plane to the baggage claim area took about one minute. Which meant that most people were spending seven minutes standing and waiting at the baggage claim. If you've ever been to an airport, you can understand how boring that can be.

So instead of trying to bring the wait time down any further, they actually made the walk to the baggage claim longer. Passengers now had to walk six times as far to get to their bags. On the surface, that sounds like a surefire way to upset people. But the reality is that complaints plummeted. Passengers were busy for most of the eight-minute wait, so even though it took them just as long to get their bags, it felt faster.

There are numerous stories about the interesting way that people perceive the passage of time. In New York, almost all the buttons you can push at pedestrian crossings aren't functional and haven't been since the 1980s. But many people still push them, believing it will save them a few seconds.

Disney, like many other attractions, hides the length of the waiting lines by twisting them in a serpentine pattern and often masking some of the line from view by strategically wrapping them around buildings. Why?

---

29 http://smashed.by/houston-airport

Because if you can't see the full length of the line, and you seem to be moving, you're less likely to become frustrated. In fact, it turns out people are happier in a longer line that moves quickly than a shorter line that moves slowly *even* when the total time waited is the same.

More than the numbers, what truly matters is how a user perceives your site. Does it feel like the site loads quickly? Do the interactions feel immediate and snappy, or delayed and sluggish? We can apply the same sort of thinking to the sites and applications we build. In fact, some very successful apps have done that.

At the end of 2011, Mike Krieger, co-founder of Instagram, gave a presentation called *Secrets to Lightning-Fast Mobile Design*[30]. During his talk, he focused on three secrets:

1. Perform actions optimistically
2. Adaptively preload content
3. Move bits when no one's watching

It's worth exploring each in a little more detail.

Perform Actions Optimistically

Let's say a visitor to your site is going to leave a comment. To do so, they click a button that submits the form. When they do, two things happen. The form, using AJAX, sends a request to the server and a loading graphic appears to tell the user their submission is in process. When the script hears back from the server that the task completed successfully, it updates the page alerting the visitor.

This is the way it's typically done, but maybe it's not the best way. That request, particularly on a high-latency network, can take several hundred milliseconds — a very noticeable delay for the person trying to submit their comment.

---

30 http://smashed.by/fast-mobile

Instagram[31] has taken a different approach to avoid that delay. As soon as the person submits the comment, it appears on the page. The request happens in the background. To the person submitting the comment, it looks like it happens instantaneously. In reality, it takes as long to process as any other form online — but the perception is dramatically improved.

Mike called this "performing actions optimistically," but others have called it *asynchronous UI*. The idea is the same: ditch the loading state and let the user feel things are moving more quickly. If the task fails, then gently alert them somehow after the fact and let them easily resubmit.

Another great example is Polar[32], the popular polling application. When you create a poll, it shows up instantly in your feed. Again, there's some clever asynchronous UI at work. What actually happens when you create a new poll is that Polar creates a temporary local copy of the poll and pushes it to the top of your feed. The temporary copy is fully functional — you can

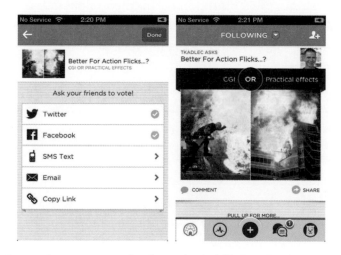

By creating a temporary local copy that is fully functional, users of Polar get immediate feedback that their poll has been submitted and avoid any performance delays that may happen in the background.

31 http://instagram.com/
32 http://www.polarb.com/

vote and comment on it and those votes and comments will get pushed to the actual poll once it's been uploaded.

In the background, Polar uploads the temporary copy to its servers. If that fails, they try again a few times before finally admitting defeat to the user. The result, once again, is that the process feels incredibly fast.

It's important to note that for both Instagram and Polar, these solutions are not exactly ideal from an engineering perspective: there's quite a bit more complexity involved. But the trade-off is that the users get a system that *feels* instantaneous.

Adaptively Preload Content

The next secret is to adaptively preload content. This doesn't mean blindly load anything and everything you can before it's needed. Instead, you need to consider what you know about user behavior and selectively load based on that. Instagram uses this technique for their photo feeds.

At first, they loaded everything in the order it appears on the page, as the browser does. But this wasn't always the best approach because that's not necessarily a correct ranking of importance for the user. Instead, Instagram chose to reprioritize loading based on where the user ended up scrolling to, using their interests to prioritize what got loaded first.

Move Bits When No One is Watching

Have you ever seen a magician perform? The tricks they do are based on illusion and distraction. Grand gestures and flashy effects misdirect you from the sleight of hand taking place right in front of you.

You can perform the same sort of trick to provide an improved experience for your visitors. In his presentation, Mike demonstrated one way you can apply this sort of approach.

When users sign up for Instagram, they are asked to fill out some basic details. While this is going on, in the background Instagram starts looking for recommendations on who to follow.

The result is that by the time the user submits the form with their account information, recommendations are presented nearly instantly.

Instagram uses the same trick on image uploads. After you select the filter for your image, you are able to choose options such as where to share the image, or to geotag it with a location. All the while, Instagram is already uploading the image in the background to reduce the time users have to wait at the end of the process.

Worth noting is that in both of the cases above, there's a very high likelihood that the person will end up moving forward to those next pages. It's a slippery slope between moving bits while no one is watching and using up everyone's bandwidth and data for pages they may never view and assets they may never need. But if there is a high likelihood that your visitor will end up needing these assets at some point, it makes sense to do a little precaching to stay a step ahead.

Beyond Technical

These are all things that are not necessarily obvious, nor are they strictly technical solutions. They require careful consideration about the user experience and a solid understanding of how users interact with an app. They also require a little bit of elbow grease, but the end result is well worth it. Luke Wroblewski (one of the brains behind Polar)[33] explained it well:

> If making temporary versions of polls fully functional and using multiple background processes to make sure uploads are successful sounds like a lot of extra effort to make things feel fast—it is. But the end result is worth it, when people create something on Polar it seems instantaneous. And in this case, perception beats reality.

---

33 http://smashed.by/luke

TASK COMPLETION

Each of the principles above are ultimately about reducing the amount of time it takes for the user to complete a given task. The importance of task completion can't be overlooked. There's the classic study conducted by UIE back in 2001[34] on the impact of the time taken to complete a task on a visitor's perception of performance. Researchers sat people down in front of ten different sites using a 56kpbs modem and gave them tasks to complete.

The surprise came when people rated the slowest site (Amazon.com) as one of the fastest when asked. The reason was that Amazon.com allowed people to complete their tasks in fewer steps.

Ultimately, this is what it comes down to: how fast the user feels the site is. You can get a long way by implementing the performance techniques so frequently cited for developers, but to influence how your users feel about the performance of your site, performance optimization has to involve the designer.

If you're a designer, consider yourself the first line of defense. Yes, ultimately the developer will have to make many of the specific optimizations, but you are the person who gets to set the stage. You must make the decisions early on that will either encourage the site to be as fast as it is beautiful, or encourage it to be beautiful, yet bloated.

Conclusion

Good performance doesn't happen by chance: it must be planned for and carefully designed. To avoid contributing to the ever increasing obesity of the Web, performance must become baked into the process from the very beginning of the process.

Taking steps like setting a performance budget, simulating poor connection speeds, and getting onto real browsers and devices as early as possible will help to make everyone involved more aware of the performance trade-offs.

---

34 http://www.uie.com/articles/download_time/

This is no longer something we can afford to offload to developers. Designers get to set the stage early on for how a site will perform. Through careful consideration, they can ensure that the site will look and feel fast.

The Web doesn't have to get heavier. We can correct its course by prioritizing performance and respecting the people who use our sites. With a little care, sites can be both beautiful *and* fast. Let's give the people who visit our sites the fast experience they so desperately want.

ABOUT THE AUTHOR

Tim Kadlec is an independent Web developer with a propensity for efficient, standards-based front-end development. His diverse background working with small companies to large publishers and industrial corporations has allowed him to see how standards-based development can be effectively utilized for business of all sizes. He writes about a variety of topics at timkadlec.com and tweets as @tkadlec.

Robust, Responsible, Responsive Web Design

Written by Mat Marquis

CHAPTER FIVE · BY MAT MARQUIS

ROBUST, RESPONSIBLE, RESPONSIVE WEB DESIGN

RESPONSIVE WEB DESIGN IS STARTING TO GET A REPUTATION — and not the kind of reputation that it rightfully deserves. When I say that I'm here to show you some of the ways we can go about building a lean, feature-rich and highly accessible responsive website that looks *and* works great for any user of any browsing context, I'm certain I've earned myself a few eye-rolls right out of the gate — and I understand that. Since Ethan Marcotte coined the term a few years ago, we've all been bombarded by sensational blog posts about the past, present or future failure of responsive Web design as a methodology: it can't do this and it doesn't do enough about that; it's useless without a certain script or server-side component. Responsive Web design has needed saving more times than Christmas, if both blogs and television holiday specials are to be believed.

The most common death knell we've heard ringing out — lately, anyway — is that every page of a responsive site is fated to weigh in at a couple dozen megabytes and there isn't a single thing that any of us can do about it. There seems to be plenty of evidence to back this up, too.

Oakley recently launched a responsive website with an 85 MB index page[1], complete with an up-front loading screen. The landing pages for the primary navigation items on time.com are in the ballpark of 3MB each. I'm glad to see so many people growing uneasy about potential bandwidth issues with responsive websites, but we have to be careful about where we direct our blame: we can't hold responsive Web design responsible for mistakes that we've been making.

Our Faulty Hammers

In another life, years and years ago, I was a carpenter. As I was just starting out, I worked with two guys who had both been at it for more than twenty years apiece. Like so many bloggers, I too had concerns about the tools we were using — concerns the other guys didn't seem to have, oddly enough. All of their dented and scarred equipment was brand new to me: heavy, awkward, impossible to manage. The hammer I was given, in particular. I was certain that it was defective, weighing as much as it did.

Now, as simple a device as it is, a hammer allows a skilled craftsman to do an unbelievable amount of work: framing an entire house, shingling a roof, building furniture, and — of course — opening beer bottles. When I was holding mine, though, it was only good for hitting my thumbs, leaving holes in walls, and sending nails careening off a roof and onto a homeowner's brand new car. Opening beer bottles it could do well enough, as I discovered soon after the chipped Lexus incident.

Our early forays into responsive Web design aren't much different from my early days of carpentry. RWD is a simple tool and it's brand new to us, though the techniques that it encompasses — a percentage-based grid, media queries and flexible media — aren't particularly new themselves. In the right hands, it can accomplish something incredible: a layout that seems as though it were tailor-made to suit any display on any device, including the ones we can't predict. Granted, we can make mistakes

---

1   http://moto.oakley.com/

with it, too. Those hulking, resource-hungry websites aren't responsive Web design's fault any more than a few dozen bent nails could be blamed on a faulty hammer. This trend is on us, and you don't see any carpenters writing blog posts about how hammers are a failed methodology because of the times they dropped one on their feet. We can do better than blaming our tools for our mistakes.

Presumptive Enhancement

We can't be faulted *too* much. You and I probably have it pretty easy, from a browsing perspective. We're developers — we have fast computers and bandwidth to spare. I'm not certain I can breathe air that doesn't have Wi-Fi in it.

That's our privileged context, though; that's what we're used to. It's comfortable. We assume high bandwidth and stable networks, because that's practically a given for us. We can safely assume that sending out a request will result in something being sent back, outside of the occasional subway tunnel. Those of us who build the Web have it the easiest on the Web, and perhaps as a result the average Web page is now roughly 1.4 MB[2].

If you've only ever experienced the Web by way of an unreliable mobile connection, pages like these are more than just a minor inconvenience: they're pages you might not be able to use at all. These pages are a part of the Web that isn't for you. Pages like these are evidence that we're building from a place of privilege. While I'm certain it isn't anyone's intent, what we've been doing lately is building a Web for *us*.

> [...] in the interwoven space-time of the web, context is no longer just about the here and now. Instead, context refers to the physical, digital, and social structures that surround the point of use.
>
> — Cennydd Bowles, "Designing with context[3]", Feb 16, 2013

2 http://smashed.by/stats
3 http://smashed.by/context

Universal access is the fundamental underlying truth of the Web. Building massive, resource-heavy sites means excluding millions of users in developing countries that only know the Web by way of feature phones or slightly better — users paying for every kilobyte they consume; users who already have to keep tabs on which sites they need to avoid day to day because of the cost of visiting them. Not some nebulous bandwidth cost, but actual economic cost.

The exclusion of these users has become something of a self-fulfilling prophecy, with some developers claiming that the lack of traffic from areas with limited bandwidth makes optimization unnecessary. An unoptimized site is unlikely to see traffic from areas with limited bandwidth *because* the site isn't optimized.

Late last year, Chris Zacharias set out to reduce the size of YouTube's 1.2 megabyte player pages, aiming to bring them below 100KB, in a project he code-named "Feather." In reducing the player page to 98KB and a mere 12 requests, he actually saw a sharp *increase* in the page's average latency. When this increased latency was plotted geographically, it was revealed that entire populations were now able to use the service despite their slower connections. A page that would have previously been too costly to render — and taken an average of twenty minutes — could now be loaded in just a few minutes.

> *[...] entire populations of people simply could not use YouTube because it took too long to see anything. Under Feather, despite it taking over two minutes to get to the first frame of video, watching a video actually became a real possibility. Over the week, word of Feather had spread in these areas and our numbers were completely skewed as a result. Large numbers of people who were previously unable to use YouTube before were suddenly able to.*[4]

> — Chris Zacharias, "Page Weight Matters", Dec 21, 2012

---

4 http://smashed.by/weight

Progressive Enhancement

Responsive Web design is, in a sense, a natural extension of progressive enhancement. Responsive Web design and progressive enhancement both aim to ensure a usable experience for all users, regardless of their browsing context. RWD is concerned more with providing users with a natural-feeling layout and presentation for accessing content, and progressive enhancement aims to ensure access to that content regardless of a browser's features and capabilities. We often see the two concepts conflated — a rare bit of Web development confusion that ends up working in everyone's favor. To many, responsive Web design extends beyond simply a flexible layout tailored by media queries, and includes such concerns as the ever-fluctuating landscape of mobile browser features, offline experiences, and network performance. These concerns are the realm of progressive enhancement for sure, but it's a blurring of lines that I'm glad to see — the kind that only serves to highlight potential issues that might inhibit users' access to the sites we build, and keep those issues at the front of our minds.

The foundation of progressive enhancement is to think in terms of an element's inherent meaning: what is the best way to express this widget in markup alone? How can we represent the intention of an element in a way that works for everyone, and then build up from there? At the core of every jQuery Mobile widget is markup that's meaningful regardless of JavaScript or CSS. The range slider[5], for example, is powered by a number input, which degrades to a text input in browsers unfamiliar with the relatively new number input. In JavaScript-capable environments, that input is enhanced to a sliding control. Whether a user receives the enhanced or the basic experience, they'll be able to input their data. When you apply this principle to an entire site, you build a site that makes sense — one that's usable — before layering your JavaScript enhancements over that.

---

5 http://smashed.by/jquerysliders

It's not hard to find figures about the number of users that have thrown the sparking knife-switch buried in their browser preferences and disabled JavaScript completely. As you might have guessed, it's fairly rare — and those figures are usually accompanied by a call to abandon progressive enhancement and cater only to the highest common denominator. But support on the Web is rarely a binary thing — even if we were to assume that a very low percentage of our users will have JavaScript disabled wholesale, relying on JavaScript for the core functionality of a site introduces a tremendous point of failure.

In chapter seven, Aaron Gustafson will discuss some of the situations where JavaScript might not be readily available to your users, but this point bears repeating. I don't have to tell you guys how atrocious the code is in most of those third-party share widgets or advertisements. What happens when your user clicks on something while waiting for a megabyte of the "Like" button to download? What happens when one of your ad tags is so catastrophically broken that the browser gives up on JavaScript altogether? Will your site function at all?

Saying that everyone has JavaScript enabled isn't much more than an excuse for developer convenience — it doesn't improve the users' experiences, just ours. Even if we could assume that a site that completely relies on JavaScript will work for every user, we're still not doing them any favors. We're still introducing the potential for a user to find themselves staring at an indefinite loading GIF or an empty page — frustrating things we've all seen plenty of times, even here, with fast and reliable internet connections. I've personally seen a number of otherwise brilliantly constructed sites time out or display a blank page as a result of an ad-blocking browser plugin: a single point of failure that halts the execution of every other script on the page, rendering the entire site unusable.

Granted, this is little more than an inconvenience for you and me. We can safely pinpoint where a problem like that comes from and work around it. For less tech-savvy users, what might only be an inconvenience for us could mean a complete loss of access to a page or an entire site.

Access is Vital

The Boston Marathon bombing took place on April 15, 2013, and like many people, I turned to the *Boston Globe* site throughout the day to find out what was going on around me — the reasons behind the constant sirens — and for reassurance that the blasts I heard all day were controlled detonations carried out by the police. Suffice to say, reliable access to BostonGlobe.com became very, very important for a huge number of people.

Given the tremendous initial surge and the sustained traffic throughout the day, and despite the tremendous efforts of the *Globe's* dev and ops teams, it's easy to understand how their servers started experiencing some issues. At peak traffic their content delivery network gave out completely, resulting in a site with no external assets: no images, no CSS, and no JavaScript.

I'm certain that more than a few of you just winced, but it wasn't the disaster you might be envisioning. The site wasn't as pretty as it could have been, true, but it worked just fine. Had the *Globe* relied entirely on JavaScript for rendering or navigation, or if the scripts and styles weren't built on a foundation of progressive enhancement, tens of thousands of understandably uneasy users would have been left at the mercy of their search engines for news.

We'll be talking about progressive enhancement as it relates to responsive Web design for the remainder of this chapter, but not strictly in the ways you might have read about it in the past. For us, it won't be a matter of simply adding functionality in unobtrusive ways, but applying that same philosophy to how we load a site's assets (JavaScript, CSS, images, and even our markup) in a way that's best suited to a user's context. We'll work towards building a responsive website that not only looks tailor-made for any display, but delivers device- and context-appropriate assets to match.

On hovering over the links in the primary navigation, BostonGlobe.com shows a drop-down containing featured articles, the most recent articles in that section, and related subsections.

Markup

In terms of our markup alone — the foundation for everything else on our site — there's a great deal of room for optimization. How do we deliver rich experiences while ensuring that the most important part of a page, the content itself, is available as soon as possible?

The simplest (though far from ideal) way to handle showing and hiding this content would be to use `display: none;` and reveal the drop-down menus when the navigation links are hovered over. But we can safely assume that a user looking to find the scores of yesterday's Bruins game wouldn't be hovering over each link in the navigation on each page of the site. Most of this content would never be visible to the user, who would still be left requesting all this markup — including the images, which would still be loaded in the vast majority of browsers, even if they were never displayed — on every single page of the site.

While we didn't want to include all that content just in case, we also didn't want to limit the user at certain breakpoints, or make assumptions based on the users' context. The drop-downs are a useful addition to the site, and worth keeping.

We needed a baseline, strictly markup means of allowing a user to opt into content on the site, which was simpler than it might sound. As one would expect, all the links in the primary navigation take the user to a landing page containing all the same content: featured articles, recent articles, and navigation for each subsection. The drop-down menus are a nice convenience, but not essential for navigating the site. It made sense to treat these drop-down menus as enhancements, and load them via JavaScript only as they were needed.

To lazily load other pieces of inessential content on the *Globe* site without introducing any barriers to access, and inspired by the approach we took to the drop-down menus, we developed a simple markup-driven JavaScript pattern named AjaxInclude[6]. AjaxInclude enhances links by using them to fetch a fragment of the linked content. The anchor tag itself serves as the fallback, ensuring that users will be able to access the underlying content whether or not JavaScript is available, but also provides all the information our script would need to fetch the related content and apply it to the page: the location of the document fragment to be used in place of the link; and how that content should be injected into the current page relative to the position of the link.

To replace the link with the injected markup:

```
<a href="/sports" data-replace="articles/sports/fragment">Sports</a>
```

To insert the content before the link's position in the source:

```
<a href="/sports" data-before="articles/sports/fragment">Sports</a>
```

To insert the content after to the link's position in the source:

```
<a href="/sports" data-after="articles/sports/fragment">Sports</a>
```

---

6 http://smashed.by/github-ajax

From a responsive design standpoint, this same script can help us avoid serving all of our content and selectively hiding it, instead allowing us to include the content only when it suits our layouts. AjaxInclude also allows us to use a second attribute so we can qualify the content's inclusion above or below a certain breakpoint.

Here, we would include the referenced fragment only at viewport widths of 30em and up:

```
<a href="/sports" data-append="articles/sports/fragment"
data-media="(min-width: 30em)">Sports</a>
```

Starting with our site's core content as our foundation allowed us to make larger decisions about how and when we could load additional assets without running the risk of leaving any users out in the cold. If all else should fail, the site's intent would still remain intact: no user would be left unable to use the site. It establishes a baseline that works for everyone, while affording us the freedom to deliver context-appropriate scripts and styles in the same way: a functional website for all, with conditional enhancements when appropriate.

This same reasoning extended a recent project, a site that featured an image carousel on every page, showing apartment listings. This would frequently mean including dozens of high-resolution images per page. But where these carousels appeared alongside a number of other vital pieces of information — potentially the users' primary concerns, certainly more so than the photographs of the listing — there was no guarantee that the user would click through the galleries upon landing on each page. Had we included all of the associated img tags in our markup and simply hidden them with CSS, it would do nothing to prevent those images from being requested. We would potentially cost our users megabytes at a time, simply to read a few snippets of text.

In this instance we applied the same "as needed" philosophy as we did with our AJAX navigation pattern: the initial photo is included with the first payload of the page, and the gallery script is initialized. Although using AJAX to fetch each individual slide while the user navigated through the gallery would end up adding a troublesome delay and harming the overall experience, we wanted to ensure that we were still responding to the user's intent.

In this instance, when the user triggered the next link, we would fetch and append all the other slides at once. This still resulted in a slight delay; the user was presented with a loading indicator upon hitting the second item in the slideshow while the other items were loaded. After a few iterations, we ended up loading the first and second photos up front. When the user clicks to the next item in the gallery — already in the markup — the third item onward is quietly loaded behind the scenes and added to the slideshow. By the time the user interacts with the next trigger again just a moment later, the third slide is ready and waiting for them. The result is massively reduced bandwidth cost for each user on the site, but a completely seamless experience at the same time.

These kinds of optimizations are matters of finesse and refinement of simple concepts — seemingly small steps with enormous potential benefits for our users.

CSS

Once we have meaningful markup as our foundation and we know that we're ensuring a usable experience for everyone, we can make some key decisions about how we deliver those experiences without leaving anyone out.

While working on the jQuery Mobile project, we quickly realized that even serving our core CSS indiscriminately could introduce the potential for a broken experience. Anyone using a feature phone or early smartphone would be poorly equipped to deal with advanced styles, even if we were to assume that the styles themselves would degrade gracefully. Simply attempting to parse the style sheet itself could introduce issues on platforms as common as Blackberry devices that are only a few years old.

We settled on the idea of serving two different levels of enhancement — sort of an experience breakpoint — after determining whether a browser is capable of handling complex layouts and enhanced functionality, or whether it's somewhere closer to a feature phone. As daunting as that may sound, this process turned out to be simpler than you might think. The first step is to split up our style sheet.

The initial style sheet is a feature phone-caliber set of styles: font sizes, block versus inline elements, a couple of solid-color backgrounds. This style sheet gets delivered to every user. Since it's served to everyone, we've recently started using the Normalize CSS reset[7] as the basis for our initial style sheet. Rather than acting as a reset that zeroes out browser default styles, it provides a sensible normalized set of defaults: useful to bundle up our enhanced styles for qualified users, while serving as a reasonable baseline for our basic styles.

The enhanced style sheet is pretty much everything else — advanced layouts, animations, Web fonts, and so on — minified and gzipped, of course.

What we end up with are two very different *looking* experiences, granted, but not different core experiences. We're not simply hiding anything, even from basic users. No one is left out in the cold. A user on an older or underpowered device will be provided with a far more usable view of the site. For that matter, they likely aren't expecting much in the way of bells and whistles in the first place: the age-old question "Does my website have to look the same in every browser?" writ large.

In the original version of Filament Group's Enhance.js[8] and early versions of jQuery Mobile, we used a series of largely unrelated feature tests to determine whether a device qualified for the basic or enhanced experience. We would set the result of these tests in a cookie, and use that variable to deliver assets throughout the user's time on the site.

---

7   http://necolas.github.io/normalize.css/
8   https://github.com/filamentgroup/EnhanceJS

Eventually we realized that the test lined up closely with support for media queries, which is the key component in our complex layouts and a far more relevant test. In addition, it gave us a native method for conditionally delivering these style sheets, removing the dependency on JavaScript.

```
<link rel="stylesheet" href="/css/basic.css">
<link rel="stylesheet" href="/css/enhanced.css" media="only all">
```

Here, the basic style sheet is linked as usual. Everyone gets that. The `media="only all"` attribute on the enhanced style sheet ensures that the style sheet is only applied by browsers that understand media queries. Of course, this means excluding older versions of IE — but we've given ourselves some options there. We can still deliver our enhanced style sheets to Internet Explorer through conditional comments, while ensuring that versions of IE prior to the minimum version we've specified get a perfectly usable basic experience. Rather than choosing a minimum version of IE to support and leaving the site broken in earlier versions, we simply provide earlier versions of IE with the basic experience.

```
<link rel="stylesheet" href="basic.css" id="basic">
<!--[ if ( gte IE 6 ) & ( lte IE8 ) ]>
        <link rel="stylesheet" href="enhanced.css">
<![endif]-->
<!--[ if ( !IE ) | ( gte IE 9 ) ]><!-->
        <link rel="stylesheet" href="enhanced.css" media="only all">
<!--<![endif]-->
```

We serve up our enhanced CSS the old-fashioned way for IE8 and above, while other browsers will still use the `media` qualified link. True, IE8 still doesn't know what to do with a media query, so we might include Filament's Respond.js[9], a lightweight script that parses and translates `min-width` and `max-width` media query support for IE 6–8.

---

9 https://github.com/scottjehl/Respond

Now, we've already gone to the trouble of ensuring that our site remains useful, if not ideal, in browsers that don't receive our enhanced styles. In this way, we've bought ourselves some breathing room: should we choose not to shim media query support for vastly outdated versions of Internet Explorer, we can change our conditional comments to only deliver the enhanced experience to IE8 and above, or serve them a separate, static-width style sheet. Support for older versions of Internet Explorer is no longer a black-and-white issue; we're no longer painting ourselves into a corner. We support older versions of IE, for certain, just differently. It just so happens we do so in the most painless possible way for us, and in a way that ensures users at the mercy of archaic browsers aren't presented with a Jackson Pollock painting of our site. It's hard to argue with that, from any angle.

There is one other catch aside from old IE support, and unfortunately one that affects all other major browsers: when we qualify our style sheets with media attributes, they aren't applied, but they will be *requested*. This makes sense since we never know if an environment is going to change. If an external monitor is plugged in or a window is resized, we wouldn't want to wait for those new style sheets to be requested. As you can see from the figure on the next page, browsers do tend to be a bit excessive about it.

These are, unfortunately, blocking requests. Even if the style sheet could never possibly apply to a user's context, the page will still be prevented from loading while the style sheet is requested, downloaded and then ignored by the browser.

We did some experimenting with asynchronously loading applicable style sheets in a project named eCSSential[10], but found that using JavaScript to request our style sheets meant sidestepping a number of browser-level optimizations. For the most part, eCSSential roughly broke even with loading CSS the old-fashioned way — better in some browsers and worse in others — but it did introduce a dependency on JavaScript.

---

10 https://github.com/scottjehl/eCSSential

	iOS6, Android 4.0, Chrome 24, Firefox, IE 9, Opera 12	Opera 11
only all	Downloaded	Downloaded
(min-width: 9999px)	Downloaded	Downloaded
(min-device-width: 9999px)	Downloaded	Downloaded
(min-device-pixel-ration: 7)	Downloaded	Downloaded
tv	Downloaded	Downloaded
handheld	Downloaded	Downloaded
dinosaur	Downloaded	No request

Requested media attribute table: Interestingly, somewhere between version 11 and 12, Opera decided that it should account for me plugging my laptop into an external brachiosaurus.

While eCSSential didn't give us the definitive way forward we'd been hoping for, it did lead to a number of bugs filed against browsers, and conversations are taking place right now about how browsers might asynchronously download inapplicable style sheets in an optimized, non-blocking way.

JavaScript

The same approach we took with our CSS applies to our custom JavaScript: we start with a basic set of scripts for everyone, and use the same test to determine whether they get the enhanced JavaScript experience: media query support.

The initial JavaScript payload includes: Filament's Enhance.js[11] to conditionally request scripts and style sheets; Modernizr[12] as our

11 https://github.com/filamentgroup/enhance
12 http://modernizr.com/

feature testing framework; and Respond.js if we've chosen to give IE8 the enhanced experience. These scripts are loaded in the head of the page, since they're either time sensitive (Respond.js) or things we need to be ready right away in case we reference them in our other scripts (Modernizr).

```
(function(win, undefined) {
    var mqSupport = "matchMedia" in win && win.matchMedia( "only all" ).matches;
    if( !mqSupport && !respond.mediaQueriesSupported ) {
        return;
    }
})( this );
```

This script checks whether the user's browser supports the matchMedia method (JavaScript's native method of parsing media queries) and then, just for good measure, it ensures that the same only all test that we're using in our CSS passes. If the native method doesn't exist, it checks against Respond.js's shimmed media query support. If you're targeting a specific minimum version of IE for the enhanced experience, this Respond.js test could be swapped out in favor of checking for the existence of an IE conditional class.

```
(function(win, undefined){
        /* This script assumes a conditional comment scheme along the
lines of the following:
        <!--[if (lt IE 8) ]> <html class="old-ie"> <![endif]-->
        <!--[if (IE 8) ]> <html class="ie8"> <![endif]-->
        <!--[if (gt IE 8)|!(IE)]><!--> <html> <!--<![endif]-->
        */
        var mqSupport = "matchMedia" in win && win.matchMedia( "only all" ).matches,
                htmlClass = document.getElementsByTagName( "html" )[ 0
].getAttribute( "class" ),
                ie8 = htmlClass && htmlClass.indexOf( "ie8" ) > -1;
        if( !enhanced && !ie8 ){
                return;
        }
})( this );
```

The trouble is, between Enhance.js, Respond.js, our Modernizr build, and our new enhancement test, we've just added four blocking requests to the head of the page. We could chuck all of these into a single file, but that's likely to cause us headaches when it comes time to update any of these libraries.

To avoid inconveniencing ourselves or burdening users with additional requests, we've recently introduced the Grunt task-running framework[13] to our development process. Grunt can be set to watch a directory and concatenate your files whenever anything changes, meaning you can keep all your libraries and custom JavaScript in separate files and work on them as usual, but link your templates to a single automatically generated "dist" file that's ready for production. It will do the same for your style sheets, allowing you to split up your enhanced CSS and organize your development environment however you'd like, but output a single concatenated file. Further, Grunt will minify all your JavaScript and CSS, lint your code for errors, run your unit tests, or run any custom task you could imagine — all done automatically, via the command line. Grunt has very quickly become an indispensable part of our development process.

With our concatenated initial JavaScript file in place, we now have a framework for conditionally loading files as needed, based on the user's context. We can asynchronously load larger JavaScript libraries, plugins and custom scripts that apply site-wide without delaying the page load. If we have custom scripts to add swipe interaction on touch devices, we can feature-detect for touch events and include those scripts, and their corresponding styles, only if they're needed. If there are any unique parts of the site with highly specific CSS or JS, we add a class to the body tag and load those page-specific scripts and style sheets only when those pages are loaded.

Remember that there will be a slight delay when loading a style sheet using this method. Be sure to limit this approach to styles for specific

13 http://gruntjs.com/

components in a layout rather than entire pages, or you risk presenting the user with a flash of unstyled content.

A Little Help from the Server

These conditional requests can add up quickly on a large project: a JavaScript framework, a few plugin libraries, scripts to add device-specific enhancements like offline storage or touch support. While they're no longer running the risk of delaying a page's core content from loading, enough asynchronous requests will still have the potential to make a site feel sluggish, and prevent our enhancements from being available to the user as quickly as they might expect.

To get around this, we're using a server-side concatenation pattern called QuickConcat[14], built to work with Enhance.js, to bundle up all our conditional scripts and style sheets into a single request.

QuickConcat is a small PHP file that intercepts and parses requests for comma-separated sets of scripts or style sheets, and assembles them into a single file for delivery to the user. For example:

```
<script src="quickconcat.php?files=js/file1.js, js/file2.js,
js/file3.js"></script>
```

Or:

```
<link href="quickconcat.php?files=css/file1.css,css/file2.css,
css/file3.css" rel="stylesheet">
```

With a bit of clean-up via an .htaccess file (or the equivalent for your server environment):

```
<script src="js/file1.js, js/file2.js, js/file3.js"></script>
<link href="css/file1.css, css/file2.css, css/file3.css" rel="stylesheet">
```

---

14 https://github.com/filamentgroup/quickconcat

We'll still use Grunt to combine our initial JavaScript files and our global CSS, since they'll never vary on the client side — where QuickConcat shines is our asynchronous requests. Rather than writing multiple `script` and `link` tags into the page and sending out a handful of requests, we can use Enhance.js to prepare a list of scripts and style sheets that apply to the user's context and request them all at once:

```
(function(win, undefined){
        var mqSupport = "matchMedia" in win && win.matchMedia( "only all" ).matches;
        if( !mqSupport && !respond.mediaQueriesSupported ){
                return;
        }

        ejs.addFile.jsToLoad( "js/lib/jQuery.js" );
        ejs.addFile.jsToLoad( "js/lib/konami-code.js" );

        // Load custom fonts > 600px
        if( window.screen.width > 600 ){
                ejs.addFile.cssToLoad( "css/fonts.css" );
        }

        if( Modernizr.touch ) {
                ejs.addFile.jsToLoad( "js/swipe.js" );
                ejs.addFile.cssToLoad( "css/swipe.css" );
        }

        ejs.enhance();
})( this );
```

When Enhance.js is invoked, all the files queued up with `ejs.addFile.cssToLoad` and `ejs.addFile.jsToLoad` are sent off as a single request, through QuickConcat.

I usually refer to QuickConcat as a pattern because it's rarely something that drops into a production environment as is. It's usually something that we'll hand off to clients for implementation in their back-end language of choice.

Thanks to QuickConcat, even if we're loading a handful of scripts and styles after the page is loaded, we're only adding two requests: one for all of our additional scripts, and one for our additional styles.

Images and Video

The subject of media asset weight holds a special place in my heart. At the time of writing, images make up roughly 64% of the average website's weight[15], and it's getting worse as more and more people plaster their sites with monstrous high-resolution images to suit the newest high-density displays. The average website's image weight alone has increased by more than 13% since January 1st of this year[16].

You likely know the basics of responsive images by heart: to make an image flexible, we first remove the width and height attributes. By setting a max-width of 100% in our CSS instead, we prevent this image from ever overflowing its parent container. As our flexible container resizes, so does the image.

Of course, this approach requires us to use assets that are at least as large as the largest size at which they'll be displayed: if an image is intended for part of a layout that could be anywhere from 300px wide to 2000px wide, you'll still need to serve an image with an inherent width of at least 2000px. That's a huge amount of wasted bandwidth and processing power for a mobile device, with no perceivable benefit to the user.

This bandwidth cost is multiplied four-fold as we update our assets to suit high-density displays. A Retina image isn't just twice as big — it's twice as big in both dimensions: a true Retina image is four times larger. We shouldn't serve those to everyone indiscriminately when the vast majority of users will see no benefit whatsoever, especially paired with the already high bandwidth cost of images that need to be able to scale up to suit desktop layouts as well as mobile layouts.

---

15 http://smashed.by/interesting-stats
16 http://smashed.by/compare-stats

At best, it would be tremendously wasteful. At worst, an older mobile browser might see all this data bearing down on it and give up entirely, leaving the page unrendered. In either case we do tremendous damage to a user's data plan, and saddle our users with a very real cost.

HTML5's `video` element makes it refreshingly simple to tailor assets to best suit a user's context. While we can't yet account for specific factors like connection speed, we can at least ensure that the assets we deliver are appropriate to the user's display. HTML5's `source` elements allow us to specify which source should apply based on the same media queries we use in our layouts, in a `media` attribute.

```
<video>
        <source src="vid-large.webm" media="(min-width: 600px)"
         type="video/webm">
<source src="vid-large.ogg" media="(min-width: 600px)" type="video/ogg">
        <source src="vid-large.mp4" media="(min-width: 600px)"
         type="video/mp4">

        <source src="vid-small.webm" type="video/webm">
        <source src="vid-small.ogg" type="video/ogg">
        <source src="vid-small.mp4" type="video/mp4">
        <!-- Fallback for browsers that don't support 'video': -->
        <a href="vid.mpg">Watch Video</a>
</video>
```

Granted, it is a *little* verbose when we need to specify multiple formats for each source; codec support is still something of a minefield[17].

In the above example, the smaller of the two video sources — in whichever format is supported by the browser — is served to any user with a display narrower than 600px. This attribute is surprisingly well-supported, despite being a little-known feature: this syntax will work in current versions of Chrome, Firefox, Opera, Safari, Internet Explorer, iOS, Windows Phone, BlackBerry and Android.

---

17 http://smashed.by/compatibility

We developed a similar means of delivering screen-appropriate images while we were working on the *Globe* site, beginning with the philosophy that the technique should err on the side of mobile: start with a mobile-sized and -formatted image, then swap that for a larger version depending on the user's screen size.

The key to this was getting the screen's width in JavaScript and relaying that information to the server in time to defer the request for the source specified in the image's `src` — otherwise, we're making two requests per image on larger screens. We could have prevented this by avoiding the use of `img src` altogether and injecting images as needed, but we wouldn't want to introduce a dependency on JavaScript in order for users to view the site's content. Instead, we ended up putting together a clever little hack that relied on JavaScript to set the screen's width in a cookie that would be sent along with the requests for the image's original `src`, allowing us to choose the most appropriate image source on the server. If any aspect of the script should fail, the original source specified in the `src` would be requested as usual. It worked well — at least, for a while.

Unfortunately, this approach didn't prove viable for long. Thanks to increasingly aggressive prefetching in newer versions of several major desktop browsers, an image's `src` would be requested before any of our custom scripting was applied — resulting in two requests for a single user-facing image.

What followed was a sordid tale of `noscript` elements and dynamically-injected base tags, `document.write` and `eval` — the Web developer equivalent of scary campfire stories. It was not pretty and, more importantly, none of it worked.

It was around this time that we formed the Responsive Images Community Group[18], and got even more people involved. Despite dragging dozens of developers into our brainstorming, it quickly became obvious that responsive images weren't something that could be solved once and

18 http://responsiveimages.org/

for all with a bit of clever JavaScript. So, we began hashing out ideas for a native solution: if HTML5 offered us a way of solving this, what would it look like?

Bruce Lawson originally proposed a markup pattern[19] for delivering context-appropriate images that fell in line with the syntax for the `video` and `source` elements:

```
<picture>
        <source src="fullsize.jpg" media="(min-width: 60em)" />
        <source src="small.jpg" />

        <!-- Fallback for browsers that don't support 'video': -->
        <img src="fallback.jpg" alt="..." />
</picture>
```

Around the same time as we presented this pattern to the WHATWG, they pitched their own idea[20] for a markup-based means of serving context-appropriate image sources: the `srcset` attribute.

```
<img src="fallback.jpg" srcset="small.jpg 320w 1x, small-hd.jpg 320w 2x,
medium.jpg 640w 1x, medium-hd.jpg 640w 2x, large.jpg 1x, large-hd.jpg
2x">
```

While the `srcset` attribute's syntax was nearly inscrutable, it did handle one part of the equation in an especially efficient way: resolution switching, using values of 1x, 2x, and so on. Furthermore, it handled the question of resolution outside of media queries, which we soon realized stood to benefit users even further.

Media queries are an absolute, at least on paper. It's hard to imagine a circumstance where a user might want to opt into a layout not suited for their display. Likewise, it takes a lot of imagination to come up with a scenario in which a user would prefer images too small or too large

---

19 http://smashed.by/bruce
20 http://smashed.by/whatwg-list

for the layout they're seeing. Image resolution, on the other hand, is a different story: if I'm on a Retina MacBook but I'm tethered to a shaky 3G connection, I'd likely prefer to opt out of huge high-resolution images.

Unlike media queries, the srcset attribute is documented as a set of *suggestions*. When making asset decisions based on a user's screen size or pixel density via media queries, we can ensure that we're never serving a larger asset than stands to benefit the user. What we can't do is use that information to make assumptions about bandwidth conditions or user preference.

By acting as a suggestion, srcset would allow browsers to introduce user settings like "always give me high-res images," "always give me low-res images," or "give me high-res images as bandwidth permits." The browser has that bandwidth information at hand, and that's where the decision should be made — not *for* the user, but *with* them.

In the following snippet, we still rely on media attributes to choose the appropriate source element. It makes sense — we'd decide our breakpoints based on a combination of factors: our layout's media queries; the weight of the images; and alternate cropping and zooming so we can better represent the focus of the image on a smaller display.

```
<picture>
    <source media="(min-width: 40em)" src="big.jpg">
    <source src="small.jpg">
    <img src="fallback.jpg" alt="...">
</picture>
```

After we've established the source element, we then present the resolution options. This is where we use a portion of the WHATWG's proposed srcset attribute to determine which resolution source is most appropriate.

```
<picture>
      <source media="(min-width: 40em)" srcset="big-sd.jpg 1x, big-hd.jpg 2x">
      <source srcset="small-sd.jpg 1x, small-hd.jpg 2x">
      <img src="small-sd.jpg" alt="">
</picture>
```

If you don't need to specify multiple resolutions for a given image source, but do want to specify a source based on the layout, you can use the `picture` element independent of `srcset`:

```
<picture><source media="(min-width: 30em)" src="big.jpg">
      <source src="small.jpg">
      <img src="small.jpg" alt=""></picture>
```

If you should only need the resolution-switching aspect, you can use `srcset` independent of the `picture` element:

```
<img src="image-sd.jpg" srcset="image-hd.jpg 2x" alt="...">
```

Not only can the two proposals harmoniously coexist and complement each other, they can still solve problems on their own.

We proposed this version of the `picture` element to the HTML WG, and a few months ago we reached First Public Working Draft[21], which means it's time for implementers to start digging into it and asking us questions. While we're making steady progress, it might be some time before we can use either of these exact markup patterns in our work.

All this doesn't do us a hell of a lot of good right now, though — I mean, this could be a while, and we've got work to do.

Fortunately, we can start using this markup today: Scott Jehl came up with a polyfill for `picture` as we were writing the specification. Picturefill[22] emulates the `picture` element's proposed behavior using `div`s and

---

21 http://www.w3.org/TR/html-srcset/
22 https://github.com/scottjehl/picturefill

data- attributes — all standards-compliant markup, with all the behavior we want from picture.

```
<div data-picture>
        <div data-source data-media="( min-width: 30em )" data-src="big.jpg">
        <div data-source data-src="small.jpg">
        <noscript>
                <img src="fallback.jpg" alt="...">
        </noscript>
</picture>
```

In the event that JavaScript isn't supported, the user will receive a standard img element. If JavaScript is available, Picturefill will parse through the attributes specified on the data-source elements, determine which one is best suited to the user's display, and inject an img tag with the appropriate source into the page. We've been using Picturefill in our client work at Filament Group for approaching a year now, and we're having great luck with it. The benefit to a developer-led standards effort is that we get a head start on polyfilling the new markup: dozens of polyfills for both picture and srcset are already available on GitHub.

Down on SouthStreet

Filament Group has rolled all the lessons we've learned about optimizing delivery of HTML, CSS, JavaScript and images into a project we're calling SouthStreet[23], named for the location of FG's office.

SouthStreet provides you with a set of tools you can use to ensure that devices get the most efficient amount of code possible, while still maintaining broad accessibility and support. We're continuing to refine SouthStreet as new approaches and techniques come to light, and all of the projects mentioned in this chapter are completely open source: feedback, suggestions and new ideas are always welcomed.

---

23 https://github.com/filamentgroup/southstreet

The day BostonGlobe.com launched, we opened the site up on a number of devices which we never tested and definitely didn't plan for in advance: a first-generation Amazon Kindle, a Nintendo DS, the Playstation 3's built-in browser, and even an Apple Newton. At no point were we presented with a blank screen: no matter the context, we could use the website to the best the device could allow.

Every time a new device shows up for the jQuery Mobile test lab, we have a look at the Globe site — and so far, we're batting a thousand. No panicked emails about updating UA strings; no worrying about new mismatched features, or unplanned display sizes. There are new enhancements we could make as new browser features and APIs roll out, of course, but our foundation is solid and we're never limited by it. It *works* everywhere, for everyone. By following a few principles for serving assets responsibly, you can do the same.

Building websites is a complicated business, and it isn't an easy one. That's the nature of the game, not the fault of any of the tools or techniques we use. The most challenging part of developing for the Web is simplifying: stripping away the inessentials. Responsive Web design can ensure that we don't hinder the inherent flexibility of the Web; progressive enhancement can ensure that we don't hinder the inherent usability of the Web. The very first page of the Web, to this day, works for users of any browsing context.

We can't expect to always get everything right; we're still going to bend a nail or two here and there. Our tools aren't perfect either. But we can do better — we can always do better — and we can use the tools we've got to build amazing things. We might be a little clumsy right now, but we're just getting started.

ABOUT THE AUTHOR

Mat Marquis makes websites at Filament Group. He is a member of the jQuery Mobile team, technical editor and author for *A List Apart*, and Chair of the Responsive Images Community Group. Mat has beaten Mega Man II on "difficult" without losing a single life. He's probably flipping out about something on Twitter as we speak, as @wilto.

ABOUT THE REVIEWER

Brian Arnold is a software developer from Albuquerque, New Mexico. He is currently a Senior Software Engineer at Bazaarvoice, and previously served as Lead Support Engineer at SitePen. His free time goes largely into playing as many different board games as possible. He also ranks in the top 2% of Rock Band Expert Guitarists. He can be found at randomthink.net and @brianarn on Twitter.

Chapter

06

Finding and Fixing Mobile Web Rendering Issues

Written by Addy Osmani

CHAPTER SIX · BY ADDY OSMANI

FINDING AND FIXING
MOBILE WEB RENDERING ISSUES

T HE PERFORMANCE CONVERSATION IS STARTING TO CHANGE.
It's no longer important just to consider how quickly a site loads but also how fast it renders and runs — this is critical on mobile where the performance of Web pages is often compared to native applications. Browsers today are able to run at the refresh rate of our devices and when they do, our pages feel a lot smoother. They're buttery, crisp and delightful to use. When they don't, and users see visual glitches in their pages, they don't like that. There's a performance smell of something being wrong with the page and it's something we need to fix.

This can be a challenge as mobile devices are underpowered when compared to our desktop systems. Rendering the page on the screen takes longer; loading network resources takes longer; decoding images takes longer; and executing scripts takes longer. Performance on mobile is almost never equal to performance on desktop. With slower CPUs and lower-powered GPUs, mobile platforms are anywhere up to five times slower than desktop today[1]. That said, graphics and mobile JavaScript have been getting better on such devices and 30 frames per second (fps) is said to be achievable for a number of use cases.

---

1 http://www.sencha.com/blog/5-myths-about-mobile-web-performance/

Now while network performance is important and JavaScript execution is usually quick, many find that rendering (painting pixels to the screen) is their bottleneck. Large sites, including Facebook[2], Flickr[3] and Pinterest[4], are starting to care about this side of performance more. They've found it can affect not only the user experience but also user engagement. Measurement is the most important part of any performance profiling and, where possible, always check your sites and apps using the tools in other browsers to double-check if your slowdown is browser-specific.

The Three Pillars of Performance

So, we've said that rendering performance is important, but just where does it fit into the overall performance conversation? The three key factors to performance on the Web are: network, compute, and render. Let's briefly review them.

NETWORK

Always keep an eye on the number of network requests your site makes. Most of the time, each file is going to end up being requested separately and these requests may have a quite large latency on them; that is, it's going to take a long time for a server to receive and process a request for a page. On mobile, they'll also keep the radio alive on your device, which is the biggest drain on power after your screen. Keeping those requests down means we can minimize how long the radio is kept on. Also keep in mind that bandwidth and latency are different things so even if you're on a 3G or 4G connection, your latency might not improve. This is one reason why best practices like concatenating your scripts, inlining CSS and using image sprites are so important.

2　http://smashed.by/fb-tweet
3　http://smashed.by/flickr-parallax
4　http://smashed.by/pinterest

A large amount of the Web's traffic is images — well over half[5] according to the HTTP Archive. In many parts of the world, users have fixed data
caps on mobile, meaning that if this cap (e.g. 1GB per month) is exceeded
the customer has to pay more. This is one reason it's important for images
to be optimized as much as possible. At the moment, newer formats like
WebP[6] offer some substantial file size savings compared to the equivalent
quality of a JPEG or PNG. I say quality because you can usually beat a
codec if you lower your quality in another format. For those lucky enough
to be running their own servers, some of my colleagues at Google recommend trying out mod_pagespeed[7] — a tool which can automatically
optimize your site, handling minification and image optimization without
any effort. I'm also happy to recommend ImageOptim[8] and JPEGMini[9] for
image optimization.

COMPUTE

We refer to JavaScript processing as "compute". All of it runs inside a dedicated engine in the browser (e.g. V8 in Chrome, JavaScriptCore in Safari,
OdinMonkey in Firefox) and in many cases these engines are blazingly
fast. One of the reasons they're so fast is that the engines keep an eye on
your code and swap it out with optimized lower-level code where possible.

JavaScript developers regularly worry about memory leaks being introduced by their code. Since we don't handle the retention and release of
memory ourselves and leave this up to the garbage collector, we have to be
careful not to do silly things like leaving references to objects we no longer
need hanging around. Memory usage from all of these hanging objects otherwise grows over time and that's basically what causes a memory leak —
the garbage collector not being able to release something because it thinks

---

5 http://smashed.by/growth
6 https://developers.google.com/speed/webp/
7 http://smashed.by/pagespeed
8 http://imageoptim.com/
9 http://www.jpegmini.com/

you may still need it. The browser developer tools in Chrome, Opera and Firefox can point out where garbage collection has occurred so you can find out where and why you're generating garbage and attempt to address this.

The last thing to keep in mind is something we call deoptimization. This happens when some of the designs you've made in code have led to the engine having to back out of an optimized path for slower code. There are tons of reasons why this can happen and it varies from engine to engine. In Chrome, you can get a little mileage using a standalone version of V8 called *d8*. It can inform you what JavaScript is being deoptimized, giving you a chance to reconsider how you've written some of your code.

RENDER

Rendering performance has only recently come under the spotlight for many Web developers and we're going to devote the rest of this chapter to understanding it. Each of your pages contains a DOM tree (representing its content and structure). Painting the DOM to pixels on the screen can be one of the most expensive operations in your page's life cycle. Any extra effort involved in doing this as your user interacts with your page can result in a visual slowdown. Lots of things can trigger this — scrolling, injecting new content into the page, layout thrashing (any changes that modify the layout of your page), interacting with the UI — pretty much any changes that need to be painted.

As we'll discuss in more depth soon, painting isn't just about user interactions. It also includes the effort the browser has to put in to decode images (if you give it a JPEG, this has to be decoded into a Bitmap), as well as resizing. If you give the browser a 1,024px wide image which you're resizing down to 360px using CSS, that's going to be a lot less efficient than simply providing a prescaled 360px wide image. Chrome's DevTools can give you some more insights into image decode times in Timeline.

Further Reading

- HTML5 Rocks: Performance
  http://www.html5rocks.com/en/features/performance
- Jank Busting For Better Rendering Performance by Tom Wiltzius
  http://www.html5rocks.com/en/tutorials/speed/rendering/
- Making a 60fps mobile Web app
  http://aerotwist.com/blog/making-a-60fps-mobile-app/
- Solving Rendering Performance Puzzles
  http://jakearchibald.com/2013/solving-rendering-perf-puzzles/

Rendering Jank and Hitting 60fps

The human eye perceives a continuous stream of information. It does not naturally see motion as a series of frames. In the worlds of animation, film and gaming, using a series of still frames to simulate motion creates some interesting perceptual artifacts — especially if the frames are played back too slowly. When the frame rate varies, our eyes perceive jerkiness and jitter rather than smoothness in the motion, and what we see appears to flicker. For an optimal user experience on the Web, animations need to be silky, scrolling[10] must be buttery-smooth and your page needs to contain little to no jank, a term that means a disruption in consistent frame rate that manifests itself visually.

You've probably experienced jank before. Have you ever visited a site where scrolling through just felt really sluggish? Or perhaps there was a lot of complex animation or new UI being dynamically introduced that blocked you from being able to do anything. It's these types of experiences that we want to avoid.

In the life of a Web page we generally perform three core tasks: fetching resources; parsing and tokenizing these resources (HTML/CSS/JS); and finally drawings things to screen. During a user's interaction with a page, only parts of it will be changed. For example, they may perform an action

---

10 http://www.html5rocks.com/en/tutorials/speed/scrolling/

changing visibility or adding an outline to an element. The actual process of updating the screen is known as a *paint*.

Changes to your page (e.g. when JavaScript modifies CSS styles) invalidate the rectangle you see on the screen and cause your browser to view it as damaged.

A paint is an expensive operation but is also one that can be difficult to avoid. You always need to draw something to the screen. The key is to make sure the regions you're painting (or repainting) are as small as possible, otherwise you may experience jank. In Chrome, we keep an eye on what in the screen needs to be changed, creating a damage rectangle with the coordinates to parts of the page requiring repainting. We save the old rectangle, prior to your changes, as a bitmap and then only paint the delta between the new rectangle and the old one. If you notice that there are particular areas of a page that require a lot of repainting, it's useful to investigate what can be done to reduce the painting cost.

On the Web, a low frame rate (and a janky experience) means that individual frames being rendered by the browser can be made out by the human eye. Giving users a jank-free experience often comes down to offering an experience that can run at 60fps on sites and Web apps, not just games and animations. At 60fps, you have 16.66ms to complete absolutely everything for Chrome to display a frame of your page — that's logic processing, painting, layout, image decoding, compositing... everything. Once you factor in miscellaneous browser processes, this number looks more like 8–10ms and blowing this budget can mean your users are more likely to see jank in their pages.

What's magical about the number 60? Well, we say 60fps as this matches the refresh rate of the devices we use today. Animations should match the refresh rate of the device they are used on. Phones are usually 55–60Hz, laptops 58–60Hz (although 50Hz in low power mode), and most monitors are 50–62Hz.

To hit 60fps, we sometimes need to go beyond JavaScript as the sole performance bottleneck for our pages and spend more time investigating paint and layout issues. Some of the core causes of jank in sites and applications include:

- Heavy paint times for your DOM elements.
- Unnecessary image resizes, because you haven't pre-scaled to the size you need.
- Long image decodes (e.g. decoding PNG or JPEG).
- Unexpected layer invalidations.
- Garbage collector runs.
- Network requests (e.g. processing an XHR).
- Heavy animation or data processing.
- Input handlers with a heavy amount of JavaScript. One common mistake is to add a lot of JavaScript to rearrange the page in an `onscroll` handler which impacts paint times.

Faster Animations

requestAnimationFrame

`setInterval` and `setTimeout` are regularly used to create animations every 16ms. This comes with its own challenges, but two are of particular note: refresh rates differ from device to device (e.g. the refresh rate on your phone may not necessarily be the refresh rate on your desktop); and timer resolution from JavaScript is only in the order of a few milliseconds.

For the next screen refresh to occur, you need a completed animation frame with all JavaScript, DOM manipulation, painting and layout to be ready. It can be really hard to get animation frames complete before the next refresh when you're working with low timer resolution and variations in screen refresh rates make this near impossible with a fixed timer. Regardless of what your timer interval is, you'll eventually move out of your timing window for a frame and will drop them, meaning users may see a visual drop in smoothness. You'll also end up doing a bunch of work to generate frames that never get shown, wasting critical battery and CPU time.

You may have noticed that we've been caring about frame rate so far when talking about rendering performance — variance has the potential to be a larger issue because, as I mentioned, our eyes notice those little glitches in motion and these tend to come with poorly timed animations. The best way to get accurate timed animation frames is to use the `requestAnimationFrame` API, currently supported in all modern browsers. When you use it, you ask the browser to give you an animation frame and your callback gets called when it's going to generate a new frame. This happens irrespective of the device's refresh rate — which is awesome.

Tom Wiltzius[11] and Paul Lewis[12] have written on HTML5Rocks about animation optimization with `requestAnimationFrame` more succinctly than I could, and they've also previously pointed out some of the other nice things it gives you that are quite relevant to mobile. For example, animations in background tabs get paused, which can conserve your battery life, and if the device can't render at the screen's refresh rate it can actually throttle animations and just generate the callback a little less regularly (e.g. 30 times a second rather than 60). Although this might mean you're halving your frame rate, it means your animation stays consistent. A constant lower frame rate is better than a varied 60Hz that drops some of its frames.

CSS ANIMATION

We've talked about `requestAnimationFrame`, but did you know that even more efficient than lighter JavaScript animation in your callbacks is no JavaScript at all? There's no perfect solution for avoiding interruptions in `requestAnimationFrame` callbacks, but you can get some mileage using CSS animations to remove the need for them. In browsers like Opera Mobile and Chrome for Android, CSS animations can be run by the browser while JavaScript is running thanks to multi-threading.

---

11 http://www.html5rocks.com/en/tutorials/speed/rendering/
12 http://www.html5rocks.com/en/tutorials/speed/animations/

CSS animations expose a few different techniques for animating. These include: transitions, which automatically animate if a specific CSS property changes; transforms, which provide methods for altering the way an element displays on screen (e.g. scaling, translation); and `@keyframe`-based animation for defining more complex animations which change over time. You should use CSS keyframe animations or transitions wherever possible, as they are heavily optimized (often GPU-accelerated) and their performance is almost universally good.

As Paul Irish has previously recommended[13], should you absolutely need to use JavaScript-based animation, use `requestAnimationFrame`. `setTimeout` and `setInterval` should be avoided like the plague. 2-D transforms typically provide a smoother experience than relying on absolute positioning and will lead to quicker paint times and smoother overall animation.

Hardware (GPU) Acceleration

The next thing we're going to look at is GPU acceleration. In the past, browsers have relied pretty heavily on the CPU to render pages. This involved two things: first, painting elements into a bunch of textures, called *layers*; and second, compositing all of those layers together to the final picture seen on screen. Over the past few years, however, we've found that getting the GPU involved in the compositing process can lead to some significant speeding up. The premise is that, while the textures are still painted on the CPU, they can be uploaded to the GPU for compositing. Assuming that all we do on future frames is move elements around (using CSS transitions or animations) or change their opacity, we simply provide these changes to the GPU and it takes care of the rest. We essentially avoid having to give the GPU any new graphics; rather, we just ask it to move existing ones around. This is something that the GPU is exceptionally quick at doing, thus improving performance overall.

---

13 http://smashed.by/translate

There is no guarantee that this hardware compositing will be available and enabled on a given platform, but if it is available the first time you use, say, a 3-D transform on an element, then it will be enabled in Chrome. Currently, the latest versions of Firefox, Safari, IE9+ and the latest version of Opera all also ship with hardware acceleration. Many developers use the translateZ hack to do just that. The other side effect of using this hack is for the element in question to get its own layer, which may or may not be what you want. It can be very useful to effectively isolate an element so that it doesn't affect others as and when it gets repainted. It's worth remembering that uploading these textures from system memory to video memory is not necessarily very quick. The more layers you have, the more textures need to be uploaded and the more layers that will need to be managed, so it's best not to overdo it.

Be very careful when manually promoting layers for mobile[14] as it can be easy to shoot yourself in the foot. Don't apply it to everything as though this may improve your performance on desktop, the cost of doing so will not be equal on mobile where you're working with a more limited GPU.

Avoiding Unnecessary Complexity

The best way to avoid rendering performance issues is to keep things simple. This advice is particularly important on mobile.

One mistake developers often make when developing for the Web is opting to create visually complex experiences (like parallax effects). This involves making visual updates to the page when you get a scroll event. The big problem here is that scroll events aren't timed to the visual updates of the browser (i.e. in a requestAnimationFrame callback). You thereby run the risk of making multiple updates inside a single render frame which can introduce jank to desktop and really slow things down on mobile.

Now, if the updates you make are really expensive (which they can be in the case of visually rich animations and parallax sites) there might be a

---

14 http://smashed.by/null

lot of areas that require painting and compositing. Doing this more than you absolutely need to is a terrible idea. In the case of scrolling, you can solve this by debouncing your scroll events. This is done by storing the last known scroll value in a variable whenever you get a scroll event and then making your visual updates in a `requestAnimationFrame` using the last known value. This will minimize layout thrashing.

This lets the browser schedule visual updates at the right time and do no more work than necessary in each individual frame. For more advice on optimizing scrolling and parallax[15], make sure to check Paul Lewis's articles.

Diagnosing Slow Paint Times

As we've discussed, the browser has to do a lot of work in order to draw things to the screen. Anything you do to increase the complexity of that task (like forcing the entire layout of the page to be recalculated) has the potential to introduce jank to your pages. You want to avoid this. So, let's talk about some tools that can help you measure these slowdowns.

Note: At the time of writing, Opera uses the same front-end developer tools as Chrome DevTools, so many of the tools mentioned in this chapter will be available there too. This may change over time.

DEVTOOLS PERFORMANCE TOOLS

In Chrome, the DevTools Timeline panel provides an overview of where time is spent loading up your Web application, such as how long it takes to process DOM events, render page layouts or paint elements to the screen. It allows you to drill down into three separate facets that can help you discover why your application is slow: events; frames; and actual memory usage. Right now, we're interested in frames mode, which gives you insight into the tasks the browser had to perform to generate a single frame (update) of your application for presentation on the screen.

---

15 http://www.html5rocks.com/en/tutorials/speed/parallax/

Timeline won't display any data by default but you can begin a recording session with it by opening your app and clicking on the gray circle at the bottom of the pane — you can also use the Command / Control+E shortcut. This record button will turn from gray to red and Timeline will begin to capture the timelines for your page. Complete a few actions inside your app (or the one suggested, such as scrolling) and after a few seconds, click the button again to stop recording.

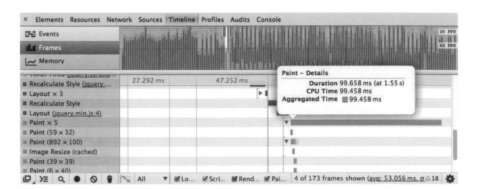

Chrome DevTools Timeline, zoomed into a set of records with some pretty heavy paint.

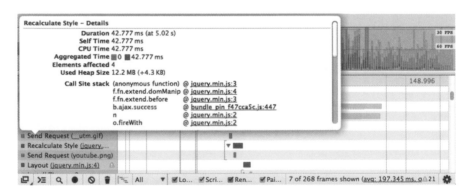

Hovering over a record will display an extended tooltip with details about the time taken to complete it. These have so much useful information in there, so do pay attention to them, especially the call stack.

The summary view (at the top of Timeline) displays horizontal bars representing the network and HTML parsing (blue), JavaScript (yellow), style recalculation and layout (purple), and painting and compositing (green) events for your page. Repaints are browser events invoked by responses to visual changes such as window resizes or scrolls. Recalculations occur when CSS properties are modified, while layout events (or reflows) are due to changes in element position.

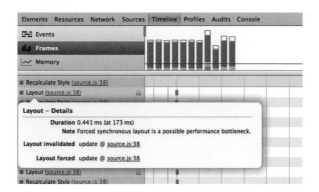

Timeline also identifies when your application causes a forced asynchronous layout and marks these records with a yellow warning icon.

Know Your Tools

Before we dive into an efficient workflow for discovering and tweaking rendering performance issues, there are a few other tools available at our disposal in Chrome that are worth noting.

SHORTCUT FOR QUICKLY HIDING DOM ELEMENTS

DevTools has a useful shortcut allowing you to easily toggle setting visibility:hidden on an element. When this style is applied to an element, it isn't painted but does maintain the page layout in an unchanged state.

To use the shortcut, select a DOM element in the Elements panel and then press the H key. When paired with paint rectangles and Timeline, you can easily evaluate which DOM elements are spending long on paint time.

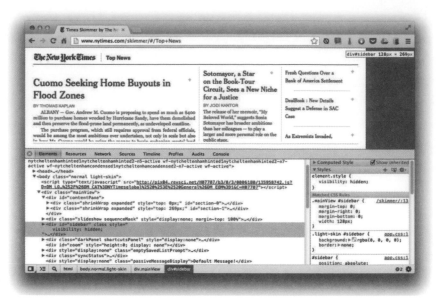

Walking through the DOM tree in the Elements panel, the H shortcut key helps identify elements with heavy paint.

CONTINUOUS PAINTING MODE FOR DIAGNOSING SLOW STYLES

Some of the reasons Chrome repaints areas of the page include: user interactions that cause style changes to DOM elements; DOM nodes being changed (forcing layout recalculation); and any other operations which cause the layout of the page to be changed.

It can be useful to understand why repaints occur in your page. "Continuous page repainting" is a feature in the Settings panel which helps identify elements that have a high paint cost on the page. It forces the page into constant-

Keep an eye on the black and green counter in the top-right corner for insights into repaints.

ly repainting, providing a counter that shows just how much paint work is being done. You can use the H shortcut mentioned above to toggle different styles (keep an eye on the counter!) to diagnose what is causing the slow-down.

SHOW COMPOSITED LAYER BORDERS

Another great setting in Developer Tools that can help here is "Show composited layer borders." This feature will give you insight into those DOM elements that are being manipulated at the GPU level.

If an element takes advantage of the GPU acceleration, you'll see an orange border around it with this on. Now as we scroll through, we don't really see any use of composited layers on this page — not when we click "Scroll to top" or otherwise. Chrome is getting better at automatically handling layer promotion in the background, but, as mentioned, developers sometimes use the translateZ hack to create a composited layer. Below is one site's home page with translateZ(0) applied to all pins. It's not hitting

With "Show composited layer borders" on, elements promoted to a new layer are highlighted with a colored border.

60fps, but it is getting closer to a consistent 30fps on desktop, which is actually not bad.

SHOW PAINT RECTANGLES

Under "Rendering" within the "Settings" cog, you can enable a feature called "Show paint rectangles" to help you visually see the area repainted in each frame. With this feature enabled, it can become easy to visualize what slows pages down. You want to keep the areas being repainted as small as possible.

In this screenshot, a paint rectangle is being drawn over the region where a div with overflow: scroll was being drawn. This is good as it's a relatively small part of the screen.

FPS COUNTER

An older but equally useful tool for visualizing frame rate and jank is the real-time frames-per-second counter. This can be enabled in DevTools by going to the Settings menu and checking "Show FPS meter."

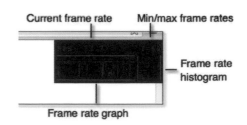

When activated, you will see a dark box in the top-right corner of your page with frame statistics. The counter can be used during live editing to diagnose what in your page is causing a drop-off in frame rate without having to switch back and forth with the Timeline view.

Keep in mind that just tracking the FPS counter may lead you to not notice frames with intermittent jank. Be careful when using the content. It is also worth noting that FPS on desktop does not equal FPS on other devices and special care should be taken to profile the performance there too.

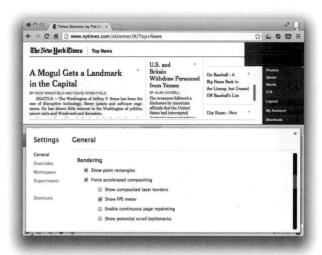

The FPS meter showing the page's current, minimum and maximum frame rates as well as a histogram of frame rate variance.

A "Find and Fix" Workflow for Mobile

It's hard to build a meaningful mobile Web experience without testing on the actual devices you support. Luckily, modern Web browsers expose tools that can profile both your rendering performance on desktop as well as your performance on connected mobile devices. This is done via remote debugging, which you'll need to set up before you can profile your pages on mobile.

SET UP REMOTE DEBUGGING

You'll normally remotely debug your pages over USB. As long as your mobile device is connected to your development machine, you'll be able to profile pages using the Timeline, as well as view and edit HTML, scripts and styles until you have an optimized page which behaves a little better on all of your target devices.

Debugging Chrome for Android using the Chrome Developer Tools.

To set up remote debugging for your version of Chrome or Opera, follow the remote debugging guide over in the Chrome DevTools documentation. You'll then be able to work through the tutorial below on either a real mobile device or your desktop.

Note that the docs linked to above will also give you two options for accessing pages you would like to debug on your device. You can either open up the page on your device's browser, or use a new feature called *reverse-port forwarding* to debug a locally hosted version of your code on your device.

OPTIMIZATION WORKFLOW

Once you have remote debugging set up, here's a workflow for diagnosing paint and jank issues:

1. Open up your page on your device, launch the Chrome DevTools and switch to the "Timeline" panel. Hit record and interact with your page the same way your user would.

2. Check the Timeline for any frames that went over budget (i.e. that are below that ideal 60fps). If you're close to the budget, then you're likely way over budget on mobile. Aim to complete all of your work within 10ms to have some margin. Note that this margin is for slower devices and you should almost certainly run this analysis on mobile using remote debugging[16] (if building for mobile, which you should be!).

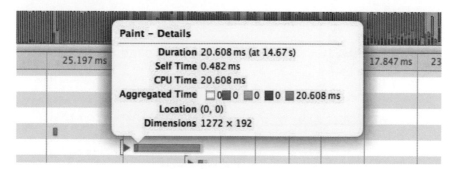

3. Once you've noticed you have a janky frame, check what the cause of it was. Was it a huge paint? CSS layout issue? JavaScript?
4. Fix the problem. If it was a paint or layout issue:
    i.   Go to Settings and enable "Continuous page repainting."
    ii. Walk through the DOM tree, hiding non-essential elements using the hide (H) shortcut. You might discover hiding particular elements makes a large difference to your paint times and frame rate.
    iii. We now know there is something about an element that has slowed painting down. Uncheck styles that could have an impact on paint time (e.g. box-shadow) for the element and check your frame rate again.
    iv. Continue until you've located the style responsible for the slowdown.
5. Rinse and repeat.

---

16 http://smashed.by/remote

Particularly on sites that rely heavily on scroll, you might discover that your main content is relying on `overflow:scroll`. This is a real challenge as this scrolling isn't GPU-accelerated in any way so the content is repainted whenever your user scrolls. You can work around such issues using normal page scroll (`overflow:visible`) and `position:fixed`.

Timeline Reference

- Composite layer: Chrome's rendering engine composited image layers.
- Image decode: an image resource was decoded.
- Image resize: an image was resized from its native dimensions.
- Paint: composited layers were painted to a region of the display. Hovering over a Paint record highlights the region of the display that was updated.
- Invalidate layout: the page layout was invalidated by a DOM change.
- Layout: a page layout was executed.
- Recalculate style: Chrome recalculated element styles.
- Scroll: the content of nested view was scrolled.

Remember, though, to test on both desktop and mobile: their performance characteristics vary wildly. Use the timeline in both, and watch your paint time chart in Continuous Paint mode to evaluate how fast you're busting your budget. Again, don't use this hack on every element on the page – it might pass muster on desktop, but it won't on mobile. The reason is that there is increased video memory usage and an increased layer management cost, both of which could have a negative impact on performance. Instead, use hardware compositing only to isolate elements where the paint cost is measurably high.

Tutorial: Getting a Jank-Free Mobile Web Experience

We've talked the talk, but let's look at a simple app with some janky animation and see if we can optimize it to be jank-free. Now, remember that the
performance of your page on mobile differs greatly from desktop performance so you'll want to make sure you have remote debugging set up for
this tutorial. Let's get started.

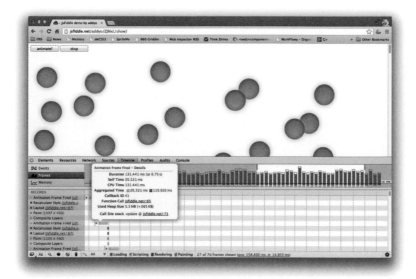

1. Open up http://jsfiddle.net/AxEJY/.
2. Click "animate!" As you can see, there is a visual break in motion,
   resulting in a suboptimal animation. We can record a Timeline
   session during the animation of this page to confirm that we have an
   issue hitting an optimal frame rate. The animation performs far worse
   on mobile than it does on desktop because we're working with more
   limited GPU.
3. Let's see what's causing things to slow down. Here's the JavaScript for
   our animation as well as the CSS:

JavaScript

```javascript
// setup
var rAF = window.requestAnimationFrame;
var startBtn = document.querySelector('.animate');
var stopBtn = document.querySelector('.stop');

// state
var running = false;

// add listeners
// start
startBtn.addEventListener('click', function(e) {
    running = true; rAF(update); });

// stop
stopBtn.addEventListener('click', function(e) {
    running = false;
});

// Set the heights for all these
// movers in simple CSS style.top
var movers = document.querySelectorAll('.mover');
(function init() {
    for (var m = 0; m < movers.length; m++) {
        movers[m].style.top = (m * 20 + 50) + 'px';
    }
})();

// animation loop
function update(timestamp) {
    for (var m = 0; m < movers.length; m++) {
        movers[m].style.left = ((Math.sin(movers[m].offsetTop +
timestamp / 1000) + 1) * 500) + 'px';
    }

    if (running){
        rAF(update);
    }
};
rAF(update);
```

CSS

```
.mover {
    background: url(http://jankfree.org/velocity-europe/examples/too-
much-layout/particle.png);
    height: 100px;
    width: 100px;
    position: absolute;
    z-index: 0;
}

input {
    z-index: 2;
    font-size: 25pt;
    height: 100px;
    width: 100px;
    display: inline-block;
}
```

ANALYZE THE RECORDING

Looking at the recording of the first few frames it's clear that each one is taking over 300ms to complete. If you hover your mouse over one of the frames a pop-up appears showing additional details about the frame.

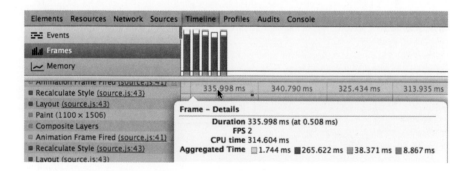

To improve rendering performance, Chrome usually batches layout changes requested by pages and attempts to schedule a layout pass to asynchronously calculate and render the requested changes.

However, if a page asks for the value of a property depending on the layout (e.g. offsetWidth or offsetHeight), the browser is forced to immediately and synchronously perform a page layout. These are called *forced synchronous* layouts and can have a pretty significant reduction on rendering performance, especially when performed repeatedly on larger DOM trees. We call this scenario layout thrashing.[17]

The Timeline can alert you when it discovers a forced synchronous layout with a yellow warning icon next to the corresponding Timeline record. If you hover over one of these records, it displays stack traces for the code which invalidated the layout and the code that forced it.

So, in our Timeline, locate an "Animation Frame Fired" record and find the yellow warning icon next to it indicating a forced synchronous layout. The icon is slightly dimmed indicating that one of its child records contains the offending code, rather than this record itself.

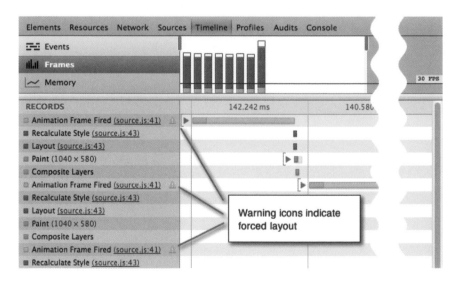

Expand the "Animation Frame Fired" to view its children.

---

17 http://smashed.by/layout-perf

The child records show a long, repeating pattern of Recalculate Style and Layout records. Each layout record is a result of the style recalculation that, in turn, is a result of the requestAnimationFrame() handler requesting the value of offsetTop for each image on the page. Hover your mouse over one of the Layout records and click the link for sources.js next to the Layout Forced property.

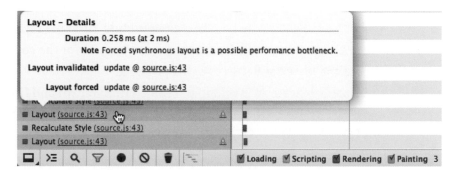

The Sources panel opens at line 43 of the source file at the update() function, which is the requestAnimationCallback() callback handler. The handler computes the image's left CSS style property on the the image's offsetTop value. This forces Chrome to perform a new layout immediately to make sure it provides the correct value.

```
// animation loop
function update(timestamp) {
    for (var m = 0; m < movers.length; m++) {
        movers[m].style.left = ((Math.sin(movers[m].offsetTop +
        timestamp/1000) + 1) * 500) + 'px';
        }
    raf = window.requestAnimationFrame(update);
};
```

We know that forcing a page layout during every animation frame is slowing things down. Now we can try to fix the problem directly in DevTools.

APPLY FIX WITHIN DEVTOOLS

Now that we have an idea about what's causing the performance issues, we can modify the JavaScript file directly in the Sources panel and test our changes on desktop or our mobile device right away.

In the Sources panel that was opened previously, replace line 43 with the following code.

```
movers[m].style.left = ((Math.sin(m + timestamp/1000) + 1) * 500) + 'px';
```

1. This version computes each image's `left` style property on its index in its holding array instead of on a layout-dependent property (`offsetWidth`).
2. Save your changes by pressing Command+S or Control+S.

VERIFY WITH ANOTHER RECORDING

The animation is clearly faster and smoother than before, but it's always good practice to measure the difference with another recording. It should look something like the recording below.

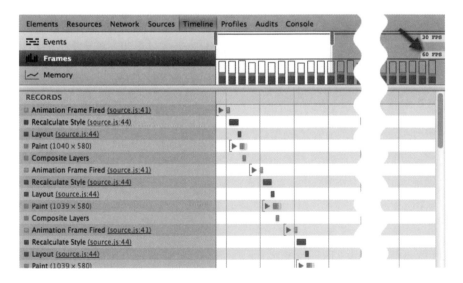

Try it out. The corrected code for this sample can be found at
http://jsfiddle.net/k4yM3/ and now performs at close to 60fps.

Pro Tips

Your JavaScript can annotate DevTools Timeline recordings using `con-sole.timeStamp()` which works whether you're using remote debugging or not. See below for "Adding result," an annotation added by our code during profiling:

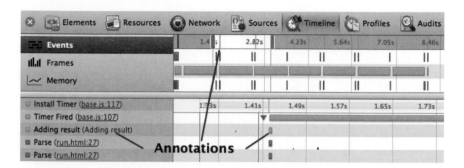

Your code can also use `console.time()` and `console.timeEnd()` to mark ranges in DevTools Timeline recordings:

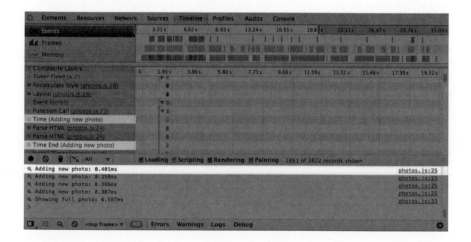

If you enable "Show CPU activity on the ruler", you can overlay the CPU activity in your Timeline recordings. With this on, the light bars indicate the CPU was busy. If you hover over a CPU bar, this highlights the region during which the CPU was active.

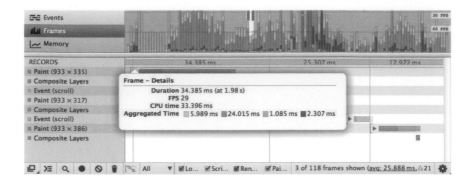

If you would like to drill down to records of a particular type, you can do this by using the Control+F shortcut (Command+F on Mac OS X) when in the Timeline. Just enter in the name of the record type (e.g. "scroll") and Timeline will only show the records containing the term.

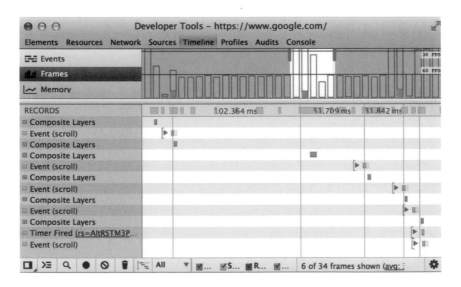

If you're wondering what those transparent bars in the Timeline mean, these hollow frames correspond to one of two things: your JavaScript on the main thread was busy doing something we forgot to show (instrument) in the DevTools; or you were bottlenecked by your GPU.

Rendering Performance Tools in IE, Firefox and Safari

So far we've discussed tools for finding and fixing rendering performance issues in Chrome. As rendering is still quite a new area for many Web developers to optimize for, the tools available for it in other browsers are still evolving but I'm excited about the direction they've been taking.

THE IE11 F12 DEVELOPER TOOLS

Many developers are surprised to hear that IE's developer tools have improved by leaps and bounds of late. In IE11, the F12 developer tools introduce a special UI Responsiveness feature for profiling perfomance issues around jank, slowness and other common problems areas like CPU and memory usage.

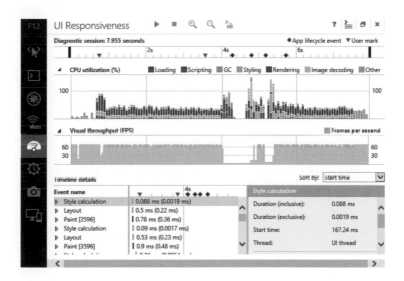

Workflow

With IE11 installed and the UI Responsiveness tool loaded, you'll be prompted to begin a new performance profiling session in the main pane.

- Select the arrow at the top of the tool to begin profiling. Keep the actions you perform to the bare minimum needed to capture the slowdown you want to investigate in your page. Anything more will run the risk of decreasing the readability of your results.
- When you've completed the interactions you wanted to capture, click "Stop profiling" or the square-shaped icon at the bottom of the developer tools to create a report from these results.

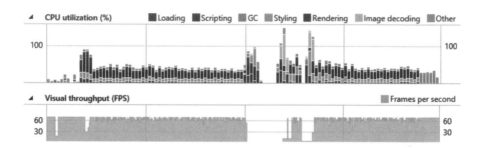

The UI Responsiveness tool comes with its own performance Timeline which you'll see next. It's a similar, but slightly different take to the one we saw in Chrome. Use this to visualize the frame-rate of the page (which IE refers to as visual throughput) and drops in this frame-rate, indicating we've dropped frames or some slowdown has occurred. It also captures how much of the CPU is being used, but this is less interesting for our purposes.

Next, you can drill down into what specific records correspond to using the Timeline Details view. The official IE11 developer tools docs cover the categories listed more comprehensively, but in short this captures: CSS and HTML parsing; network requests; script evaluation; image decodes; animation frame callbacks; and of particular interest to us: layout and rendering. Layout in this context refers to changes to the DOM that caused the dimensions or position of elements to change and rendering refers to visual changes to the DOM that caused regions of the page to be repainted. The details summarized include the dimensions and coordinates of the render layer that was affected.

To learn more about the F12 developer tools, check out the official documentation[18] and their guide to the UI Responsiveness[19] tool.

FIREFOX

The Firefox nightlies have a feature called *paint flashing* which can also be used to determine what regions of the page the browser is repainting. With paint flashing turned on, each region is tinted with a random color making it really easy to distinguish one region from another. Regions with really heavy paint flashing are the ones that are going to cost you, so try to minimize them as much as possible.

Enable paint flashing

1. Be sure to have Firefox 11 or higher installed (Beta, Aurora, or Nightly).
2. Go to about:config.
3. Accept the warning that is displayed.
4. Right-click and select New → Boolean.
5. Type nglayout.debug.paint_flashing.
6. Set the option to True. That's it!

---

18 http://smashed.by/f12
19 http://smashed.by/uiresp

WEBKIT/SAFARI

Apple has also been doing interesting work in the WebKit nightlies. If you grab one of the recent releases you'll find that two new tools are exposed to help improve rendering performance.

The first is that the Web Inspector recently introduced a layer details sidebar for getting insights into WebKit's compositing of elements. It highlights layer information for a selected DOM element (if it's been promoted to a layer) as well as layers for descendant elements.

When you select a layer in the sidebar, it displays a pop-over summarizing the reasons the layer was created (promoted). Depending on the type of page you're working on, eliminating layers can be a good way to reduce your page's graphics performance overhead.

The quickest way to view layer information for a page is to inspect the document body and review the child layers. You're then able to narrow down the list by inspecting descendants that are even deeper. Similar to Chrome, you can also show compositing layer borders, done in the DOM tree's navigation bar, which overlays your page to provide a clearer visualization of layers and the number of times they are being repainted.

Show Reasons for Compositing

- Grab the WebKit nightlies.[20]
- Make sure to switch off "Use WebKit Web Inspector."
- Hit that shiny "Layers" button. Boom!
- Reasons for layer promotion are displayed on hover.

The second is that you can display the number of times a layer was (re) painted, helpful for understanding what parts of your page may be getting excessively painted due to behavior in your scripts.

Show Paint Counts of Layers

- Under Layers → Show composited layer borders.
- Like Chrome, it displays layers promoted to a composite layer.
- However, it also displays the number of times a layer was painted!

---

20 http://nightly.webkit.org/

Conclusions

Jank-free experiences are critical for the mobile Web to come anywhere close to what users are accustomed to with a native app. That's how high the bar is and you can rise to the challenge of clearing it.

But building amazing experiences on the mobile Web takes more than just a good designer and fancy CSS — you absolutely must care about performance. Users expect a native feel, and smooth animation that never drops a frame can give it to them. When your pages scroll slowly, animations stutter and effects lag heavily... that's jank and it can impact your user experience and engagement.

Keep in mind that performance can vary massively between browsers and a performance smell in one might not be present in another. Use their developer tools to see what's really happening under the hood.

Check that your style recalculations aren't changing more styles than you expect. Keep your paint areas small. If you notice lots of large or full-screen paints, there may be a problem. Reduce unnecessary image resizing because even one large resize can make you miss 60fps.

If all goes well, you'll make your users happy with more fluid, silky smooth experiences, regardless of the device they're using. You'll have cleared that jank-free bar and can give yourself a well-deserved pat on the back.

To learn more about optimizing the paint performance of your pages, check out Jankfree.org and remember, if you think you have a performance problem on mobile, don't guess it — test it!

ABOUT THE AUTHOR

Addy Osmani is working on the Chrome team at Google, building and advocating for tools to help improve developer productivity and satisfaction. His personal projects include TodoMVC, which helps developers compare JavaScript MVC frameworks and AuraJS. He's also written *Developing Backbone.js Applications* and *Learning JavaScript Design Patterns.*

ABOUT THE REVIEWER

Sindre Sorhus is passionate about creating things and moving the Web forward. He is an eloquent JavaScript developer and Open Source monomaniac from Norway, and the creator of many Open Source projects and Node.js modules. He is currently infatuated on fixing front-end development with Yeoman, Bower, Grunt and TodoMVC.

Chapter

07

Designing Adaptive Interfaces

Written by Aaron Gustafson

CHAPTER SEVEN · BY AARON GUSTAFSON

DESIGNING ADAPTIVE INTERFACES

D ESIGN, AS A CONCEPT, IS A TRICKY LITTLE BEAST. On the one hand, a well-designed object should be attractive, but on the other it must also be easily understood and highly usable. For a design to be successful, these two facets must be in balance. When aesthetics trump usability, the resulting work serves the designer — by being a vehicle for self-expression — not the consumer. Similarly, when a project sacrifices aesthetics for usability, the resulting work can be uninspiring, pedestrian even. People will use it, but they won't love it.

> Pleasurable designs are not necessarily usable. But need these attributes be in conflict? Why not beauty and brains, pleasure and usability?

> — Don Norman, *Emotion & Design: Attractive things work better* [1]

Etymologically speaking, "design" originates from the medieval Latin *designare*, to mark out. Classically, it has been synonymous with the act of indicating. From the very beginning, design has been about more than just

---

1 Don Norman, "Emotion & Design: Attractive things work better"; http://smashed.by/emotion-design, 2002.

aesthetics; it has been about illuminating content and making it easier for the consumer to accomplish key tasks. We design to solve problems.

To create truly exceptional designs, we must not only reduce the friction inherent in completing a task, but we should make it (dare I say it) fun! We must reconcile aesthetics with usability.

We're Empathetic

Design does not exist in a vacuum. It is not art on a wall. Designs are meant for interaction. For use. And who is the user? Sometimes it's us, but unless we are lucky enough to spend all day building stuff that's meant solely for our own consumption, we are probably building for someone else.

It's hard to design for someone else. After all, we're complex creatures with unique perspectives, objectives and needs. It's incredibly difficult to put aside our own biases and approach a problem from someone else's point of view.

Thankfully, however, we are hardwired with the capacity to do so.

Throughout the 1980s and 90s, Giacomo Rizzolatti and a group of neurophysiologists in Parma, Italy, were studying the neurons that control hand and mouth actions. To test these neurons, the researchers would place electrodes in the ventral premotor cortex of a macaque monkey and record the firing of individual neurons as the macaque reached for peanuts from a bowl.

Purely by happenstance, a macaque was still hooked up to the recorder when a research assistant walked into the room and grabbed a peanut. Much to everyone's surprise, the very same neurons fired when the macaque saw the peanut plucked from the bowl as when the monkey performed that same action. Through what have come to be known as mirror neurons, the macaque was able to share in the experience, despite not actually partaking in it. That's the root of empathy.

"Empathy" stems from the Greek *empatheia* meaning state of emotion and is defined by Merriam-Webster as:

The action of understanding, being aware of, being sensitive to, and vicariously experiencing the feelings, thoughts, and experience of another [...] without having the feelings, thoughts, and experience fully communicated in an objectively explicit manner.

We often rely on user research to establish and maintain empathy with our customers. We may conduct this research by sending a small team into the field to meet our customers where they live and work. Or we may assign one person to look at our site's analytics data to glean insight. Or, for better or worse, we may just go with our gut and assume we know what our users want.

Regardless of how (or whether) we conduct research, it is important that we never lose sight of the fact that real people will be using our interfaces. Data is great, but it's impossible to empathize with data.

What Do We Know?

Data, especially analytics data, can be enlightening, but it can also lead us to false assumptions.

Scenario: We do not see any non-JavaScript users in our stats.
Assumption: All of our users have JavaScript, so we don't need to support a non-JavaScript use case.
Follow-up Questions: Did we check to see if our analytics software is configured to track users without JavaScript turned on? Does the site work at all without JavaScript? What is the experience like while a user waits for JavaScript to be read and executed? How do you handle SEO? (Hint: search spiders don't execute JavaScript.)

Scenario: We do not see any users browsing our site on a Blackberry 5.
Assumption: We have no Blackberry 5 users and can stop supporting it.
Follow-up Questions: How does the site look and function on a Blackberry 5? If it is a bad experience, would you consider coming back?

As you can see, a simple stat does not tell us everything. Also, in both of these scenarios, our initial design and implementation choices may have unintentionally shaped the stats: JavaScript for stats + no JavaScript = no stats; bad Blackberry 5 experience = Blackberry 5 users go elsewhere. When decisions (strategic or accidental) shape them, the stats become less useful and we run the risk of driving away potential customers. Instead, we should strive to grow our customer base by treating everyone as we would want to be treated: with respect.

The fact is that when users come to our site, we know very little about them. Sure, we can read the *user agent (UA) string* sent in the request from their browsers, but that only tells us so much (if it is even telling us the truth. UA strings are easily spoofed).

A UA string can't tell us if they visit our site on a Blackberry 5, have $5 to spend on our product or $5 million. A UA string can't tell us if users don't have the same domain knowledge or level of education as we do. A UA string can't tell us if they have poor vision and need to be able to enlarge the text. A UA string can't tell us if they have a broken arm, are mousing with the non-dominant hand, and aren't as accurate at clicking as they otherwise would be. A UA string can't tell us if a user has installed a browser plugin that will bring our carefully constructed JavaScript framework to its knees. A UA string can't tell us if the high pixel density device being used is connecting over a mobile network and the user may not want that 7MB photo.

There are so many possibilities to consider beyond what we know (or think we know) about users when they visit our site. Instead of trying to nail it down and control every detail, we should take advantage of the inherent fluid and flexible nature of the Web. We should focus on building an experience that is universally accessible and then capitalize on opportunities presented by different devices, platforms and technologies to enhance that experience. You know: *progressive enhancement*.

Progressive enhancement keeps the design open to the possibilities of sexiness in opportune contexts, rather than starting with the "whole" experience that must be compromised.[2]

Brick by Brick, Row by Row

We don't know what the future has in store for us, but we know that what has worked in the past will work in the future. That's the promise of the Web: future-friendliness[3]. Embracing the past — real links, forms that submit to an action page, body elements brimming with actual content — doesn't hold us back: it provides us with a solid foundation to build even more incredible experiences.

When people get excited thinking about a Web interface, they are often getting excited about some fancy animation effect or dynamic widget. I have no problem with that. As designers — of content, data, pixels, interactions or code — we *should* be excited about how we help people accomplish what they set out to do. But often, we get caught up in trends, tactics and technology — the things we think are cool, fun, interesting, or likely to garner us some industry attention — and we lose sight of our users and their needs.

I've been amazed at how often those outside the discipline of design assume that what designers do is decoration—likely because so much bad design simply is decoration. Good design isn't. Good design is problem solving.

— Jeffrey Veen, *The Art and Science of Web Design*

There's nothing wrong with a slick interface for folks with the latest and greatest browsers as long as we consider what the experience looks like for someone without access to that technology. It's tempting to focus on building the flashy version and then go back to patch it to work reasonably

---

2 Ben Hoh, "From degradation to enhancement": http://smashed.by/redesigning-society, Jan 30, 2012.
3 http://futurefriend.ly/

well in less-capable browsers (*graceful degradation*[4]). And if we let our stats deceive us into believing we don't need to worry about non-JavaScript users or specific older browsers, we may even call it a day and assume anyone who visits on those browsers is going to have a bad experience (or no experience at all).

Obviously, that's not a very good demonstration of user empathy. We need to build solid, universal experiences that will work without the bells and whistles and then add on the flashy bits when we know the browser can actually use them. Support RGBa colors? Awesome, let's tweak the look and feel a bit. Got gesture support? Great, let's upgrade the interface to make it work with swipe.

Smartly built interfaces offer a *continuum* of experience. In case you're unfamiliar with the term, a continuum is a collection of steps from point A to point B where each step varies by a minute degree. For a simple example, consider the continuum from a peanut to a Peanut M&M:

1. First, there's the peanut, a natural and tasty snack in its own right.
2. Next comes the chocolate-covered peanut, a definite improvement on the original. The smooth, rich chocolate coating complements the peanut beautifully.
3. Finally the package is complete: the candy shell provides texture and a touch of sweetness that rounds out the experience perfectly.

Each step in this continuum from peanut to Peanut M&M is a perfectly valid snack option, but each (in my opinion at least) is also a significant improvement on the previous step.

We should strive to create interfaces that operate like this. Each step in the process of building an interface should add to the experience. In the end, independent users may have differing experiences of the interface, but no one is denied access to a good experience.

---

4 http://en.wikipedia.org/wiki/Fault-tolerant_system

The peanut to Peanut M&M continuum.

The Layer Cake, Revisited

When the Web standards movement was young, we were encouraged to separate the code controlling our content, presentation and behavior. We did that in order to make our sites more maintainable, our pages smaller, and our markup cleaner. And it worked. Amazingly well, in fact.

Progressive enhancement asks that we take that concept a step further and considers these three layers of the Web standards cake comprising many smaller layers of experience.

Why? As you're no doubt keenly aware, the browser ecosystem is incredibly diverse. One browser accessing our sites today may only support a subset of HTML4 tags, while another may support all of HTML4 and some HTML5, and a third may support only HTML4 and some microformats. One may support only a handful of CSS2 properties, while another supports most of CSS2 and CSS3 colors, and a third supports all of that in addition to CSS3 animations and media queries. JavaScript support is similarly all over the map. A quick look at Peter Paul Koch's Acid 3 test matrix for WebKit[5] reveals that not all browsers are created equally, even when they are based on the same underlying rendering engine. Sure, overall standards support is far better now than it was when I built my first Web page back in 1996, but that doesn't mean they all support the same standards.

We all know the answer to the classic question: do websites need to look exactly the same in every browser? The answer is *No*[6]. But why stop there? We must take it a step further: do websites need to function exactly the same in every browser? No.

---

5 http://www.quirksmode.org/webkit_mobile.html
6 http://dowebsitesneedtolookexactlythesameineverybrowser.com

We could never hope to create (and test) unique experiences for each combination of these capabilities any more than we could test our websites in every browser on every device ever made. We'd never sleep and we'd never launch anything. But we can think about experience as a continuum and architect our interfaces to adapt to the capabilities of our users' devices in order to ensure a positive experience — even if it's not an identical one.

As the mobile first movement has reminded us, we need to focus on the core use case for a page or interface and build up the experience from there. And, while we craft that experience, we need to make sure none of our design or technical decisions undermine it. The layers of a typical Web experience break down like this:

0. The Core

Text content and basic interactive elements that form a universally usable foundation (links, forms, etc.). Our copywriting (even microcopy like labels and error messages) must be both clear and appropriate.

1. Semantics

HTML markup that illuminates the content of the core experience and conveys the meaning of the words. Each element we choose should enhance the semantic meaning of the content. We should never choose an element that could obscure the meaning of our content or confuse a reader (e.g. using a div, span, or even an anchor when it should be a button). We should also employ ARIA landmark roles to more easily guide our users who rely on assistive technology around the page.

2. Design

CSS that establishes a visual hierarchy, enhances the reading experience (through the use of vertical rhythm, comfortable line lengths, etc.), and reinforces the brand. Each design decision we make should enrich the experience and should never subvert the core by reducing access to content or obscuring it through the use of low-contrast text or visuals.

3. Enhanced Interaction

JavaScript, in concert with advanced HTML-based interactive elements (e.g. details/summary, advanced input types) and related CSS styles, that enhances the usability of an interface. Enhanced interactions should *humanize* the interface and reduce any friction inherent in completing the specific task. The JavaScripts we write and use should manipulate the document to introduce the necessary markup and styles to create the enhanced interface, thereby reducing the size of the page for non-JavaScript users.

No style or coding decisions we make should limit assistive technology's access to the core experience if the JavaScript is executed. Our JavaScripts should also introduce and update the ARIA attributes necessary to provide assistive technology with useful details about the interface and what is happening as a user interacts with it.

Each layer not only serves a technical purpose, but a human one. Every decision we make, every key we press, affects our users' experience. With empathy as your guide, you're more likely to make the right call.

Considering Constraints

The world of Web-enabled devices is extremely diverse and seems to get more so every day. With each new platform, browser and rendering engine having its own complex matrix of technical features and constraints, attempting to craft a universally great experience can seem like a daunting endeavor. Again, looking at an interface as serving a core purpose helps maintain our sanity.

HOW DOES IT READ?

First and foremost, we need to consider how an interface reads. Have you ever used a screen reader? How about a text-based browser? Ever read email as plain text? When we strip away the design, the semantics and the interactive affordances of an interface, what we are left with is the core: text, enhanced with hyperlinks. If our interface is functional in this context, we're almost guaranteed it will be usable on pretty much anything.

Text-only can seem impossible when we're concentrating on advanced content displays, but with a little thoughtful consideration of the interface, we can find ways to literally spell out that which is visually conveyed. Take a timeline, like the one on the right, for instance: What is a timeline, but an ordered list of events grouped around markers in time?

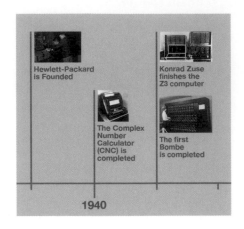

Timeline from the Computer History Museum.
http://www.computerhistory.org/timeline/

```html
<h1>Timeline of Computer History</h1>
<ol>
  <li>
    <h2>1939</h2>
    <ul>
      <li>
        <figure>
          <img src="images/1939_HewlettPackard.jpg" alt=""/>
          <figcaption>David Packard and Bill Hewlett in their Palo Alto,
California Garage</figcaption>
        </figure>
        <p>Hewlett-Packard is Founded. David Packard and Bill Hewlett
found Hewlett-Packard in a Palo Alto, California garage. Their first
product was the HP 200A Audio Oscillator, which rapidly becomes a popular
piece of test equipment for engineers. Walt Disney Pictures ordered eight
of the 200B model to use as sound effects generators for the 1940 movie
"Fantasia."</p>
      </li>
    </ul>
  </li>
  <li>
    <h2>1940</h2>
    <ul>
      <li>
        <figure>
          <img src="images/1940_complex.jpg" alt=""/>
```

```
      <figcaption>The Complex Number Calculator (CNC)</figcaption>
    </figure>
    <p>The Complex Number Calculator (CNC) is completed. In 1939,
Bell Telephone Laboratories completed this calculator, designed by
researcher George Stibitz. In 1940, Stibitz demonstrated the CNC at an
American Mathematical Society conference held at Dartmouth College. This is
considered to be the first demonstration of remote access computing.</p>
      </li>
    </ul>
  </li>
  <li>
    <h2>1941</h2>
    <ul>
      <li>
        <figure>
          <img src="images/1941_zuse_z3.jpg" alt=""/>
          <figcaption>The Zuse Z3 Computer</figcaption>
        </figure>
        <p>Konrad Zuse finishes the Z3 computer. The Z3 was an early
computer built by German engineer Konrad Zuse working in complete
isolation from developments elsewhere. Using 2,300 relays, the Z3
used floating point binary arithmetic and had a 22-bit word length. The
original Z3 was destroyed in a bombing raid of Berlin in late 1943.</p>
      </li>
      <li>
        <figure>
          <img src="images/1941_luring-bombe.jpg" alt=""/>
          <figcaption>Bombe replica, Bletchley Park, U.K.</figcaption>
        </figure>
        <p>The first Bombe is completed. Based partly on the design of
the Polish "Bomba," a mechanical means of decrypting Nazi military
communications during WWII, the British Bombe design was greatly
influenced by the work of computer pioneer Alan Turing and others. Many
bombes were built.  Together they dramatically improved the intelligence
gathering and processing capabilities of Allied forces.</p>
      </li>
    </ul>
  </li>
  <!-- content continues -->
</ol>
```

In a text-only context, this example is quite easily understood. Additionally, it works pretty well on a small screen, where real estate is at a premium. But, if we want to enhance the timeline with JavaScript to make it into a more engaging experience, we can test to see if that enhanced experience makes sense given the constraints of the browser and device used to access the content. If the conditions are right, JavaScript can inject additional markup, rearrange elements on the page, hide visually redundant content (in an accessible way), and insert a new set of style rules to govern the look and feel of that upgraded interface.

When thinking about different ways to experience content, I like to sketch out a *UI construction flow*. You can think of a UI construction flow as a roadmap for the build process of a page. It outlines the different potential experiences along the continuum and helps us better visualize how they all fit together. It also gives us an opportunity to explore the constraints we need to consider for that interface. To the right, you'll find a sample diagram for the timeline:

Simple Timeline UI Construction Flow

The constraint of offering a text-only experience is a crucial first step toward ensuring everyone can use our websites, but it is only the first of three constraints I use to guide my work. The second constraint I embrace is the network.

SIP, DON'T GULP

Bandwidth. Latency. Simultaneous connection limits. Each of these facets of the network has an effect on the experience of loading and interacting with a site. These affect every connection, but on mobile networks they have an even more profound effect (more on that in a moment).

For years, Web performance luminaries have been telling us to concatenate our files, build sprite maps, compress our images, and minify everything. Reducing the number of requests to the server makes a huge difference in the speed of delivering content to a browser. And, of course, smaller files will download more quickly.

Most of us jumped on the Web performance bandwagon pretty quickly. It just made sense. But can we do more?

Mobile networks present an interesting challenge because they typically suffer from high latency, and roaming users may jump from cell tower to cell tower, experiencing a wide variety of service stability and availability. The more quickly we can deliver our experiences to our customers, the more likely they will be able to use them before they lose connectivity in a dead zone or wind up dropping from 4G speeds to Edge.

Then there's the money issue. Few mobile data customers are lucky enough to have an unlimited usage plan. Most users are paying by the bit and the larger our site is, the more it costs them to view our content. Anything extraneous we send to our customers is tantamount to a tax on accessing our content or service, and we aren't even the one reaping the financial benefits.

This is why it is critical that we focus on the core purpose of a Web page or interface when we build it. Mat Marquis' now famous tweet (see on the right) says it all. I don't think anyone has more clearly articulated the tension between a marketing department's vision for a page and the customer's. Sure, we want our pages to be beautiful, but there are trade-offs we need to be aware of. In the end, we should be empathetic toward the people who visit our websites so they become (and remain) our customers.

Mat "Wilto" Marquis on twitter.com

To that end, let's consider a typical newspaper website. Most newspaper sites contain one or more pages that display a number of articles in aggregate. The homepage is a typical location, but newspaper section landing pages often function similarly.

Each of these contexts contains multiple instances of a teaser module. Universally, the teaser module contains a headline, byline and lede. But sometimes it also contains a small thumbnail to draw our eye or hint at what we might find on the full article page.

The "Latest News" section on Nooga.com

As visually appealing as these thumbnail images might be, they are merely complementary to the core purpose of the teaser: getting us to click through and read the full article. Furthermore, thumbnail images like these create additional problems:

1. Externally referenced images require an additional download (and all of the networking-related overhead that involves), making the page take longer to render, while simultaneously costing consumers more money to view the content over a metered network.

2. Images embedded using data URIs are typically three times larger than their binary equivalents, leading to a larger HTML payload which may be faster to download, but actually costs metered network customers more to view than external images.

3. In narrower layouts, these images can actually make reading more difficult, defeating the whole purpose of the content to begin with.

Those are some pretty powerful arguments against having any teaser thumbnails, right?

Well, studies have shown that some images — relevant images with story appeal[7] — can actually engage readers, so we shouldn't throw them out entirely. Instead, we should scrutinize each image's content to determine whether it actually adds anything to teaser. Once we've separated the useful from the useless, we can concentrate on addressing the issues above.

If readability is our chief concern, we might be tempted to link to the images in the traditional way and hide them with CSS when the browser is less than twice the thumbnail width. The problem with that strategy is that the browser will still download the images even though they are not being displayed. That's not very respectful of our customer's time and money.

A better strategy to use is called *lazy loading*.

You may be familiar with lazy loading as a concept from the JavaScript world, where additional code is loaded into a Web page as needed. But there's no reason to reserve that technique for JavaScript. We can lazy-load anything that is ancillary to the core purpose of the page: images, HTML, CSS, etc. In fact, this is exactly what many news sites (e.g. the Guardian, the Boston Globe, and the BBC) have begun to do. When it comes to lazy loading images, my current preference is to take an empty paragraph and assign it a data-* attribute pointing to the image I may want to load if the conditions seem right:

```
<p data-image-src="/path/to/my.jpg"></p>
```

I use some simple CSS to hide this paragraph by default:

```
[data-image-src] {
        display: none;
}
```

Then I use JavaScript to test a few conditions and decide what to do. A UI construction flow for this approach looks like the figure below:

---

7 http://smashed.by/the-truth

Obviously, without JavaScript the script won't run and the paragraph just sits there, invisible. Sure, it is a bit of extra markup to download, but it beats a hidden image or (worse yet) a hidden embedded image.

If JavaScript is available, the script is run and can test for things like browser width[8], currently employed media query[9], network speed[10], and even whether or not the user is on a metered connection[11]. The usefulness and reliability of network-related testing are currently dubious at best, but I am hopeful they'll get there in the future.

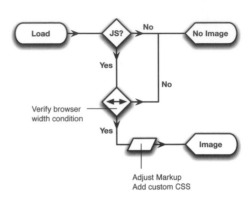

Lazy Load Images UI Construction Flow

For simplicity's sake, let's say we know the thumbnail images are 200px square and we want to load them if the browser window is at least twice as wide (400px). The JavaScript for that would look something like this (comments in the code are there to help you understand what's going on):

```javascript
// self-executing function
(function(){
        var
        // set the threshold
        threshold = 400,
        // collect the window width
        browser_width = window.innerWidth ||
                        document.body.offsetWidth,
        // prototype image for reuse
        image = document.createElement('img'),
        // get all paragraphs
```

---

8 http://smashed.by/win-width-height
9 http://adactio.com/journal/5429/
10 http://smashed.by/network
11 http://www.w3.org/TR/netinfo-api/#attributes-1

```
paragraphs = document.getElementsByTagName('p'),
// count the paragraphs
i = paragraphs.length,
// instantiate loop vars
p, src, img;

// are we over the threshold
if ( browser_width >= threshold )
{
        // make sure we have an empty alt for accessibility
        image.setAttribute('alt','');

        // reverse looping through the paragraphs is faster
        while ( i-- )
        {
                // reference the paragraph
                p = paragraphs[i];
                // collect the image path
                src = p.getAttribute('data-image-src');
                // do we have a path?
                if ( src != null )
                {
                        // clone the prototype image
                        img = image.cloneNode(true);
                        // set the source
                        img.setAttribute('src',src);
                        // append it to the paragraph
                        p.appendChild( img );
                        // flag the paragraph as having an image
                        p.setAttribute('data-image-loaded','');
                }
        }

        // release DOM references
        image = paragraphs = p = img = null;
}
}());
```

That takes care of the initial load of the page. On a narrow screen (<400px) the thumbnails won't be loaded, but on a wider screen they will be dynamically requested and added to the page.

```
<p data-image-src="/path/to/my.jpg" data-image-loaded>
  <img src="/path/to/my.jpg" alt=""/>
</p>
```

The paragraph itself is shown by keying into the dynamically assigned data-image-loaded attribute:

```
[data-image-src][data-image-loaded] {
  display: block;
}
```

Comparing potential JavaScript and JavaScript-less experiences of a news teaser.

Of course, mobile devices can be held in either landscape or portrait orientation and users often switch to suit the task they are trying to complete. To provide the best possible reading experience, again demonstrating empathy, we should really take the interface a step further and let it adapt. We can do that by listening for changes in the window size using a function. Here's the one I'm currently using:

```
window.watchResize = function(callback)
{
  // used to track the timer
  var resizing;
  // this runs when resizing has stopped
  function done()
  {
    // stop the timeout
```

```
    clearTimeout( resizing );
    resizing = null;
    // run the callback
    callback();
  }
  // track the resize event
  window.onresize = function(){
    // if we are currently resizing, clear the timeout
    if ( resizing )
    {
      clearTimeout( resizing );
      resizing = null;
    }
            // set the done function to execute when the resize completes
            resizing = setTimeout( done, 50 );
  };

  // run the callback once
  callback();
};
```

With a function like watchResize, it becomes easy to track changes in
browser size so we can update the interface in ways CSS alone can't.

To introduce this more dynamic functionality to the earlier script, we
would start by moving the browser_size variable to the global scope so it
is available to any other adaptive UI scripts we might want to write. We'll
update it in real time using watchResize:

```
// watch browser width on resize
var browser_width = 0;
window.watchResize(function(){
    browser_width = window.innerWidth ||
    document.body.offsetWidth;
});
```

With browser_width being updated live, we can revisit the original script and
make it more adaptive by having it check the width as orientation changes:

```
// lazy-load images
window.watchResize(function(){
  var
  threshold = 400,
  image = document.createElement('img'),
  paragraphs = document.getElementsByTagName('p'),
  i = paragraphs.length,
  p, loaded, src, img;
  if ( browser_width >= threshold )
  {
    image.setAttribute('alt',");
    while ( i-- )
    {
      p = paragraphs[i];
      src = p.getAttribute('data-image-src');
      // check to see if the image is already loaded
      loaded = p.getAttribute('data-image-loaded');
      // Do we have a path?
      // Is the image already loaded?
      if ( src != null &&
           loaded == null )
      {
        img = image.cloneNode(true);
        img.setAttribute('src',src);
        p.appendChild( img );
        p.setAttribute('data-image-loaded',");
      }
    }
    image = paragraphs = p = img = null;
  }
});
```

The main differences between this version and the previous one are:

1. The function is now being passed into watchResize as a callback.
2. We are no longer assessing browser_width within the scope of the function.
3. We are checking the data-image-loaded attribute to see if an image has already been loaded for the given paragraph so we don't double-load images if a user continually reorients the screen.

Finally, we can move our display CSS rule set into a media query to ensure any images that were lazy-loaded when a device was in a wider (e.g. landscape) orientation aren't displayed when the screen is too narrow (e.g. portrait):

```
@media only screen and (min-width:400px) {
  [data-img-src][data-image-loaded] {
    display: block;
  }
}
```

As you can see, by being empathetic to our users and cognizant of the price they pay to access our content, we can create amazing adaptive experiences for them without much extra effort.

Comparing potential orientation-appropriate experiences of a news teaser.

NO JAVASCRIPT, NO PROBLEM

JavaScript can do some nifty stuff, but planning for its absence is equally important. After all, JavaScript availability is not guaranteed in every browser. Even if JavaScript is supported by the browser, there are many circumstances in which our carefully crafted JavaScript may be unable to run and they are completely beyond our control. For example:

- JavaScript code delivery could be being blocked by an overzealous firewall.
- JavaScript may be disabled by the user — either manually or via plugin — in an effort to stop annoying ads, pop-overs, and the like.

- That third-party JavaScript library we included and which was working yesterday has been upgraded and introduced a bug.
- The user installed a browser add-on that contains an error or creates a conflict with our code.
- The user is still waiting for the page assets to finish downloading and our JavaScript can't execute until they do.

I love JavaScript, but I also realize that it is quite fragile. Unlike writing code that will execute on our servers, which we control, JavaScript code is executed in places and on systems that we have no control over and on which we cannot guarantee its successful execution.

If my JavaScript code fails to execute, I don't want to be the one getting a call in the middle of the night because something's broken. I want the website, Web application, or any other sort of Web thang[12] that I create to be robust. I want it to keep going like the Chrysler Imperial in a demolition derby[13].

As you saw in the previous lazy loading example, I set up the resting (a.k.a. JavaScript-less) state so that the necessary information was in place for the JavaScript to act without creating problems for users who did not have JavaScript enabled. But when JavaScript is available and my code is executed, the page is manipulated to create the best possible experience for readers.

This approach to JavaScript is often referred to as unobtrusive because it doesn't get in the way. On one hand, JavaScript

Pumpkin Pie

OVERVIEW	INGREDIENTS	DIRECTIONS	NUTRITION

Whether you're hosting a festive party or a casual get–together with friends, our Pumpkin Pie will make entertaining easy!

Original recipe yield: 1 × 9-inch deep dish pie

Prep Time: 10min
Cook Time: 1hr
Ready In: 1hr 10min

Photo by *Paul Goyette*, licensed under *Creative Commons*.

A simple recipe displayed as a tabbed interface.

---

12 http://www.webthang.co.uk/
13 http://smashed.by/demo-derby

is not required to access the core experience, but on the other, the bits of JavaScript-related markup are not injected into the content in a distracting or confusing way.

The thumbnails are a pretty simple example of this, but let me give you another one: a tabbed interface. It's a pretty common gadget consisting of a series of content panels that are displayed one at a time when the corresponding tab is activated.

When looking at this from a semantic point of view, the panels of content could be ensconced in separate section elements with the tabs as list items within an ordered list. Pretty simple and straightforward, right?

What if there is no JavaScript to make it function as a tabbed interface? In that case, it really shouldn't look like a tabbed interface, as that would render the bulk of the content visually inaccessible, which isn't very considerate.

Pumpkin Pie

OVERVIEW
Whether you're hosting a festive party or a casual get-together with friends, our Pumpkin Pie will make entertaining easy!

Original recipe yield: 1 × 9-inch deep dish pie

Prep Time:	10min
Cook Time:	1hr
Ready In:	1hr 10min

INGREDIENTS
1 (9in) unbaked deep dish pie crust
½ cup white sugar
1 tsp ground cinnamon
½ tsp salt
½ tsp ground ginger
¼ tsp ground cloves
2 eggs
1 can (15oz) pumpkin puree

The same recipe, linearized.

Without JavaScript, the list of links and the sections aren't really all that necessary either; they don't add much to the page in terms of meaning and are just extra markup to download. It would be nice to save those bits for places where they are actually useful, for microformats and the like.

Stripped of all cruft, what we have in this example is a recipe that consists of several titled sections.

If you're like me and get all nerdy about semantics, you've probably already realized that those titles should be headings (let's say h2s) and heading levels create a natural document outline[14].

---

14 http://html5doctor.com/outlines/

(If you have no idea what I'm talking about, hit "View Document Outline" in the Web Developer Toolbar[15] to see the outline of any Web page.)

The great thing about a document outline is that it implies sections. Knowing that, we can write a simple JavaScript to parse that content, dynamically build the additional markup for the tabbed interface, trigger the inclusion of some basic CSS rules to lay it out, and add in some accessibility enhancements via ARIA when JavaScript is available.

Tabbed Interface UI Construction Flow

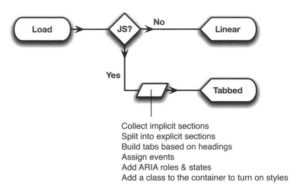

Collect implicit sections
Split into explicit sections
Build tabs based on headings
Assign events
Add ARIA roles & states
Add a class to the container to turn on styles

Diagraming the process of building a tabbed interface
using a UI construction flow.

I won't exhaust you with the code to do this, but you can check out the script I've been evolving for this purpose over on Github[16] if you're interested.

So now we have an interface that adapts beautifully based on JavaScript availability; but tabbed interfaces don't always work nicely on narrow screens, especially when the tabs don't fit. To truly call this tabbed interface adaptive we need to consider the experience in different form factors.

Taking a lesson from the lazy-loaded image example we just discussed, we could adjust the JavaScript code to include a test to see whether the

---

15 http://chrispederick.com/work/web-developer/
16 https://github.com/easy-designs/tabinterface.js

section headers will fit horizontally when rendered as tabs. If they fit, the script can proceed and build out the rest of the interface. If not, the script can stop where it is and leave the linear content as it is. This test could even be a live check (using a function like `watchResize`) that triggers the construction and destruction of the interface components as the browser size or device orientation changes.

Again, by putting ourselves in our users' shoes, we can discover that there are many meaningful ways to interact with our content. And placing those in a continuum can create an impressive adaptive interface.

Building Blocks

Despite how daunting they may seem at first blush, complex problems can always be broken down into simpler ones. The same is true of complex Web pages and complex interfaces.

It's easy for me to get overwhelmed when first presented with an elaborate interface. When I begin to pick it apart into smaller page components and discrete interactions, however, I begin to breathe a little easier.

Components are great because they can be built and tested individually, yet can be combined in myriad ways to meet the challenges of even the most complicated of interface requirements. Often teams will organize these components (or design patterns) into catalogs called *pattern libraries*.

Each component in a pattern library exists in isolation, with its own requirements, capabilities and documentation. This allows it to be iterated without affecting other UI elements in use on a website or across a family of Web properties.

For me, the starting point for any adaptive component is the UI construction flow I've mentioned a few times. Most are simple sketches on a sheet of paper or a whiteboard that illustrate the different content states and under what circumstances changes in the presentation or interaction method occur.

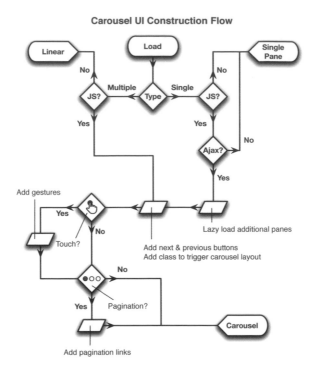

UI construction flows can get really complicated, as
this sample one for a carousel demonstrates.

At the simpler end, we have ones like the lazy loading image example.
At the complex end, we can end up with sprawling flows for a carousel.

I find UI construction flows not only help me organize my thoughts
around the different ways to present and interact with content, but they
also help me communicate my ideas to others.

CREATING ADAPTIVE COMPONENTS

In my experience, component-based development can be done well in
isolation, but it excels in small, integrated, collaborative teams. You don't
need to hop on the Lean UX or Agile bandwagons, but having a diversity of
perspectives on an interface is really helpful.

It's especially helpful when the different members of that team have different spheres of expertise. A product manager, content strategist, UX designer, visual designer, front-end engineer, and back-end developer all bring different, but valuable ideas to the table.

Not only will each person be able to shed light on the positive or negative effects each decision may have on his or her primary area of concern, but each will likely empathize with our users in a slightly different way.

In my office, UI construction flows are generally the low fidelity first pass we use for organizing our thoughts and making sense of the different interaction paradigms. From there, we move into rough sketches.

Our team tends to sketch on paper or whiteboards, but you may be more comfortable in OmniGraffle, Photoshop, Illustrator, or any of the many wireframing and prototyping tools out there.

Use whatever makes you comfortable and efficient, but be conscious to not get bogged down in details. Sketches are a low-risk way to flesh out the experiences in a UI construction flow.

Next, we begin prototyping in HTML, CSS and JavaScript, referencing the low fidelity spec we assembled in the UI construction flow and our sketches. On occasion, we will stub out some back-end functionality if we need to reference an API or something, but often we fake that with static JSON files.

We use the prototype to see if the ideas we came up with actually make sense and operate as we'd expect. If something falls apart in a certain context or doesn't work in a certain form factor, we regroup and try something else.

We iterate on the prototype until we are generally happy with the different behaviors and then we begin to flesh out the design, tune the code for performance, and hook it into back-end functionality as necessary.

The result is a living, breathing adaptive component that can be added to the pattern library and dropped into whatever context we need.

A VERITABLE BUFFET OF INTERACTION

As a tool, pattern libraries have been with us for quite some time. Most JavaScript libraries have their own UI patterns (e.g. YUI, jQuery UI, Dojo Digits) and several standalone UI frameworks such as Bootstrap and Foundation have captured the popular imagination of late. But I am a firm believer that one size does not fit all. Don't get me wrong, I think tools like Bootstrap can be really helpful for prototyping and testing interactions, but I hate the idea of deploying a site built entirely on it. I feel this way for many reasons, some of which I'll summarize here:

0. Verbosity

In an attempt to create a universal UI framework, the code behind the scenes is often bloated or requires that we bloat our code in order to make use of their grid system or widgets.

1. Excess

In most cases, a UI framework (or even a JavaScript library for that matter) includes more options and components than we actually need for our sites. And, if we don't remove unused CSS and JavaScript, it can create performance issues for our customers.

2. Philosophy

Buying wholeheartedly into a UI framework locks us into a narrow way of thinking and building, which may not align with our way of thinking or how our team operates. For instance, Bootstrap is made to be responsive, but it comes from a desktop-first perspective, rather than a mobile-first one.

3. Aesthetics

UI frameworks have a certain aesthetic and it can sometimes be difficult to escape that. Failure to break out of the stock UI mold means our sites end up looking almost identical to every other site out there that's using that framework.

It may sound like I have no love for UI frameworks, but that's not the case. While I don't advocate their use on public websites, I do think they present valuable learning opportunities. The same goes for other publicly available pattern libraries[17].

Seeing what others have done helps ensure we don't miss anything when we work on our own pattern libraries — ones that directly meet our company's or our clients' needs. In his discussion of responsive deliverables[18], Dave Rupert echoed this very point: "Responsive deliverables should look a lot like fully-functioning Twitter Bootstrap-style systems custom tailored for your clients' needs."

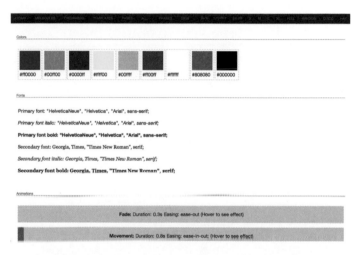

Brad Frost's PatternLab is an excellent tool for helping create
and maintain pattern libraries and then combine those patterns
into page templates: http://demo.pattern-lab.info/

Pattern libraries are a godsend for everyone on the team, from upper management to the grunts pounding out pages. They provide a consistent catalog of components that can be plucked out and incorporated into a

17   http://smashed.by/pattern-libraries
18   http://smashed.by/rd
19   https://github.com/bradfrost/patternlab

mock-up or prototype. They act as a clearinghouse for code snippets and documentation to help front-end engineers work more quickly and efficiently. And they allow the QA team to test discrete components rather than having to diagnose issues when these components become deeply entwined.

Pattern libraries are also a boon for users. When a website is built using a pattern library, it imbues the site with a consistency and predicability that makes it easier for them to do what they need to do.

They don't need to spend time trying to figure out how to fill out a particular form or interact with a particular widget because each instance is familiar to them. It's reassuring.

Plus, pattern libraries make it much easier to get everyone on the dev team up to speed when a component is upgraded or an API changes, because it is the central repository of information for everyone who works on the website. After all, a pattern library should evolve over time. It should be a living document of numerous independently evolving modules. It should not sit there like a monolith, but should be shaped and molded as we continue to better understand our medium, the Web, and our users' interaction with it.

The Future is Messy, Embrace it

We live in very interesting times. It seems every day a new device surfaces, a new browser, a new interaction model. It's hard to keep track of it all and mind-boggling to imagine creating siloed experiences for each new thing that comes along. Like chasing screen sizes: it's a fool's errand. At a certain point we need to let go and focus on what really matters: people.

We design — content, user flows, interactions, interfaces, APIs and experiences — to help people do what they need to do as quickly and efficiently as possible. We work hard so they don't have to.

We're here to solve problems. To do that, we need to become one with our customers. We need to empathize with them and experience their struggles as if they were our own.

With that insight, we can craft amazing experiences for them. We'll strike that perfect balance between aesthetics and usability. We'll build experiences up from the core, following the progressive enhancement philosophy. We'll make our work more consistent and flexible by embracing pattern libraries. And, no matter what devices companies throw at us, we'll rest assured our customers will be well-served.

ABOUT THE AUTHOR

Aaron Gustafson is the Founder & Technical Lead of Easy Designs, a content-focused Web consultancy that specializes in delivering great user experiences irrespective of device or platform. He is an Invited Expert to the W3C, is the former Manager of the Web Standards Project (WaSP), served as Tech Editor for A List Apart, and wrote the oft-lauded *Adaptive Web Design: Crafting Rich Experiences with Progressive Enhancement*.

ABOUT THE REVIEWER

Nicholas C. Zakas is a Staff Software Engineer at Box. He is the author of *Maintainable JavaScript* (O'Reilly, 2012), *Professional JavaScript for Web Developers* (Wrox, 2012), *High Performance JavaScript* (O'Reilly, 2010), and *Professional Ajax* (Wrox, 2007). He blogs regularly at http://www.nczonline.net/ and can be found on Twitter via @slicknet.

Image credits

1st Image from *Adaptive Web Design: Crafting Rich Experiences with Progressive Enhancement*, http://adaptivewebdesign.info, Easy Readers, 2011.
2nd Image from *The Computer History Museum*, www.computerhistory.org/timeline/

Chapter

08

How to Fix the Web
Obscure Back-End Techniques
and Terminal Secrets

Written by Paul Tero

CHAPTER EIGHT · BY PAUL TERO

HOW TO FIX THE WEB

OBSCURE BACK-END TECHNIQUES
AND TERMINAL SECRETS

I MAGINE THAT YOU WAKE UP ONE MORNING, reach groggily for your laptop and fire it up. You've just finished developing a brand new website and last night you were proudly clicking through the product list. The browser window is still open, the Widget 3000 is still sparkling in its AJAXy newness. You grin like a new parent and expectantly click on "More details". And nothing happens. You click again, still nothing. You press Refresh and get that annoying swirling icon and then the page goes blank. Help! The Internet is gone!

We're going to cover a lot of ground in this chapter, from routers to servers, from error logs to PHP hacks. I'll start with the worst case scenario and work inwards, exploring the infrastructure of the Internet and the make-up of a Web server, imparting lots of little tips and commands along the way, opening up a new perspective on how websites can stop working — and be fixed.

The End of the World

It is unlikely that civilization has collapsed overnight, especially if you are a light sleeper. You can verify this with a battery-powered radio. An apocalypse would certainly make the news and perhaps qualify for a full-blown government warning. All stations should be reporting it, assuming there are any left; it would be really, really bad news if not.

In the US, many broadcasters participate in the Emergency Alert System, which theoretically allows the President to address the nation within 10 minutes, though it might be vulnerable to hackers.[1] France uses air raid sirens for its Signal National d'Alerte[2] and Japan's J-Alert uses loudspeakers.[3] All are part of the United Nation's International Early Warning Program. This is important, especially now that the International Decade for Natural Disaster Reduction (the 1990s) is long over.[4]

You should be able to ascertain pretty quickly if your website woes are related to this. If not, move on to the next section.

Infrastructure

The Internet depends on electricity. Your hosting company probably has an uninterruptible power supply (UPS) which will take over instantly in the event of power failure. It can provide power to your Web server for a few minutes, long enough to have a diesel generator ready to take over.[5] The major networking equipment connecting your Web server to the Internet is probably protected with UPSes and generators as well. And your laptop should survive for a few more hours if fully charged.

Your wireless router, however, will cease to function. It is the weakest link. You can get around it by checking the Internet via your smartphone, which should work as long as your nearest tower has back-up power, and

1 Lucian Constantin, "Emergency Alert System devices vulnerable to hacker attacks, researchers say", Computer World, Feb 13 , 2013. http://smashed.by/emergency

2 Le Signal National d'Alerte, Institut Français des Formateurs, Risques Majeurs et protection de l'Environment, Mar 28, 2007. http://smashed.by/national-alert

3 "Japan Launches Alert System For Tsunamis And Missiles", Terra Daily, Feb 9, 2007. http://smashed.by/alert-system

4 A-RES-44-236 General Assembly Resolution 44/236, United Nations General Assembly, Dec 22 , 1989. http://smashed.by/un-solution

5 "UPS and Generators - How long can they run for?", Power Continuity. http://smashed.by/power-continuity

there is a route to the Internet through other working towers. It might be very slow though, especially if everyone in your neighborhood has also had the same idea. If your website is still gone, then the problem is a bit more personal.

Networking

Power outages aren't the only things which upset broadband routers. They have many inventive ways of failing, as does all the other networking equipment between you and your website, and all the copper and fiber-optic cable in between.

To explore networking issues, you'll need to run some commands. Much of this information is also available through various menus, but the command line gives you more data more quickly. On Mac OS X, go to Applications → Utilities and run Terminal. In Ubuntu Linux, the terminal is under Applications → Accessories. In Windows, go to Start → All Programs → Accessories and choose Command Prompt.

YOUR IP ADDRESS

Every computer connected to the Internet has a numerical IP (Internet Protocol) address. To find out yours, run the command ifconfig on Mac and Linux and ipconfig /all on Windows:[6]

```
$ ifconfig
eth0      Link encap:Ethernet  HWaddr 00:10:dc:75:d9:5b
          inet addr:192.168.0.11  Bcast:192.168.0.255  Mask:255.255.255.0
          inet6 addr: fe80::210:dcff:fe75:d95b/64 Scope:Link
          UP BROADCAST RUNNING MULTICAST  MTU:1500  Metric:1...
lo        Link encap:Local Loopback
          inet addr:127.0.0.1  Mask:255.0.0.0
          inet6 addr: ::1/128 Scope:Host
          UP LOOPBACK RUNNING  MTU:16436  Metric:1...
```

---

6 Linux users may need to run /sbin/ifconfig or sudo ifconfig. sudo is used to run a command as the super user and is discussed later in the chapter.

This says that the computer (Linux in this case) has two network interfaces. The `eth0` is the one which communicates with the Internet via a cable. If this computer had wireless there would also be an `eth1` or `wlan0` interface. The loopback interface `lo` is used as a shortcut for communicating with itself. Each interface has an IP address on the local network. The important line here is `inet addr:192.168.0.11`. This gives the computer's IP address. If you have a cable attached and wireless turned on, you may have two active interfaces and two IP addresses, but it's usually just the one. Macs tend to call these interfaces `en0` and `en1`. Windows is more verbose and uses sexy names like "Ethernet adapter Local Area Connection".

DHCP

How does your computer know its IP address? Especially on a home or wireless network, you do not need to enter this information yourself. When your computer first connects to your home network, it sends out a request to every other device on the network, something like: "Can someone please give me an IP address?"

Your broadband router should dutifully respond and assign your computer an IP address. As you probably know, routers are the devices that hold the Internet together. Unlike laptops and desktops, routers have more than one network interface, more than one cable (or wireless point) attached to them and so more than one IP address. In your home or office, the router is the little box which provides your connection to the Internet via your broadband service.

The method used to assign an IP address is Dynamic Host Configuration Protocol (DHCP). If there is no IP address when you run `ifconfig` or `ipconfig`, you can force your computer to retrieve new DHCP settings. On Windows, run `ipconfig /release` followed by `ipconfig /renew`. On a Mac, run sudo `ipconfig set en0 DHCP`, and on Linux use sudo `dhclient eth0`[7].

---

7   Some Linux distributions may use a different client such as dhcpcd.

On Mac and Linux, the actual command is prefaced by sudo[8] which forces you to put in the root password for the computer. You must also specify which interface to renew, usually eth0 on Linux and en0 for Mac.

If this was successful, then voilà! You're a tiny bit closer to being back on the Internet. If not, check your broadband router. It may be off, disconnected or broken, or it may just need resetting.

DEFAULT GATEWAY

You know your broadband router was alive at some point in the recent past because it gave you an IP address. But that could have been up to three days ago: is it still there now?

Every computer on the Internet also has a default gateway[9]. This is basically the IP address of the piece of networking equipment at the other end of your network cable or wireless connection. It is your computer's gateway to the Internet. Every time you request anything from the Internet, it goes via this gateway. To find our your default gateway, run netstat -nr on Mac and Linux, and route print (or ipconfig again) on Windows. You will get something a bit like:

```
Destination   Gateway       Genmask         Flags  Metric   Ref    Use Iface
192.168.0.0   0.0.0.0       255.255.255.0   U      0        0      0 eth0
0.0.0.0       192.168.0.1   0.0.0.0         UG     100      0      0 eth0
```

In the Destination column above, the 0.0.0.0 (or the word "default") means anywhere and the G in the Flags column stands for "Gateway". The default gateway of this computer is therefore 192.168.0.1. For people at home or in a small office this is probably the internal IP address of the broadband router.

---

8 Especially on Linux, not all users are allowed to run sudo and sometimes it won't ask for a password, for example, if you have already run it recently. Also beware that sudo can be dangerous as it allows you to run anything. You can inadvertently delete and stop things that should be left alone.

9 It's possible to have more than one default gateway, e.g. if you are connected to a virtual private network.

You can use the ping command to see if it is up and available. Type ping 192.168.0.1.

```
$ ping 192.168.0.1
PING 192.168.0.1 (192.168.0.1) 56(84) bytes of data.
64 bytes from 192.168.0.1: icmp_seq=1 ttl=64 time=1.31 ms
64 bytes from 192.168.0.1: icmp_seq=2 ttl=64 time=0.561 ms
64 bytes from 192.168.0.1: icmp_seq=3 ttl=64 time=12.6 ms
```

The "64 bytes from 192.168.0.1" represents a successful reply. If you get a reply, then your broadband router is reachable. If not, then check it again. On Mac and Linux the replies will go on forever until you press Control + C. On Windows, it will quit after the fourth ping.

BEYOND THE ROUTER

To go beyond your router, you will need the traceroute command on Mac and Linux, and tracert on Windows. This command traces a route through the Internet, reporting each networking device (router) it comes across. IP addresses are formed of four numbers from 0 to 255[10]. Pick an IP address out of a hat and try it:

```
$ traceroute -q 1 -n 1.2.3.4
traceroute to 1.2.3.4 (1.2.3.4), 30 hops max, 60 byte packets
  1  *
  2  80.3.65.217  9.163 ms
  3  213.105.159.157  11.158 ms
  4  213.105.159.190  11.215 ms
...
 13  72.14.236.149  98.484 ms
 14  209.85.252.47  104.071 ms
 15  *
 16  *...
```

10 There are newer long IPv6 (version 6) addresses which have 8 blocks of 4 hexidemcial digits separated by colons, but you are unlikely to come across these in 2013.

The -q 1 option on Mac and Linux tells the command to try each router only once. The -n tells it not to bother looking up the human-readable name for each router, which makes the command much slower. This option is -d on Windows, so use tracert -d 1.2.3.4.

Each step above is known as a hop in networking jargon. The first hop is the broadband router. It is probably configured not to provide any information about itself, so traceroute just shows an asterisk. The second hop takes it outside the local network to the other side of the broadband router.

At each subsequent hop sits another router, probably with many network interfaces and many IP addresses. Each router has a routing table like the one above. Its table contains rules like: if the destination starts with 0 to 91, then send the packet down interface eth1 (the Use Iface column); if it starts with 92 to 128, use eth2.

This example goes 14 hops before reaching a dead end, either because the IP address is blocked or not in use.

That is about as far as numbers alone can take us. Hopefully you've established that civilization is still going at least a couple networking hops beyond your front door. You've also learned how to use the useful networking commands ifconfig, ping and traceroute. To explore further, you'll need DNS.

The Domain Name System

Smashing Magazine could have gone with http://80.72.139.101 as its main website address rather than http://www.smashingmagazine.com. It would have had two advantages: it would have used less space on business cards; and it would still have worked when DNS was down. However, Smashing's marketing people may have objected, and their customer base would have been limited to people with extremely good memories.

The domain name system makes the Internet more human-friendly by translating between domain names like www.smashingmagazine.com and IP addresses like 80.72.139.101. DNS is a big hierarchical distributed database. You are probably aware that there is no single computer which knows all the translations and which everybody else consults. Rather, it is a huge network of computers each of which know a few translations, and know who else to ask if they don't.

YOUR LOCAL DNS SERVER

Every computer knows about a local DNS server. It is one of the crucial bits of information your broadband router provides via DHCP: your IP address; your default gateway's IP address; and your local DNS server's IP address.

When you type a website address into your browser, your computer first asks its local DNS server to translate it into an IP address. To find out your DNS server, run the command cat /etc/resolv.conf on Mac and Linux[11], or ipconfig /all on Windows. On Mac and Linux, the cat command displays a file, and the file /etc/resolv.conf contains your domain name servers. The file looks like:

```
$ cat /etc/resolv.conf
nameserver 194.168.4.100
nameserver 194.168.8.100
```

NSLOOKUP

To diagnose DNS problems, first check that your local DNS server is alive with ping. If it is, then you can use the nslookup command to see if it's responding correctly. nslookup stands for name server lookup and is used like this:

```
$ nslookup www.smashingmagazine.com
Server:      194.168.4.100
Address:     194.168.4.100#53
Non-authoritative answer:
Name:        www.smashingmagazine.com
Address:     80.72.139.101
```

---

11 Some versions of Mac OS X (Mountain Lion) do not use /etc/resolv.conf but you should be able to find the information within System Preferences from the Apple menu.

This command tells you the DNS server used (194.168.4.100) and the IP address you are looking for (80.72.139.101). If nslookup didn't respond, then your Internet woes lie with your local DNS server[12]. If you are at home or in a small office, your DNS server is probably provided by your broadband company.

They generally provide two or more of them, so it's unlikely that they will all fail. If you happen to know the IP address of a different name server, you could query that instead (nslookup www.smashingmagazine.com 194.168.8.100), but it may well refuse to talk to a stranger. You'll probably need to complain to your broadband company about the problem instead.

FREE ADVERTISING

Have you ever typed in a website address incorrectly and come up with a branded page from your broadband provider? Instead of admitting "I don't know", your local name server is sneakily replying with an alternative IP address of its choice, promoting the broadband company it is owned by. It's interesting to see that the marketing people are into DNS, and a shame that their technical colleagues didn't stop them, as this sort of practice makes some automated networking processes more difficult.

Broadband company intercepting a non-existent website.

---

12 This is not a definitive diagnosis. This chapter presents a simplified account of many networking and server processes, problems and solutions. It could be that some other bit of DNS software on your own computer or a DNS relay on your router is failing.

A FULL JOURNEY

Having confirmed that your local DNS server is working, you can tentatively try to establish human-friendly contact with the Internet using traceroute with a domain name instead of an IP address, and leaving out the -n option. The command is tracert on Windows. This will report a readable name for each router.

```
$ traceroute -q 1 www.smashingmagazine.com
traceroute to www.smashingmagazine.com (80.72.139.101), 30 hops max, 60
byte packets
 1  *
 2  brig-core-2b-ae6-725.network.virginmedia.net (80.3.65.177)   10.542 ms
 3  popl-bb-1b-ae14-0.network.virginmedia.net (213.105.159.157) 13.934 ms
 4  popl-bb-1c-ae1-0.network.virginmedia.net (213.105.159.190) 14.454 ms
 5  nrth-bb-1c-ae7-0.network.virginmedia.net (62.253.174.137) 15.982 ms
 6  nrth-tmr-1-ae1-0.network.virginmedia.net (213.105.159.30) 16.215 ms
 7  fran-ic-1-as0-0.network.virginmedia.net (62.253.185.81)   36.090 ms
 8  FFMGW4.arcor-ip.net (80.81.193.117)   39.064 ms
 9  92.79.213.133 (92.79.213.133)   47.404 ms
10  92.79.200.190 (92.79.200.190)   45.385 ms
11  kar-145-254-15-178.arcor-ip.net (145.254.15.178)   40.421 ms
12  145.253.159.106 (145.253.159.106)   46.436 ms
13  1-3-frr02.continum.net (80.72.130.170)   49.321 ms
14  1-6-frr04.continum.net (80.72.130.158)   47.194 ms
15  www.smashingmagazine.com (80.72.139.101)   48.081 ms
```

This reveals much more about the journey packets of data take. After it leaves your local network, the first few hops in any traceroute are probably owned by the local broadband company, Virgin Media in this case. If the traceroute stopped here, then it would be an issue for them resolve. You could phone them for more information.

Once the traceroute leaves your broadband provider, it enters a no man's land of big inscrutable networking devices. In this case they are owned by Arcor, a subsidiary of Vodafone. If the traceroute fails here, it may represent a fairly major networking problem and there's not much you can do.

Eventually, it will reach the hosting company for the website in question (Continum.net in this case). If it fails there, then the fault may lie with your hosting company. Or it may simply be that the traceroute is blocked by a firewall. Or that your website has moved.

MOVING WEBSITES

It's unlikely that your website has moved to a different server without you knowing, especially as you were just working on it last night, but you can double-check this.

Every DNS server keeps a cache of every domain name it has been asked for. This saves clogging up the Internet with requests for things that rarely change. The downside is that if someone changes the IP address for a domain like www.smashingmagazine.com, it can take 24 to 48 hours for all the caches to clear so that everyone in the world knows the new IP address.

To ascertain that you have the latest information, you first need to find out the local name server for the domain name you are querying. To do this, give nslookup the option -type=ns, like this on Mac, Linux and Windows:

```
$ nslookup -type=ns www.smashingmagazine.com
Server:         194.168.4.100
Address:        194.168.4.100#53
Authoritative answers can be found from:
smashingmagazine.com
        origin = a.regfish-ns.net
        mail addr = postmaster.regfish.com...
```

The origin (or sometimes primary name server) is the local DNS server for www.smashingmagazine.com. You can use nslookup again to query this server directly:

```
$ nslookup www.smashingmagazine.com a.regfish-ns.net
Server:         a.regfish-ns.net
Address:        79.140.49.11#53
Name:   www.smashingmagazine.com
Address: 80.72.139.101
```

Compare this to the nslookup on your local DNS server. It no longer says "non-authoritative". This is now the authoritative reply. It's the same IP address, so we know that www.smashingmagazine.com didn't suddenly move last night.

On Mac and Linux, you can use the dig command to find out exactly how long your local DNS server has cached this translation for. It stands for domain information groper. Windows users will need to search for an online dig tool as Windows doesn't natively support this command:

```
$ dig www.smashingmagzine.com
...
;; ANSWER SECTION:
www.smashingmagzine.com. 246   IN      A       80.72.139.101...
```

The 246 is the number of seconds before the local DNS server's cache expires and it has to rediscover the IP address for smashingmagazine.com.

YOUR BROADBAND ROUTER REVISITED

Now that DNS is working, you can find out what the world thinks of you. You have already discovered your computer's own IP address above. But that may not be the one that it uses on the Internet. If it starts with 192.168 or 10, then it is definitely not a public address. Those IP address ranges signify local IP addresses for use within your internal network only.

When your computer sends a request to the Internet, it first goes to your default gateway (your broadband router), which also has a local internal IP address such as 192.168.0.1. But your router has another public IP address as well. Your router wraps up your request and resends it from this public IP address instead.

Therefore, your broadband router's public IP address is basically your public IP address. This is how the rest of the Internet sees you as you browse. This is the IP address that will show up in log files in any of the websites you visit. Consequently, anybody else using the same broadband router will have the same public IP address as you. Your router handles all of this using a process called *network address translation*, making sure requests and information go out and come back to the right local IP address.

You can find out your broadband router's public IP address by visiting a website like whatismyipaddress.com. Alternatively, you can run the command `curl ipinfo.io/ip` on Mac or Linux, or `wget -O- -q ipinfo.io/ip` on Linux. Both `curl` and `wget` retrieve a Web page (http://ipinfo.io/ip) from the Internet. The `-O-` option (that's a letter O, not zero) tells `wget` to output the result to the screen (signified by a single hyphen) rather than save it to a file, and `-q` tells it to do it quietly. `curl` automatically outputs to the screen. To use `curl` on Windows you have to download and install it first. All these methods go outside your local network and look back. There is no way to find out your router's public IP address from the inside. The output is quite simple:

```
$ curl ipinfo.io/ip
85.106.118.199
```

WHERE ARE THEY?

Websites like whatismyipaddress.com and ipinfo.io do more than just tell you your public IP address. They also provide geolocation services. It is interesting to take the IP addresses from the traceroute mentioned earlier on page 187 and copy and paste them in. Geolocation guesses at the physical location of the router, and can also tell you who owns the IP address. The address 62.253.185.81 is in southern England but the next one crosses the Channel to 80.81.193.117 in Frankfurt, Germany. This type of geolocation relies on databases of IP address ownership.

In fact, there are websites which can map this all out for you, such as DNStools.ch[13] and YouGetSignal[14]. The starting points for these traceroutes will be the Web server hosting the tool, rather than your own computer.

---

13 http://smashed.by/visual-traceroute
14 http://smashed.by/visual-tracert

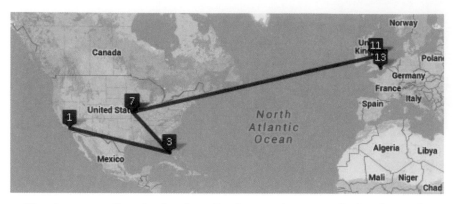

Visual traceroute from Los Angeles to London covering 7,904 miles in 4.8 seconds.

Above is an example of the distance and time taken between a Web server in Los Angeles and the BBC website in London.

Connecting to Your Server

So, civilization and its Internet are both up and running. What's gone wrong? Your website lives on a computer somewhere out there, probably in a big air-conditioned room full of other computers, with multiple fire doors and an awful lot of colorful cabling. This computer is colloquially known as a Web server.

Imagine for a moment that your Web server is the nation of France. If you want to send a large item of furniture to somewhere in France, it will be wrapped up tight on a container ship and sent off across the sea. It will arrive in one of France's major ports, maybe Marseille or Bordeaux or Le Havre. It doesn't really matter to you which port it goes through, but it does matter to the shipping company. Computers are similar, except they are a bit smaller and have 65,535 ports.

On computers, some ports are assigned specific functions. On a Web server, port 80 receives and replies to Web browsing requests. Ports 25 and 110 deal with email. A typical Web request would involve a high-numbered (usually random) port on your computer sending a request to port 80 at 80.72.139.101, something like: "Hey you, send me the Web page /index.html."

TELNET AND NETCAT

The telnet command allows you to mimic a container ship and connect to a specific port on a server. Windows does not have telnet by default, but you can enable it on Windows 7 by going to Start → Control Panel → Programs → Turn Windows features on or off → Telnet Client.

Since we're dealing with a website problem, and since the Web server is almost always on port 80, try telnetting to port 80:

```
$ telnet www.smashingmagazine.com 80
Trying 80.72.139.101...
telnet: Unable to connect to remote host: Connection refused
```

Mac and Linux support an alternative command: netcat. It is more specifically suited for networking tasks and supports additional features like proxies. This chapter will focus on telnet, however, as it also works on Windows. Add -v to netcat to make it verbosely tell you what it's doing.

```
$ netcat -v www.smashingmagazine.com 80
netcat: connect to www.smashingmagazine.com port 80 (tcp) failed: Connec-
tion refused
```

Uh oh.

Except, not really. I faked the issue above. Smashing Magazine wasn't really down. But I will use www.smashingmagazine.com as an example domain throughout this chapter. Suspend your disbelief and pretend that Smashing has moved into the Widget 3000 market and has sequentially fallen victim to just about every networking and website problem imaginable, and subsequently overcome them.

CONTROL PANEL

Whenever your Web server receives data on port 80, it sends it to a piece of software for processing. Confusingly, that software is also called a *Web server*. By far the most common type of Web server software is Apache.

According to W3Techs in June 2013, it had a market share of 65.2%.[15] Microsoft's Internet Information Server (IIS) is second with 15.7%, just in front of nginx at 14.3%.

Web server software shouldn't ever stop working. But if it does you can, hopefully, just restart it again. The quickest way to do this is using a control panel provided by your server. Windows servers (34.3% market share in June 2013[16]) are often managed by Remote Desktop or VNC which allow you to take control of the server's screen, keyboard and mouse, and change settings directly on the server.

The rest of this chapter, however, will focus on Linux and UNIX servers (65.7%), which are usually managed via a Web interface such as Plesk, CPanel or Webmin. These management tools are really just websites, but running on a different port. Plesk, for example, usually runs on port 8443, CPanel on 2082 or 2083 and Webmin on 10000.

Dig deep into your email folders and look for the URL, username and password for your control panel. Log in and find the screen which allows you to restart your Web server software. In Plesk, look for "Services management" (in Server or Tools & Settings) and press the Play button next to "Web Server (Apache)".

Restarting a Web server with Plesk.

---

15   "Usage of Web servers for websites", W3Techs. http://smashed.by/web-servers
16   "Usage of operating systems for websites", W3Techs. http://smashed.by/operating-sys

SSH

If port 80 is down, there's a good chance that the control panel won't be available either. You will need to log in to the server and issue commands directly. For this there is Secure Shell (SSH). SSH is like the text-only version of Remote Desktop. It allows you to open a terminal window on the server. From a Linux or Mac desktop or laptop, use the command ssh. From a Windows computer, download and run PuTTY.

You'll need the username and password for your server, contained in the same email as above. On a Linux server, root is the most powerful administrative user. For security reasons, the SSH user from your email will often be something less privileged. When you run SSH, you have to provide the username as part of the command. It will ask you to accept a security fingerprint and enter a password:

```
$ ssh root@www.smashingmagazine.com
The authenticity of host 'www.smashingmagazine.com (80.72.139.101)' can't
be established.
RSA key fingerprint is 00:5a:cf:51:83:46:0b:91:29:ef:2c:1d:c9:59:e9:ab.
Are you sure you want to continue connecting (yes/no)? yes
Warning: Permanently added 'www.smashingmagazine.com,80.72.139.101' (RSA)
to the list of known hosts.
root@www.smashingmagazine.com's password: ...
```

If successful, you'll end up with a welcome message and a terminal prompt:

```
Linux dedivps-13236 2.6.10-091stab048.3 #1 SMP Fri Dec 7 17:06:14 GMT
2012 x86_64
Last login: Thu May  2 07:20:11 2013 from cpc1-brig18-2-0-cust123.3-3.
cable.virginmedia.com
root@dedivps-13236:~#
```

Note that this will only work on Linux or UNIX servers that have an SSH server which accepts connections, and the rare Windows servers that have opted to install it. For most other Windows servers, you'll need Remote Desktop instead. If you can't get at your server via a control

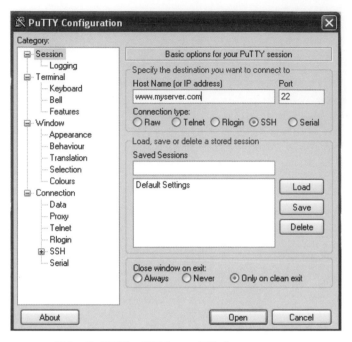

Using PuTTY for SSH from a Windows computer.

panel or SSH, your options are very limited. There's a slim chance that an overenthusiastic firewall is getting in the way, or that you're experiencing a denial of service attack. Or else you'll need to contact your hosting company and ask for help.

FIREWALLS

Firewalls are bits of hardware or software that filter incoming and outgoing data. These filters are applied according to the source and destination IP address and port. So, for example, a firewall should allow all requests going to the server's port 80 or else nobody will be able to get to the website. But it may block all requests to port 8443 (Plesk), port 22 (SSH) or port 3389 (remote desktop) except from a few known and trusted IP addresses.

You can sort of tell if there's a firewall in your way depending on how the connection fails. To test if SSH is being blocked, you can run the command ssh or use telnet as above to port 22:

```
$ telnet www.smashingmagazine.com 22
Trying 80.72.139.101...
telnet: Unable to connect to remote host: Connection refused
```

"Connection refused" means that your data reached the server but was probably refused entry for non-firewall reasons. For example, SSH may be turned off or running on a different port. The message "Connection timed out" or no message more strongly indicates a firewall block. If it does connect, press Control +] to get to the telnet> prompt and then type quit to quit.

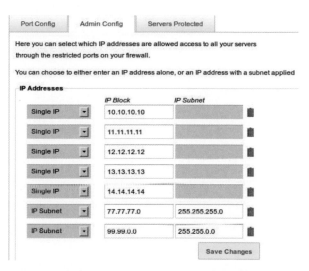

So if you have a firewall (that email should tell you), you need to make sure that SSH is allowed

Many firewalls maintain a list of trusted IP addresses.

and that your public IP address is in the list of trusted ones. Even if you know your IP address was in the list yesterday, it may have changed today, particularly if you have had broadband issues recently. The public IP addresses assigned to home routers can stay the same for months on end, and then suddenly change. How and why and when depends on your broadband company and your neighbors. The only way to avoid this is to pay extra for a static or fixed IP address.

DENIAL OF SERVICE

Imagine that the Widget 3000 suddenly goes viral. The Queen of England is filmed throwing one at the winner of X Factor and suddenly everybody in the world wants to own one. You might think "Fantastic!" But unless your server infrastructure is prepared to go from 100 visits an hour to 100 million, you probably won't actually sell very many. All those visitors accessing your website at once will grind the network and your server to a halt. The first few thousand visitors may receive half a Web page, the rest will be staring at blank browsers.

And when you try to `telnet` to your server as above, it will also sit there waiting — no refusal but no entry either. This is roughly what happens in a *distributed denial of service* (DDoS) attack. All those hackers who have spent the last 15 years finding holes in Internet Explorer were not working in vain. They have managed to plant Trojan horses on millions of computers worldwide. When they issue the command, all those computers suddenly try to send data to and request data from your Web server, overwhelming it and making it unreachable.

Unless you are running a bank or a spamming operation, or have managed to make some clever and determined enemies, it is unlikely to happen to you. Let's assume `telnet` has instead connected successfully.

Checking Your Server

Now you're in business. You've got a terminal window open on your server waiting for your every command. From now on, all the commands are being issued on your Linux server, not your laptop. Other types of UNIX server, including Macs, may have different commands or the same commands with different options.

LISTENING TO PORT 80

The first step is to figure out which software should have responded when you tried to `telnet` to port 80. For that, you can use the `netstat` command

to display all the networking information about your server. Add -tlpn
to the command to make it show only TCP connections that it is listening
for, along with the numeric port and the program they belong to. On some
systems the p option requires super user access, so the commands below
also do a sudo.

```
$ netstat -tlnp
Active Internet connections (only servers)
Proto Recv-Q Send-Q Local Address   Foreign Address State   PID/Program name
tcp      0       0 127.0.0.1:53    0.0.0.0:*        LISTEN  4290/named
tcp      0       0 127.0.0.1:5432 0.0.0.0:*         LISTEN  3507/postmaster
tcp      0       0 0.0.0.0:3306   0.0.0.0:*         LISTEN  7117/mysqld...
```

This shows only an abbreviated output. It normally shows all the ports
which the server is listening to, and there can be between 10 and 100 of
them. When running any command, you can whittle down its output
using the grep command. grep filters the output and only shows lines
containing a word or phrase you have specified. The vertical bar | makes
a pipe, piping the output of one command (netstat) into the input of
another (grep). Try this instead:

```
netstat -tlpn | grep :80
tcp6   0    0 127.0.0.1:8005    :::*    LISTEN    22885/java
```

This runs netstat and shows only results containing :80. This server has a
java process listening to port 8005 but no Web server running.

Which Web Server

When a Linux server starts up it looks in the directory /etc/init.d and
runs the scripts there to launch its software. This varies among Linux
distributions, and on other UNIX flavors like BSD this might be /etc/rc.d
or /etc/rc.d/init.d. This is similar to the Startup menu folder in Windows.

You can see what your server starts using the ls command which lists the files in a directory. The -l shows a long format with permissions, owners, size and date created.

```
$ ls -l /etc/init.d
total 368
-rwxr-xr-x 1 root root  7621 Sep 13  2012 apache2
-rwxr-xr-x 1 root root  3281 Oct  5  2012 bind9
-rwxr-xr-x 1 root root  2444 Jan  1  2011 bootlogd
-rwxr-xr-x 1 root root  5364 Nov  1  2011 courier-imap
-rwxr-xr-x 1 root root  3753 Dec 19  2010 cron...
```

You are looking for a Web server software package such as apache2, httpd (the old name for Apache) or nginx. You can use grep again with the -e option which tells it to use a regular expression. In regular expressions, the vertical bar means "or" so this displays any files containing "apache" or "http" or "nginx". The bar must be escaped with a backslash:

```
$ ls -l /etc/init.d | grep -e "apache\|http\|nginx"
-rwxr-xr-x 1 root root  7621 Sep 13  2012 apache2
```

RESTARTING THE WEB SERVER SOFTWARE

The files in /etc/init.d are called *shell scripts*. The commands you've been using on Mac and Linux up till now form part of a C-type language which also includes setting variables and running loops. As in JavaScript, the semicolon at the end of each line is optional, but if you use it, you can cram several commands onto a single line. Here is a simple for loop on the command line:

```
$ for i in 1 2 3; do echo Line $i; done
Line 1
Line 2
Line 3
```

To see a complex shell script, take a look at some of the startup scripts in /etc/init.d. Use the less command to view a file. Press space to view the next page or q to quit from less.

```
$ less /etc/init.d/apache2
#!/bin/sh
set -e
SCRIPTNAME="${0##*/}"...
```

The reason we're really here, though, is to restart the Web server software. If you logged into ssh as the administrative user root, you can run the restart command directly. In this case, you will have been typing your commands after a # instead of a $. If not, you'll need to prefix it with the sudo command, which says do some command as the super user. You'll need the root password to hand for sudo. To tell the Web server software to start, run:

```
$ sudo /etc/init.d/apache2 start
Password:
Starting apache2...
```

Hopefully this will fail with a useful error message. Hopefully, because then you will know why it crashed in the first place, and you can plug the error message into Google to find out how to fix it.

If it was unlucky enough to work, then your Web server is now running. All the scripts in /etc/init.d run as background processes, or daemons in UNIX parlance. This means that you can start them and they will stay running even after you exit from ssh, turn off you computer and go to the beach. This is unlike commands like traceroute and ls which do their thing and finish. You can run netstat again to double-check the Web server is now running. Notice the d at the end of apached. It stands for daemon.

```
netstat -tlpn | grep :80
tcp        0        0 :::80                :::*      LISTEN      18201/apached
tcp6       0        0 127.0.0.1:8005   :::*      LISTEN      22885/java
```

WEB SERVER ERROR LOGS

If it failed to start and didn't give a friendly error message, the next place to look is the error logs. These are usually in the /var/log directory named after the software. Run ls /var/log to double check. For example, Apache's logs are in /var/log/apache2.

```
$ ls -l /var/log/apache2/*log*
-rw-r----- 1 root adm 1944899 May  5 09:59 /var/log/nginx/access.log
-rw-r----- 1 root adm  538152 May  4 02:40 /var/log/nginx/access.
log.2.gz
-rw-r----- 1 root adm   28647 May  5 08:18 /var/log/nginx/error.log
-rw-r----- 1 root adm    5701 May  4 02:35 /var/log/nginx/error.log.2.gz
```

This shows that Apache has an access log and an error log. Both logs are zipped up around 02:30 each morning. The next command first changes into the /var/log/apache2 directory with the cd command, and then uses tail to view the last few entries in a log file.

```
$ cd /var/log/apache2; tail error.log
```

To look at a gzipped log file, use the zcat command to output it and pipe through tail. The -20 shows the last 20 lines.

```
$ zcat error.log.2.gz | tail -20
```

Or better yet, just look for errors using grep. Use zcat with the -f option to display both normal and zipped log files. Then pipe the output through grep to search for the word "error" case insensitively:

```
$ zcat -f error.log* | grep -i error
```

This command may produce a lot of output. If a Matrix fan happens to walk past your computer right now, they'll be impressed to see all that raw data whizzing by. It won't help you much, though, so pipe it through less:

```
$ zcat -f error.log* | grep -i error | less
```

less is powerful. You can press arrow keys or j to go down, k to go up, /something to search for "something" and h to see a helpful list of all the commands. If you can narrow down the moment of failure of your Web server to a few hours, you can use less to navigate to that part of the log file.

SYSTEM LOGS

There are several other useful log files in /var/log such as syslog (the system logger) and dmesg (bootup messages). They all use a similar date format so if you can narrow down the time when you suspect something went wrong, you can search them all at once. This command changes to the /var/log directory and then outputs all the files using zcat -f. The [234] in grep is borrowed from regular expressions and matches the numbers 2 or 3 or 4. So this will display any error messages in any of the logs that took place on May 5 between 02:00 and 04:00 in the morning:

```
$ cd /var/log; zcat -f * | grep "May  5 0[234]:" | less
```

OUT OF SPACE

If your Web server software still won't start and the error remains elusive, there are a couple common problems you can explicitly check for. Your server could have run out of hard drive space. Use the command df to show disk file usage. The -h shows things in human-friendly form (with M for megabyte and G for gigabyte instead of really big numbers):

```
$ df -h
Filesystem            1M-blocks      Used Available Use% Mounted on
/dev/simfs              20.4G        9.8G    10.6G  49% /
tmpfs                    1.6G           0     1.6G   0% /lib/init/rw
tmpfs                    1.6G           0     1.6G   0% /dev/shm
```

If that was a problem, then a quick solution is to find and delete really big files. The find command is very powerful. The -size option tells it to look for files of at least the given size, and the -printf option tells it to print the size (%12s, where the 12 directs the print area to be 12 characters wide to help line things up), last modification time (%t), directory (%h), file name (%f) and then a new line (\n). To view all files over 10 megabytes try:

```
$ find / -size +10M -printf "%12s %t %h/%f\n"
445631888 Mon Mar 18 13:38:07.0380913017 2013 /var/www/huge-file.zip
```

If you are absolutely sure that this file is superfluous, then you can use the following command to delete the file and free up space quickly. Be warned that there is no going back. The rm command does not have a trash folder from which you can restore things later: $ rm /var/www/huge-file.zip

OUT OF MEMORY

To check your server's RAM usage, run the free command, again with -m to show in megabytes:

```
$ free -m
                total       used       free     shared    buffers     cached
Mem:             3067       2673        393          0          0        819
-/+ buffers/cache:          1853       1213
Swap:               0          0          0
```

This server has 3GB of total memory and 393MB free. This is fine as Linux likes to use a lot of its memory. It's the buffers/cache line which you should focus on. If this is nearly all used, then your system may be struggling to cope.

To find out what is hogging all the memory, use the top command. It shows a real-time display of system CPU and memory usage. Unfortunately this will also run very slowly if your server is under strain, but it may tell you what's causing the problem.

```
$ top
  PID USER        PR  NI  VIRT   RES   SHR S %CPU %MEM    TIME+  COMMAND
22885 tomcat6     20   0 2061m  159m  2644 S    1  5.2 780:41.85 java
    1 root        20   0  8360   568   536 S    0  0.0   0:52.30 init
    2 root        20   0     0     0     0 S    0  0.0   0:00.00 kthreadd/10086
    3 root        20   0     0     0     0 S    0  0.0   0:00.00 khelper/10086
14579 root        20   0 40900  3124  1668 S    0  0.1   1:30.27 nginx...
```

If something is being a memory hog, you can restart it or kill it. However, be sure you know what it is first. You may crash the server completely, or lock yourself out, or stop an important database amalgamation which your efficiency-unaware colleague started three days ago.

First of all, try to find a friendly way of restarting an errant process. Many services can be restarted nicely by issuing a restart command to the shell script which started them, such as:

```
$ sudo /etc/init.d/apache2 restart
```

If that isn't available, search online for how best to restart or shut it down gracefully. If you still have no luck, then to kill a process, press k and type in the number from the process ID (PID) column. It will ask for confirmation and then try to kill the process. If you are not root, it may say "Operation not permitted", in which case you'll need to run sudo top instead.

The PID is used to identify a piece of software running on a computer. Each instance of an application, program or software has a unique PID. If the process refuses to go away, you can press q to leave top and try the kill command instead. Give it the more extreme -9 option. top sends the friendly signal 15 (termination). Signal 9 goes straight for the kill.

```
$ sudo kill -9 22885
```

Run top again. If some other similar process has taken over the memory-eating honors, then you have only killed a child process. You will need to find out the parent which spawned the misbehaving child in the first place, because killing the parent will also stop all the children. The ps command can be used to display information about a specific process. Normally it does not show the parent process ID, so you need to add the -o option and specify that the output should show the parent process ID ppid and the full command that started it:

```
$ ps -o ppid,command 14579
  PPID COMMAND
  6950 nginx: worker process
```

This nginx process is not the main one.

```
$ ps -o ppid,command 6950
  PPID COMMAND
     1 nginx: master process /usr/sbin/nginx
```

A very low parent PID means that this process is the daddy[17]. Killing process 6950 will kill the main nginx process and all its children.

There is an easier way to do this. You can search for processes using pgrep and kill them with pkill. The -l tells pgrep to list the process name as well. For example:

```
$ pgrep -l nginx
6950   nginx
14579 nginx...
```

And then go in for the kill with sudo pkill nginx. A further way to search for processes is using ps with the aux option as in ps aux | grep nginx. Easier, but you wouldn't have learned about the wonder of top.

---

17 Process ID numbers are assigned in order, so a low number really only means that the process was started just after the server booted.

Speaking HTTP

At this stage, your Web server software is hopefully up and running. If it did crash, you've restarted it, found out the reason and taken steps to prevent it from happening again.

You can now double-check your Web server is up and running by telnetting to port 80 from your laptop again. This time it should say "Connected" and then wait for your request. Web servers understand HTTP (hypertext transfer protocol). After a connection is established type GET / HTTP/1.1 to tell the server you would like to GET (as opposed to POST) the home page / and that you speak version 1.1 of the protocol.

Press Enter and then type Host: followed by the host name. This line is only necessary on servers which host more than one website. HTTP does not know that you telnetted to www.smashingmagazine.com. As far as it is concerned, you telnetted to 80.72.139.101 and it needs to know which of its many websites you are interested in. Press Enter twice to make the request. You should get back a long stream of text and HTML:

```
$ telnet www.smashingmagazine.com 80
Trying 80.72.139.101...
Connected to www.smashingmagazine.com.
Escape character is '^]'.
GET / HTTP/1.1
Host: www.smashingmagazine.com

HTTP/1.1 200 OK
Date: Thu, 09 May 2013 13:25:52 GMT
Content-Type: text/html; charset=UTF-8
Transfer-Encoding: chunked
Connection: keep-alive
X-Powered-By: PHP/5.2.17
Content-Length: 25023
Content-Type: text/html

<html>
<head><<...
```

These lines are mostly HTTP headers. The HTTP/1.1 200 OK says that the server also speaks version 1.1 of HTTP and gives the successful HTTP response code 200. Other common responses are 500 for Internal Server Error and 404 for File Not Found. It then continues with the HTML. If the Connection header specified "keep-alive" then telnet will wait for your next request and you'll need to type Control +] and then "quit" to exit. If the Connection header said "close" then it will finish by itself and say "Connection closed by foreign host" at the bottom.

FINDING YOUR WEBSITE

The 200 code means that your home page is okay, and you should be able to visit it in your browser. However, it may not show what you expected, and your fabulous Widget 3000 page may still be absent.

VIRTUAL HOSTS AND STREAMS

As mentioned above, many servers host multiple websites. One of these is the default website. It is the website you get when you visit the server by IP address http://80.72.139.101/ instead of by name, or when you leave off the Host: line in the HTTP request while telnetting. The rest of the websites are known as virtual hosts. Every one of these websites has a physical location on the server known as its document root. To further investigate your website woes, you need to discover its document root.

Fortunately and sensibly, most server management packages like Plesk store their virtually hosted websites according to their domain name, so you can usually just find directly on the domain name. The / in the command below tells find to search the whole file system, the -type d looks only for directories, and the -name part searches for any directories containing "smashingmagazine". The asterisks are wild cards. You'll need to either escape them *smashingmagazine* or put them in quotes "*smashingmagazine*":

```
$ find / -type d -name "*smashingmagazine*"
find: '/var/run/cups/certs': Permission denied
find: '/var/run/PolicyKit': Permission denied
/var/www/vhosts/smashingmagazine.com
/var/www/vhosts/smashingmagazine.com/httpdocs...
```

If you run this command as a normal unprivileged user, you will probably see lots of "Permission denied" as find tries to explore forbidden places. You are actually seeing two types of output here: stdout for standard output and stderr for standard error. They are called *output streams* and are confusingly mixed together.

You have already encountered the pipe symbol | for piping the output stream (stdout) of one command into the input stream (stdin) of another. The symbol > can redirect that output into a file. Try this command to send all the matches into a file called *matches.txt*:

```
$ find / -type d -name ^"*smashingmagazine*" > matches.txt
find: '/var/run/cups/certs': Permission denied
find: '/var/run/PolicyKit': Permission denied...
```

In this case, all the stdout is redirected into the file matches.txt and only the error output stream stderr is displayed on the screen. By adding the number 2 you can instead redirect stderr into a file and just display stdout:

```
$ find / -type d -name ^"*smashingmagazine*" 2> matcherrors.txt
/var/www/vhosts/smashingmagazine.com
/var/www/vhosts/smashingmagazine.com/httpdocs...
```

There is a special file on Linux, UNIX and Mac computers which is basically a black hole where stuff gets sent and disappears. It's called /dev/null, so to only see stdout and ignore all errors:

```
$ find / -type d -name ^"*smashingmagazine*" 2> /dev/null
/var/www/vhosts/smashingmagazine.com
/var/www/vhosts/smashingmagazine.com/httpdocs...
```

The end result is that this find command tells you roughly where your document root is. In Plesk, all the virtual hosts are generally stored within the /var/www/vhosts directory, with the document roots in /var/www/vhosts/domain.com/httpdocs.

THE LONG WAY

You can find the document root more accurately by looking through the configuration files. For Apache servers, you can find the default website's document root by looking through the main configuration file which is usually /etc/apache2/apache2.conf or /etc/httpd/conf/httpd.conf.

```
$ grep DocumentRoot /etc/httpd/conf/httpd.conf
DocumentRoot "/var/www/html"
```

Somewhere inside this conf file will also be an Include line which references other conf files, which may themselves include further conf files. To find the DocumentRoot for your virtual host, you'll need to search through them all. You can do this using grep and find but its a long command, so we will build it up gradually.

First, we will find all the files (because of the -type f) on the whole server (the /) whose names end in "conf" or "include". The -type f finds only files and the -o lets us look for files ending in "conf" or "include", with surrounding escaped parentheses. As above, the errors are banished into the ether:

```
$ find / -type f \( -name \*conf -o -name \*include \) 2> /dev/null
/var/spool/postfix/etc/resolv.conf
/var/some file with spaces.conf
/var/www/vhosts/myserv.com/conf/last_httpd.include...
```

This is not quite complete as any files with spaces will confuse the grep command we are about to attempt. To fix that you can pipe the output of the find command through the sed command which allows you to specify a regular expression. Regular expressions are a huge topic in their own right. In the command below, the s/ /\\ /g will replace all spaces with a slash followed by a space:

```
$ find / -type f \( -name \*conf -o -name \*include \) 2>/dev/null | sed
's/ /\\ /g'
/var/spool/postfix/etc/resolv.conf
/var/some\ file\ with\ spaces.conf
/var/www/vhosts/myserv.com/conf/last_httpd.include...
```

Now you can use a backtick to embed the results of that find command into a grep command. Using ` is different than | as it actually helps to build a command, rather than just manipulating its input. The -H option to grep tells it so show file names as well. So, now we will look for any reference to "smashingmagazine" in any conf files.

```
$ grep -H smashingmagazine `find / -type f \( -name \*conf -o -name \*in-
clude \) 2> /dev/null | sed 's/ /\\ /g'`
/var/www/vhosts/smashingmagazine.com/conf/last_httpd.include: ServerName
"smashingmagazine.com"...
```

This may take a few seconds to run. It is finding every conf file on the server and searching through all of them for "smashingmagazine". It may reveal the DocumentRoot directly. If not, it will at least reveal the file where the ServerName or VirtualHost is defined. You can then use grep or less to look through that file for the DocumentRoot.

You can also use the xargs command to do the same thing. It also allows the output from one command to be embedded into another:

```
$ find / -type f \( -name \*conf -o -name \*include \) 2> /dev/null | sed
's/ /\\ /g' | xargs grep -H smashingmagazine
/var/www/vhosts/smashingmagazine.com/conf/last_httpd.include: ServerName
"smashingmagazine.com"...
$ grep DocumentRoot /var/www/vhosts/smashingmagazine.com/conf/last_httpd.include
DocumentRoot "/var/www/vhosts/smashingmagazine.com/httpdocs"
```

The end result, hopefully, is that you've definitively found the document root for your website.

You can use a similar technique for nginx. It also has a main conf file, usually in /etc/nginx/nginx.conf, and it can also include other conf files. However its document root is just called "root".

APACHE CONTROL INTERFACE

With Apache, there is yet another way to find the right conf file, using the apachectl or newer apache2ctl command with the -S option.

```
$ apachectl -S
VirtualHost configuration:
80.72.139.101:80        is a NameVirtualHost
        default server default (/usr/local/psa/admin/conf/genera-
ted/13656495120.10089200_server.include:87)
        port 80 namevhost default (/usr/local/psa/admin/conf/genera-
ted/13656495120.10089200_server.include:87)
        port 80 namevhost www.smashingmagazine.com (/var/www/vhosts/
smashingmagazine.com/conf/last_httpd.include:10)...
```

If this whizzes by too fast, you can try piping the results through grep. It won't work, however, because grep only operates on stdout and for some reason apachectl outputs its information to stderr. So, you have to first direct stderr into stdout and then send it through grep. This is done by redirecting the error stream 2 into the output stream 1 with 2>&1, like this:

```
$ apachectl -S 2>&1 | grep smashingmagazine
        port 80 namevhost smashingmagazine.com (/var/www/vhosts/smas-
hingmagazine.com/conf/13656495330.08077300_httpd.include:10)
```

This also reveals the conf file which contains the DocumentRoot for this website. As above further grep or less will reveal the DocumentRoot.

CHECKING THE DOCUMENT ROOT

Now that you've found the document root, you can snoop around to make sure it's alright. Change to the directory with cd:

```
$ cd /var/www/vhosts/smashingmagazine.com/httpdocs
bash: cd: /var/www/vhosts/smashingmagazine.com/httpdocs: No such file or
directory
```

If you get the error message "No such file or directory", that is bad news. Either the DocumentRoot has been incorrectly set or your whole website has been deleted. If it is there, you can list the files with ls. The -a also shows hidden files which start with a dot, and -l displays them in long format with permissions and dates:

```
$ ls -al
drwxrwxrwx  8 nobody   nogroup  4096 May  9 14:03 .
drwxr-xr-x 14 root     root     4096 Oct 13  2012 ..
```

Every folder will at least show these two entries. The single "." is for the current directory and ".." is for the parent directory. If that's all there is, then the directory is empty. While you're there, you can double-check you are in the correct place. Create a new file using echo and again using the > symbol to send the output to a file.

```
$ echo "<h1>My test file</h1>" > testfile.html
```

This will create a file called *testfile.html* containing a bit of HTML. You can use your browser or telnet or curl or wget to see if the file is where it should be.

```
$ curl http://www.smashingmagazine.com/testfile.html
<h1>My test file</h1>
```

If that worked, then well done, you have found your website! Remove that test file to clean up after yourself with rm testfile.html and keep going.

BACK UP AND RESTORE

The `tar` and `zip` commands can be used to back up and restore. If your website is missing, then restoring won't help you much unless you have previously backed up. So go back in time and back up your data with one of the commands below. To go back a whole day:

```
$ gobackintime 86400
It is now Sat May 10 20:30:57 BST 2013
```

Just kidding — but it would be nice! The `tar` command stands for tape archive and comes from the days when data was backed up on magnetic tapes. To create an archive of a directory, pass the `cfz` options to `tar` which will create a new archive in a file and then zip it in the gzip format.

```
$ tar cfz backupfile.tgz /var/www/vhosts/smashingmagazine.com/httpdocs
tar: Removing leading `/' from member names
```

All Mac and Linux computers support the `tar` command and most also have `zip`. To do the same with `zip`:

```
$ zip -r backupfile.zip /directory/to/backup
```

To see what an archive contains, run:

```
tar tfz backupfile.tgz
var/www/vhosts/smashingmagazine.com/httpdocs/
var/www/vhosts/smashingmagazine.com/httpdocs/.htaccess...
```

Or for `zip` format:

```
unzip -l backupfile.zip
Archive:  test.zip
  Length      Date    Time    Name
--------- ---------- ----- ----
        0  2012-05-28 00:33  var/www/vhosts/smashingmagazine.com/httpdocs
      234  2012-05-28 00:33  var/www/vhosts/smashingmagazine.com/httpdocs/.htaccess
```

Both `tar` and `zip` strip the leading slashes when they backup. So when you restore the files, they will be restored within the current directory. To restore them in the same location they were backed up from, first restore them in the current directory and then move them into place with `mv`.

```
$ tar xfzv backupfile.tgz
var/www/vhosts/smashingmagazine.com/httpdocs/...
```

The "v" above stands for verbose and causes `tar` to show what it's doing. `zip` has a similar option:

```
$ unzip -v backupfile.zip
Archive:   backupfile.zip
 Length    Method    Size Cmpr    Date      Time   CRC-32    Name
--------   ------   ------- ---- ---------- ----- --------   ----
       0   Stored        0   0% 2012-05-28 00:33 00000000   var/www/vhosts/
smashingmagazine.com/httpdocs/...
```

Website Errors

Let's assume your website hasn't actually disappeared. The next place to look is the error log file.

FINDING THE LOG FILE

When using a server management package like Plesk, each website probably has its own log file. You can find it by grepping for the word "log" in the conf file you identified above. The -i means case-insensitive.

```
$ grep -i log /var/www/vhosts/smashingmagazine.com/conf/last_httpd.include
    CustomLog /var/www/vhosts/smashingmagazine.com/statistics/logs/ac-
cess_log plesklog
    ErrorLog  "/var/www/vhosts/smashingmagazine.com/statistics/logs/er-
ror_log"...
```

There is also a server-wide log where any non-website-specific errors go. You can find this in the main conf file:

```
$ grep -i log /etc/apache2/apache2.conf
ErrorLog /var/log/apache2/error.log...
```

HTACCESS ERRORS

It is very easy to screw up a website. You can quite readily bring down a very big website by removing a single character from the .htaccess file. Apache uses the file *.htaccess* to provide last-minute configuration options for a website. It's most often used for URL rewriting rules that look like this:

```
RewriteRule   ^products/.*/([0-9]+)$   products/view.php?id=$1   [L,QSA]
```

This rule says to rewrite any URL in the form "products/widget-3000/123" to the actual URL "products/view.php?id=123". The L means that this is the last rule to be applied and QSA means that Apache should attach any query string to the new URL.

URL rewriting is often used for search engine optimization so that Web managers can get the name of the product into the URL without actually having to create a directory called "widget-3000". However, make a single typo and your whole website will give a 500 Internal Server Error.

The `tail` command will display the last 10 lines of a log file. Give it a -1 to display the single last line instead. An .htaccess problem will look like this:

```
$ tail -1 /var/www/vhosts/smashingmagazine.com/statistics/logs/error_log
[Thu May 06 11:04:00 2013] [alert] [client 81.106.118.59] /var/www/
vhosts/smashingmagazine.com/httpdocs/.htaccess: Invalid command 'Rewi-
teRule', perhaps misspelled or defined by a module not included in the
server configuration.
```

Or give it the -f option to follow the log file, showing any additional log entries as they happen:

```
$ tail -f /var/www/vhosts/smashingmagazine.com/statistics/logs/error_log...
```

You can grep for all of these types of errors:

```
$ grep alert /var/www/vhosts/smashingmagazine.com/statistics/logs/error_log
[Thu May 06 11:04:00 2013] [alert] [client 81.106.118.59]...
```

PHP PARSE AND RUNTIME ERRORS

Many websites use the LAMP combination: Linux, Apache, MySQL and PHP. A common reason for Web pages not showing up is that they contain a PHP error. Fortunately, these are quite easy to discover and pinpoint.

There are two broad classes of PHP errors: parse errors and runtime errors. Parse errors are syntax errors and include leaving off a semicolon or forgetting the $ in front of a variable name. Runtime errors include undefined functions or referencing objects which don't exist.

Like .htaccess errors, parse errors will cause an HTML response code 500 for Internal Server Error, often with a completely blank HTML page. Runtime errors will give a successful HTML response of 200 and will show as much HTML as they have processed (and flushed) before the error happened. You can use telnet or wget -S or curl -i to get only the headers from a URL. So now, copy and paste your erroneous page into a command:

```
$ curl -i http://www.smashingmagazine.com/products/widget-3000/123
HTTP/1.0 500 Internal Server Error
Date: Sun, 12 May 2013 17:44:49 GMT
Server: Apache
Vary: Accept-Encoding
Content-Length: 0
Connection: close
Content-Type: text/html
```

PHP ERROR SETTINGS

To find the exact error, you need to make sure errors are being reported in the log file.

There are several PHP settings which cover errors. display_errors determines if errors are shown to the website visitor or not, and log_errors says whether they will appear in log files. error_reporting specifies the types of errors that are reported: only fatal errors, for example,

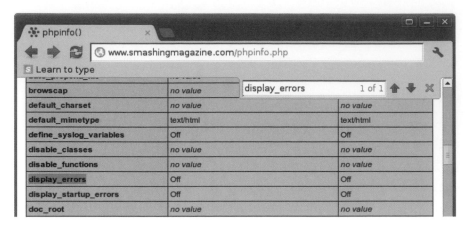

phpinfo function showing configuration settings.

or warnings and notices as well. All of these can be set in a configuration file, in .htaccess or within the PHP script itself.

You can find out your current settings by running the PHP function phpinfo. Create a PHP file which calls the function and visit it in your browser:

```
$ echo "<?php phpinfo()?>" > /var/www/vhosts/smashingmagazine.com/htt-
pdocs/phpinfo.php
```

The two columns show the website and server-wide settings. This shows that display_errors is off, which is good, because it should be off on live websites. It means that no PHP errors will ever be seen by the casual visitor. log_errors on the other hand should be on. It is very handy for debugging PHP issues.

The error_reporting value is 30719. This number represents bit flags or bit fields. This is a technique for storing multiple yes/no values in a single number. In PHP there are a series of constants representing different types of errors.[18] For example, the constant E_ERROR is for fatal errors and has the value 1; E_WARNING is for warnings and equals 2; E_PARSE

---

18 "Predefined Constants", PHP.net. http://smashed.by/errorfunc

is for parsing or syntax errors and has the value 4. These values are all powers of two and can be safely added together. So the number 7 means that all three types of errors should be reported, as E_ERROR + E_WARNING + E_PARSE = 7. A value of 5 will only report E_ERROR + E_PARSE.

In reality, there are 16 types of errors from 1 for E_ERROR to 16384 for E_USER_DEPRECATED. You can type "30719 in binary" into Google and it will give you the binary equivalent: 0b111011111111111. This means that all errors are switched on except the twelfth, which is E_STRICT. This particular setup has also been given a constant E_ALL = E_ERROR + E_ WARNING + E_PARSE + etc = 30719. From PHP version 5.4.0, E_ALL is actually 32767 which includes all the errors include E_STRICT.

If your error_reporting setting is 0, then no errors will show up in the log file. You can change this setting in the file php.ini, but then you have to restart Apache to make it have an effect. An easier way to change this setting in Apache is to add a line in a file called .htaccess in your document root: php_value error_reporting 30719.

Or you can do that on the command line, using the double arrow which appends to an existing file or creates the file if it doesn't exist:

```
$ echo "php_value error_reporting 30719" >> .htaccess
$ echo "php_value log_errors On" >> .htaccess
```

Refresh your erroneous Web page. If there is a PHP error in your page it should now show up in the error log. You can grep the log for all PHP errors:

```
grep PHP /var/www/vhosts/smashingmagazine.com/statistics/logs/error_log
[Sun May 12 18:19:09 2013] [error] [client 81.106.118.59] PHP Notice:
Undefined variable: total in /var/www/vhosts/smashingmagazine.com/htt-
pdocs/products/view.php on line 10...
```

If you have referenced variables or array indices before assigning them values, you may see thousands of PHP notices like the one above. It happens when you do things like <? $total = $total + 1 ?> without initially setting $total to 0. They are useful for finding potential bugs, but they are not show stoppers. Your website should work anyway.

You may have so many notices and warnings like this that the real errors get lost. You can change your error_reporting to 5 to only show E_ERROR and E_PARSE or you can grep specifically for those types of errors. It is very common to chain grep commands together like this when you want to filter by multiple things. The -e option below tells the second grep to use a regular expression. This command finds all log entries containing "PHP" and either "Parse" or "Fatal".

```
$ grep PHP /var/www/vhosts/smashingmagazine.com/statistics/logs/error_log
| grep -e "Parse\|Fatal"
[Thu Jul 19 12:26:23 2012] [error] [client 81.106.118.59] PHP Fatal er-
ror:  Class 'Product' not found in /var/www/vhosts/smashingmagazine.com/
httpdocs/library/class.product.php on line 698
[Sun May 12 18:16:21 2013] [error] [client 81.106.118.59] PHP Parse er-
ror:  syntax error, unexpected T_STRING in /var/www/vhosts/smashingmaga-
zine.com/httpdocs/products/view.php on line 100...
```

SEEING ERRORS IN THE BROWSER

If you are tracing a runtime error rather than a parse error, you can also change the error_reporting setting directly in PHP. And you can quickly turn display_errors on, so you will see the error directly in your browser. This makes debugging quicker, but means everyone else can see the error too. Add this line to the top of your PHP page:

```
<? ini_set ('display_errors', 1); error_reporting (E_ERROR | E_WARNING); ?>
```

These two functions change the two PHP settings. The | in the error_reporting call is a bit OR operator. It effectively does the same as the + above but operates on bits, so is the correct operator to use with bit flags.

Any fatal errors or warnings later in the PHP page will now be shown directly in the browser. This technique won't work for parse errors as none of the page will run if there's a parse error.

BIT FLAGS

Using bit flags for error_reporting avoids having 15 separate arguments
to the function for each type of error. Bit flags can also be useful in your
own code. To use them, you need to define some constants, use the bit OR
operator | when calling the function and the bit AND operator & within
the function. Here's a simple PHP example using bit flags to tell a function
called *showproduct* which product properties to display:

```php
<?
define ('PRODUCT_NAME', 1);
define ('PRODUCT_PRICE', 2);
function showproduct ($product, $flags) {
   if ($flags & PRODUCT_NAME) echo $product['name'];
   if ($flags & PRODUCT_PRICE) echo ': $' . $product['price'];
}
$product = array ('name'=>'Widget 3000', 'price'=>10);
showproduct ($product, PRODUCT_NAME | PRODUCT_PRICE);
?>
```

This will display "Widget 3000: $10" in the browser. This is a rather
superficial example of bit flags. Usually there are far deeper, more constant
system processes.

INFINITE LOOPS

PHP's error reporting may struggle with one class of error: an infinite loop. A
loop may just keep executing until it hits PHP's time limit, which is usually
30 seconds (PHP's max_execution_time setting), causing a fatal error. Or
if the loop allocates new variables or calls functions, it may keep going until
PHP runs out of workable memory (PHP's memory_limit setting).

It may, however, cause the Apache child process to crash, which means
nothing will get reported, and you'll just see a blank or partial page. This
type of error is increasingly rare, as PHP and Apache are now very mature
and can detect and handle runaway problems like this. But if you are about
to bang your head against the wall in frustration because none of the

above has worked, then give it some consideration. Deep within your code, you may have a function which calls some other function, which calls the original function in an infinite recursion.

DEBUGGERS

If you've gotten this far, and your page is still not showing up, then you're entering more difficult territory. Your PHP may be executing validly and doing everything it should, but there's some logical error in your programming. For quick debugging you can var_dump variables to the browser, perhaps wrapping them in an if statement so that only your IP address sees them:

```
<? if ($_SERVER['REMOTE_ADDR'] == '85.106.118.199') var_dump ($product); ?>
```

This method will narrow down an error but it is ungraceful and error-prone, so you might consider a debugging tool such as Xdebug or FirePHP. They can provide masses of information, and can also run invisibly to the user, saving their output to a log file. Xdebug can be used like this:

```
<?
ini_set ('xdebug.collect_params', 1);
xdebug_start_trace ('/tmp/xdebugtrace');
echo "This will get traced.";
xdebug_stop_trace();
?>
```

This bit of code logs all function calls and arguments to the file /tmp/xdebugtrace.txt. It displays even more information when there is a PHP notice or error. However, the overhead may not be suitable for a live environment, and it needs to be installed on the server, so it's probably not available in most hosting environments.

FirePHP, on the other hand, is a PHP library that interacts with an add-on to Firebug, a plugin for Firefox. You can output debugging information and stack traces from PHP to the Firebug console.

Security Issues

By this point, you should have some HTML reaching your browser. If it's not what you expect, then there's a chance that your website has been compromised. Don't take it personally (at first). There are many types of hacks and most of them are automated. Someone clever but unscrupulous has written a program which detects vulnerabilities and exploits them. The purpose of the exploit may simply be to send spam, or to use your server as part of a larger attack on a more specific target (a DDoS).

SERVER HACKS

Operating systems are very complex pieces of software. They may be built from millions of lines of programming code. They are quite likely to have loopholes where sending the wrong message at just the wrong time will cause some kind of blip which allows someone or something to gain entry. That's why Microsoft, Apple, Ubuntu and others are constantly releasing updates.

Similarly, Apache, nginx, IIS and all the other software on a typical server is complicated. The best thing you can do is keep it up to date with the latest patches. Most good hosts will do this for you.

A hacker can use these flaws to log in to your server and engineer themselves a terminal session. They may initially gain access as an unprivileged user and then try a further hack to become the root user. You should make this as hard as possible by using good passwords, restrictive permissions, and being careful to run software (like Apache) as an unprivileged user.

If someone does gain access, they may leave behind a bit of software which they can later use to take control of your server. This may be detectable by an anti-virus scanner or something like the Rootkit Hunter, which looks for anomalies like unexpected hidden files. But there are also a few things you can do if you suspect an intrusion.

The w command shows who is currently logged in to a server and what they are doing:

```
$ w
 20:44:32 up 44 days,  7:51,  2 users,  load average: 0.07, 0.03, 0.05
USER     TTY      FROM              LOGIN@   IDLE   JCPU   PCPU WHAT
root     pts/0    cpc1-brig17-2-0- 17:54    1:02m  0.15s  0.13s -bash
root     pts/1    cpc1-brig17-2-0- 20:44    0.00s  0.02s  0.00s w...
```

The last command shows who has logged in recently in date order. Pipe it through head to show only the first 10 lines.

```
$ last
paul     pts/0       :0.0              Sun May 12 17:21   still logged in
paul     tty7        :0                Sun May 12 17:20   still logged in
reboot   system boot 2.6.32-41-386     Sun May 12 17:18 - 20:48  (03:29)
fred     tty7        :0                Sat May 11 10:10 - down   (01:12)
```

It tells you who has logged in and for how long, plus any terminal session they have open. down means until the server shut down. Look for unexpected entries and consult your host or a security expert if you are in doubt.

PHP HACKS

More common are hackers who gain entry though vulnerabilities in PHP scripts, especially popular content management systems like WordPress. Anybody can write a plugin for WordPress and, if it's useful, people will install it. When writing a plugin, most developers think primarily about the functionality and little about security. And because WordPress allows file uploading, hackers who find vulnerabilities can use them to upload their own PHP scripts and later take control of a computer.

These PHP scripts can use the PHP mail function to send out spam on demand, but they can also try to execute commands in much the same way as you can via a terminal session. PHP can execute commands with its exec or system functions. If you do not need to use these functions, it is advisable to disable them. You can do this by adding the `disable_functions` directive to your server's php.ini file (or php5.ini for PHP 5) or to the file php.ini within your document root. If you search for "php disable functions" in Google, you will find a whole list of functions which should be disabled in this way:

```
disable_functions=fpassthru,crack_check,crack_close...
```

A quick check you can make for this type of hack is to look for all PHP files modified recently and make sure there are no anomalies. The `-mtime -1` option tells find to only consider files modified within the last day. There is also `-mmin` for minutes. This command searches all websites within /var/www/vhosts for recently modified files ending in "php" or "inc":

```
$ find /var/www/vhosts -mtime -1 \( -name \*php -o -name \*inc \) -printf
"%t %h/%f\n"
Sun May 12 21:20:17.0000000000 2013 /var/www/vhosts/smashingmagazine.com/
httpdocs/products/view.php
```

PHP hacks are difficult to detect because they are designed to not stick out. One method hackers use is to gzip their PHP and then encode it as base64. In that case, you may have a PHP file on your system with something like this in it:

```
eval(gzinflate(base64_decode('HJ3HkqNQEkU/ZzqCBd4t8V4YAQI2E3jvPV8...
```

Another method is to encode text within variables and then combine them and evaluate them:

```
$unywlbxc = " uwzsebpgi840hk2a jf";
$hivjytmne = "  jqs9m4y 1znp0  ";
eval ( "m"."i". "croti"...
```

Both these methods use the PHP `eval` function, so you can use `grep` to look for `eval`. Using a regular expression with `\beval\b` means that the word "eval" must have a word boundary before and after it, which prevents it being found in the middle of words. You can combine this with the find command above and pipe through less for easy reading:

```
$ find /var/www/vhosts -mtime -1 \( -name \*php -o -name \*inc \) | sed
's/ /\\ /g' | xargs grep -H -e "\beval\b" | less
/var/www/vhosts/config.php:eval(gzinflate(base64_decode('HJ3HkqNQE...
```

If you do find this type of hack in your website, try to discover how they got in before completely removing all the tainted files.

ACCESS LOGS

Along with error logs, Apache also keeps access logs. You can browse these for suspicious activity. For example, if you found a PHP hack inside an innocuous looking file called *test.php*, you can look for all activity related to that file. The access log usually sits alongside the error log and is specified with the CustomLog directive in Apache configuration files. It contains the IP address, date and file requested. Search through it with grep:

```
$ grep -e "\(GET\|POST\) /test.php" /var/www/vhosts/smashingmagazine.com/
statistics/logs/error_log
70.1.5.12 - - [12/May/2013:20:10:49 +0100] "GET /test.php HTTP/1.1" 200
1707 "-" "Mozilla/5.0 (X11; Ubuntu; Linux i686;...
```

This looks for GET and POST requests for the file test.php. It provides you with an IP address, so you can now look for all other access by this address, and also look for a specific date:

```
$ grep 70.1.5.12 /var/www/vhosts/smashingmagazine.com/statistics/logs/er-
ror_log | grep "12/May/2013"
70.1.5.12 - - [12/May/2013:20:10:49 +0100] "GET /products/view.php?so-
mething HTTP/1.1" 200 1707 "-"...
70.1.5.12 - - [12/May/2013:20:10:49 +0100] "GET /test.php HTTP/1.1" 200
1707 "-" "Mozilla/5.0 (X11; Ubuntu; Linux i686;...
```

This kind of debugging can be very useful for normal website errors, too. If you have a feedback form on your website, add the user's IP address to the message. If someone reports an error, you can later look through the logs to see what they have been up to. This is far better than relying on vague secondhand information about reported problems.

It can also be useful for detecting SQL injection attacks, whereby hackers try to extract details from your database by fooling your database retrieval functions. This often involves a lot of trial and error. You could send yourself an email whenever a database query goes wrong and include the user's IP address. You can then cross-reference with the logs to see what else they have tried.

Last Resorts

William Edward Hickson is credited with popularizing the saying: "If at first you don't succeed, try, try, try again."[19] Hickson was a British educational writer living in early Victorian times. His advice is not appropriate for the modern Web developer, lying in bed on a Saturday morning, drowning in frustration, staring at a blank Web page, preparing to chuck an expensive laptop against a brick wall.

You've now been through all the advice above. You've checked that the world hasn't ended, verified your broadband box, tested the Internet and reached your server. You've looked for hardware problems and software problems, and delved into the PHP code. But somehow or other, your Widget 3000 is still not there. The next thing to do is...

HAVE BREAKFAST

Get out of bed and take your mind off the problem for a little while. Have some toast, a bowl of cereal, something to drink. Maybe even indulge in a shower. Try that new lavender and citrus shampoo you bought by mistake. While you're doing all this, your subconscious is busily working on the

---

19   Oxford Dictionary of Quotations (3rd edition), Oxford University Press, 1979

website issue, and may unexpectedly pop a solution into your thoughts. If so, give it a try. If not...

ASK FOR HELP

Check the level of support that you are entitled to by your hosting company. If you are paying $10 per month, it's probably not much. You may be able to get them to cast a vague glance in your direction within the next 72 hours. If it's substantially more, they may log in and have a look within the next few minutes. They should be able to help with hardware or software issues. They won't help with Web programming issues. Alternatively, ring a colleague or freelancer. If you are still stuck...

PREPARE

...to release some nervous energy. Find one of those squidgy balls that you can squeeze mercilessly in your hands, or a couple pencils to use as drumsticks, or a pack of cigarettes and a pot full of coffee. And then try the last resort to any computing problem...

REBOOT

When your laptop or desktop goes wrong, a common solution is to reboot it. You can try the same trick on your Web server. This is a quite risky. Firstly, it may not solve the problem. If it's a PHP error, then nothing will change. If, however, your issue is caused by some obscure piece of software becoming unresponsive, then it may well help, though it may not fix the problem permanently. The same thing may happen next week.

Secondly, if the reboot fails then you will be really stuck. If the server shuts down but fails to start back up again, then someone may have to go and press the power button on the physical machine. That someone is an employee of your hosting company, and they may be enjoying their breakfast too, in a nice comfortable office somewhere. They may have left their jumper at home. They may not want to enter the air-conditioned bunker where all the servers are kept. You will be thoroughly dependent on their response time. Given all the risks, the command is:

```
$ sudo /sbin/reboot
Broadcast message from admin@thisserver.com (/dev/pts/1) at 13:21 ...
The system is going down for reboot now.
```

The `reboot` command causes the server to shut down and then restart. That may take a few minutes. Soon after issuing the command above your SSH session will come to an abrupt end. You will then be left for a few nervous minutes wondering if it will come back up again. Use the tools you prepared above.

While you are waiting, you can issue a `ping` to see if and when your server comes back. On Windows use `ping -t` for an indefinite ping:

```
$ ping www.smashingmagazine.com
PING www.smashingmagazine.com (80.72.139.101) 56(84) bytes of data.
Request timeout for icmp_seq 0
Request timeout for icmp_seq 0
Request timeout for icmp_seq 0...
64 bytes from www.smashingmagazine.com (80.72.139.101): icmp_seq=1 ttl=52
time=39.4 ms
64 bytes from www.smashingmagazine.com (80.72.139.101): icmp_seq=1 ttl=52
time=32.4 ms...
```

You can breathe a sigh of relief when `ping` finally responds. Wait a couple more minutes and you'll be able to use SSH again and then try to view the Widget 3000 in your Web browser.

Conclusion

This has been an epic journey, from the end of the world to a single misplaced character in a file. Hopefully, it will help you through the initial few minutes of panic when you wake up one morning and the beautiful product page you created last night is gone.

Some of the reasons and solutions above are very rare. The most likely cause is simply a slight malfunction in your broadband box. Running out of disk space or getting hacked are the only other things that are in any way likely to happen in the middle of the night when nobody else is working on the website. But throw in other developers, server administrators and enthusiastic clients — and anything is possible.

Good luck!

ABOUT THE AUTHOR

Paul Tero is a website and computer programmer living with his family in Brighton, England. He grew up in California and studied computer science at UC Berkeley, before moving to Brighton in 1997. He currently mostly works for Existor, the company which makes Cleverbot, a quirky artificial entity which talks back. And he writes occasionally and enjoyably for Smashing Magazine.

ABOUT THE REVIEWER

Ben Dowling is a British software engineer who lives in Mountain View, California. He loves writing code, learning, and launching new products. He is currently a software engineer at Facebook. Prior to that he was lead server engineer at Lightbox.com, co-founder of Geomium. He blogs at coderholic.com and also tweets as @coderholic.

ABOUT THE REVIEWER

Sergey Chikuyonok (@chikuyonok) is a Russian front-end Web developer and writer with a big passion for optimization: from images and JavaScript to working processes and time-savings on coding. He is the developer of the Emmet (ex-Zen Coding) tool.

ABOUT THE REVIEWER

Sean Coates (@coates) has been developing web applications professionally for over a decade. In the past, he's worked as Editor in Chief of PHP Architect magazine, where he also organized PHP conferences. He's long been a contributing member of the PHP community, having worked heavily on the PHP manual in addition to maintaining PEAR and PECL code, and contributes to open source projects.

The Next Steps for Web Typography

Written by Marko Dugonjić

CHAPTER NINE · BY MARKO DUGONJIĆ

THE NEXT STEPS FOR
WEB TYPOGRAPHY

I T'S A CLICHÉ, BUT NEVERTHELESS IT'S TRUE — for many Web designers, this is a time of extreme excitement and personal reward, whether through pioneering new methods and techniques, using technology to automate previously manual processes (where they were possible at all), or establishing new rules and standards. In some respects it's an adventure into the unknown. And do you know what? We are not even halfway there! To be able to design and optimize for each and every angle and perspective known today is next to impossible. There are so many new discoveries about us as individuals and collectively in the fields of biology, psychology, sociology and evolution, that the sentence "There are so many things that have to be done" takes on a completely new meaning. No Web design project is ever complete and there's always room for improvement, whether it's fixing minor usability issues, conversion tweaking or optimizing performance.

Typography is no exception. Indeed, we inherited a lot from our sister field, graphic design, but there are also a myriad of options that haven't been possible until recently. Pardon my enthusiasm, but for me — both as a Web user and as a Web producer — these times are quite exciting!

Here is a quick overview of what we will cover. First, the big picture, the things I wish I'd known much earlier. Not many code examples here:

- Not too frightening context models,
- A list of actors that participate in content creation and publishing.

Then practical details, with plenty code examples and tips:

- Preparation, typefaces and the typographic design in general
- Organization and performance
- Typesetting
- Advanced techniques

Before we get started, one thing to bear in mind is that practicing typography as an isolated discipline can be very intoxicating, especially when diving straight into the tiniest of typeface particularities and historical anecdotes. As the Web in its purest context is multifaceted, let's start by observing typography as an integral part of the bigger picture.

The Big Picture: Universal Typography

In 2012, Tim Brown, type manager at Typekit[1] presented his talk "Universal Typography[2]" in which he explained the nature and the challenges of a Web design process.

He argued that in print design, where the medium and physical variables are inherently fixed, on investigating the options open to you, you can determine the best typographic setup; that is, a typeface, font grade, font weight, font width, letter size, line length, line spacing, hierarchy and layout. And once you have decided, you're more or less done. At the end, there is a single design which is unchangeable. It is permanent. The work

---

1 http://typekit.com
2 http://universaltypography.com/

is then sent off to a print shop and the final result is a physical object that — in absolute terms — looks consistent to everyone.

A book, a magazine or a leaflet have consistent dimensions. Width, height, thickness and weight are the same everywhere in the world. More importantly, we know how to use printed objects, even though in comparison with the digital environment, our options are fixed or more limited. For example, we cannot read text on paper in suboptimal lighting conditions, and we can realistically only carry a limited quantity of printed content with us at any one time.

With Web typography today, there is a vast number of combinations. That's why Brown proposes we investigate our options thinking in terms of acceptable ranges instead of fixed points.

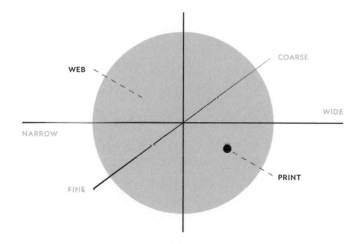

It's easier said than done, however. The Web typographer needs to understand all the facets of context in order to conduct extensive research and find appropriate solutions. The system of axes along which our ranges sit can be quite frightening and it's ever-growing, especially as technology advances and new behavioral patterns are discovered. But worry not. Most of the variables can be addressed and dealt with using a little patience, an occasional look back into history, and a tiny bit of courage to question the status quo.

Think about the responsive nature of any particular web experience as a continuum of being. Along this continuum, on one axis, the experience can grow wide or narrow. Along a different axis, it can be near or far. Along a still different axis, it can be coarse or fine. There are many axes.

— Tim Brown, *"Breakpoints and range rules"*[3]

Simple Multifaceted Model

If we are only concerned with the medium and content, we can then typeset along the basic seven axes that describe the device itself and the basic connection between the device and the reader. These axes are:

- reading distance (viewing distance)
- screen dimensions (viewport width and height)
- content hierarchy
- information density
- pixel density (resolution)
- device orientation
- screen aspect ratio

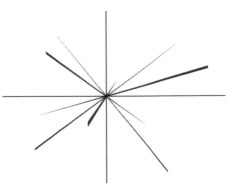

If you think this is already too much, don't worry — that is a normal reaction and you are a completely normal person. Don't let this discourage you, though, and take it as a sign of professional evolution. We should be happy that there's a new toy in our sandbox every morning! It *is* possible to typeset for the Web within this model. It can be done. We can account for the extremes and provide appropriate solutions to create satisfactory results. For the purpose of this journey, we can call this set of methods: *Responsive Web Typography.*

---

3 http://nicewebtype.com/notes/2012/01/27/breakpoints-and-range-rules/

Zoom out a Little More

Carrying on with our theme of creating lists, let's zoom out even further. In February 2013, Cennydd Bowles wrote an article "Designing with Context"[4] on different flavors of context.

- Device
- Environment
- Time
- Activity
- Individual
- Location
- Social

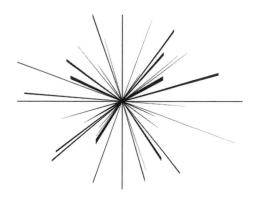

Some comfort is to be had from the combination of these two models despite their explosive mix. What else to say, other than "Congrats on your new job!"

These flavors are very easy to remember thanks to their handy abbreviation: DETAILS. They don't influence typesetting directly, but are food for thought when we make decisions on a more strategic level. In general, UX methodologies can help us understand business goals, the target audience's needs, and find a sweet spot where universality meets originality.

CONTENT

To begin, let's utilize (customer) journey mapping, a tool from the UX field to illustrate the content publishing process from the design perspective. From its conception in the author's mind to the full understanding and comprehension in the reader's, content is on a journey. It is manipulated, tweaked, improved and stylized to send a message across in the most successful manner. This is done by a line of actors which take part in the process and influence the reading experience:

4 http://www.cennydd.co.uk/2013/designing-with-context

- author
- editor
- Web designer
- type designer
- Web font hosting
- OS rendering engine
- browser (or an eBook reader)
- reader

Just being aware of the number of parts and parties involved is an ac-complishment in itself. The sooner we start taking into account all of these factors, the sooner we will be able to let go of the illusion that we can create a one-size-fits-all design. Web typography and Web design in general are about creating the best possible conditions for the majority of users, as long as we are able to preserve adequate experiences for the edge cases. Less than perfect results are acceptable for users at both ends of the bell curve, as long as information is accessible and typography is edible.

In the following sections, we will investigate how typography can be improved at each stage in the content journey.

First, Structure the Content

Having taken stock of the whole picture, with the realization that typog-raphy on its own cannot fix broken patterns missed earlier in the design process, it becomes easier to set up the project with a solid foundation. The foundation for every Web design project is HTML and I'll probably requote many smart people out there when I say CSS-less HTML is the first break-point. An unstyled HTML document that is correctly structured is accessible by default. By using proper semantic markup and by establishing relation-ships between different parts of the content with elements like header, foot-er, section, article and aside, we can create structure and meaning. Even by applying all that markup, the document can still be rendered and it can easily adapt to its container, the browser window.

We all know how to markup a basic HTML document. Yet, there's still so much content on the Web which is not properly structured. For example, the abbreviation element, the non-breaking space, the thin space, the hair space, all of which are still heavily underused. Proper spacing before and after punctuation in initials, initialisms and truncations, even ratio or date and time expressions, can tremendously improve the texture, supplying just the right amount of pause for uninterrupted reading. *E.R.Burroughs, 18.04.2013, e.g.* and *2:3*, as well as *E. R. Burroughs, 18. 04. 2013, e. g.* and *2 : 3* are equally wrong. Instead, we should use the thin space and the hair space between characters. For example:

```
E.&#8202;R. Burroughs
24. 2. 2013.
24.&#8202;1. 2013.
e.&#8202;g.
2&#8202;:&#8202;3
```

E.R. Burroughs	E. R. Burroughs	E. R. Burroughs
24.2.2013.	24. 2. 2013.	24. 2. 2013.
24.1.2013.	24. 1. 2013.	24. 1. 2013.
e.g.	e. g.	e.g.
2:3	2 : 3	2:3

A couple of examples of properly set spaces.

The situation with quotations ("…" instead of "…" and '…' instead of '…') and line pauses (dashes) is a little better now — at least in Web design publications — but we rarely see appropriately applied ranges, for instance *Zagreb–Split* or *9AM–5PM* (both spaced with an en dash), on a mainstream website.

Provide content creators (including yours truly) with tools to help improve their texts by encouraging the proper use of a writing style. There

non-breaking space		
narrow non-breaking	&#8239;	
en-quad	&#8192;	
em-quad	&#8193;	
en-space		
em-space		
three-per-em space	&#8196;	
four-per-em space	&#8197;	
six-per-em space	&#8198;	
figure space	&#8199;	
punctuation space	&#8200;	
thin space		
hair space	&#8202;	&hairsp;
medium mathematical	&#8287;	

A table of spaces available in HTML.

are quite a few reference websites for writers that provide a good starting point for us all, for instance The Chicago Manual of Style Online[5], The Oxford Guide to Style[6] or the more specific UK Government Digital Service content principles[7]. And every Web typographer should write an essay or an article at some point in their career — at least to change perspective and learn how content conception works.

I also encourage you to write. You may not be Tolstoy, but shared thoughts can inspire friends you haven't met yet.

— Jeffrey Zeldman, Offscreen #3, 2012.

5 http://www.chicagomanualofstyle.org/home.html
6 http://smashed.by/oxford-style-guide
7 https://www.gov.uk/designprinciples/styleguide

Working with Editors and Art Directors

In recent years we have witnessed a rise in the use of Web art direction. Naturally, it first started on the personal blogs of Web designers, but now many online magazines have a person onboard who double-checks how content looks and if there are any orphans or widows left, whether they role is art direction, proofreading or anything else. You'll think, "Why should I care? It's the Web!" I know, I know — we have to embrace the fluidity of the Web. But fixing a widowed word at the end of a paragraph is easily done either manually or with a preprocessor[8], by entering a simple   or   between the two last words, so there's really no excuse for not doing so. In editorial environments the chief editor and the art director work together to rephrase, break and reshuffle content in order to facilitate readability[9]. The same process can be applied to every website that goes out. After all, messages need to be edited — both in content and in form — so that they reach the receiver.

Work more closely with content creators and CMS developers to ensure proper text markup is applied, and provide guidelines for establishing rhythm and balance, especially if there are different content types — such as text, photos, videos, graphs or tables — mixed and matched together.

We can go further and design bulletproof templates for whatever markup is generated by the CMS; for example, restrict floated images, ignore font styles and custom bullets. Help develop a CMS that supports content objects that, besides supporting an extensive metadata scheme, also support content sequencing and hierarchy[10].

If this isn't possible, then, at the very least, extend the original content object with specialized sub-objects, a feature now available for some years in a few robust CMSes, for instance in eZ Publish[11].

---

8   http://smashed.by/widont
9   I love Jason Santa Maria's definition of readability: "Do I want to read it?", http://vimeo.com/34178417
10 Gerry Leonidas, The Newest New Typography", http://player.vimeo.com/video/73444208
11 http://ez.no

Get your developers to build a safety net with rigid edit forms that limit design explorations and preserve semantics throughout the CMS. Consult the editor and establish a system of placeholders for the article equipment, such as introductions, important facts (e.g. the most important number), pull-quotes or side-notes and account for different combinations. This might seem redundant, but if content hygiene and style consistency is important, this is the way to do it. If National Public Radio[12] developed an API for its content[13], so too can the rest of us[14].

(Responsive) Web Typographer

As Andrew Clarke once wrote[15], "Responsive Web Design is web design, done right." Likewise, responsive Web typography is Web typography done right. We use the responsive adjective temporarily, just as we one used the phrase *CSS based layouts* until everybody and their neighbor's dog realized that tables were bad for laying out pages. Suffice to say, nowadays everybody refers to layout as *layout*.

The primary role of typography is to provide an interface for the message to be put across to the receiver. How you say it is often more important than the information itself. However, Web typography is not only about browsing font catalogues and smelling freshly baked type specimens (don't tell me you never do that!?). Web typography is primarily concerned about making information accessible, legible and readable. That is why understanding micro-typography is essential. If content can't be read comfortably, style doesn't matter.

There are cases when we can superimpose style over substance. If the content's only purpose is to achieve a short term attraction and a one time call to action, then style *can* be the first thing we should consider, but more

---

12 http://www.npr.org/
13 http://blog.programmableweb.com/2009/10/13/cope-create-once-publish-everywhere/
14 Karen McGrane, Adapting Ourselves to Adaptive Content", http://smashed.by/adaptivecontent
15 http://the-pastry-box-project.net/andy-clarke/2012-january-3/

often than not and especially on the Web, content should be accessible and readable not only now, but in the future, too. At least, that's the idea.

As professional matchmakers between content and the reader, we must understand what has to be covered to design for the reading experience[16]. As we get to know the content, context and the user, consider all of the variables and understand the constraints, limitations and flavors of all the ingredients in a project, as ultimately our choices are informed as a result of covering all of these bases and avoiding the traps. In other words, type-setting is a very rational practice.

Erik Spiekermann likes to say that you only need a color and a typeface and you have a brand. Once we remove all of the flourishes and decorations, the type remains, thus forming the bare essence of visual communication. This is far more evident now that we design for ridiculously cramped mobile screens and adaptive environments. There's no room for intensive visual treatments and add-ons, because it's not viable to carry all that baggage across different media.

Furthermore, we need to relearn how to design for the Web with fewer visual devices and with fewer building materials. After we remove all of the lines, backgrounds, texture and layout, the only thing left is content. That's why typography is so important. Since typography is the face of content, everything else can be stripped down, but typography always stays.

Fortunately, typography is an old and established discipline and there are plenty of resources to learn from. Below is a selection of recommended books, listed approximately in order of ease to read.

- *Inside Paragraphs* by Cyrus Highsmith
- *Thinking with Type* by Ellen Lupton
- *Stop Stealing Sheep and Learn How Type Works* by Erik Spiekermann and E.M. Ginger
- *Detail in Typography* by Jost Hochuli

---

16 http://www.smashingmagazine.com/2013/02/18/designing-reading-experience/

- *The Elements of Typographic Style* by Robert Bringhurst
- *The Stroke* by Gerrit Noordzij
- U&lc: *Influencing Design and Typography*

Meet Type Designers

In May 2013 Jessica Hische wrote an incredibly easy to follow essay "Upping Your Type Game"[17] about selecting typefaces, stressing the importance of selecting a few type designers and sticking to their typefaces. I couldn't agree more. Not only do different typefaces from the same designer usually work well together, but talking to your favorite type designer can bring another perspective into your own process. Type designers have tons of testing and feedback under their belts and we both share the common pain of the publish once, work everywhere imperative. For example, we use @media queries to adjust our designs to different screens; they use hinting to translate bezier curves into a pixel grid. We are frustrated with fragmentation and an ever-increasing number of breakpoints and tweakpoints that are difficult to maintain; they are frustrated with manual hinting at every letter size. We have different browsers; they have different rasterizers. In short, we have a lot in common and they can be a perfect friend if you need a shoulder to cry on.

Type designers can advise you as to what could be the best letter size for your design, how to compensate for the lack of fine spacing control in CSS, what typeface works best in a given situation. They will have a different view on things, because they've seen their typefaces used in many more scenarios than we have. They know who their influences are before they start creating a typeface. And ultimately, they know the history, because they have been part of it.

Small foundries are very easy to reach, but so too are the bigger foundries with their representatives readily available on social networks and at the conference next door.

---

17 http://jessicahische.is/talkingtype

Make it your mission to talk to a type designer or a type manager next time you attend a conference.

If you don't have a chance to meet a type designer in person, Typophile forums[18] are great places to ask questions and get plenty of answers. Elliot Jay Stocks' 8 Faces magazine[19] features interviews with type designers who — apart from giving an insight to their way of thinking — provide the reader with an elaborated selection of their favorite typefaces.

Still not convinced? Here's a comforting self-reflecting quote from Chris Schwartz of Commercial Type[20]:

Back to my earlier question: "How do I think my work will be influenced by the 'new' medium of the Web?"

— Chris Schwartz, Ampersand conference, 2013.

Font Delivery and Distribution

Another group Web designers should talk to are Web font hosting services and distributors. In doing so, Web designers have an opportunity to influence these groups to tailor their services to meet the needs of the market, so that in return they can deliver even better results to their clients through the use of type. We are past the point of having to explain the importance of consistent cross-channel brand experiences to our clients. Brands known world-wide, such as Red Bull or The Guardian are good examples to showcase should you ever require references to reinforce your message.

Web font hosting services also play a key role in the delivery of fonts across the full range of Internet-enabled devices. They are on the business end of the latest technological advances, as they work closely with font foundries to deliver the best possible results.

18 http://typophile.com/
19 http://8faces.com
20 http://commercialtype.com/

They *will* often listen if you have a special request. For example, sub-setting (removing all unnecessary glyphs) is one of the most convenient methods of reducing the font file size and speeding up Web type perfor-mance. If you need a particular subset for a project (for instance, small caps or a lining figures subset), a Web font hosting company might be able to create and deliver a separate font file and make your website feel lightning fast. While that particular service might not be available free of charge, it might not be as expensive either — especially if you can significantly increase the performance of a website.

With the adoption of Web fonts becoming more common and wide-spread, many font foundries have begun to appreciate and understand the importance of performance, resulting in numerous foundries offering Web font services via their own reliable CDNs. Foundries such as Hoefler & Frere-Jones[21], Just Another Foundry[22], Monotype Imaging[23], Typonine[24] and Typotheque[25] have all recently entered the fray and join the usual suspects such as Adobe Edge Web Fonts, Fontdeck, Google Fonts, Typekit, Webink and Webtype who all primarily promote other foundries' Web fonts.

OS Rendering Engine

There's little you can do to influence OS manufacturers, but it's useful to know how different rendering engines affect typography and what we can do to improve legibility. There are currently three major OSes that render type differently: Windows, Mac OS X and iOS. On Apple's OSes both type and Web designers have little control, because the rendering engine com-pletely ignores hinting. This results in somewhat thicker letterforms, but that's acceptable as rendering is reliable and consistent.

---

21 http://www.typography.com/cloud/welcome/
22 http://justanotherfoundry.com/
23 http://www.fontslive.com/
24 http://typonine.com/
25 https://www.typotheque.com/

On Windows, we can improve how type appears on the screen by se-lecting the appropriate font format. For IE6–8 — which use GDI (Windows Graphic Device Interface) ClearType subpixel rendering — the only viable options at smaller sizes are well-hinted[26] TrueType Web fonts. However, there is one problem. GDI ClearType improves rendering only along the horizontal axis, because red, green and blue subpixels are only available in that direction. To better understand the effects of this, zoom into a screen-shot of text and observe the orange and blue halo around a curved letter, such as O. The halo is only present in the horizontal direction and is the result of subpixel rendering.

On the vertical axis ClearType uses the most primitive black-and-white rendering (instead of grayscale rendering, which is an interme-diate anti-aliasing solution). The effect is easily noticed at the top and bottom of curves in some letters, like o, p and b, where steps and jags ruin the shape, especially when display type is set at a large size. As GDI ClearType is dependent on good hinting, and well-hinted fonts are hard to find, using tried and tested fonts such as Georgia or Verdana for body copy combined with a Web font for headlines and subheads at larger sizes makes perfect sense.

PostScript fonts — which use a different type of hinting — are better for large sizes and oval shapes in IE6–8. Unlike TrueType fonts, Post-Script fonts are not rendered with GDI ClearType, but instead fall back to grayscale rendering, which yields better results in the vertical direction, thereby improving the overall appearance of shapes. Some foundries and services, such as JAF[27] and Typekit, deliver different formats depending on the use of the typeface.

Self-hosted Web fonts can be embedded with two different formats for IE6–8, using TrueType font files for content elements set at smaller sizes (about 14px and below) and PostScript font files for elements set at

---

26 Hints are built-in instructions that ensure correct positioning of character shapes within the pixel grid.
27 http://justanotherfoundry.com/

larger sizes (about 18px and up). The full procedure of converting files for different uses is well-explained in the wax-o blog article "Font-face rendering problem in chrome and firefox: use postscript outlines"[28]. A word of caution: double-check the font's EULA to ensure you are allowed to make such changes.

For proper subpixel anti-aliasing, the rendering engine takes information about the background into account, and so text that sits on a transparent or semi-transparent layer needs to be anti-aliased against the color that shows through from the layer in the background. Apple even disables it on the Mac OS X translucent menu bar. So, if rendering seems a little off, opacity at less than 100% combined with a difficult background might be the reason.

Finally, in my research I came across a few unofficial sources who claimed iOS ditched subpixel rendering in favor of standard anti-aliasing, because subpixel rendering is only possible in a native direction. Supporting subpixel anti-aliasing in only one direction would obviously ruin consistency in different device orientations. Indeed, if you take a screenshot from within an iOS device and zoom in, you will see the light gray pixels in place of the orange and baby-blue pixels.

However, if you zoom into a photo taken with a simple smartphone camera, the orange and blue colored fringes are evident. For instance, on Retina iPhones, the horizontal subpixels BGR (blue, green, red[29]) sequence is clearly visible when viewed in portrait, while on iPads the same sequence occurs when viewed in landscape (with the volume control buttons facing up).

I should probably stop at this point, because I can only speculate that the built-in screenshot app flattens the edge pixels to the respective shades of gray. But whatever seems to be the case, when it comes to typography ignore the device specs and trust your good judgment.

---

28 http://smashed.by/postscript

29 While displays exist in different sub-pixels patterns, for instance horizontal RGB, horizontal BGR, vertical RGB and vertical BGR — horizontal RGB is the most common. http://en.wikipedia.org/wiki/Subpixel_rendering

Browsers

Different browsers use different defaults to handle typography. I know, tell me something new. However, the situation is not as horrible as it used to be back in the early 2000s, because browser vendors now listen to — and collaborate with — designers and developers. Even the once closed IE development team released a couple of nifty typography demos that can be found at Use The Whole Font[30].

As important as it is to stay in the loop with the latest updates, it's also essential to participate with feature requests, bug reports, case studies and compatibility tests. Many conferences and meet-ups for Web developers are sponsored by browser vendors and they usually send a technical evangelist to present the latest developments. Talk to them during the breaks, via email or social networks. Even if they may not have the answer to your particular question, they will certainly forward you on to someone within their organization who will. The best conversation starter with a technical evangelist is to have a ready-made test page with both live examples and screenshots. Easy!

The main differences in typographic defaults across browsers are in supported font formats, font loading behavior and legibility options. A discussion about font formats would well exceed an already intensive chapter (I did warn you I was enthusiastic about the topic), but I'll explain how to manage differences with loading behavior a little later. Let's just focus on legibility and rendering for a moment.

text-rendering Property

If you haven't been sleeping under a rock for the past few years, you are then probably familiar with the text-rendering CSS property[31] that can be set to enable kerning and ligatures. While Internet Explorer and Opera don't support text-rendering at the time of writing, it is applied by default

---

30 http://ie.microsoft.com/testdrive/graphics/opentype/
31 https://developer.mozilla.org/en-US/docs/Web/CSS/text-rendering

in Firefox. The auto value in Firefox is treated as optimizeLegibility (which enables kerning and common ligatures, but slows down the page load and scrolling), while in Chrome and Safari the auto value is treated as optimizeSpeed (which disables kerning and common ligatures in favor of better performance).

This property has been reported to cause a number of issues, though. text-rendering can dramatically slow down page loads if applied to longer texts. Throw in a font-variant: small-caps; and some custom letter-spacing and it occasionally produces unpredictable results. My rule of thumb has been to apply text-rendering to headlines and subheads only, or simply filter out the less capable devices via media queries. An orthodox standardista in me has another minor issue — this property is actually not part of the CSS standard, but rather the SVG standard. Interrobang!

The same effect can be achieved using the more suitable and future-friendly properties font-kerning and font-feature-settings:

```
body {
        -webkit-font-kerning: normal;
        -moz-font-kerning: normal;font-kerning: normal;
        -webkit-font-feature-settings: "liga";
        -moz-font-feature-settings: "liga", "kern";
        font-feature-settings: "liga", "kern";
        /* IE 10 supports the standard property name */
    }
```

Browser-specific Legibility Improvements

For the unsung heroes among us who feel comfortable with managing different CSS rules for different browsers, there are a few tricks we can apply to improve the appearance of fonts.

The easiest way to tweak rendering in Safari and Chrome in Mac OS X is with the -webkit-font-smoothing property and its values of none, sub-pixel-antialiased (the default), and antialiased. The antialiased value results in thinner glyphs, but with less than optimal rendering of diagonal lines, so it's best avoided with italics:

How razorback-jumping frogs can level six piqued gymnasts!
All questions asked by five watched experts — amaze the judge.

How razorback-jumping frogs can level six piqued gymnasts!
All questions asked by five watched experts — amaze the judge.

How razorback-jumping frogs can level six piqued gymnasts!
All questions asked by five watched experts — amaze the judge.

Different results side by side. Check out the
`-webkit-font-smoothing` test page by Christoph Zillgens[32].

```
body { -webkit-font-smoothing: antialiased; }
```

`text-shadow` improves text antialiasing in Chrome on Windows. The shadow has no effect on the Mac:

```
body { text-shadow: 1px 1px #fff; }
/* Replace the color with the background color */
```

Legibility in Firefox can be improved by adding a combination of text shadows[33]:

```
body { text-shadow: 0px 0px 0px #777, 0px 0px 1px #ddd; }
```

How razorback-jumping frogs can level six piqued gymnasts! All
questions asked by five watched experts — amaze the judge.

How razorback-jumping frogs can level six piqued gymnasts! All
questions asked by five watched experts — amaze the judge.

How razorback-jumping frogs can level six piqued gymnasts! All
questions asked by five watched experts — amaze the judge.

Different rendering with text-shadow in Firefox.

---

32   http://files.christophzillgens.com/webkit-font-smoothing.html
33   http://dribbble.com/shots/99803-text-shadow-hackery

text-size-adjust Property

Most modern browsers implemented a text inflation algorithm to fix the mobile experience for websites that sport a fixed layout (D'oh!). We can opt out from this behavior with the text-size-adjust property. However, if the value is set to none, it will prevent zooming in[34], so be extra cautious when using it.

```
body {
        -webkit-text-size-adjust: 100%;
        -moz-text-size-adjust: 100%;
        -ms-text-size-adjust: 100%;
        text-size-adjust: 100%;
}
```

Readers of the World

When designing for print, no matter how big the edition is, it's still limited. Designing for the Web means designing for everyone, everywhere and — in theory — anytime in the future. Unlike with print editions, we cannot plan and control the distribution of websites that we build. Designing for an international audience means understanding there are significant differences.

The work that goes into maintaining a multi-lingual website, such as BBC World Service[35] is simply astonishing. Not only are there different writing directions, but also cultural particularities too, such as the prohibition on depictions of living beings for the purpose of worship in Islam. Taking such factors into consideration certainly places even more emphasis on typography.

Unlike cursive writing based on the Latin alphabet, the standard Arabic style is to have a substantially different shape depending on whether it will be

---

34   http://smashed.by/webkit-text-size
35   http://www.bbc.co.uk/worldservice/languages/index.shtml

connecting with a preceding and/or a succeeding letter, thus all primary letters have conditional forms (allographs), depending on whether they are at the beginning, middle or end of a word, so they may exhibit four distinct forms (initial, medial, final or isolated).

Source: http://en.wikipedia.org/wiki/Arabic_alphabet

Even if only the local audience is to be targeted and the designer is familiar with the language, it is crucial for the designer to go out and observe people. You don't have to be trained to conduct comprehensive user interviews or contextual inquiries. A less formal approach is completely acceptable. Simply spend some time among the general public and you should get a valuable insight into people's behavior. Pretend that you are a spy. Stand near a kiosk to see what newspapers are read and how cover pages influence buying choices. Observe how much time people spend reading a book in the park. Learn what kinds of topics are consumed and in which contexts. Public transportation is ideal for this, as people usually isolate themselves while diving deep into content, whether it's text, music or video. Visit a library or watch people in the waiting room at the doctor's or hairdresser's. These are all methods of research for any design project.

When we design with typography, a good test is to simply ask someone to read the text out loud. If they struggle with otherwise easy to read text and the reading pace is uneven, that's a sure sign something is standing in the way. The solution might be as simple as tweaking letter-spacing, shortening the line length or widening the gutter between two columns.

Another great test is to present a person with a document and ask them to find some information buried within it as quickly as possible. Or you can ask them to read text within a limited timeframe and then ask them a set of questions to test whether they were able to find and comprehend all of the important facts.

While it's not necessary to undertake this kind of research on each and every project, observing how people read and share content usually improves your perspective and understanding.

So, can we measure if a design is successful? Dr. Kevin Larson of Microsoft and Dr. Rosalind Picard of MIT conducted research to explore the effect of good typography. In a study "The Aesthetics of Reading"[36] (PDF) they divided 20 participants into two groups. Each group had to read a document, with one group receiving a well-typeset version, and the other receiving a poorly typeset version. They conducted two studies to confirm the results. Any ideas as to the outcome?

Well, here comes a little surprise. The reading time and comprehension was the same in both groups. However, the group who read the well-typeset version performed better when it came to relative subjective duration — they underestimated the reading time more — and so were more capable of completing creative tasks, such as the candle task[37] and the remote associates task[38] (even though the results in the later test were not statistically reliable). In plain English, good typography induces good mood.

Now that We are All Friends...

You should be convinced by now that design is not just a solitary activity. We can best learn about a project's needs if we go out, exchange ideas and watch users on both sides of the content journey. Learn to see the big picture and the decisions about technology, performance or type selection will become much easier to make. Keep your eyes open and patterns will start to emerge. Once you become comfortable in spotting them, you will learn that there are oceans of details you can cover to improve typography. So now let's look at the more practical methods.

PRACTICAL DETAILS

To establish a design direction, we first need to evaluate the content. Apart from reading the text, which should be the most obvious first step, we can gauge text

---

36 http://affect.media.mit.edu/pdfs/05.larson-picard.pdf
37 http://en.wikipedia.org/wiki/Candle_problem
38 http://www.remote-associates-test.com/

with a few handy formulas. Such numeric values can be used to compare text to other similar pieces and give us a better understanding about the text.

Article readability stats[39] is a PHP script that calculates various text properties. It can be easily embedded in your CMS of choice and can therefore automatically calculate reading time, automated readability index and reading ease for every article on a website.

Reading rates range anywhere from under 100 words per minute to a few thousand. An average adult reads 250 words per minute with 70% comprehension[40], so reading time is calculated by dividing the number of words in the text by 250. Simply throw the content for your project into a local installation of your favorite CMS and run it through the script to observe the results based on that average rate. Of course, if the reading rate for your project is different than 250, use the value that suits your target audience to asses the text.

From there on, if it seems that the text won't fit the time format in the expected context (for instance, a 30-minute train ride), we have a few options:

1. Talk to the author and editor to rearrange the text to fit the required time format. This can be done by shortening the article to fit the format or by breaking up the article either into sequels or separate smaller articles that can exist on their own.
2. Break the main text with subheads and pull-quotes. Remove all explanations and examples from within the text and place them outside of the main body as side-notes. This way, readers who are familiar with the topic can quickly run through the article and those who need additional explanation can use side- and footnotes to learn more.
3. Provide the reader with navigation aids such as subheads, metadata and different structures for complementary elements (for instance, lists, data tables and graphs), so they can get important information fast.

---

39 http://www.maratz.com/blog/archives/2012/07/26/article-readability-stats-with-php/
40 Smith, Brenda D. "Breaking Through: College Reading", 7th Ed. Longman, 2004

Macrotypography

After we have qualified content, depending on the findings, we can take a different approach to setting up *macrotypography*.

If the text is easy to read, i.e. scores high at Flesch-Kincaid Reading Ease[41] or low at Automated Readability Index[42] — it means it can be read rather quickly. In this case, there's room for varieties in style. You can select a typeface with plenty of character and layout the document in an unusual way to add interest. The elements can be mixed and matched, as the reader will be able to understand the story.

One such example is a poster (or a website) for an event. The set of information on a typical poster is well-known and clear. For instance, a typical conference website features speakers, attendees, sponsors, topics, schedule, location and a ticket form. Yet, besides providing the visitor with information, its purpose is to stand out in the forest of similar events. Because it serves as a communication tool for some other content (the event), and it's expected to be memorable on a visceral level, we can select a typeface with character.

On the other hand, if the text or the matter is complicated, the layout should be sound and stable and in this case any quirkiness or unexpected typographic extravagance can break the flow of thought. Such text can be broken into components with extensive use of illustration and infography, numbered image captions and clear document outlines. A document that is difficult to read or understand benefits from robust structure.

The easiest way to set up the structure is with our old friends block paragraphs, numbered lists, a clear grid and generous gutters.

For instance, step-by-step how-tos are easiest to follow if each step is accompanied with a clear photo or illustration. It's easy to mess things up here, too. The natural direction of reading for westerners is horizontal, left to right, so it's always better to design each step as a horizontal pair

41 http://en.wikipedia.org/wiki/Flesch-Kincaid_Readability_Test
42 http://en.wikipedia.org/wiki/Automated_Readability_Index

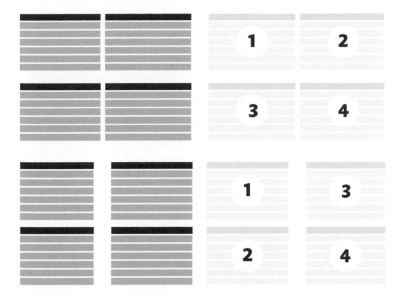

instead of stacking images and text on top of one another. For better clarity, the image and the textual explanation should sit side by side, even if this means using a smaller image to make it fit comfortably into the available horizontal space. There is a big difference between a photo with a caption and a photo as a visual aid for text. In the former case, the photo is the main content, the main point of interest. In the latter case, the image acts as a mere helper, an extension that adds clarity to the main text. If needed, we can always provide a link to a bigger version.

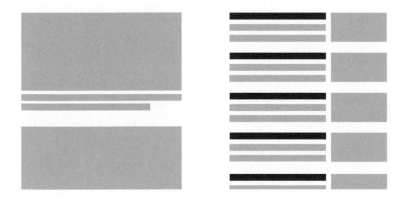

Combining Typefaces

Here comes the fun part — selecting typefaces. The art of choosing and combining typefaces is well-covered in the pocket guide Combining Type-faces[43] by Tim Brown. However, as Brown himself says, it takes practice. A lot of practice.

Once you are able to recognize the classification of any typeface you see, it becomes very easy to combine typefaces, simply because by the time you are able to see the difference, you've learned plenty of other things about typefaces and typography in general. Sorry for the bad news, but the shortcut to successfully selecting and combining typefaces is 10,000 repetitions.

Seriously, the art of selecting typefaces is an art of narrowing down your choices. Your project needs are your criteria. The better you know the project, the pickier you become. After discarding all typefaces that don't have a full character set available, that miss some styles and weights, that won't look as good in a range of sizes, and that are generally rude in the company of other typefaces — you are left with only a few reasonable choices and in the end you only have to pick from a group of two or three.

To select a typeface, we must know how big the pond is. If we watch and recognize only a handful of typefaces all the time, we cannot invent something radically new and we end up with the same conventional de-signs over and over again.

The first step in studying typefaces is to become familiar with the clas-sification of typefaces and the history of typography. It is crucial to study and investigate typefaces from all classifications, even the ones you think you would never use.

For starters, focus on well-established professional typefaces. These are popular for a reason. They work in demanding environments and they resist ageing.

---

43 http://www.fivesimplesteps.com/products/combining-typefaces

*The common mistake is to choose a beautiful typeface, one that looks
attractive, thus favoring form over function. This is putting the cart over
the horse. However strange this sounds, the 'look' of the typeface should be
your least concern.*

— Alessandro Cattaneo, Yves Peters, Jon Tan, Smashing Book #1

A good place to start is visiting various lists:

* Typedia's Explore section lists all type designers and foundries. Start
  with the most popular designers first and then study typefaces by
  each designer: http://typedia.com/explore
* The folks at Typekit created a number of lists that will help you find
  alternatives to common typefaces: https://typekit.com/lists
* FontBook for iPad is another great resource. Fonts are grouped by
  genre, which is super useful if you are looking for a typeface that
  should meet your target audience's expectations:
  http://www.fontshop.com/blog/newsletters/fontbookipad/

Develop Your Type Library

For a seasoned typographer, purchasing typefaces is a big commitment. It's
comparable to buying new clothes in that they should ideally match items
we already have in the closet, and have some durability. Purchase sets that
complement your existing library, otherwise, you may find yourself with
a typeface that will probably never be used, resulting in a couple hundred
dollars' worth of merchandise being thrown out the window.

Successful chameleon designers are very rare and in reality we all have
a distinctive style. Some of us are better at designing one-pagers, while
others are better at designing multifaceted information systems. Some
designers specialize in Web shops, others in Web applications. That's why
it's very important to find and work with a set of typefaces that suit your
particular style and the type of projects you are usually commissioned to

work on. Don't think that famous designers use tons of different typefaces. On the contrary, if you compare their most successful projects, they all use a limited selection of fonts.

It will not be uncommon for you — or any designer for that matter — to end up using fonts from the same foundry or type designer over and over again, because the familiar underlying structure of respective glyphs along with the common DNA will probably best fit your personal typesetting style.

Managing a font library would be a pain without font management software like Fontcase[44] or Linotype FontExplorer X Pro[45]. Once you classify fonts in your library, previewing and testing them should be relatively straightforward. Suffice to say, create a backup of your preference files!

Find Inspiration

Train yourself to spot and recognize typographic patterns. Everywhere we go, we carry our smartphones, so take photos of any interesting typography you spot on the street, in libraries or in book stores. Other valuable sources of inspiration are printed newspapers, fashion magazines or leaflets found in hotel lobbies. Collect each one you see and write a comment about why you took it on a Post-it note. Still not carrying a block of Post-its on your trips? Here's an incentive to start doing so.

Last, but not least, purchase as many specimens as you can and subscribe to every typographic newsletter out there. Over time, you will have a pretty nice reference full of proven and reusable type combinations created by experienced designers and typographers. One autobiographical piece of advice, a form of nostalgia if you will — be extra careful not to be caught drooling over the legs of some rational serif or displaying the beaming smile of a first-time kisser while touching engraved stationery.

---

44 http://www.bohemiancoding.com/fontcase/
45 http://www.fontexplorerx.com

History of Typefaces

A very common piece of advice given by experienced typographers to new-comers is to learn about the history of a typeface. What does that mean? What does a period such as the Renaissance have to do with the project being worked on? Learning about how typefaces came to be through history can also help us understand the anatomy of typefaces. Many type designs were the result of technology and the practical needs of that time. For instance, a typeface with ink traps looks ridiculous on screen, unless its used as a display type to convey a particular message. A typeface that was reproduced in the age of photosetting, when typefaces were designed a little softer, can look less than satisfactory on screen utilizing a rigid grid.

In the creative world, everything is neo-something-from-the-past and everything is a remix[46]. It's natural to reuse old metaphors and design on the shoulders of our glorious predecessors. When a trend emerges, it's useful to learn about its origin. In May 2013, Yves Peters, the editor at Font Feed[47], gave a talk on Trajan Pro as a movie poster typeface[48]. He explained how this trend came to be and foresaw the new trend of using Gotham in movie posters. Both typefaces became popular based on their previous successes — Trajan Pro being a font used in a movie that won an Oscar and Gotham being the official font of President Obama's 2008 election campaign.

Since everything is just another iteration of some previous idea, we can draw connections to the original idea and use a typeface that matches the given period.

Sometimes knowing about the history can help you establish more of a direct connection, too. For example, Arno is a typeface inspired by the early humanist typefaces of the fifteenth and sixteenth centuries, named after the Florentine river. It also proved to be a great match for a website offering

46 http://everythingisaremix.info/
47 http://fontfeed.com/
48 http://vimeo.com/72435170

luxury villas for rent in Dubrovnik, Croatia[49]. Knowing that Dubrovnik in the past has had strong cultural and economic connections to Venice and Florence — which influenced the city's development and prosperity in the fifteenth and sixteenth centuries — made it very easy for us to select Arno as the main typeface for the website.

CSS Organization and Performance

A well-structured HTML document is accessible and satisfies all the basic requirements for the reader, even without CSS. Text can be zoomed, selected, copied and shared. Letter size by default is big enough to be comfortably read at arm's length and the layout is flexible. So the fallbacks are already present and we only need to ensure the enhancements we add don't stand in the way, especially if the browser is less capable or the connection speed is poor.

That said, the best way to manage responsive typography with CSS is to handle the micro-typography and the most common defaults in the main CSS file, while placing all of the breakpoint-specific typography into separate files.

The main CSS file should contain the default rules for:

- font stack
- document hierarchy
- relative letter sizes for headlines, subheads, captions and side-notes
- best-guess line height based on the optimal line length
- maximum widths for content elements

A breakpoint-specific CSS file can contain:

- different typographic scale values based on information density
- line height overrides based on increased (or decreased) line length
- layout-specific rules

49 http://dubrovnikapartmentsvillas.com

The first thing that's always recommended is to reset margins and padding. Whether you prefer to use Eric Meyer's reset.css[50] or a more radical asterisk reset, the goal is to take full control over the document. It might seem like overkill at first, but it forces us to revisit all of the elements and to take care of the tiniest of details.

```
* { margin: 0; padding: 0 }
html { font-size: 100%; line-height: 1.5em; }
```

Since the ideal line length is somewhere around 66 characters[51], we can limit the maximum width of the basic block of text to 33em, given that an average character width is around half an em. To keep things relatively safe and simple, the bottom margin on block level elements can be set to the same value as the line height, which in this case is 1.5em. This way, we preserve the vertical rhythm — a repeating pattern our brains are used to — helping our eyes to jump double the line height and not some arbitrary length, that's off-rhythm.

```
article { max-width: 33em; }
p, ul, ol, dl, table { margin-bottom: 1.5em; }
```

We can also extend the `max-width` rule a little more for international audiences. Based on Vasilis van Gemert's article "*Logical Breakpoints For Your Responsive Design*"[52], Jordan Moore came up with the idea of language-based line lengths[53]. Since the ideal line length might vary from language to language, we can apply language-specific line length maximum values:

```
article { max-width: 33em; }
:lang(de) article { max-width: 40em; }
```

---

50 http://meyerweb.com/eric/tools/css/reset/
51 http://smashed.by/66char
52 http://www.smashingmagazine.com/2013/03/01/logical-breakpoints-responsive-design/
53 http://www.jordanm.co.uk/post/44359705696/responding-to-language

BASELINE GRIDS

To help us compose to a vertical rhythm, we can create a repeating pattern in the background and adjust the baseline grid to our needs. We used to create a GIF for this, but today we can dynamically create gradients in CSS.

```
html {
    background-image: -webkit-linear-gradient(top, #fff 0, #fff 95%, #f00
95%, #f00 100%);
    background-image: -moz-linear-gradient(top, #fff 0, #fff 95%, #f00
95%, #f00 100%);
    background-image: linear-gradient(top, #fff 0, #fff 95%, #f00 95%,
#f00 100%);
    background-repeat: repeat-y; background-size: 100% 24px;
/* Background size height equals rendered line height at the respective
breakpoint */
        }
```

Web designers find it very hard to compose to a vertical rhythm and I agree. It's not the easiest skill out there to master, but this doesn't mean we should give up.

Daniel Eden and Matt Wilcox each developed jQuery plugins[54][55] that calculate bottom margins of images that fall out of the rhythm. With more and more solutions like these, there is no excuse not to align everything to a baseline grid. At first, it's a struggle, but over time, composing to a baseline grid becomes second nature.

Fonts as a Progressive Enhancement

With a fair share of browsers still unable to handle Web fonts optimally (e.g. Android 2.2–2.4) or lacking support for more advanced features (e.g. data URI in IE6–8), Web fonts should be considered a progressive enhancement. They still don't work optimally outside the box and to make them work properly we occasionally need to use complicated syntax.

---

54 Baseline.js by Daniel Eden https://github.com/daneden/Baseline.js
55 jQuery Baseline Align by Matt Wilcox https://github.com/MattWilcox/jQuery-Baseline-Align

By default, the browser doesn't have to download a font to render a Web page, it will use what's already available there. Our custom Web font is an override and as such can sometimes render some unwelcome effects, like the *flash of unstyled text (FOUT)*.

Google and Typekit collaborated to create the Web Font loader[56], a JavaScript library that works with most Web font services as well as with self-hosted fonts. It is very simple to use and, in the case of Typekit, it's already built into the standard embeddable snippet. If you are self-hosting or using another service, the following code should be pasted into the <head> of the document:

```
<script type="text/javascript">
        WebFontConfig = {
                custom: {families: 'Font Family Name', 'Another Font Fa-
mily'], urls: 'http://domain.com/fonts.css']}
        };

        (function() {
        var wf = document.createElement('script');
        wf.src = ('https:' == document.location.protocol ? 'https' :
'http') + '://ajax.googleapis.com/ajax/libs/webfont/1/webfont.js';
        wf.type = 'text/javascript';
        wf.async = 'true';
        var s = document.getElementsByTagName('script')[0];
        s.parentNode.insertBefore(wf, s);
        })();
</script>
```

Then you have three classes at your disposal: `.wf-loading`, `.wf-active` and `.wf-inactive` that are set on the <html> element. The most interesting class is `.wf-loading` which is used to control what happens until the Web font is downloaded and applied to text. Here's an example:

---

56 https://developers.google.com/fonts/docs/webfont_loader

```
.wf-loading h1 { visibility: hidden; }
/* — or — */
.wf-loading h1 { font-family: 'A fallback font'; }
```

When creating font stacks, the best results are achieved if: selected type-faces belong to the same classification; and each respective character covers the same amount of physical space. This means an appropriate fallback font will posses the following qualities, sorted by importance:

- matching x-height
- similar character width
- similar letter space

A bulletproof font stack should contain the first choice typeface, the nearest alternative, platform-specific alternatives, universal alternatives and finally a generic alternative. If you are self-hosting Web fonts, the great Font Squirrel Webfont Generator[57], among other options, lets you fix vertical metrics and resize glyphs to match the x-height of the selected Web-safe font (Arial, Verdana, Trebuchet, Georgia, Times New Roman and Courier).

Subsetting

We can dramatically improve performance by reducing the file sizes of Web fonts and by reducing the number of HTTP requests (we'll come to that in a minute). It is also common for a font file to contain multiple scripts that are neither always necessary nor required. If only a subset of glyphs from a font file are needed, why download the whole font?

Some Web font services offer subsets, like small caps or lining figures as separate fonts. Others let you select the character ranges you require prior to exporting. While this is a great step forward, in most cases it's still not always possible to subset fonts on a glyph-by-glyph basis.

---

57 http://www.fontsquirrel.com/tools/webfont-generator

If Web fonts are self-hosted, we can subset them with FF Subsetter[58] or the aforementioned Font Squirrel. Both tools let you select and preview characters that you require in the font, as well as remove hinting, kerning and optional glyphs, such as old-style numerals. Even though all these options are available, that doesn't mean they have to be utilized. Be careful not to cripple the font by removing punctuation, hyphens, spaces and other common non-alphabetic symbols. If the built-in kerning is removed, the typeface will look less than satisfactory on Windows. Even the text-rendering or font-kerning properties won't know how to handle kerning pairs properly. Clearly, we should never sacrifice the quality of rendering, so there will be times when you'll have to face the facts and simply use a Web-safe font.

Base64 Encoding

Another way to optimize performance is to reduce the number of HTTP requests by including a Web font as a Base64-encoded string in the main CSS file. Data URIs are supported in modern browsers (IE9 and up), so you can serve separate font files for IE8 and the predecessors, or omit Web fonts in older browsers. Some high profile websites, like The Guardian and GOV.UK use this method to serve their Web fonts.

```
@font-face {
        font-family: "My Font";
        src: url("data:font/opentype;base64,[base-encoded font here]");
}
```

Again, Font Squirrel is a great service that does all the heavy lifting for you. It can subset and Base64-encode fonts, export all necessary font formats, create a CSS file with fallback options for older browsers, as well as create a sample specimen.

---

58 http://www.subsetter.com/

Content-based Media Query Breakpoints

To determine where to introduce breakpoints, we can refer to a quote by Jeremy Keith[59], co-founder and technical director at Clearleft:

> *Breakpoints should not be dictated by devices, but by content. Let the content decide when to expand and then adjust your designs.*

In practice, this means that we can start with the default media query-less, 100%-wide column of text, with or without an aforementioned max-width limit. This way the content will fill up the screen on sizes smaller than the max-width limit and leave more room for additional columns on screens wider than the max-width value. When it hits the max-width mark, we have two options. First, we can start increasing the white space (for instance, with the margin: auto; rule) until there's enough room to comfortably fit in a new column. Second, we can introduce a new breakpoint right away, shrinking the original column to an acceptable minimum, while fitting a new column into the remaining space.

There is an important trade-off when selecting between these two options. With more controlled layouts, the information density is much lower, which might be counter-effective, especially in Web applications or anything else that is supposed to provide plenty of information quickly. On the other hand, it's much harder to keep the line length within optimal limits with fully flexible layouts, and it usually results in many more breakpoints and tweakpoints being set. As always, your project's needs should influence this decision.

Calculating the ideal line length is not the easiest of things to do. That's why Trent Walton proposes adding asterisks after the 45th and 75th characters in a paragraph[60], which makes life easier when observing content that reflows at different breakpoints.

---

59 http://www.lukew.com/ff/entry.asp?1393
60 http://trentwalton.com/2012/06/19/fluid-type/

Some users zoom into websites. To allow for proportional scaling with zoomed-in text, we can use ems instead of pixels as proposed by Lyza Gardner in her article "*The EMs have it: Proportional Media Queries FTW!*"[61]. The effect takes place when text is zoomed in and the lower breakpoint condition is met. For example, let's say our ideal breakpoints for a project are at 600, 800 and 1,000 pixels. If we divide pixel values by the root font size, which in this example will be 16px, the em-based query values would be 37.5, 50 and 62.5ems respectively.

```
@media only screen and (min-width: 37.5em) { } /* 600px */
@media only screen and (min-width: 50em)   { } /* 800px */
@media only screen and (min-width: 62.5em) { } /* 1000px */
```

Despite the fact they have changed the way we plan and build websites from the ground up, media queries are still not the final solution. They are perfect for introducing different layouts, but the content units should behave in a certain way depending on their available space, not just going by the overall screen size. One typical example is a data table that can be easily turned into a definition list on a small, 300px wide screen, but at the same time can't be rearranged in the same manner when placed in a narrow, 300px-wide sidebar on a bigger screen. Can you see the problem here? How can we query that? [62]

Andy Hume came up with the concept of responsive containers[63] which he elaborates on his blog, so I won't go into the exact details here. For now, rest assured that the problem was detected and some smart people are working on the solution. Fingers crossed it becomes part of the CSS standard.

---

61 http://blog.cloudfour.com/the-ems-have-it-proportional-media-queries-ftw/

62 There's a handful of jQuery plugins available, e.g. http://kumailht.com/responsive-elements/

63 http://blog.andyhume.net/responsive-containers/

White Space Hierarchy

There are three white spaces within a paragraph that are interdependent — letter space, word space and line space. If any one of the three is changed, all the others should be reassessed, too. By preserving the hierarchy between the white spaces, we can achieve the best reading experience for various scenarios (variable tempo, different line lengths).

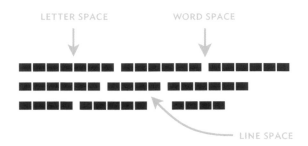

Illustration of white spaces

Font Size, Leading and Measure

Another fundamental relationship is the interconnection between font size, line height and line length. The line length is dictated by a combination of font size and the available horizontal space within a container. The longer the line, the more space we need between successive lines and vice versa. As a result of these dependencies, if any of the three is changed, all the others should be reassessed, too.

As every Web designer knows, the satisfactory line length is between 45 to 75 characters per line[64]. It's a common thing among Web designers to space such lines with a line height of 1.5ems, give or take. The trouble is, we can barely fit 40 characters on a mobile screen. The line height of 1.5 combined with such a short line length results in too generous spacing. If a paragraph looks like a list, reduce the spacing between lines.

---

64 http://smashed.by/webtypo

Line height for each breakpoint is adjusted according to the line length rendered at that breakpoint. Short line lengths require tighter line spacing, because the reader's eye doesn't have to travel much to reach the next line of text. As line length gets longer, more line spacing is required.

Line height for each breakpoint is adjusted according to the line length rendered at that breakpoint. Short line lengths require tighter line spacing, because the reader's eye doesn't have to travel much to reach the next line of text. As line length gets longer, more line spacing is required.

How tight is too tight? Test this with a row of letters q or p followed by a row of bs or ds. For international audiences you might want to enter an upper-case with a diacritic, for instance Š.

Obviously, there are natural boundaries for both line length and line height. While we need to reduce line height at short line lengths, we should be careful not to clash extenders in consecutive rows.

Line length can be easily controlled with min- and max-width in CSS, but there is currently only one fixed value available for line height in CSS. In spite of that, we *can* tweak font size, line height and bottom margin with media queries, depending on the line length at any given breakpoint. The paragraph code at different breakpoints would look something like this:

```
@media only screen and (min-width: 37.5em) {
    p {
        font-size: 1rem; /* 16px */
        line-height: 1.4;
        margin-bottom: 1.4em; /* = line-height */
    }
}
@media only screen and (min-width: 50em) {
    p {
        font-size: 1.125rem; /* 18px */
        line-height: 1.45;
        margin-bottom: 1.45em; /* = line-height */
    }
}
```

```
@media only screen and (min-width: 62.5em) {
        p {
                font-size: 1.312rem; /* 21px */
                line-height: 1.5;
                margin-bottom: 1.5em; /* = line-height */
        }
}
```

Still, this is not the best solution and it greatly depends on the number of breakpoints. The more breakpoints we introduce, the better the experience is. But wouldn't it be easier if such mathematically simple rules were applied automagically?

Molten Leading

In "Molten leading (or, fluid line-height)[65]", Tim Brown proposed range rules for line height in CSS, which would enable designers to specify line height limits and let the browser reflow the text following the changes of the fluid width of the container. He suggested a new pair of CSS properties min- and max-line-height, which would behave similarly to min- and max-width. As we will see later in the chapter, the CSS3 Working Draft introduced another approach for dealing with range values.

Based on Brown's idea, Mat Marquis made Molten Leading[66], a jQuery plugin that solves that problem. The syntax is as easy as:

```
$('p').moltenLeading({
        minline: 1.4,
        maxline: 1.7
});
```

Paragraph Styles

If the text is straightforward and linear, and thoughts are tightly connected, we can use an alternative more intimate way to divide paragraphs.

65 http://nicewebtype.com/notes/2012/02/03/molten-leading-or-fluid-line-height/
66 https://github.com/Wilto/Molten-Leading

This becomes especially handy at small screen sizes, where not many bits of information compete for the reader's attention.

```
p { margin-bottom: 0; }
p + p { text-indent: 1em; }
```

This example is just a simple trick to cram more content into a screen without sacrificing readability. To learn about many more options to style paragraphs on the Web, definitely check out Jon Tan's "*12 Examples of Paragraph Typography*"[67] and the Web typography chapter he co-authored in Smashing Book #1[68].

Letter Spacing

By default, letters on screen can appear too close to one another, especially on high pixel density screens. This can be improved quite easily by using the letter-spacing property. Mobile Safari on the iPhone accepts letter-spacing increments of 0.01ems, which comes in handy on iOS devices.

While IE7+ and newer versions of Firefox are capable of rendering such tiny increments, the coarseness of the 96dpi screen usually produces less than satisfactory results, so it's better to reserve such nuances for high-dpi screens only.

```
@media only screen and (-webkit-min-device-pixel-ratio: 1.5),
   only screen and (min-device-pixel-ratio: 1.5) {
      p  {
            font-size: 1rem;
            line-height: 1.5;
            letter-spacing: 0.01em;
            word-spacing: 0.01em;
         }
   }
```

---

67 http://v1.jontangerine.com/silo/typography/p/
68 https://shop.smashingmagazine.com/smashing-book.html

Correctly spaced letters and words should be invisible to a non-trained eye, so if the average reader can spot the gaps between letters, you probably went too far.

Hyphenation and Justification

To equalize individual line lengths, paragraphs can be set justified. To prevent gaps between words in a justified setting, the text should be hyphenated. Basic hyphenation and justification is possible in all modern browsers:

```
p {
        text-align: justify;
        -webkit-hyphens: auto;
        -moz-hyphens: auto;
        -ms-hyphens: auto;
        hyphens: auto;
}
```

Unfortunately, this is not enough and the result is far from acceptable. Apart from hyphenation, the line rhythm in a justified paragraph should be preserved with a combination of variable word spacing, letter spacing and character widths. We can get away without using variable character widths, but variable spacing is a must for a properly justified paragraph. This is yet another example where min- and max- properties could come into play, for instance:

```
p {
        text-align: justify;
        min-word-spacing: -0.05em;
        max-word-spacing: 0.1em;
        min-letter-spacing: -0.01em;
        max-letter-spacing: 0.02em;
}

/* A concept code */
```

CSS3 Text Module Level 3 Working Draft [69] proposes the new spacing-limit value type, which represents optimum, minimum, and maximum spacing in word-spacing and letter-spacing. The syntax in this case would be:

```
p {
        text-align: justify;
        word-spacing: 0 -0.05em 1em;
        letter-spacing: 0 -0.01em 0.02em;
}

/* optimum, minimum, maximum respectively */
```

Another problem with hyphenation is the lack of fine-grained control over the severity and occurrence of hyphenation. It's considered a type crime when more than three successive rows are hyphenated. Additionally, Robert Bringhurst, the author of *The Elements of Typographic Style* [70] suggests that at least three characters of the hyphenated word should be taken to the next line.

CSS3 Paged Media Working Draft [71] proposed a few interesting properties (there are more, but I've found these to be the most important):

- hyphenate-before specifies a minimum number of characters in a word before the hyphenation character
- hyphenate-after specifies a minimum number of characters in a word after the hyphenation character
- hyphenate-lines specifies a maximum number of successive hyphenated lines in an element

If these were supported by browsers, the subsequent set of CSS rules would look like this:

69 http://smashed.by/spacing
70 http://smashed.by/bringhurst
71 http://smashed.by/hyphen

```
p {
        hyphens: auto;
        hyphenate-before: 2;
        hyphenate-after: 3;
        hyphenate-lines: 3;
}
```

CSS Text Level 4 Editor's Draft from 2013[72] proposes the extension to hyphenate-before and hyphenate-after in the form of a hyphenate-limit-chars property which would take three values: the required minimum for the total characters in a word; and the minimum number of characters in a word before and after the hyphenation. The same draft renames the hyphenate-lines property to hyphenate-limit-lines which at the time of writing is supported in IE10 and Safari.

For now, the best results for the user are still achieved ither with manual hyphenation. To manually hyphenate text, simply insert the soft hyphen ­ (or ­) wherever is convenient. If there's a need for a word break, the browser will insert the hyphen character. It works as advertised in all modern browsers.

```
oto&#173;rhino&#173;laryngo&#173;logy

p { hyphens: manual; }
```

COMBINING PSEUDO-ELEMENTS WITH THE CONTENT PROPERTY

I'm a big fan of combining pseudo-elements with the content property.[73] Even though they are not supported in older browsers, we can use them to achieve a better control over hanging symbols, quotation marks and multi-level numbering.

---

72 http://dev.w3.org/csswg/css-text-4/#hyphenation
73 http://www.w3.org/TR/CSS21/generate.html

Hanging Symbols and Numbers

Instead of relying on the `list-style` property which we cannot control, we can use the `:before` pseudo-element to add bullets or en dashes before text in list items and regain full control over such symbols. Options are now limitless and one that immediately comes to mind is using a different shade of gray for the hanging bullet.

```
li {
        list-style: none;
}
ul li:before {
        content: "–"; /* en dash */
        float: left;
        margin-left: -1em;
        color: #999;
}

ol { counter-reset: item }
/* "item" is an arbitrary variable, by default equals zero */

ol li:before {
        content: counter(item) ". ";
        counter-increment: item; /* equals item++ */
        float: left;
        margin-left: -1em;
}
```

Quotation Marks

Following the same principle from the previous section, we can add a pinch of elegance to blockquotes.

```
blockquote:before {
        content: """;
        font-size: 4em;
        color: #eee;
        float: left;
        margin: -.33em 0 0 -.5em;
}
```

```
/* — or — */

blockquote p:first-child: before {
        content: """;
        font-size: 4em;
        color: #eee;
        float: left;
        margin: -.33em 0 0 -.5em;
}
blockquote p:last-child: after { content: """; }
```

To provide a pair of quotation marks for each respective language along with their nested alternatives, we would use the :lang selector:

```
q:lang(de) { quotes: '„' '"' ',' '"' }
q:lang(en-gb) { quotes: "'" "'" '"' '"' }
q:lang(en-us) { quotes: '"' '"' "'" "'" }
q:lang(fr) { quotes: '« ' ' »' '"' '"' }
q:before { content: open-quote }
q:after  { content: close-quote }
```

Each language has its own set of rules, so I encourage you to check out "Non-English usage of quotation marks" [74] at Wikipedia.

Automatic Multilevel Numbering

Automatic numbering in multilevel content provides readers with an easy to follow outline and enforces hierarchy. With automatic numbering, styling ordered list items in a "1., 1.1., 1.1.1." fashion becomes ridiculously easy.

```
ol { counter-reset: item }
ol li { display: block }
ol li:before {
        content: counters(item, ".") ". ";
        counter-increment: item;
}
```

---

74 http://en.wikipedia.org/wiki/Non-English_usage_of_quotation_marks

Vladimir Simović goes a little further and explains how to apply automatic numbering to headings[75] which is very useful for eBook publishing.

```css
body { counter-reset: subhead1; }

h1:before {
    content: counter(subhead1) " ";
    counter-increment: subhead1;
}
h1 {
    counter-reset: subhead2;
}
h2:before {
    content: counter(subhead1) "." counter(subhead2) " ";
    counter-increment: subhead2;
}
h2 {
    counter-reset: subhead3;
}

h3:before {
    content: counter(subhead1) "." counter(subhead2) "."
        counter(subhead3) " ";
    counter-increment: subhead3;
}
```

HIERARCHY

You never would have guessed! Typography can help with inaugurating a document structure, too. Subheads provide the reader with a clue about the content that follows; side- and footnotes provide us with additional explanations of the key terms inside the text; and captions provide descriptions for figures, data tables and graphs. All these elements form part of the typographic hierarchy.

---

75 http://smashed.by/css-headings

Modular Scales

The most common way to establish hierarchy is with a typographic scale. Tim Brown created Modular Scale[76], an online calculator that returns a series of related values based on a given body copy size and any of several common mathematical scales and musical intervals. The calculator is named after the typographic concept of the same name. As Brown said in his article "*More Meaningful Typography*"[77]:

> *A modular scale is a sequence of numbers that relate to one another in a meaningful way.*

For the purpose of this chapter, I selected 16px as the ideal text size, and the 2:3 perfect fifth scale, which gave me an array of useful values: 7.111, 10.667, 16 (the initial value), 24, 36, and 54. Translated to rems and applied to subheads and captions in CSS, they look like this:

```
h4 { font-size: 1rem }
h3 { font-size: 1.5rem }
h2 { font-size: 2.25rem }
h1 { font-size: 3.375rem }

caption { font-size: 0.667rem }
small   { font-size: 0.444rem }
```

Subhead Styles

While a typographic scale combined with different font weights is a great way to establish hierarchy and balance on large screens, such variety can stand in the way on small screens. With large screens there are many more informational elements and the main content can often compete with advertisements and other related or unrelated content.

---

76 http://modularscale.com
77 http://www.alistapart.com/articles/more-meaningful-typography/

On smaller screens there are only a few elements on the screen at the same time and the signal-to-noise ratio is far better. A 36px subhead that looks good on a desktop monitor, might be slightly over the top on a smartphone.

So, meet style variations. Instead of progressively increasing the font size for each heading level, we can use italics, small caps and all caps at the same letter size to establish text hierarchy. Add bolds into the mix, and we have a palette of at least six styles.

ALL CAPS   **ALL CAPS**

SMALL CAPS   **SMALL CAPS**

italic   ***italic***

Six distinctive styles with font style variations

While all caps and italics are styled easily with CSS, small caps are relatively new in Web design. Web fonts contain small caps subsets less often than not. In essence, there are three alternatives to applying small caps:

1. Apply the CSS3 OpenType feature rule.
2. Load a separate small caps font file.
3. Create faux small caps.

```css
.subhead-1 {
    -moz-font-feature-settings: "smcp";
    -ms-font-feature-settings: "smcp";
    -webkit-font-feature-settings: "smcp";
    -o-font-feature-settings: "smcp";
    font-feature-settings: "smcp";
    text-transform: lowercase;
}

.subhead-2 {
    font-family: small-caps-typeface;
    text-transform: lowercase;
}
.subhead-3 {
    font-weight: 500;
    font-size: 80%;
    text-transform: uppercase;
    letter-spacing: .125em;
}
```

One possible scenario in responsive typography is switching between style variations and a scale for subheads. For instance, we can set a range of styles at the same size for small screens — where a single content unit is in view and the signal is clear — and create more contrast with a typographic scale for larger screens where there's much more noise.

Subheads are a great opportunity to add style to a composition. For an extensive list of options, check out my article "Setting subheads with CSS[78]" and the accompanying demo page[79].

Data Tables

Tables are becoming a very common element on the Web, handy for comparing numerical data, as well as creating connections between arrays of information. As such they are almost unavoidable in Web applications.

For a clean-slate table, we can use the `border-collapse` property and the `cellspacing` attribute. Preserve the vertical rhythm by adding the bottom margin rule and, where necessary, override the bottom margin in breakpoint-specific CSS files.

```
<table cellspacing="0" cellpadding="0" />

table {
        border-collapse: collapse;
        border-spacing: 0;
        margin-bottom: 1.5em;
}
```

Horizontal borders are easy on the eye and will add clarity, so we can create such borders using the `border-bottom` or `border-top` property. Next, we set some padding to let the data breathe, keeping in mind the harmony of the vertical rhythm. For any column that contains numerical data, we can align the data to the right so that the values can be easily read and matched up to one another — singles under singles, tens under tens, and so on.

---

78 http://blog.typekit.com/2013/07/25/setting-subheads-with-css/
79 http://webdesign.maratz.com/lab/subheads/

```
th, td {
        border-top: .1em solid #ccc;
        padding: .65em 1em .75em; /* .75em = 1.5em/2 */
        vertical-align: top;
}

.numeric {
        text-align: right;
        font-feature-settings: 'tnum';
}
```

Some popular typefaces on the Web, for instance Proxima Nova and Georgia don't support fixed width lining numerals. In that case, you might want to consider other alternatives, for instance Anonymous Pro[80] by Mark Simonson. It's free and available at a Web font host service near you, or a good old Web-safe font such as Courier New, Trebuchet MS or Verdana.

Setting tabular figures with OpenType fonts is the best option for tabular data. Activate them with the `font-feature-settings` property.

Another CSS rule that would be useful for tabular data — still in working draft — is character-based alignment in a table column[81]. When the alignment character is specified, it is centered along a single column-parallel axis and the text is shifted accordingly. This is especially convenient for styling an array of numbers with a separator, for instance decimal numbers. At the time of writing, this rule is still not supported in browsers.

```
td { text-align: "." center }
```

When a large unexpected chunk of data fills the table (for instance a long URL), it can fall out of its designated area and break the layout. To keep the table from falling apart, we can use the CSS rule `table-layout: fixed` and set the maximum width to the table, for instance 100%. This should keep the table contained within the parent element.

---

80 http://www.marksimonson.com/fonts/view/anonymous-pro
81 http://www.w3.org/TR/css3-text/#character-alignment

```
table {
        border-collapse: collapse;
        border-spacing: 0;
        table-layout: fixed;
        max-width: 100%;
}
```

ADVANCED TECHNIQUES: PIXEL DENSITY AND GRADES

We have already looked at different rendering technology in different OSes, but device manufacturers, led by Apple, introduced another variable to us: screen resolution. Pixel density affects the appearance of type on a given device. Take, for example, the evident differences in type rendering on iPhones and iPads which are all made by the same manufacturer. Imagine what happens when you add more densities into the mix.

As an additional issue both on iOS Retina[82] and Windows ClearType[83] screens, when the device orientation is changed, the stack of subpixels is not parallel with the line of text anymore, but instead it's perpendicular to it. Because of that, the rendering engine cannot rely on the layout of subpixels for subpixel anti-aliasing.

I've already introduced you to the vague topic of anti-aliasing on iOS devices, but regardless of whichever theory is true, there's still an issue of text appearing less elegant in landscape orientation on both iPhones and iPads. I suppose at this point you might want to go out to your balcony and scream to the sky, so please go on — I don't mind.

Feeling better? Shall we continue?

Since designing for the screen is very similar to designing for newspapers, many solutions to our problems can be found in the print design world. Back in the day, type designers invented graded fonts, slightly adjusted variants of the same type style, which helped book and newspaper designers better control the ink performance on different paper qualities.

---

82 http://www.muleradio.net/thetalkshow/6/
83 http://smashed.by/cleartype

The quick brown fox jumps over the lazy dog.

ALL, EXCEPT RETINA

The quick brown fox jumps over the lazy dog.

RETINA LANDSCAPE

The quick brown fox jumps over the lazy dog.

RETINA PORTRAIT

iA graded fonts

In print design there is rough paper; in Web design there is a coarse low resolution screen, so the same approach can be applied. Designers at Information Architects[84] led by Oliver Reichenstein use graded fonts[85] to normalize the appearance of text across different resolutions. They embed three different grades:

- the default, non-Retina grade
- the Retina landscape grade
- and the Retina portrait grade

Since you are a CSS-literate, the code is self-explanatory:

```
@font-face {
    font-family: '-graded font';
    ...
}

@media only screen and (min-device-pixel-ratio: 1.5) {
@font-face {
    font-family: '+graded font';
        ...
    }
}
```

---

84 http://ia.net
85 The comprehensive list of graded fonts can be found at Typophile forums
http://typophile.com/node/81483 — you will be amazed at the selection.

```
@media only screen and (min-device-pixel-ratio: 1.5)
and (orientation: portrait) {
    @font-face {
    font-family: '++graded font';
    ...
    }
}
```

Reading Distance, Revisited

We currently assume reading distances are based on the devices' form factors. Device manufacturers decide on the reference pixel, making numerous assumptions as to how the device will be used at the uniform reading distance. That is, we only read from a smartphone when it is held with the palm facing towards the face, read from a tablet when held with both hands, and always sit exactly 70cm away from our desktop screen.

We need something better, a way to detect the physical relationship between the user and the device and to readjust typography accordingly. We already have the technology to measure reading distances so we can readily detect and calculate how far the object is from the device with sensors that are already available in devices.

Firefox OS and Firefox for Android both support the Proximity API[86], which detects how close the device is to any other physical object, by accessing the proximity sensor. In Firefox implementations, it currently works at distances of up to 10cm, but if it could be expanded to return accurate values for distances within arm's reach, we could use that value to increase or decrease the letter size and adjust paragraph spacing accordingly. Working with proximity API is straightforward. The `DeviceProx-imityEvent` interface provides information about the distance between the device and a nearby object, while the `UserProximityEvent` currently returns a boolean value if the user is close to the device.

---

86 https://hacks.mozilla.org/2013/06/the-proximity-api/

```
window.ondeviceproximity = function (event) {
        var prox = "Proximity: " + event.value + " cm";
        prox += "Min. value supported: " + event.min + " cm";
        prox += "Max value supported: " + event.max + " cm";
        proximityDisplay.innerHTML = prox;
    };

    window.onuserproximity = function (event) {
        var userProx = "User proximity - near: " + event.near;
        userProximityDisplay.innerHTML = userProx;
    };
```

Another example is capturing objects with a plain old Web camera. By combining the getUserMedia API with face recognition algorithms, we can detect the user's face and calculate the distance between a user and the screen[87].

Whatever the sensor technology is, once the reading distance is
available, we can use it as a complementary query to screen size @media
queries to deliver better typography. A few combinations and their respective setups come to mind:

- A smartphone at palm distance (small size, short measure, tight leading)
- A smartphone at lap distance (small to medium size, short measure,
  medium leading)
- A tablet at palm distance (small size, medium measure, normal leading)
- A tablet at lap distance (small to medium size, medium measure,
  medium leading)
- A tablet at desk distance (medium size, short measure, tight leading)
- A laptop at lap distance (small to medium size, medium measure,
  medium leading)
- A laptop at desk distance (medium size, measure and leading)
- A desktop screen at desk distance (medium to large size, medium
  measure, medium leading)
- A desktop screen at wall distance (large size, measure and leading)

---

87 http://webdesign.maratz.com/lab/responsivetypography/

These different typographic combinations shouldn't be applied in real time, because in that case the interface would scale up and down right in front of the user. Obviously, that would be completely useless. Instead, the device could apply a slightly different setup each time the user loads a page, and measure especially if the user tries to readjust the reading distance by moving the device away from or closer to their face.

All that data could be collected, stored and used to run a series of multivariate tests in the background, without ever interrupting the user. Gathered statistics could help us to better determine what the optimal setup is at each reading distance. The device could recognize each particular user, recalibrate and apply the optimal typographic setup for them. Not to mention the look on your optician's face when you dump all your stats onto her desk. Who's a nerd now, huh?

Did we hit the roof on the Web? I don't think so!

IT'S NOT THAT HARD

You'll agree that each presented technique is quite simple observed in isolation. The complicated part in Web typography is keeping in mind all the axes and creating the best possible setup for a given situation. But if you prioritize, you can achieve pretty decent results with very little effort.

First, markup the text with correct punctuation, dashes, quotes and spacing. Second, take care of the default paragraph by balancing the letter size, line length and line height. Aim for even texture. Even if it feels unexciting, the use of proper characters and spacing will establish soundness. Third, create proper hierarchy so the reader can actually make it through to the end. Finally, if you have enough time, tweak the style subtleties — think of it as icing on the cake.

How do you become comfortable with designing typography? As a daily exercise, use one font in black or white on a background color and try to express different moods using variable sizing, macro and micro white space and adjusting the arrangement of elements. Another exercise is to try different strategies for establishing hierarchy and experiment with supplementary furniture, such as captions or pull-quotes — using only one typeface. This way you will learn what each type family is capable of and what can be accomplished with CSS.

I dare you to learn to live without flourishes, the bling and the gloss, to undesign Web sites and make them lightweight and accessible in both appearance and performance, as well as being cross-platform. Resist the seduction of beautiful counters and spines, and delay browsing typefaces until you have built a solid foundation.

Always keep in mind that typography serves content and we serve the user — not the other way around. Typeset content first, because the stark reality is that Web typography is not about selecting fonts, it's about making information accessible, legible and readable. We all have an innate tendency to make things eye-pleasing, so once you have learned to cover the essentials, you will instinctively know how to add just the right volume of appeal.

Good luck!

ABOUT THE AUTHOR

Marko Dugonjić is a designer, speaker and author based in Velika Gorica, Croatia. As the creative and user experience director at Creative Nights, he improves customers' digital experiences for both local and international clients. He founded FFWD.PRO, a micro-conference for internet professionals. His favorite pet project is Typetester, an online tool for testing screen fonts.

ABOUT THE REVIEWER

Tim Brown is a designer, writer, speaker, and toolmaker, with a focus on typography. Formerly a web designer at Vassar College, he is now Type Manager for Adobe Typekit, a curator for A List Apart, and the author of Nice Web Type (@nicewebtype on Twitter).

The Two Faces of Content Strategy

Written by Corey Vilhauer

CHAPTER TEN · BY COREY VILHAUER

THE TWO FACES OF
CONTENT STRATEGY

BALANCING THE NEEDS OF USERS AND EDITORS

I N 2005, I CREATED MY OWN WORDPRESS BLOG. It wasn't easy. It took what felt like a monumental amount of learning — learning I did on my own time, relying on a continuous cycle of trying and failing my way toward each small success. It was barely a success, but it launched, and I took on the task of creating something interesting on a daily basis.

This was my first brush with self-publishing, in which I wrested the reins of publication from the essayists and journalists whom I admired, forcing myself into the public eye. I did it to practice writing, to sharpen it like one might sharpen an axe, chopping through the thicket toward fame, fortune and maybe a Pulitzer, if I was lucky. Instead, I ended up reinventing myself as a Web professional, combining the two loves of my life: words and technology.

This was my choice. I had moved from audience to editor. I was now behind the machine.

That was eight years ago. Since then, we have seen websites become more complicated. We have improved our methods. We have focused on user-centered information architecture, then user-centered content strategy, then refocused again on a user-centered, multiscreen, *everything-is-everywhere* strategy.

Our attention on users — on the audiences and customers we rely on to make our products and content a success — took a long time to coalesce. But here we are! The golden age of Web design! Where content is taken seriously! Where users get a seat at the table! Where everything is rainbows and chocolate cake and there isn't an oatmeal raisin cookie to be seen!

Except.

Except for those who may not have had the same desire to take apart the Web and get behind it. Except for the people who take the things we make and fold them into their everyday job. Except for the editors who struggle with the weight of a new CMS, or the trivialities of workflow change, or the political turmoil that comes with a new website.

Along the way, these people all made the same move I did — from audience to editor — and they all take part in the creation of Web content. But we've been so focused on making usable websites for our customers that we somehow forgot that we also need to walk editors and bosses and co-workers through the process, too.

There are two faces to content strategy: the people we're targeting (our users), and the people who are doing the targeting (our editors). We're responsible for making great websites. But we're also responsible for making websites that are usable from the editor's standpoint. We are the people who make the Web; we are also those responsible for helping those who sustain it.

A Renewed Focus on People

Just as I discovered with that first WordPress blog, people who maintain and create content are faced with leaps in technological advancement, complicated new systems, and an inherent change in their workflow. As we better understand how people access the Web, we find our current methods aren't working as well as we had hoped — that we're forced to adapt both how we do things and *what we do in the first place*. We raise the banner for structured content. We adopt content tools like GatherContent[1], or editorial tools like Editorially[2]. We lobby for more dedicated content strategists within our organizations.

We start to ask for change. And against that change comes resistance.

These are not easy things to take on. When Chip and Dan Heath, authors of *Switch: How to Change Things When Change is Hard*[3], say "Change isn't an event; it's a process," they're warning us that people aren't hardwired to switch directions on a dime. In our jobs, within our teams, in whatever situation we find ourselves, our worth is defined by what we do.

Imagine you're working with a Web content editor at a major university. As part of the Web design process, we push for changes to how the home page is laid out, or how content flows through the system, or what CMS is used. We may also suggest advanced technologies like personalization, and we ask the content editor to take a deep look into a new taxonomy so they can efficiently pull content blocks in from across the website.

We're not just redesigning a website. We're also rebuilding their process, which, in turn, redefines their role at the university. Change means more than just the simple adaptation of how we create a spread-sheet or what it means when we say "content audit." It's a full-scale meta-morphosis in what we mean to our co-workers, bosses and partners.

Jonathan Kahn, principal at Together London, says "We've got plenty of ideas, we work with skilled people, and our tools get better every day—but until we start changing our organizations' culture, we won't achieve our objectives."[4] This means changing our expectations of what content work really is and who's in charge. Because we're all in charge now.

---

1 https://www.gathercontent.com
2 https://editorially.com
3 Heath, Chip & Dan; Switch: How to Change Things When Change Is Hard, http://smashed.by/switch
4 Kahn, Jonathan; "Start Changing Your Organisation's Culture Using Storytelling & Startup Techniques", http://smashed.by/cult-video

EMPATHY

Good content requires empowered and engaged people. Good content needs people to read it, and it needs people to create it. Without people, there is no content. Content strategy, at its heart, is people strategy.

Yet we still see content work banished to the back offices, left for IT or the copywriter or the marketing department (people who *already* have plenty to do, thanks). Such buck-passing is a sure sign that our discipline is still fighting to reach maturity. We still spend too much time looking for the right methods and workflow, and not enough time figuring out how the vast changes in Web content will affect not just the jobs of those who are tasked with creating content, but also every other job in the company.

So, those of us who help create or redesign websites must take into account the needs of our websites' audiences and the people who will create content, every last one of them — which is to say: *everyone*. To do that, we must put ourselves in their shoes and work with empathy for their situation.

We hand our content needs to an editor[5] with the expectation that everything will be perfect, but each editor is responsible for additional tasks that may not involve creating or maintaining Web content, tasks that require time and attention. Every new content need — every addition to the content workflow, and every new analytics system, every new CMS platform — eats into that time and that attention.

This is where we come in as content strategists.

Two Paths Converge

To keep things simple, the people engaging with a website can be divided into two camps: those who will use the website; and those who will maintain the website.

---

5   When I talk about editors throughout this chapter, I refer not just to the traditional editor, but to anyone who will handle content duties during the creation and governance process. An editor could be a co-worker, a client, a boss, a freelance copywriter, someone from a different department, a member of an advisory board, or they could be an actual editor. The content process is a wild, woolly mess, even when it's well organized, and because of that we have all become, in some sense, editors of the Web.

On one hand, you have the users, the audiences and customers we need to make our company or content a success. Our goal with this group is simple: provide value and communicate a message. On the other hand, you have the editors, the people who make this content, creating experiences and stories that resonate with website users. Users ask for information and products. Editors ask for attention and patience.

Thanks to the traditional advertising method of the big reveal, we've been trained to think that there is a kind of constant struggle between editor and user; that an editor's artistic sensitivity and personal views are held back by data and search engines and user feedback, while users ignore anything that's not of immediate relevance and only respond to big, bold and dumb.

Our editors deserve more respect, as do our users. In reality, the two groups are separated by nothing more than a few lines of code and an Internet connection. They play complementary parts in the Web creation process — supply and demand, create and consume — representing two paths that, instead of diverging, move in the same direction with constant interchanges.

When we create a website, we go through the following stages:

- *Discovery*: Who is this website for and why will they visit?
- *Strategy*: How do we lead users to their goals?
- *Execution*: What do we say to our users?
- *Governance*: How do we keep this website relevant?

The methodology on the editorial end follows a similar path:

- *Discovery*: Who is creating content for this website and why?
- *Strategy*: How do we help the company and editors reach their goals?
- *Execution*: What do our editors say and how do we help them say it?
- *Governance*: How do we stay on track after launch?

Different tasks, different goals, but the same direction. The discovery stage is concerned with *who* and *why*. The strategy stage is concerned with *how*, while the execution stage is concerned with *what*. Finally, governance gives us more insight into *where* and *when* by giving us a set of editorial tools and guidelines to live by once the initial website is live.

With these two paths, we can begin to figure out exactly how to reach our audiences and give them what they need, all while keeping in mind the issues that may sprout up on the other side of the content process. Let's take a look at where these two paths most often meet throughout some of the basic steps of content strategy.

DISCOVERY: WHO AND WHY?

Successful content relies on a deep level of understanding in both audience makeup and user goals. Developing successful content requires an additional level of understanding in how an organization works, who can be pulled out as content champions, and what form our network of content editors will finally take. This is done through asking a lot of questions and undertaking a lot of probing during an initial discovery meeting.

Before any real content work can begin, we sit down with all relevant parties and determine audiences and perceived outcomes: who will visit our website and what they expect to get out of it. This "audiences and outcomes" process gives us a wonderful opportunity to ask some editorial questions as well.

The discovery process is the most crucial stage in building an empathetic relationship with a Web editorial team. It's necessary for editorial buy-in. It's necessary for effective involvement. And it helps build warm and fuzzy feelings throughout the project. It's all about figuring out who's going to use the website on both sides of the process.

Audiences and Outcomes

First of all, let's get this out of the way: we are not the audience. We may be a frequent flier, but that doesn't mean we can speak for every airline passenger. We may have kids, but that doesn't mean we can speak for every parent. We may be a huge fan of the newest Daft Punk album, but that doesn't mean we can speak the multitudes who also enjoy the new Daft Punk album. So we must find and talk to the people who *can* speak for these audiences: the audiences themselves.

We begin by gathering everyone in for a big information-gathering discovery meeting. The meeting might take 30 minutes, it might take several hours. What matters is that it happens, and that the right people are involved. This means you need to find someone from every relevant area of the organization. The list might include, but is not limited to, representatives from:

- Marketing
- Creative/Web
- IT
- Product Development
- Front-line Service
- Executive Board
- Business Development

The range of attendees is wide on purpose. Every area of the company has a different lease on Web content, and they all work differently to make Web content happen.

Members of IT can talk about their needs and limitations, especially as it relates to content workflow, while someone from product development or sales can discuss the murmurs they hear outside of the company. Front-line service is key to capturing the thoughts of disgruntled users or customers, while the executive board will shed light on potential business strategy and will appreciate being part of the project.

Different voices bring different solutions. If your initial discovery meeting involves just a few members from marketing, you're going to run into trouble.

With this group in the room, it's time to solidify our audiences and the outcomes those audiences expect. Create two lists and begin sorting all of the audiences and all of the perceived outcomes into two columns. Then, start asking questions. For example:

- Who do you feel are your website's audiences?
- Which audiences are not represented well enough, and what are they looking for?
- Who else is competing for your audiences' attention?
- What drives your business, and how does your audience help achieve positive results?
- What audiences are part of a strategic initiative? Are there any secondary audiences that the company seeks to invest in?

Let's imagine we're going through this process with a small university. As you field answers, your audience list might start looking like this:

- Potential students
- Current students
- Parents
- Alumni
- Athletic fans

And the outcomes may be:

- Sign up for a university tour
- Find information on applying for school
- Learn more about the residence halls
- Apply for financial aid
- Read news about university projects funded by alumni
- Read scores for the football team

These audiences will be further separated by need — after all, a potential student could be non-traditional, graduate, online or post-secondary — and the outcomes will overlap across the audiences. You'll end up with a long list of audiences, a long list of outcomes...and you'll gather a lot of information that doesn't fit in, either. Because when a group of editors and marketing professionals starts talking about their customers and content, they also start talking about the failings of their current systems, the struggles they have with internal politics, and the initiative they've been pushing to implement for years.

Jackpot. Time to talk about editorial process.

(For a deeper look into audiences, outcomes and personas read my article for A List Apart[6], or check out the book that inspired the article: *Online and On Mission*[7], by C. David Gammel. For a great primer on how, when and what to ask during discovery interviews and audience interviews, read *Interviewing Users: How to Uncover Compelling Insights*[8] by Steve Portigal.)

When Editors Become Audiences

Remember when I wrote, "we are not the audience?" I take that back. Because it's at this point — when user audience research turns into workflow gripes — that the fun stuff starts to surface: the editorial audiences.

Editors get content from all corners of the organization. They may be represented by a single person, or they may be a department's worth of staff. They could be the CEO, or they could be a handful of interns. Editors differ depending on the organization, industry and website, which makes them as important a website audience as any.

While we've got the group together for the initial discovery meeting, now's the time to ask some sticky questions. Talk about department siloing, about faulty workflow, and that one person who has a hard time

---

6 "Audiences, Outcomes, and Determining User Needs", http://smashed.by/user-needs, 28. Feb. 2012
7 Gammel, C. David; "Online and On Mission" , http://smashed.by/online-mission
8 Portigal, Steve: "Interviewing Users: How to Uncover Compelling Insights", http://smashed.by/itv-users

understanding the WYSIWYG editor. Talk about everything, because this is your best chance to create editor- and user-friendly content and architecture before it's too late.

Trust me. They will talk, if given the chance. This is because content work requires some level of ego; it's writing and creating, after all, even if it's only a basic FAQ or press release. When faulty processes or staff frustration lead to less than stellar content, those responsible for putting the content on the Web are going to take offense.

So start sussing out annoyances and dive deeper. What causes these annoyances? What can we do to fix these frustrations? If someone in marketing mentions they can't make all the changes they'd like because there aren't enough editors, ask what kind of skills they're missing and try to figure out if there's a way to spread the work around. If a certain department has trouble getting content on the website, ask about that department's process and whether or not it's an issue of resources or simply a bad case of apathy.

Armed with this information, we can create a similar list of audiences and outcomes for editorial workflow. For example, a university might see the following editorial audiences:

- Departmental directors
- Web steering committee
- Staff and faculty
- Marketing
- Undergraduate admissions
- Editorial staff

Each of these internal groups has a different role in the Web content process. By identifying all of the players, we can get a better sense of where snags might be, and how to untangle them before they become larger internal content conflicts.

Once we've determined all of the editorial audiences, it's up to us to make sure each is represented, both within any strategic content plan and as a part of the overall website discussion. We know, we know: committees are hard to work with. But dealing with committees is easier than scrambling to make changes for departments or stakeholders who stick their nose into the project at far too late a stage. Mike Monteiro, author of *Design is a Job*[9], talks about the necessity of grabbing the right mix of people:

> *"Going into a project, you need to know who on the client side provides input, who gives feedback, and who approves. You may have a better idea of who these people should be than your client. ... As important as it is to have a small feedback group reviewing design decisions, it's even more important that it's the right group."*

Each of your editorial groups plays a huge part in determining editorial workflow and project sustainability. By figuring out what makes each group tick, we can present solutions that fit the project's expectations.

Auditing the Existing Process

With our audiences — both external and editorial — in mind, it's time to figure out what we have to work with. This is an exercise in resource allocation, but it is also a major trial in patience.

We're already used to diving into a project armed with a spreadsheet and several hours of droning music, ready to inventory every last PDF and policy page. We do this to gain a sense of where we are. What areas of the website are under-represented? What content is sitting idle and mucking up search results? Why do we still link to the program for the 2002 Annual Christmas Program?

The goal of this inventory is to:

---

9 Monteiro, Mike "Design Is A Job", http://smashed.by/alap-job

- Determine the current direction of the website, as well as gain a good understanding of the project scope.
- Gain exposure to the voice and tone of the website's content.
- Find relationships between pages and current website information architecture.

Yet this focuses only on external audiences: how people find things and whether those things are relevant. We also need to figure out how content lands on the website where it does, when it does and how it does.

Which means, in addition to standard inventory fields like "ID," "Page Name" and "Content Type," we also have to start determining "Content Owner," "On-site Expert" and whether or not a page is static or changing. In so doing, we'll create a de facto editorial workflow, a workflow that needs its own element of editing as well.

In content strategy, we so often talk about getting rid of *ROT* (redundant, out-of-date, trivial) content. Workflow requires this as well. As we're going through website content, we should also look at areas where workflow has become redundant, out-of-date or trivial. Some examples of this might be:

- Sending non-legally binding copy to the legal department for approval,
- Running all content through a department supervisor instead of empowering the content team to make their own edits,
- A focus on time-based content production over relevance — in other words, posting for the sake of posting,
- A lack of editorial governance in reviewing old content or archiving out-of-date content.

This workflow audit (like the content audit) is going to weed out the bad parts and help us make good strategic decisions.

Strategy: How

Strategic planning is often handled from a user perspective (What are our audiences' goals? How can we help achieve them? What content do we need?); which is fine, except that we need to do more to answer the questions under the surface. In addition to how to achieve goals, we need to determine who can create the content. Along with working out what content we need, we need to establish who can maintain it.

Melissa Rach and Kristina Halvorson define strategy as "an idea that sets the direction for the future."[10]A strategy is not a document; it's the idea behind the document. Which means it encompasses much more than a document ever could — it's made of culture, workforce, tools and, most of all, people.

Therefore, our strategic plans must embrace a little bit of both worlds.

At Blend, our strategic content plans set out the following high-level concepts:

- Reiteration of website audiences and objectives
- Analysis of current content issues and proposed changes
- Gap analysis of content needs and proposed additions
- An action plan for proposed website messaging
- An action plan for proposed website structure
- An action plan for proposed website governance
- Measurements for success

You'll notice that apart from the proposed website governance plan, nearly all of those items are user-facing strategies. Yet, there's a hidden purpose to all of this analysis and strategy: we are throwing these ideas out not just to see if they'll work with website users, but also to see if they'll be accepted by editors.

---

10 Halvorson, Kristina, and Rach, Melissa; *Content Strategy for the Web, Second Edition*, http://content-strategy.com

Each messaging plan comes with workflow suggestions: find someone to become keeper of the style guide; or determine one person who can run A/B testing on website content. Structural suggestions pull in editorial workflow issues from across departments; for example, if we build a news feed, will someone maintain it?

It's these governance and workflow issues that pose the largest hurdles in the process. Remember: people don't like change. And this is often the stage of the project where we start suggesting changes to their existing jobs.

Our job is to ease the change. Lay out all expected outcomes and show what changes are needed. Personally meet people who may have to take on extra duties and explain the benefits of those duties. Work with managers to ensure they understand the amount of extra work or the change in skill set required for each new initiative. But most of all, get people on board early.

ASSIGNING ROLES

Who should be involved with Web content? Everyone.

Who *can* be involved? A select few who hold the password and have the time to work on the new website. Who *will* be involved? That's a subject that can be both simple and complicated at the same time. Which is kind of the point of an interdisciplinary content team.

We talk about interdisciplinary content teams because, at their heart, every group of collected content workers is in some way interdisciplinary. They play on their own experiences, their own backgrounds and their own thoughts to create complex content systems for our websites. They don't always get along, but they combine their efforts to create a better mix than any of the pieces could on their own.

There's a concept called *informed simplicity* that comes into play when building and assigning roles within a content team. Matthew Frederick, in his book *101 Things I Learned in Architecture School*, says informed simplicity is "founded upon an ability to discern or create clarifying patterns within complex mixtures."[11] He likens it to pattern recognition, but with a twist, whereby we move past the teeming mass of conflicting interests and find places where they can come together in harmony.

If this sounds a lot like the quagmires we wade through trying to keep all of our website users happy, you're not mistaken. Just like we spend hours and hours organizing and testing and reorganizing the content on our website to provide the fastest view to all pertinent audiences, we must also, through trial and error, determine who will work best within an organization's content team.

You start by bringing back your group from the initial discovery session. One by one, go through each part of the proposed strategic plan. Ask questions about ownership and ability. Who does this already? Who else could do it? How many people do we have working on this project? How many hours can we pull from other departments? Where are opportunities for us to hand over content to a subject matter expert in order to save time on our end?

With these questions, you can create an initial workflow plan. It can be as simple as a Word document with everyone's responsibilities by position, or as complex as a spreadsheet with exact hours and tasks. Simple is better, however. Step Two Designs, which has undertaken extensive research on developing intranet content teams and evaluating workflow, warns against overly complicated workflow processes. James Robertson, managing director of Step Two Designs, writes that "simple workflow can be useful, with one or two steps between the author and the published page… Beyond this, however, workflow can prove to be ineffective or even problematic."[12]

We typically develop a chart that shows relative content flows, very much like the one displayed below.

---

11   Frederick, Matthew; *101 Things I Learned in Architecture School*, http://101thingsilearned.com/Architecture/101TILArchitecture.html

12   Robertson, James; "What Every Intranet Team Should Know,, http://smashed.by/step2

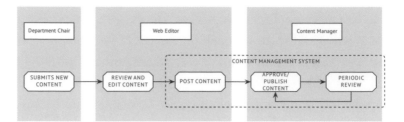

Then, we prepare for it all to change.

Workflow should always be iterative. It depends on ability and current staffing. There's a need for constant revisions, and these revisions must be built into the process. Whether content is created using Agile or Lean methods, or any other existing or created process, it must be reviewed periodically. Check the machine for leaks. Tune it up. Repurpose the parts that aren't working.

And when things get tight, start prioritizing tasks. That is, if you didn't prioritize from the get go.

DON'T TRY TO DO IT ALL

Let's make this clear from the beginning: not every client or project team will be equipped to handle every part of a project. Assigning roles and determining strategy may require more than just a knowledge of the content and a handful of user outcomes. It will require understanding the skill set of each user. And it will require understanding when to say enough is enough.

Believe it or not, we don't need to throw our full methodology at every project. The first time I realized this was when I worked with a small non-profit organization funded entirely on donations. They had no money for a project, yet I still dove straight in with the full package: full content inventory, full audit and strategic plan, detailed wireframes and website map, editorial calendar with weekly updates. We had agreed to donate our time, and I felt strongly about the organization, so why wouldn't I give it my all?

Here's why. I went way over their heads.

It wasn't that they couldn't understand the plan; they just couldn't understand why I had spent so much time on it. The website had 20 pages total, and they had a skeleton crew of volunteers running the organization. They had no need for detailed content plans — they just needed insight and direction on how to reach their audiences. They had no need for a weekly content calendar — they barely had enough staffing to make it to weekly meetings. They were a non-profit group. They were friends. They took my contribution as the overzealous ramblings of a content fanatic.

But what if this was a paying client? What if this was someone who had agreed to spend a full 50% of their marketing budget on a new web-site? What if you delivered a pointless deliverable because you thought that's what they needed?

It's going to go over their heads, too — as soon as the anger subsides. Because you're not just wasting their time and money, at that point: you're unknowingly sabotaging their internal team by demanding more project buy-in than they can handle. We all have methodologies, but none of them are one-size-fits-all. They're expandable and contractable, movable and skippable. They should be designed to work in parts, to be scaled back, and to be adjusted for the needs of the current project.

Give someone every tool in the toolbox, and they'll spend most of their time trying to figure out which screwdriver to start with. Our tools will differ on every project, and that's the thing to focus on — we need to understand and empathize with the situation in order to provide more than just a cookie cutter solution from our methodology.

Execution: What

With a strategic plan in place, we now turn to creating actual website content, a task typically handled over what seems like a thousand days with input from 17 million people.

Creating content (words, video, organization, relationships, sidebars, tutorials — whatever it may be) takes shape back in the discovery phase, when we start talking about website messaging, brand standards and existing content. But now we are ready to get specific and turn our messages and outcomes into actual words on a page.

Except, who's going to make that content?

Your website editors. That's who.

And if you've never been lucky enough to work with a 10,000-page content migration, or if you've managed to steer clear of any complete content makeover project, I'll let you in on a little secret: execution is messy, stressful and completely overwhelming.

EMPATHY FOR THE DEVIL

Page after page. Sentence after sentence. Every image needs the right tags, and every video needs the right embedding, and should the heading go here or there?

Content creation can be as labored an act as the term itself, mired in politics and revisions and the smallest of details, over and over again. But the devil is in the details, as they say. And that's what we need to focus on with any website content project: the details. The details help us pull content across the website through metadata, and they inform microcopy and small interaction decisions during testing, and they might even help us notice the unfortunate spelling of our "*pubic* relations department."

And while we may not necessarily be in charge of every detail of a project — after all, we're in this to empower website editors to create a website that's usable long after launch — we are responsible for creating an environment that promotes careful, usable content, from important home page content to the smallest microcopy. Here are some ways in which we can help:

Put someone in charge

Every project needs a leader who can organize and delegate tasks. This leader can take two forms: either a natural leader connected to the project who understands it and can work with various departments (think: marketing director, lead content editor, etc.); or someone from outside the project who can bridge the gaps created through siloing and politics (think: a content strategy consultant).

This seems so simple, right? Yet we still struggle with teams that have too many cooks in the kitchen — and too many content sources claiming precedence. Nothing frustrates the process more than unnecessary work, so make sure someone is in charge of determining where content comes from, where it goes, and (most importantly) what's important.

Rely on subject matter experts

I don't know anything about flywheel engines or computer chips or cupcakes or whatever it is we're making websites for this week. That's not my job as a content strategist, though. My job is to help those who *do* know about flywheel engines or computer chips or cupcakes create content that's usable.

Remember: we aren't responsible for knowledge within the domain. We are responsible communicating that knowledge in a way that's both usable and useful for that domain's audiences. We do this by relying on the relationships we have within the project, asking good questions and conceding to expertise, instead of running in with all of the answers predetermined.

Know when to hold 'em, and know when to fold 'em

Internal politics. Apathetic co-workers. A reliance on outdated methods that appeal to a certain section of the organization. These are serious problems, and they really pop up when we begin figuring out the details of website content. Who gets to be on the home page? Who gets to have the biggest bio? Why haven't you talked about *this* department yet?

When we start work on a project, we're often bombarded with information. But the information is biased. It's all connected to specific goals and departments within the company, and it's all competing for the same area on the website. The worst part? These competing nuggets of information can all be reframed to fit our website's message hierarchy. For example, if a person really wants the university library link to be one of the top headings on the website, that person can certainly make a case for it using our existing criteria.

Our goal in this case is to reframe the conversation, taking advantage of that person's goals and making allowances were possible. For instance, imagine a university website where four different departments are vying for the same website real estate. You have options. You can show them data that refutes their claim, which can backfire if future gut feelings can't be summed up with relatable numbers. You can give in and save the fight for a larger battle, which could anger and alienate other departments. Or, you can filter out some of the voices by finding passion projects.

Ultimately, each department or stakeholder is super-focused on a few ideal things. Make an allowance here or there based on those passion projects, all while pointing out the vast amount of information you have to deal with. Be empathetic to their needs and give a little bit, all while helping them empathize with your situation.

Use editorial tools to help communicate

Often, the biggest difficulty we face isn't in organizing people and creating workflow — it's simply finding a way to give everyone access to changes and comments within our own content. Thankfully, this is a problem being worked on through several online Web applications.

There are solutions for Web content planning, such as GatherContent, that help you collaborate on site maps, content models and other pre-development needs. Once that site's gone live, there are collaborative editorial applications like Editorially or Poetica that promise to create a single source for content feedback.

And, seriously. Given the issues we all run into when gathering a thousand word documents from seven different departments and organizing them into something usable, we can only assume that more people are going to make more online solutions. We're right on the edge of a content tool explosion.

Develop with a CMS that's easy for editors to use

Well, now we're just being silly, right? Maybe not. Let's talk about developers.

WORKING WITH DEVELOPERS

Despite the fact that nearly every content strategist has some issue with the inconsistencies of content management systems, we all rely on some kind of content management solution to make our jobs easier and our editors' jobs relatively painless.

I say relatively, because while we'd never expect editors to go back to manually marking up each HTML page, that doesn't mean today's CMS solutions are optimal. They're not. But we can make them better. As long as we have a good relationship with our developers.

The content strategist/developer rift has been talked up for years. "Developers don't understand the needs of editors and are always looking for fast solutions, not correct solutions," say the content strategists. The developers answer, "Content strategists develop impossible, complicated solutions that we then have to implement, as though they have no knowledge of how databases or programming work." And it's true, in some sense. Content strategy is just now reaching a critical mass on structured, database-driven content, while developers are coming around to the benefits and efficiencies of a content-first approach.

These stereotypes are just that, though. Stereotypes. When it comes down to it, developers and content strategists work perfectly together. Developers want to know what kinds of copy are going to be on the website, and how they're going to interact. Content strategists benefit from working closely with developers to create a CMS experience that editors can understand and use.

Which brings us to the art of content modeling and how we can help create editor-centric CMS mechanisms — even within existing CMS packages — by simply listening to our editors and gleaning what content fields they might need.

First, imagine a basic block of content: a university department page, for example. The page is designed to give access to all content within that department. The biology department page might have links to biology research, a list of biology majors, a staff listing, and more. It will also have basics like a title, introductory paragraph, phone number and office location.

Taking this example, we can dive down into the details. What fields are needed? What will an editor need to update, and what content would work better populated through tags or categories?

In this case, we need to make fields for attributes that live on the page: the title, introductory paragraph, phone number and office location. So the editors don't need to manually enter every single major or research project, we will also need to pull in majors, research news, staff and classes that are categorized within "biology."

Yet, the CMS will probably also add fields that aren't relevant to the editing experience: publish date, page ID, page language, sort index and permissions, for example. These fields can be confusing to an editor who has to weed through the irrelevant just to change a block of copy, but they're crucial to making changes within the CMS.

Our job is to help bridge this gap.

Lullabot's Jeff Eaton talks at length about the relationship between content and development, reminding us that editors aren't going to be happy with the typical rigid CMS system. In his article, "When Editors Design: Controlling Presentation in Structured Content," he says that "providing editors and writers with more control over the presentation of their content is where many well-intentioned content models break down."[13] For this reason, Eaton says, "some teams go to the opposite extreme. They pile dozens of custom fields onto each content type to capture every possible presentation option, or they give editors a menu of carefully tailored visual templates to choose from for each post."

This is where collaboration between developers and content strategists is so important. It's also where collaboration between developers and editors becomes crucial.

Remember, we content people aren't interface designers, but we can work between the two camps to help organize fields for editors while still developing a structured content model that the developers can build upon.

That's exactly what we want: a website that both editors and developers continue to use, especially after launch.

Governance: When and Where

So the website's been launched. Now what?

Easy. Begin by ditching the assumption that the website is finished. Because no website is ever actually finished. Ever. None. No way.

In a traditional content strategy sense, this is where we begin talking about data analysis and content testing and A/B testing and all of the post-launch governance tools we've begin implementing over the years. Yet, these tools mean nothing without a heavy dose of editor education — education that's just as important as any content model we could devise.

13 Eaton, Jeff; "When Editors Design", http://smashed.by/content-structure

EDUCATING AND ITERATING

"Education?" you might ask. "Yes," I'll answer. Education.

Not just CMS training. Not a course on Web writing. I mean the understanding that we as content strategists — and Web creators as a whole — have a duty to keep up with the industry in order to pass it's benefits to those who use the websites we make.

Governance is the point when creators and editors merge, when trial and error testing and constant use unearth the issues we couldn't have planned for at the beginning of a project. It also marks the point in the project when we hand over expertise to the editors. It's their website now. It's their content, their domain knowledge. As they become more familiar with the website, and as we get less familiar with their process, as it organically changes throughout the life of the now live project, we lose the ability to help.

We mustn't lose that ability. We can't be strangers. We have to check in.

This comes with a cost, both in time and money. And yes, this means extra work once the website has launched. Our involvement has to move beyond "get it up and get it out."

The solution is to think beyond launch. Be it an internal project estimated on time, or a client contract estimated in overall cost, every project contract should include a few hours of monthly check-up. Go through the discovery meeting script again, asking questions about the current workflow, what's working, what's not. What can we do to alleviate the problems? What extra training do you need now that you've jumped in and have gotten use to how things run?

Don't skimp on that portion of the contract. Explain the benefits clearly, and don't allow it to be removed. It's that important.

Changes will need to be made. If not, you're apparently the perfect content strategist. And last I checked, no one's perfect.

Rethink the Editorial Calendar: Editorial Triggers

We often think of editorial calendars as tools to help bring new content to our users. They're a necessary governance tool that requires the bulk of our editorial attention. But, let's be honest, not every company needs an editorial calendar. Most of our content is not rolled out on a periodic basis, but as needed.

Enter editorial triggers.

Less editorial calendar and more editorial *timeline*, editorial triggers don't focus on forcing content into a daily or weekly schedule, but instead create guided paths to getting content completed as necessary. They borrow heavily from David Allen's *Getting Things Done*[14] methodology, breaking each project into a series of tasks and assigning them a timeline when relevant, and they take the editorial strain away from periodic change for change's sake.

For example, new product launches for your project may not occur at set intervals. Instead, they happen when the product is ready to launch — regardless of what the editorial calendar says. In this case, an editorial trigger for new product content takes us away from the rigidity of a calendar and into the flow of our product life cycle, using the following steps:

New Product Content — Maximum time: 5 days. Immediate Action.
1. Gather information on new product based on New Product copy deck (Web content editor, 2 days)
2. Upload initial content to website using placeholder images (1 day)
3. Approval needed: Initial approval of content required (product managers)
4. Take final image for product and create for all sizes (design, 150px, 300px, banner)
5. Final Approval (product manager/Web content editor, 1 day)

---

14 http://smashed.by/things-done

We know this editorial trigger takes five days maximum, and we know who is involved in the process. A new product like this requires immediate action, so we know it becomes a priority over any existing work.

What's more, because this trigger is only pulled when necessary, we don't have to watch a deadline come and go because we expected to work on new product content despite there not being a new product to work on.

This is not to say that the editorial calendar is dead; on the contrary, the editorial calendar is necessary to check for editorial triggers. Instead of focusing on publishing on a specific date, the calendar is repurposed to handle both scheduling content and content review, the most overlooked portion of any governance workflow.

What this gives us is a balance between editorial needs and editorial resources. We're able to keep up on content, and plan for future editorial initiatives as they arise. Editors are happy. The website content is being updated. And now we're diving head first into an editor-centric content workflow.

Content Strategy for the People, by the People

Websites are made up of code, design and messages, all three of which are created to serve a purpose. And while those purposes differ from company to company and project to project, they all have one thing in common: they are made of people. People behind the scenes, pulling the levers and writing copy. People responsible for creating new products and new brand standards. People making corporate-level decisions and people handling the grunt work of daily change.

So while it's logical to focus on keeping our website users happy — to acknowledge their needs, context and the demands on their time — it also makes sense to keep website editors happy. Keep them in the loop, helping them understand the content process, and make a smoother Web workflow to make better websites.

It takes more than just empathy, though, more than putting ourselves in their shoes. It takes *action*.

When we say empathy, we also mean *perseverance*; not only putting ourselves in the shoes of those we create for, but also making sure we don't give up on them if they don't immediately understand our process, or when it seems like they're resistant to change.

We mean *empowerment*, doing what we can to make teams and co-workers and bosses and everyone involved feel like they're not just implementing some random change, but that they have skin in the game. They have the power to facilitate change on their own. The website is theirs, ready to be shaped into something awesome.

We mean *passion* — for the project and the industry, passion for solving the problems that will undoubtedly arise. We need to be able to say, "Yes, this is a lot of work right now, but it's going to be OK. It's going to make your customers happy. It's going to make your team happy."

And finally, we mean *humility*, a trait we often overlook. There are two faces to content strategy, just as there two faces to every part of the Web process. Where there are two faces, there are two opinions, so we must admit, often, that — *shudder* — we're wrong. That we didn't fully understand the relationship between departments, or that we were overzealous with the changes we proposed.

If there's anything we're charged with doing, it's to remember the difference between knowing how to do something and communicating how to do that thing. We can create the best website we can, with design that's out of this world and Pulitzer-level content. But it's worth nothing if we can't communicate to our clients and teams how to use it. It's worth nothing if we create for the user, but forget to create for the editor.

Content strategy is not a singular discipline, and the Web isn't some kind of exclusive club. Our industry has been forged in a mix of disciplines, each of which have adapted to the current situation to create better, more readable, nimbler and certainly more effective websites.

I am a content strategist. You are a content strategist. Everyone who works on a website, who works with words, who works in communication or journalism or public relations is, in essence, also a content strategist at some point in their career.

I am also a website user and an audience. So are you. We're on both sides of the coin. Which is why it's up to us to create better content models and editorial calendars, not to mention better Web editing software and content management systems, to make sure the great Internet things we make can be taken care of, at launch and beyond. Empathy is just a buzzword until it's paired with a corresponding action. So let's start taking action.

ABOUT THE AUTHOR

Corey Vilhauer is User Experience Strategist at Blend Interactive, a Web shop in the heart of the Midwest, where he specializes in content strategy, information architecture, and editor/end user quality assurance. Corey is a recovering advertising copywriter and productivity junkie. Despite these hardships, he still likes to write at length about methodology, empathy and small business content strategy at www.eatingelephant. com Elephant (http://www.eatingelephant.com) and about other things at Black Marks on Wood Pulp (http://www.blackmarks.net).

Chapter

11

Supporting
Your Product

Written by Rachel Andrew

CHAPTER ELEVEN · BY RACHEL ANDREW

SUPPORTING YOUR PRODUCT

Most of your competition spend their days looking forward to those rare moments when everything goes right. Imagine how much leverage you have if you spend your time maximizing those common moments when it doesn't.[1]

— Seth Godin

I never intended that technical support would become part of my job. As one of the founders of Perch[2] (a self-hosted content management system), however, technical support is one of the most important parts of my day-to-day work. When I talk to other developers about our move from being a service business, developing projects for clients, to becoming a product company, I typically get two responses. The first is to express how great it must be to only work on our own product; the second is to ask whether the support is a nightmare!

Perch is self-hosted: our customers download the software and install it on their own hosting and local development environments. Unlike a software-as-a-service application, we have very little control over the environment into which our software is installed, and PHP Web hosting can be a fairly hostile environment.

---

1 Seth Godin, "Winning on the uphills", http://smashed.by/winning, 21 July 2009.
2 http://grabaperch.com

Our typical customers are Web designers, many of whom have never used a CMS, or installed something that relies on a MySQL database before.

So even if our product is incredibly usable and bug-free, we will always have people with crazy hosting configurations or who are just unsure how to get started.

Something that has always surprised us is the importance placed on support by our customers. Early on, we took to marking as favorites on Twitter the nice things people said about us, so we could display them on the website. It was notable how many of those tweets were not about features of the product, but about the support we gave. How you treat customers who turn up in support will make a huge difference in how they feel about your product or service. Does their customer experience make them feel valued? Do they really feel that their call, ticket or email really is important to you?

Providing a good customer experience is really important in support. The customer may make that initial contact feeling annoyed about your product. They have an issue, and it isn't doing what they wanted it to. Your aim should be not only to solve their problem, but to leave them feeling more positive about your product than they would if they hadn't had the issue that brought them into support in the first place.

The Hidden Value of Customer Support

I hope anyone reading this book understands that customer support and a focus on customer experience are important in their own right. Therefore, much of this chapter will deal with how we actually provide support.

Before I talk about the nuts and bolts of actually giving support, I'd like to start by talking about the hidden benefits great customer support can bring to your product or service. In addition to shaping a great experience for customers, support can make people confident to try your product in the first place; it can be a fantastic marketing tool; and it can be a source of market research and product development information.

BUILDING CONFIDENCE TO TRY A NEW PRODUCT

Just the fact that you offer support at all can be a huge selling point. In our case, we sell a commercial product that has many free competitors. Purchasing a license entitles customers to free and unlimited support, so our customers can rely on someone being there to help them. Our customers use our product to provide services to their own customers and need to have confidence in getting help quickly if they encounter difficulties. They can't wait for days to receive help when their website has to go live the next day, and they need to be sure they won't end up missing a deadline because of slow — or no — support.

There are a number of open-source competitors to Perch, not least the behemoth that is WordPress. Support for these products, however, is often by way of a community forum, where you might get help, but as you haven't paid any money, it is down to some kind soul being willing to help you free of charge. The inclusive support we offer, therefore, can be a huge selling point to move the customer from wondering whether they should pay for a CMS solution, to parting with the money for a license fee.

SUPPORT CAN BE YOUR BEST MARKETING TOOL

One of the reasons I write and talk about support is because of the huge part it has played in the success of Perch. It is the thing people talk about the most, and speaking to the developers of the product, not just technical support staff is a big part of that. Support really can be your best marketing tool, because people talk about the experiences they have.

As I've already outlined, offering support may be a significant differentiator between your product and free alternatives. Hearing from existing customers that the promise of support rings true underlines that promise far more than your own marketing materials ever could.

SUPPORT AS A MARKET RESEARCH TOOL

One customer well taken care of could be more valuable
than $10,000 worth of advertising.[3]

— Jim Rohn

For word about your product to spread, support doesn't only act as a marketing tool and talking point — it can also be a great place to find out what people want from your product. You can spend a lot of time and money doing market research, sending out and analyzing surveys, when an excellent source of information is right there in your support channels.

The more you engage with customers, the clearer things become and the easier
it is to determine what you should be doing.

— John Russell, former V.P., Harley-Davidson

Sometimes customers want to make suggestions or request features directly, so it is important to show you are open to comments and give people ways to do this. We provide a feature requests forum that also affords other customers the opportunity to read a request and comment on it, perhaps adding a new use case or, at the very least, demonstrating that this request is relevant to more people than the single user who proposed it.

Some companies take this a step further, using support systems such as UserVoice[4], which allow customers to vote for feature requests that have been posted by others. I'll talk a bit more about handling feature requests later in this chapter.

In our experience, it is important to take note of non-explicit feature requests; the times, for example, when you have to tell a customer that your

---

3 http://smashed.by/care
4 https://www.uservoice.com/

product doesn't do a certain thing. Keeping a record of those helps you see if the lack of a certain feature is encountered again and again.

Even less obvious are the points where customers have to jump through a few hoops to make something work in your product. In Perch, there are a lot of things you can do by writing a small amount of PHP, but many customers don't know PHP. We can save people the trouble of working out what to do by adding a simple function for frequently required tasks, allowing customers to just grab the code from examples in the documentation. This is the reason why I think it is very important that the product's developers also help out with support. Unless you see these types of issues come in, and think like a developer to solve them, they may get missed.

Customer support can be seen as a distraction by developers, as Josh Emerson from Clearleft explains, "Customer support can be very distracting. It has a tendency to pull you away from work and take you out of a state of flow." However, he also understands the benefits of involving developers in supporting the customers whom they write code for: "The major benefit of having a developer handle customer support is that it allows them to directly make changes to improve the product based on customer feedback."

I strongly believe that developers should be involved in support. In a larger company, however, you can manage people's time so they help with support without it becoming a distraction when they are writing code. For example, at 37signals all of the developers are involved in support, with everyone taking it in turns to spend a day working with customers.

Later in this chapter I'll discuss the tools that you can use to do technical support, but when setting up any system I would advise finding a way to collect all these types of feature requests and ideas that customers mention. They represent a goldmine of information when working out what features you'll add to future versions of your product.

In addition to feature requests for future capabilities, watch out for those that are already present but the customer just hasn't discovered yet.

This is a huge challenge for us because when we demonstrate the simplicity and speed of Perch for simple use cases, we sometimes fail to promote some of the more complex tasks it is capable of. Customers asking for current features indicate where this is happening. Often what's needed is better documentation, and you might want to check your marketing and sales information to ensure that features are listed in places people might try to find them.

Managing Feature Requests

I get support tickets that are nothing short of extortion.

— Andrey Butov

As I have described above, not all support tickets or posts to your product's forum will be issues that you can resolve, close before moving on quickly. Many tickets will essentially be feature requests, especially in the early days of your product. If you launched with a small feature set to test the water, you will soon get a lot of requests for features and additions.

The above quotation from Andrey Butov was something he said in an edition of the Bootstrapped podcast[5] that he hosts with Ian Landsman. Butov spoke about supporting his mobile products and how customers have threatened him with a one-star review in the App Store if a certain feature wasn't added. I'm glad I don't operate in that world, but we do have to manage customers who see one particular feature as vital, despite theirs being the only request for it. How can you manage such requests and keep the customer happy?

I have already mentioned my top tip for managing feature requests: make sure that you log who asks for what, whether as a direct request or when you have to tell a customer that your product doesn't do what they'd like.

---

5 http://bootstrapped.fm/

This log is important as it allows you to check whether a feature is indeed requested by a lot of different people, or whether it just seems that way because of one or two noisy people repeatedly asking for it. Once you have that list of requested features and can see what is floating to the top, you have something to work with.

PROTECTING THE CORE USE CASE

Perch has very much been driven by customer requests. We launched with a product quite different in scope to what it is today. At launch we had a simple content editor — no ability to add new pages or resize images, and no API, so no add-ons or ability for users to develop them.

With new pages, for example, we had assumed that our target market would want to protect the website architecture as designed and not want clients to add new pages all over the place. However, our customers had other use cases in mind and the ability to add new pages became a top feature request, something we added to the product fairly early on.

It is vital that you maintain control of your product and protect it from feature bloat as you try to fulfill customer requests. Remember that it is perfectly acceptable for your product not to be a perfect fit for everyone.

If you try to cater to every possible need then you're likely to end up with a product that's difficult to use, with so many options that people find it hard to get started. In our case, that would mean ending up like so many other CMS products of the type we try to provide an alternative to.

We deal with this by strongly protecting our core, basic use case — a use case that hasn't changed in the four years since we launched. Once Perch is installed, to start editing content on a page you need to include the Perch runtime and then add a Perch content tag to your page.

Then, all you need to do is reload that page in your browser and the region will show up in the admin area where you can select a template and start editing.

```
<?php include('perch/runtime.php'); ?>
<!doctype html>
<html lang="en">
<head>
    <meta charset="utf-8" /><title>Perch Example Page</title>
</head>
<body>
    <?php perch_content('Content'); ?>
</body>
</html>
```

We never want the experience of getting started with the product to become more complex than that. However, our customers see almost every feature request as an addition to perch_content — the tag that declares a Perch region on your page. They want to pass an ever increasing number of variables when creating a region, which would leave us with something like the following on the page, and users would have to make a whole bunch of choices just to get started.

```
<?php include('perch/runtime.php'); ?>
<!doctype html>
<html lang="en">
<head>
    <meta charset="utf-8" />
     <title>Perch Example Page</title>
</head>
<body>
    <?php perch_content('Content','index.php','article','html',true,'ti-
tle','ASC','singlepage',true,'index.php.true,1,true,',','admin,hr','tit-
le,text'); ?>
</body>
</html>
```

We want people to get started simply and then discover the more complex features as they need them. So, while we log these requests, we don't implement them in the way the customer has requested. That might work for that particular customer, but it would damage the experience of so many others.

In the case outlined above, there are ways people can declare regions in code and add additional options to regions — using alternative tags — so you can often use these requests to prompt thinking around a solution. If we can provide a frequently requested feature in a way that doesn't damage our basic use case, then, assuming we don't burn up a lot of development time for a very rare use case, we generally will.

However, you need to make that call on a feature-by-feature basis. If your product has an API, as Perch does, you can add extra features by way of plugins for the core product, and make the API available so people with specific needs can develop their own functionality.

I see this need to protect the core use case as a potential problem when using a public system that enables upvoting. There might be a popular feature request that just doesn't sit well with the core use case you want to protect. Not addressing it may cause people to believe that you are not listening.

I spoke to Ian Landsman of UserScape[6], which develops helpdesk application HelpSpot[7], the system we use for our customer support. I asked him if certain features weren't included because they were outside the scope of support, or issues that software shouldn't attempt to solve. He said:

> Absolutely. In fact HelpSpot takes this more seriously than most. Many of our competitors have lots and lots of other features that, to me, fall outside of customer service, like network monitoring, asset tracking, CRM functions, network password resets and so on. Obviously, some people like the all-in-one solution, but we'd much rather build something that's very focused on one specific problem and solves it well rather than be all things to all people.

When you do have to push back on a feature, perhaps because it doesn't fit the product or is useful only to a small minority, you do risk upsetting a

---

6 http://userscape.com/
7 http://www.helpspot.com/

customer. This is especially true if you have the requester of that feature is very vocal. We've experienced that scenario once or twice, and the customer has then accused us of not listening to our customers. I find that really hard to deal with because we spend all day listening to our customers and trying to make the best product for them.

What I have to remember in such cases is that we don't add a feature because we do listen to and understand our customers; including that feature would not benefit the majority, or may even be detrimental to many people's use of the product.

I see this as the main downside of having the developers of a product also supporting it. As the founder of a company and developer of a product you can't help but feel emotionally attached to it. When customers accuse you of not helping them, or tell you your product is terrible because it doesn't do a certain thing, it can be hard to deal with. That is the time to walk away, take a deep breath and look at your list of lovely things that people say!

When adding features based on customer requests, you have to ensure that you always remember your base of happy customers. The people who like your product and use it without issue never show up in support. Keep them in mind when planning additions and don't let the views of a noisy minority draw you away from a product that a silent majority are paying for and using quite happily.

Managing Difficult Customers

The customer is frequently "wrong". They are also a human being, so they deserve empathy, respect and the best possible advice we can give, even if that means pointing them to a competitor who would fit their needs better. It can be really easy to get caught up in the words that someone is using, rather than the intent — they reached out because they need some help.

— Jim Mackenzie, 37signals

While moving from client work to a product is something that many of us aspire to, it isn't quite the client-free utopia you might imagine. As developers launching a product, we went from dealing with very few clients over the course of a year to having thousands of customers to take care of. The majority of customers happily use our product and we rarely hear from them, although there are some names that we know very well in support.

When I talk to my peers about Perch and support, they tend to ask about how we deal with customers who take up all of our time and ask question after question. There are days when it feels as if we are just building some websites one ticket at a time, but I thought it would be interesting to take a look at our actual sup-

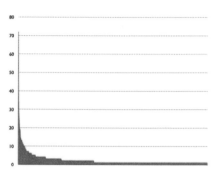

The long tail of customer support.

port statistics. Only 26% of our customers have ever raised a support ticket and only 10% have raised more than one ticket. Once we get to the more frequent requesters, we find that 10% of requests are made by the same 10 people and in fact 2% of requests are from one customer.

The graph above demonstrates that there is a long tail of customer support reflected in the majority of customers who never contact support or do so only once. We also have a very small number of customers who contact us a lot. In their defense, those top support requesters also have a lot of licenses and so have developed a lot of projects using our software. The idea that we will be swamped by people wanting basic help, or help with related issues such as their CSS, hasn't really held true. Yes, we do spend a significant amount of time helping some customers with poorly configured PHP hosting, or answering questions better suited to a CSS forum. Yet, most of our customers we never hear from at all. We know they are using Perch and many of them have a large number of licenses, but it must just be working for them.

As long as your product has been accurately described and advertised, and your support materials are good, most customers should not need to use support at all. However, you should expect a few to become frequent faces in your ticket system.

THE END CLIENT PROBLEM

As Perch has become a more mature product, one set of difficult customers has started to appear, and for products like ours they're probably only going to increase. Because our software is installed by our customers for their clients, we have started to be contacted by those end clients, the people or company who had the CMS installed by a Web designer. How we have dealt with this makes for a case study in how to deal with the very specific situations that show up in support of certain products.

We can generally identify someone as an end client when we see a support request that reads something like: "How do I add an image to my 'About' page?" or "I can't log into my Perch." We usually ask people whom we suspect to be an end client, "Did you install Perch yourself?" We then get to hear the story of how their website was developed by a designer who has disappeared, or with whom the client has fallen out. Sometimes the client doesn't want to pay for updates and thinks they should be able to manage things themselves from now on. We had one client get in touch who was trying to transfer a license because, sadly, their designer had died. The more established Perch becomes as a product, the more of these situations we have to deal with.

The end client situation poses a few problems. First is the legal one of who owns the license. Our contract is with the person who bought the license: if that was the Web designer then our contract is with the designer. No matter how hard done by the client is (or thinks they are), we can't just give them control over the license, so we have to explain they need to contact the designer and get the designer to place a license transfer request with us.

Another issue is that we assume Web designers will be supporting their clients. We are not set up to support people using Perch as an editor, as we don't know anything about individual installations due to the CMS being self-hosted. We have to tell end clients that unless they have the basic skills in HTML, CSS and general website building and are able to follow our support materials, they need to find another designer.

We have dealt with sourcing those designers for end clients by way of our registered developer program. The Perch customers who sign up to this typically are experienced with and like the product. We can then send that list to the end clients as a start in finding someone to help them — we know that these experienced customers of ours have the understanding of the product to help them out. Hopefully, we all do well: we get to keep that person using our product; a designer gets a new, grateful client; and the end client gets help with their website.

This situation is only likely to be relevant to you if you offer tools or a service that people use to provide their own services. If, like us, you are in that situation, it pays to consider how to deal with people with whom you do not have a contract, but who are still users of your product and may well come to you for help if the relationship with the person who actually deployed your product breaks down.

DIFFICULT CUSTOMER, OR CULTURAL CLASH?

Customers are human and humans can view situations in unexpected ways.
— Marilyn Suttle[8]

Despite our best efforts, we have had the occasional incident where a customer has felt we were being unhelpful or even rude, and these have tended to be due to misinterpretation of our replies based on the fact that we are British and speak English, and our customers are from all around

---

8   Marilyn Suttle, "Customer Perceptions Matter More than the Truth", http://smashed.by/truth

the world. Even where English is a first language — which isn't the case for many of our customers — there is still scope for cultural differences to create confusion when discussing issues in support.

Our most extreme example of this came from a support ticket that Drew responded to. The customer was having difficulty with some part of the software and in one reply Drew referred to having a *mental model* of how something worked. This response made the customer furious and Drew couldn't see why. I read the thread and also couldn't understand why the customer had got so upset, and then it dawned on us: the customer thought that Drew had called her a mental model! Perhaps she was a model, we don't know. But we are not in the habit of calling our customers names.

Most areas of confusion are not as extreme as that, but it pays to use language that is as clear and simple as possible in support. The person you are responding to may have English as a second language, may find following written instructions difficult for whatever reason, or may simply not understand your sense of humor or colloquialisms from your part of the world.

One of the challenges of being a business offering a digital product is that you essentially become an exporter from day one. Traditional businesses will often be quite well established before they start to export to new markets. When selling a digital product, you have the advantage of being able to sell worldwide with little extra outlay, but it does mean that you have to learn very quickly how to cope with customers who may not speak your language well, or have different expectations of you based on what is normal in their culture.

CUSTOMERS WHO REALLY NEED A DIFFERENT PRODUCT

We have a few customers who are not from our target market, and are not the sort of person we have in mind when we make decisions. Perch was always aimed at professional Web designers and developers, so we assume our users know HTML and CSS. We don't assume they understand PHP, or how to set up a database or any of the more technical parts of using a content management system. But we do expect them to know how to develop a static HTML website.

We have, however, picked up a number of customers who use visual development tools such as Dreamweaver and Freeway Pro, and who don't know HTML. When such person contacts us prior to buying our product we always explain that Perch requires HTML and CSS knowledge. If they then go on and buy, however, it can be quite difficult to support them.

We have recently raised the price of the product, making it perhaps slightly less attractive to the hobbyist, and aiming more at the professional market. We would need to make a number of compromises to make Perch usable for people without any HTML knowledge. We don't want to compromise the product in that way because we want the product to be a tool for professional use, and to attract professional designers and developers to it. There are other website building tools out there that would be a better fit for the non-coder.

Supporting customers who are not a good fit for your product is difficult, as to meet their requests and needs could mean becoming a different product. Good sales material can help, as well as clear indications of who the product is for, with typical use cases. However, our experience shows that even when we tell a potential customer directly that we don't think Perch is for them, they sometimes still go on to buy a license.

REALLY DIFFICULT PEOPLE

We've found that by being friendly and professional we don't have a huge number of problems with truly difficult customers. Probably the hardest support conversations are with the noisy person with the very specific feature request that we have explained we are not going to fulfill.

We offer unlimited free support, which I feel releases us from some of the potentially tricky conversations we would have if people paid per incident. It doesn't matter what the issue is: if we can help we do, or we help the customer get help (for example, if the issue is with their host).

There are, of course, some people who are impossible to please. As long as they are a rarity rather than the norm, it is likely the problem is with them — not you or your product. My advice is to remain objective at all times, treating the difficult customer in the same way as any other customer, and working to solve their problem.

Support Pricing Models

In the previous section I mentioned that we provide free and unlimited support at Perch. Support always incurs a cost in terms of your or your employees' time. How you recoup that cost will depend on the pricing model you decide on. You will find models that range from free support included with purchase, support subscriptions, and per incident models, where you pay each time you place a support request.

We are often asked why we decided on offering free and unlimited support, rather than a paid support subscription or per incident support. An important reason for not choosing a pay per incident model or a subscription is that we feel that we should not benefit from people needing support. Not every support request is related to a failing in the product or documentation, but by offering free support we place the onus on us to make sure people have a great experience.

As I have already shown, the customer who expects us to help build their website one ticket at a time is very rare. Making people pay for support essentially penalizes everyone, because a few people need a lot of help.

We also wanted our product to fit easily into the sales process for the average Web design job. Typically, designers quote on a project basis, including any costs for scripts and services used. If they then needed help and had to pay for that help, they might not be able to pass that cost back to their client.

We have always wanted our pricing to be fair and easy to understand. So when we decided on the price of Perch, we had to work out how much we needed to make to be able to afford to support it as well as develop it. With a new product that was obviously a bit of a guess, but if you want to offer inclusive support you need to factor that time in when setting your price.

For SaaS applications, customers usually pay monthly for the service, so you already receive a recurring payment which generally includes support. In this case, you need to ensure that the monthly charge covers the time needed to offer that support.

While we feel that offering free and inclusive support with a license for Perch is the best solution, other companies in our space have moved away from that model. The ExpressionEngine[9] CMS used to operate under a similar model to Perch but recently moved to a paid model. ExpressionEngine users get three months of support included when they first buy a license, but then must pay for continued support with a subscription at various levels.

These support plans are a mixture of a subscription and per incident support. A plan includes a number of urgent tickets, though you can also purchase additional urgent tickets if you need them. Ellis Labs published a blog post[10] detailing why they moved to this system, which gives some insight into their decision making. The key driver seems to have been economic, and they state:

> *The cost to provide an ongoing service isn't well-supported by one-time purchases, and the disconnect only grows more severe as the number of one-time purchases increases.*

Based on our experience, I would disagree that offering inclusive support is impossible. Despite a Perch license being a one-time purchase, customers return to buy additional licenses. What we have seen is that we often give far more support for the initial license purchase than would be expected for the price of a license, yet because our customers go on to buy a license for each website they build, over time it balances out. I have

---

9 http://ellislab.com/expressionengine
10 http://ellislab.com/blog/entry/rethinking-tech-support

included the Ellis Labs information here because I think it interesting to compare the approaches of two companies that are quite similar in terms of the type of product sold and support requirements.

Another model used by some companies offering a self-hosted system or desktop product is to combine a one-off cost for the software with a yearly support fee that also includes updates to the product. HelpSpot uses this pricing model for support and updates.

With a subscription model, quite often the initial purchase includes one year of support; if you wish to continue to receive support and upgrades, then you must renew the support part of the license. With this model, however, you can continue to use the software even if you do not require continued support for it. We don't often use support from Help-Spot, although we do like to keep the software up to date with any upgrades. I am very happy to pay my yearly support subscription as I know the work that goes into a product and I'm glad that the product continues to be developed and supported.

Whether you charge explicitly for support or bundle it with your one-off or monthly charge, the cost of support has to be absorbed somewhere along the line. When you make pricing decisions for your product, be sure to account for the time it will take. If you feel that support is draining your resources, it will be far harder for you to feel happy about going the extra mile for a customer.

Customers can be upset if the support or pricing model changes in a way they feel is detrimental to them. That isn't to say you shouldn't change it if you realize your current model isn't working for you, but it is worth putting some serious thought into your initial decision because if you can get it right first time it saves potential bad PR around a move.

Strategies to Minimize Support

Collectively you can find very telling patterns [...] if lots of people are asking where to find something then you probably have a design problem there.

— David Goss

Providing some amount of support is inevitable. However clear your documentation, someone will need help to get started; however careful your testing, some bug will slip through. So a sensible strategy for support should also include attempts to minimize the number of requests that come in. We have been very successful with this approach at Perch; despite a large increase in license sales and new customers over the course of the past year, the number of support tickets that we are dealing with has remained fairly level.

How are we managing this? For Perch, we attempt to design support requests out. If people regularly have to request support for a particular area of your product, is it possible to remove or change the thing that causes those requests, rather than assuming them to be inevitable? As an example, we were receiving a number of tickets every week where first time users installed Perch, reached login, and then saw the following message: "Sorry, your license key isn't valid for this domain."

The updated screen gives instructions to the user.

These users had missed the part of the email sent with their license details that explained they needed to log into their account on our website and configure the domains they were using Perch on. It would have been easy for us to sit back and complain about users who don't read, and continued to deal with the tickets as they came in.

However, this issue meant that a first-time user had a slower start than we would like, as they had to post a ticket and wait for us to answer, and we were spending time responding to the same request over and over again. We made these requests disappear with a simple change to the messaging on that screen. Rather than just tell the user they had done something wrong, we told them how to fix it. This meant that our customer could quickly get started with our product rather than needing to wait for support.

Particularly with a technical product, it will not always be possible to prevent people getting stuck. What seems obvious to a more technical user can be baffling to a beginner. So, if you are frequently answering questions about a specific part of your product, there may be things you can do to help people with it.

While many of our customers are very used to installing and using a content management system of some type, perhaps having come from using WordPress, we have a significant number for whom Perch is the first CMS they have installed. If your experience of Web development to date has just been flat HTML files, then any system, no matter how straightforward, is going to involve learning new concepts. We found that we were stepping people through the initial stages of using Perch. Once they had grasped the concepts we often didn't hear from them again — they just needed some help to get started.

We reduced the frequency of these requests by creating a set of tutorial videos. These help the newcomer to Perch through the initial setup and basic implementation on a website. We have found that these greatly reduce the amount of initial handholding we need to do. Having a variety of support materials will ensure that your customers can learn in a way that is appropriate for them.

No FAQs Policy

We have always tried to avoid the frequently asked questions page, which tends to end up being merely an expedient place to push customers toward, and a way to avoid trying to solve a problem from even occurring.

The previous example of our login page is a great example of this. It would have been really easy for us, had we had a FAQ area, to just put that information there. However, this information is already detailed on our website and in the post-purchase email, yet people were still missing it.

I don't think adding it to a FAQ page would have done anything other than providing yet another place for people to not look for the information, so it wouldn't have actually mitigate the real problem.

We believe that where possible the problem causing people to get in touch with support should be fixed, or an explanation sensibly placed in the documentation. Simply sticking things into a FAQ page is rarely the best approach.

TOOLS FOR SUPPORT

I think anyone starting a business that will require customer support should set themselves up with a proper scalable system from the start — make it work for having just 1 support "agent" but also make sure it will still work if you suddenly have 10. Just pointing support@mycompany.com to your own inbox is a bad way to start. When that transition happens, it probably means you are growing so there'll be plenty of other stuff going on, so you don't want to be dealing with migrating helpdesk systems and changing processes at the same time.

— David Goss

There are a huge range of options available to help you manage customer support requests. From simply offering support by email to SaaS helpdesk apps, how do you choose the best method of supporting a product?

When launching a small product or service, often the first thing that people do is to post a support@ email address and deal with the issues right there in the inbox. The problem with email support with no other system backing it, is that it is very hard to scale. If several people all log into the same mailbox, you will need to enforce some kind of system to make sure that requests don't get missed (because everyone thinks someone else will look at it), and that requests don't get answered twice (as two people jump on the email at the same time).

If you have a very small team, perhaps with one person taking responsibility for dealing with email, this might work. If you see the need to scale your support at any point, however, then my advice would be to look at what systems can be put in place to ensure that you are not reliant on a single inbox as your system. Many helpdesk products allow customers to contact you via email, so moving away from email as a method of managing requests does not mean that your customers will need to log into and post to a support forum. The system can be completely transparent to the user.

Support Statistics

Something that a helpdesk system can often do is provide statistics about the support tickets raised: the figures I quoted earlier came directly from our support system. By being able to discover trends in support, you can see if a feature in your product or service has caused a spike or a drop in the number of tickets. You can get some idea of how your support requirements need to grow to meet the needs of an increasing number of customers. This can help you to plan for hiring additional support staff ahead of time, and check that the revenue you will have at that point will be sufficient to cover that expansion.

In addition to giving you a basis for long-term planning, statistics can help you plan the day-to-day support needs. When we deliver a major new version, we see a large spike in the number of tickets as people upgrade and try out new features. Knowing that this occurs means that we don't plan to do anything that would make it difficult to do support in the few days after a release.

CANNED RESPONSES

A canned response is a standard reply to a standard question, that can be quickly sent when that question is asked. We find these very useful for common situations where a customer has not given us enough information at first to be able to help them. For example, Perch has a diagnostic report available in the software, and we ask that customers requesting support paste this into their ticket as

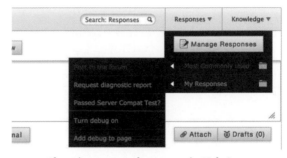

Choosing a canned response in HelpSpot.

it gives us a lot of information about the particular environment that our product is running in. If the customer has not added that information we can, with one click, send out a response asking for it.

Some product owners and those providing support worry that canned responses might remove the personal touch. Josh Emerson from Clearleft voiced this concern saying:

> *I spend a lot of my time replying to customers with very similar solutions [...] I often consider automating my customer response in some way, but I'm concerned that by offering a more automated solution, the quality of our response would suffer. I hate to contact a company and get a generic response that does not answer my question. I especially hate it when the email pretends to come from a real person.*

He goes on to say, "I'm sure there are better solutions, such as filtering and sorting emails to speed up my work, potentially prepopulating the most likely response, but with a human verifying that the response is correct before sending it."

I think that using tools to ensure people with the same question get the same answer is a beneficial thing. In addition to saving you time and preventing you from writing the same answer over and over again, you can craft good clear responses to common questions. Ideally, these sorts of questions are also answered in your documentation but, as we all know, not all users will read the documentation no matter how clear it is.

Like Josh, I wouldn't want to send entirely automated responses to people requesting help, but canned responses can save a great deal of time in typing the same reply over and over again. When the reply requires looking up some links in the documentation, the time you can save is substantial over the course of a week.

The system we use allows us to edit the response before sending it, so I sometimes use the canned response as a starting point and also add some information that I can see is relevant to a particular customer. A good system should let you use your template responses as a starting point, rather than relying completely on a standard response to each customer.

SELECTING A HELPDESK PRODUCT

The solution that is right for you must be driven by the type of support you need to do. There is a wide range of helpdesk systems, each trying to solve the problems of providing support in a particular way. This chapter can't attempt to review all these systems, as any such review would be projected through the lens of what I feel is important. Therefore, I suggest that before you start trying out systems, you should consider what sort of support you want to offer to your customers; you can then assess each system against those requirements. For example, if you plan to offer phone support, can those tickets be logged in a system? Some systems assume you are offering Web-based support only. Is social media support within the system valuable for you? Is there anything about the types of responses you need to give that you should check is supported? Before setting up trials of the various systems, consider the following things:

- What are the methods (phone, email, Twitter, Facebook, logging into a ticketing system) we want people to contact us by?
- Are support requests usually short questions and answers, or do you expect longer threads discussing an issue back and forth?
- Should support be public, private, or a mixture of both?
- If you use a public system, should customers be able to comment on and advise each other?
- Do you need to be able to collect specific information when a customer posts a ticket?
- Do you need to be able to verify a customer's status in any way? This is important if you have limitations around support.
- Do you need to integrate support with any other systems?

In our case, one of the important features is that the system allows us to post code examples into tickets and forum responses. Much of our support involves helping someone with their templates or custom PHP. Some systems had very poor support for doing this. When we asked for advice as to how to get round the issue they suggested that we get all of our customers to use a third-party tool for displaying code snippets. In our eyes, that just put up an additional barrier for people wanting help. What might seem a very small thing became a deal breaker for us with some of the popular systems.

We would also advise caution when having a completely public system where customers can help each other out. People often post secure information — things like database connection details — into the public domain. Customers don't always realize that their ticket will be public.

Another issue we found was that if a customer replied to another with incorrect advice, the original poster wasn't always aware that the response wasn't official support. As we try to craft a good support experience for our customers this was a concern to us. Our current system has a forum and a separate ticketed support area. We encourage implementation requests, CSS problems and feature requests to be posted to the public forum where we and other Perchers can respond. Quite often, if a request is really to do with a third-party jQuery plugin or a certain editor such as Dreamweaver, other customers know more about this than we do!

Many support systems have an API so you can link up other systems that you use or develop extra functionality that is specific to your requirements. As David Goss, who supports the e-commerce website for Thackerays[11], explains:

> We've gotten on very well with Zendesk. It's flexible enough so we can set up the workflow and processes as we want them, but the really useful thing is the API, so we can do a lot of stuff automatically from the back end of the website. For example I'm making a change to our "payment failed" page at the moment so if a customers payment fails there's a button for them labelled "Help – I don't know why my payment failed" and that will generate a ticket with all their order and payment details attached to it and email them to let them know we're looking into it for them.

> Also being more proactive is something I'm working on. Most helpdesk systems are based on the premise that a customer has a problem and reports it to the company, but if we see a problem before the customer does, like maybe their delivery gets delayed a day or something they ordered is out of stock, we want to open a ticket on their behalf, let them know what's happening and ask what they'd like to do, as automatically as possible. With the API this is actually going to be pretty easy to get done.

---

11 http://thackerays.co.uk

Try to make the experience of receiving support as simple as possible. The large helpdesk systems all do a fairly similar job, with slightly different features and focus. They can help you create fairly complex systems for your support operation. If you have very simple support needs then a full helpdesk might seem like overkill. I believe this is why many companies stick with just managing email support in their inboxes. However, there are smaller solutions out there as companies seek to solve support issues in new ways. One such solution comes from the developer of the HelpSpot system we use, and it's interesting because it's a new product in the same space as HelpSpot, but designed to fill this need for smaller, simpler systems.

Snappy[12] is a brand new product, but I mention it here as I think it has a lot of potential for anyone reading this thinking that a big solution is unnecessary but who would like to have something in place to help manage email requests. Snappy simply manages email tickets and responses in a modern and streamlined way. Your customers can send you emails and you can reply by email, but Snappy solves that immediate problem of tracking what has been responded to.

RESPONDING TO A TICKET IN SNAPPY

I think solutions like Snappy have a lot of potential for developers of small products. I can see this being a great solution if you support a mobile app, for example, where questions tend to be fairly straightforward. Ian wrote a blog post[13] about some of the thinking behind Snappy, which is interesting coming from someone who has also developed a larger helpdesk solution.

As the theme of this book is facing the future, I think including new breed support systems is important and I'll be very interested to see how Snappy and other systems that get away from traditional helpdesks develop. It is also interesting that a new system goes back to email at its core. Email is definitely not dead for most customers, and is often the easiest way for them to talk to us.

---

12 http://www.besnappy.com/
13 http://www.ianlandsman.com/2012/08/28/building-a-better-human-helper

Using Social Media To Support Your Product

If you make customers unhappy in the physical world, they might each tell 6 friends. If you make customers unhappy on the Internet, they can each tell 6,000 friends.

— Jeff Bezos

Big companies have jumped on Twitter and that having support representatives monitoring and helping people there is a great way to turn around customers' negative experiences quickly. When the representatives actually have power to help on Twitter then they can, in full view of other customers and potential customers, solve a problem and turn an unhappy customer about to vent their frustration to Twitter followers into a happy one.

Twitter was a natural place for us to talk about Perch and to talk to our customers and potential customers as Drew and I were already active there. We use the @grabaperch account to update people on any new software releases or tutorials and documentation and reply to questions. We also have a Facebook page and find that while people often like and share our posts, they tend not to chat or ask questions there as they do on Twitter.

We see Twitter as a really important way to communicate with customers. However, it isn't always the best place for providing support.

For us, responding to a support ticket often involves posting code. That isn't going to be possible in the 140 characters allowed in a Twitter message. Occasionally, all the person needs is a link to something in our documentation, and that can be dealt with on Twitter. So it really depends on what type of response is required.

Twitter can be ideal for quick answers, such as pointing someone to the right place in the documentation. Providing technical support on Twitter or Facebook might not be appropriate. By ensuring that people talking about your product or needing support get a response, you demonstrate that you are there to help. In addition, supporting people in such a visible way promotes your product and can help to encourage a sense of community.

Several helpdesk products have some form of social media integration. For example, Zendesk can turn a tweet into a support ticket, which can be useful to monitor the track that a request has taken. We haven't felt the need to have such tight integration between our helpdesk and social media activity, though many companies find this sort of integration helpful, in particular when dealing with a lot of support that originates from a social media channel.

37signals uses Twitter extensively when supporting its products, and while its chosen helpdesk system has Twitter integration, the team found it wasn't working out for them:

> *Since we got serious about Twitter, we've mostly used the built in Twitter functionality that our support tool (Desk.com) provides. When I asked the team how it was working for them a couple months ago, the general reaction was tepid. The consensus was that while it gets the job done, it was rather slow to use, and the large number of retweets and links to SvN posts mixed in makes it hard to get people with urgent questions answers promptly. Most of the team was using it, but no one was happy about it.*[14]
>
>   — Noah Lorang, 37signals

The series of posts about the Twitter tool used by 37signals is a fascinating look at how a company can take a small part of their support operation and really tailor the experience for support staff and customers. It also shows that even where you have selected a particular system for support, if part of it doesn't fit your needs you don't need to completely change to a different system. Instead, you can use an alternative approach in that area.

---

14   Noah Loang, "Behind the Scenes: Twitter, Part 1", http://smashed.by/scenes, 13 November 2012.

Another way to use Twitter is to be proactive in monitoring what people say about your product and jump in where appropriate. We have saved searches set up for terms such as Perch CMS and sometimes will contact someone talking about us, even when they haven't directly replied to @grabaperch. Used carefully this can be a good way of encouraging someone into support, rather than just asking their friends and peers for advice.

It also works very well for us in terms of pre-sales as we can ensure their questions are answered. You need to take care not to come across as spammy when doing this, however; we tend to just say, "Let us know if you have any questions" and then leave it up to them to respond to us if they want to.

A Final Thought

Always remember that support is about helping people have a great experience with your product or service.

Support is a vital part of a successful product. It can be beneficial to the product, even a source of customer research and a way of advertising. The ultimate aim of customer support, of course, is to help your customers get the most out of your product or service, to solve their problem quickly and get them back to doing whatever it is they purchased your product to do.

> *You have to be a nice person to do support well. You have to want to help people. Everything else — how to phrase your emails, how to use the helpdesk software, the technical knowledge — it can all be taught. You just have to care enough to get it right, and to keep caring, even when you are in a bad mood, or the servers are on fire.*
>
> *— Jim Mackenzie, 37signals*

If you approach support with the needs of the customer in mind, even when you don't have a perfect answer for them, you may find that it starts to become an enjoyable part of what you do, rather than the chore that many people believe it is.

Next Actions for Future-Friendly Support

I've assembled a to-do list and some further reading on the themes in this chapter.

For the New Product or Service Just Exploring How to do Support

1. Think about the type of support you will offer. Will it mostly be quick replies or will you need to give lengthy technical help? Where will requests come from: email, phone, social media, anywhere else?

2. Think about who will be doing the support now and in the short to medium term. What would you need to do if the product or service became an overnight success? Can you put at least part of that infrastructure in place to begin with?

3. Create a requirements list for support using my thoughts in the section on 'Selecting a Helpdesk Product'.

4. Use the information gathered above to research support solutions and create a shortlist of those that fit. These will be the solutions you can demo thoroughly before making a choice.

5. Write up a document detailing what tone you want to use in support, and make sure everyone who does support can access it.

For the Established Business Wanting to Enhance Its Support Offering

1. Make a list of the top five to ten issues that arrive in support.

2. From that list, can you identify something that you could stop being a problem by some change to your product or service? If so, make that change.

3. In that list is there something that could be better explained in your documentation or support materials? If so, make that change.

4. Identify five support requests that are really feature requests, whether explicit requests or areas where you have had to tell a customer that your product does not fulfill a certain requirement. For each request, consider if it is something that could: damage your core use case and should not be implemented; could be quickly implemented; or could be added to the long-term plans for the product. Don't forget to let customers know when you have implemented their suggestions.

5. If you have a FAQ page, are there issues that could be documented or dealt with in the product itself to stop them being frequently asked?

6. Revisit the above process regularly!

7. Are you using your support system to its full potential? Spend some time looking at any features you don't use. Can you improve your use of the system, perhaps by making use of an API to tailor your customer experience?

LINKS AND FURTHER READING

- Support Ops: a website and podcast with lots of practical technical support help and information. http://supportops.co
- Customer Complaints and Types of Customers: an academic paper from the University of Florida that details the types of personalities your customers might have, and how to deal with them. http://smashed.by/complaints
- The Help Scout blog is the blog of a helpdesk product but has a number of excellent articles about the business of doing customer support: https://www.helpscout.net/blog/
- 37signals blog contains a number of really useful posts about how they approach support: http://37signals.com/svn/support
- An article on Smashing Magazine that discusses customer experience in depth: http://smashed.by/like-to-love
- Bootstrapped, a podcast by Andrey Butov and Ian Landsman, creator of HelpSpot and Snappy: http://bootstrapped.fm/

ABOUT THE AUTHOR

Rachel Andrew is a front- and back-end Web developer, author and speaker. She has written several Web development books, including chapters for Smashing Books. She also writes about business and technology on her own site at rachelandrew.co.uk. In addition to offering consultancy services through http://edgeofmyseat.com, Rachel is also one of the developers of the content management system, Perch.

Chapter

12

The Design
of People

Written by Nishant Kothary

CHAPTER TWELVE · BY NISHANT KOTHARY

THE DESIGN OF PEOPLE

I AM GOING TO GET YOU FIRED!" yelled Prakash[1], the heavyset, smooth-talking and very politically savvy engineering manager, so loudly that I could feel my desk vibrate. I'd just returned from lunch and was clearing out my inbox when he marched in looking like Mount St. Helens right before it erupted. He was livid that my executive status report (a weekly report that I sent to all the stakeholders of our project, including the vice-president of the company) announced that the overall project status was "red", compliments of Prakash's team letting a few critical milestones pass. In other words, we were going to miss our launch date, again. We were over six months behind schedule now.

My brain flashed back six months to a conversation with my manager, John. "We need to chat," John began cautiously. I instantly braced for bad news. Thanks to his lackluster bedside manner, it went south pretty quickly from there. In the next thirty minutes he delivered a message in almost undecipherable corporate-speak that amounted to: You really suck at your job, it's making me look bad, and if you don't get your act together soon, I'm going to have to fire you.

---

1 All names have been changed to protect the guilty.

It hit hard because I had been working 70–80 hours a week and giving it my all in an environment that was as dysfunctional as a chimpanzee community with two alphas. We were understaffed, overspent, under tremendous pressure from the market, in the crosshairs of the CEO and, to make matters worse, I was fresh out of college and learning the ropes. And I was pretty green: that's software industry-speak for naive. In a nutshell, the project had gone to hell, and I was the perfect fall guy.

"I don't know what I need to do to fix things anymore. I need you to walk me through this," I said with resignation to John. Begrudgingly — after all, he was burning the candle at both ends, too, and really didn't have time to deal with his pesky employees. He started making a list of action items for me on the whiteboard. One of them was: Fix ownership column for each milestone in status report. Each milestone in the status report was to have one clear owner. One could debate the true owner for many of the milestones, and my default in such situations was to list myself as the owner. I was, after all, ultimately responsible for getting the project out the gate. So, when we missed a milestone, it was generally seen as my fault. And I didn't care.

"You don't own anything. You have no control over when one of those items is late or on track. You only have influence. Ultimately, someone else is responsible for each of those pieces, and you simply need to report their progress toward completion of their line-item," said John matter-of-factly. He instructed me to remove my name from the owner column for approximately twenty-five of the milestones my status report tracked.

I cringed.

It wasn't the first time I'd heard this. In fact, I'd rejected these words from the leading project management books. I philosophically disagreed with the tactic because, from a practical perspective, I reasoned, it simply shifted blame and generally ignored seeking out a solution to the overarching problem: the project had gone off the rails.

But things change when you have a gun to your head.

I transferred the commandments from the whiteboard to my notepad and left John's office that day determined to save my job.

And now here we were.

As I watched Prakash — the key to many of our critical organizational problems and, in fact, the true owner of the most critical milestones on the project — hyperventilate, I couldn't help but smirk. Success, even when it comes in this deranged form, still releases the same happy hormones into the blood stream. My amygdala (the most ancient part of our brains that, among other things, is responsible for the fight or flight response) slowly crossed its arms across its large pectorals with a smug grin on its face, leaving my imminent response in the capable hands of my neocortex: the newest part of our brain responsible for some of our most complex decision-making.[2]

"Dude. I'm just the messenger," I shrugged with deliberately practiced nonchalance. "You gave me these dates a few weeks ago. You didn't hit them. Now, if you're telling me that we can still ship on time irrespective of your items being late, then let's talk!" He just stared at me with rage and wonder for the next few seconds as his mind tried to work out how the tables had been turned. Then, abruptly, his amygdala took over again. He yelled some incoherent gibberish, swore at me one last time and stormed out of the office.

The product eventually shipped three months later, a full nine months behind schedule[3], to lackluster reviews and angry customers. Reeling from the epic death march, most of the team quit and left for other jobs. I received a good performance review at the end of the project, and was then assigned to one that was even more visible and important to the company. I had, after all, done my job "well".

I quit a few weeks later.

2 Bruce Schneier, "Risk and the Brain", 2008, http://smashed.by/risk

3 Underestimating the time estimated needed to ship a product is a cliché as old as the software industry itself. Among the many factors, one that weighs heavily is known as optimism bias. Tali Sharot's TED 2012 talk is a great starting point to learn about it: http://smashed.by/ted-time

The Goal of this Chapter

My account, even if a little extreme, is hardly unique. We've all been there in one capacity or another: a hard-to-deal-with co-worker, an incompetent boss, a micro-managing client, seemingly deranged leadership, design by committee... the list goes on.

There are myriad ways to slice and analyze my story. Some will empathize with it and express anger over dysfunctional work environments. Some will point a finger at bad leadership. Some will focus on the alleged worthlessness of middle management. Some will attribute the failures to the process — perhaps you should have used Agile methodologies. And some will suggest that I was, in fact, the true culprit and should have been fired; after all, I had led the project.

None of these analyses are wrong. In fact, they're all right. And there are many more I haven't mentioned that would apply as well. But no matter how much we analyze such situations in our postmortems and vow to avoid them at all costs in the future, we just can't help but frequently find ourselves in similar predicaments. While we have amassed a tremendous number of tactics and patterns that often help us narrowly avoid dysfunctional situations, we have a poor understanding of the root of the problem and, as a result, very little control over our destinies.

After years of working my way through more dysfunctional situations than I'd like to remember, I have firmly settled on a belief (in fact, it is the only belief I hold sacred anymore): almost every problem we face at work (and play) begins and ends with one or more people.

While we run off to fix processes, hire experts, solicit feedback from users, increase the number of code reviews per week, switch our programming methodologies, churn out more mock-ups, get blue in the face explaining our strategies to stakeholders, and implement a thousand other makeshift fixes, the real solution continues to elude us. Creatures of habit that we are, we simply shut our eyes and swim harder upstream until we find ourselves spent and jaded, ready to quit our jobs. But as someone wise once said, "The definition of insanity is doing the same thing over and over and expecting different results."

The goal of this chapter is simple: to introduce you to the human being as the center of every success or failure in our lives. But not in that tired way we're all guilty of where we commiserate and vent on Twitter. Or the way where we publish blog posts about the bureaucratic deadweights that are the true bottlenecks to innovation. Or even that way where we write articles, chapters and books that disseminate best practices for dealing with said deadweights. We've done it all before, and we'll surely do it again. But right now, let's resist the convenient cover of insanity. Let's stop putting more lipstick on the pig, and instead explore why the pig is so darn ugly in the first place. That is, let's talk about the root of the problem instead of the symptoms.

Grab a seat (and a drink).

Too Many Cooks don't Spoil the Broth

A few years ago I happened to find myself in charge of the redesign and consolidation of a set of very popular developer community sites, a project we'll dub Project Unify. We were combining five different sites, each of which had been serving a different target audience, and run by a different internal team. Together, the sites served thousands of unique types of media: everything from HD videos to short blog posts. Some organized their content in the form of shows; others featured live streaming content. The media came in all shapes, formats and sizes. The visual tone and information architecture of each website was different. By most measures, it was a complicated redesign.

To make matters worse, there were a ton of stakeholders across the company who were going to be involved in this project: hosts of the various shows, developers working on the different sites, the founders of the sites, managers, and even a few executives. And most of them weren't very happy about the existence of this project, for it meant that their day-to-day lives were about to change. Not to mention, they liked how things were.

I had tried to limit myself to smaller projects with fewer stakeholders after my experience with Prakash and team, and this was my first big project since then. I was nervous — after all, swimming with sharks and coming out alive is hardly a good predictor of your ability to survive the next expedition. But I was also excited. Thanks to an initial book recommendation from a friend, I'd ended up immersed in the world of human behavior — cognitive psychology, behavioral economics, neuroscience, anthropology, evolutionary biology and so on — and had amassed enough knowledge to warrant an experiment with a larger sample size.

Project Unify was a good opportunity for my career, but an even better one to put some of my newfound knowledge to the test.

THE PSYCHOLOGICAL EFFECTS OF FAIR SYSTEMS

In *Sway: The Irresistible Pull of Irrational Behavior,* Ori and Rom Brofman wote, "A group of researchers asked hundreds of felons from Baltimore, Detroit and Phoenix to fill out a survey. The first part of the survey consisted of factual questions, such as the nature of their conviction and the length of their prison sentence. In part two, the survey moved on to the questions about perceptions of fairness: How were you treated? How did you like the judge? Were the lawyers nice to you?" The researchers were attempting to deduce what factors affected inmates' perceptions of the fairness of the justice system.

What factor do you think most affected their perception the most? The length and severity of the sentence, right? Not quite.

The researchers found that respondents placed as much weight on the legal process as they did on the outcome. "One of the factors weighed most heavily by respondents was how much time their lawyer spent with them. The more time he or she spent with them, the more satisfied the respondents were with the ultimate outcome," wrote the authors. This is surprising because one would expect that inmates who were slapped with longer sentences after having spent a great deal of time with their lawyers would be more disgruntled. But the exact opposite was true. "Although the outcome might be exactly the same, when we don't get to voice our concerns, we perceive the overall fairness of the experience quite differently," concluded the authors.

Designers are prone to hiding from their stakeholders. Each of us has our reasons, but most of them are grounded in the fear of being told how to design something. But researchers have found time and again that fulfilling someone's need to be heard has more influence on their perception of the outcome of a situation than the actual outcome.[4] And if you're smart about it, you can both influence stakeholders into cooperating and create the design you believe to be right for the project at hand. On Project Unify I forced myself to make time for one-on-one conversations with around twenty stakeholders. I wanted them to meet me and get to know me. The meetings ranged from getting lunch together to letting developers wireframe their vision of the website on their whiteboards. I always kicked off the meetings with, "So, tell me what you think we should be doing for Project Unify?"

And boy did they.

Some vented about politics and bureaucracy (I joined in). Some vehemently disagreed with the project's existence (I empathized and reminded them about our pay grade). Others felt it was time for a professional designer to take this on (I hid my imposter syndrome[5] symptoms). Some focused on a specific aspect they really cared about (I took notes). And there were those who were just happy to be out getting a coffee during work hours (my type of people). It was an intense week.

But by the following week, the timbre of Project Unify was a solid

---

4   Ori Brafman, Rom Brafman, Sway: The Irresistible Pull of Irrational Behavior, 2 Jun 2009, pp. 121-125.
5   The Impostor Syndrome is a psychological phenomenon in which people, despite external evidence of their competence, remain convinced that they're frauds and don't deserve the success they have achieved.

positive. Stakeholders were cautiously optimistic, even excited to launch into such a contentious redesign. The turnaround in attitude far exceeded my expectations, so much so that informal one-on-ones have become an indispensible part of my designer repertoire.

A tremendous amount has been written about stakeholder interviewing on the Internet. I trust you will be able to search your way to the articles. But before you start creating checklists of interview questions about brand strategy, success criteria and user personas, consider for a second that while we need information from stakeholders, they need security from us. They need to be heard, and this need, when left unfulfilled, justifiably jeopardizes the project at hand in unfathomable ways. And the worst way to treat someone hoping to be heard is to walk in with a clipboard and a checklist. There will be time for that later. First, focus on what's important: the little things.

It is the little things, after all, that can have the biggest effects.

ANCHORING GOOD BEHAVIOR IN DESIGN REVIEWS

Getting stakeholders to feel optimistic about a project is one thing, but translating that optimism into useful and favorable feedback is entirely another.

There is a fascinating concept in psychology known as anchoring. *Anchoring* is a psychological phenomenon whereby humans rely heavily on the first piece of information they're offered (known as the anchor) in making subsequent decisions.[6] Dan Ariely, behavioral economist and author of a few of the most fascinating books on human behavior, provides a fundamental example on anchoring in his first book *Predictably Irrational: The Hidden Forces That Shape Our Decisions*: "A few decades ago, the naturalist Konrad Lorenz discovered that goslings, upon breaking out of their eggs, become attached to the first moving object they encounter.

---

6   Daniel Kahneman, "Anchors", Thinking, Fast and Slow, 2 Apr 2013, pp. 119-129.

Lorenz knew this because in one experiment he became the first thing they saw, and they followed him loyally from then on through adolescence."[7]

Over the past few decades, researchers have confirmed the role of anchors in all walks of life through seemingly bizarre findings: we are more likely to marry people whose names start with the first letter as our own, pick products whose brand names share the first three letters with our own, give favorable reviews to people who share our birthdate, and more.[8] In fact, the effects of anchoring extend even into the moral realm as Ariely demonstrated in his latest book, *The (Honest) Truth About Dishonesty: How We Lie to Everyone—Especially Ourselves*. Ariely conducted a study showing that you could almost eliminate cheating on tests — that is, you could literally make people more honest — by simply having students sign a simple honor code right before they took a test.

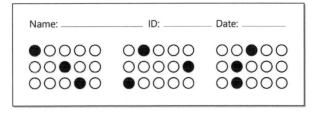

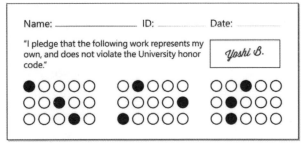

A regular exam bubble sheet (top) and a modified bubble sheet with honor code signature slot (bottom).

7　Dan Ariely, "The Fallacy of Supply and Demand", Predictably Irrational, Revised and Expanded Edition: The Hidden Forces That Shape Our Decisions, 2 Apr 2013, p. 27.

8　David Eagleman, "Mind: The Gap", Incognito: The Secret Lives of the Brain, 15 May 2012, pp. 55-75.

Back on Project Unify, I wondered to myself if I could use the power of anchoring to shepherd a very large and diverse group of stakeholders through the design review process without the drama and conflict we've come to expect in such situations. Was there anything I could do or say that would anchor the individuals in the group to focus on providing logical feedback rather than reacting from the emotion that they (and all of us) would naturally feel from looking at new colors, shapes and patterns that would be part of the new design? I thought it was worth trying and came up with a simple solution.

Right before my design team started working on the new design, I sent an email to the entire group of stakeholders. The email was structured as the customary piece of correspondence that explains the design process, but within it were hidden several anchors.

Let's walk through this email together.

THE EMAIL: YOU ARE GETTING SLEEPY, VERY SLEEPY

I've tried my best to reproduce the email in its original form but, inevitably, a few names and details need to be changed to protect the privacy of all involved. That said, none of the changes take away from the discussion at hand.

> From: Nishant Kothary
> Sent: Friday, May 01, 5:48 PM
> Subject: How to provide feedback
>
> Folks –
> Apologies in advance for the long email; if you think I've forgotten someone, please email me instead of adding them yourself. My intention is to keep the group limited to the core stakeholders. I will be soliciting feedback from others as needed.

Notice that the email was sent after hours on a Friday. This may not be an option for all projects, but I've found it increases the odds (unscientifically, of course) that your recipients will read the email in a positive frame of mind (first thing on Monday before the stress of the week kicks in).

I also note here that stakeholders are encouraged to not designate others at the company as stakeholders. That decision needs to be made by me. However, in return for this, they get to be part of the limited group of core stakeholders. A fair trade.

So, yes, hello again! We are entering the most critical design phase of the project — information architecture — and will be delivering wireframes soon. We're running a really tight schedule for the deliverables and this includes feedback loops, too. In this email, I'd like to get everyone on the same page about what's coming and how to remain involved. To that end, I've compiled a set of FAQ's, milestones and some instructions on how to provide feedback when the time is here.

There is one tiny element of anchoring here — "*and this includes feedback loops*". It set the expectation that the act of providing feedback would be bound to a tight schedule (much like the act of actually designing the site).

FAQ's

Will you be reviewing the wireframes with each of us? Nope. Doing reviews with individuals or even on a per team (John's team, Erics's team, etc.) basis is not feasible and also unnecessary. Instead, I'm going to share the wireframes with you electronically. They will also be posted on the Project Unify wall (I request that you stand in front of it to capture your feedback instead of printing the set of wireframes). I expect legible feedback through email. More on that towards the end.

May I drop by or just schedule a call with you to provide the feedback? No and no. :) There are quite a few of you, so it's not very scalable. If you deem the feedback important enough, then I would expect that it'd be worth your time to take 30 mins to type up a clean bulleted list of comments.

Next, an FAQs section as shown on the page before: Again, I'm emphasizing fairness. The takeaway is that we are all part of the team and we all have to contribute equally.

> *What if I don't understand some part of the wireframe?* I think this is going to be unlikely; a wireframe, after all, is simply a skeletal representation of the site with the color, fancy graphics, and real typography pulled out. But, there are always exceptions, and in those cases, I suggest you send me a quick email and I'll try to get back to you.

This is a message of support for anyone who happens to be feeling anxious about the process. There is an escape hatch, but it has constraints (I'll help you over email).

> *If I don't hear back from you, should I be offended?* No. With the volume of email that I expect to receive, I won't be able to respond to everything and everyone. You are going to have to trust that I've heard you and will do the needful to make your feedback actionable (and in many cases, I will be discarding it, or tabling it for future releases so we can hit our ship dates).
>
> *What if I don't see a feature that I really wanted in the site (and I even told you about it)?* Put it in your feedback email (discussed below), but bear in mind a couple of things, (a) it may have been tabled for future releases because this release is about getting a solid foundation in place and not all the bells and whistles, (b) it was a cool feature/idea but not necessarily worth investing in for the business.
>
> *Do I have to do this and will it reflect badly upon me if I have nothing to say to you?* Heck no. You've heard of the saying, "Too many cooks spoil the broth", right? You will actually be increasing our chances of success by not chiming in (and don't take that to mean, "Your feedback is stupid anyway, so bugger off"; I am just alluding to the fact that there is always a higher probability of finding sane solutions when you reduce the number of inmates running the asylum even if it could come at the regrettable cost of some valuable features and interactions).
>
> *If I don't provide feedback, will this project fail?* No. It's my (and the design team's) job to catch all the UX issues. If we're doing our job well, chances are that we will not be surprised by any of your emails (either we'll have already caught what you're pointing out and accounted for it, or we'll have discarded/tabled it with some objective-sounding justification).

There are several anchors hidden within this section: reviewing designs individually isn't feasible; providing written feedback is important; design is often subjective; the big picture is more important than individual features; "trust me"; and more.

Next up, a milestones section, but not just for various stages of design, but for providing feedback as well.

MILESTONES

Note that the above schedule is subject to change because of how tight things are right now. Also, I'll provide more milestones moving forward based on how this process goes. Mark your calendars!

- *Friday, May 8* — First round of wireframes will be distributed via email and posted on the Project Unify wall.
- *Monday, May 11 by noon* — Feedback due via email (described below)
- *Wed, May 13* — Second round of wireframes will be distributed via email and posted on the Project Unify wall.
- *Thurs, May 14 by end of day* — Feedback due via email

Holding stakeholders to milestones for providing feedback is not a new concept, but one we often stray away from because we generally don't know how to argue for it. The best argument is generally simple arithmetic. The design timeline itself was extremely tight for Project Unify. The design team had nine days (counting the weekend; this was definitely a burn the midnight oil project) to produce the wireframes for the new site. In comparison, the stakeholders had three full days to provide feedback. All in all, this proved to be another excellent anchor, and also a way to control scope.

Finally, the most important section : how to provide feedback. While most of this section is process-oriented, the final bullet point — "Your feedback must be actionable, rational and reasonable. In other words, focus on specifics of the wireframes and not wishful/nice-to-have things" — stands out. While it wasn't equivalent to an explicit signature (remember, Ariely had subjects physically sign an honor code before they

PROVIDING FEEDBACK

It's pretty simple. Send it via email and keep the following in mind:

- Send the feedback to me only. Do not send it to the entire group.
- Don't use any fancy fonts or formatting.
- Lists are good and required. Use bulleted lists for different points.
- Keep each point concise.
- Break questions out into their own section. In other words, you could have two sections in your email — Questions & Feedback.
- Your feedback must be actionable, rational and reasonable. In other words, focus on specifics of the wireframes and not wishful/nice-to-have things.

I think that's about all I've got right now. Let me know if you have any questions/concerns.

Cheers,
Nishant

proceeded to take the test), I hoped that this final point, combined with written and verbal acknowledgements from all the stakeholders in the following days would nudge the stakeholders to behave more rationally.

A better solution, in hindsight, would have been to have stakeholders individually respond with a digital signature of sorts to pledge their rationality; some email software like Microsoft Outlook allows you to enforce a binary response ("I accept" or "I do not accept") from each recipient upon receipt of the email. Also, if the Brafman brothers' report on inmates' perceptions of the legal process had broader applicability, then not only would this kick-off email succeed in inspiring fruitful participation in the process, but stakeholders would feel positive about the entire experience irrespective of the outcome.

So, the question is: did it work?

The Results

Simply put, yes. But it was the process and not the outcome that left me in admiration of the research that enabled the outcome. Sure, we successfully designed the website in three weeks. By any reasonable measure, this bordered on impossible given its scope. But what I found most fascinating was that the stakeholders not only provided feedback on time, but also offered incredible insights in a way I hadn't witnessed earlier in my career.

Many stakeholders went above and beyond in explaining their rationale when they disagreed with design team choices. Some provided helpful historical information to aid us in making the right design decisions. Others used their deep subject matter expertise to provide context for the changes they suggested. Developers specifically focused on the feasibility of implementing certain aspects of the proposed design. And a non-trivial number of stakeholders voluntarily pulled themselves out of the process. You got the sense that everyone was not only invested in the project, but also focused on moving the process forward. Particularly when the times got a little hairy.

For instance, at a later phase of the project, the art direction — specifically, a shade of teal that was a part of the art board — was met with some resistance. In such cases, stakeholders (even the best designers) often focus heavily on their personal feelings towards the art, as in "I really don't like this!" But, there's no way to truly weigh such feedback, and such situations typically tend toward heavy contention. The Project Unify group members, after acknowledging their visceral distaste for the color, focused on providing actionable and rational feedback: everything from suggestions on tweaks to the color, to its disconnect from the company brand. The stakeholders acted like ideal designers.

Now, you're probably wondering what was the essence of the email — what can you take and apply to the next project kick-off email that you send? There are obvious no-brainers that we've all picked up along the way from basic project management books; for example, by outlining the process clearly I reduced uncertainty, provided actionable next steps and, in turn, improved the chances that this project was going to succeed. While it's impossible to know exactly else what really helped and what had a neutral effect on this specific project, here are the core principles that I personally took away:

1. *Anchoring*

   The email set expectations about the design process with an eye on encouraging desirable behaviors among participants. It did so by employing the power of anchoring repeatedly.

2. *Fairness*

   The design process framed in the email employed what we know about the effect of fair systems in inspiring positive human behaviors.

3. *Honor Code*

   The phrasing and choreography of the email capitalized on the anchors that specifically influence short-term human morality.

4. *Social Coordination*

   The email unified the team by making the style of the feedback something that all stakeholders shared in common.

5. *Social Norms*

   The email removed me from the top of the accountability hierarchy and instead replaced my position with the project. If one person were to ignore the directions, they would be hurting the project instead of me.

It is worth mentioning that it wasn't an entirely smooth ride. There were a few stakeholders who turned in feedback far past their deadlines. When I rejected their feedback on the grounds that the time had passed, they escalated to the executive sponsor (and original founder of the sites). Fortunately, thanks to past experience, I had put some air cover (support from the most senior influencer on the project) in place before the project kicked off. He dismissed such escalations, in turn adding another strong psychological force to the forward momentum of Project Unify.

At this point, we'll stop talking about other people and start looking at our problems' roots from another angle. After all, there's a hard limit on what you can learn from even the best observations and discussions about other people. As the old proverb goes, "Nothing ever becomes real until it is experienced." Sure, we've used the word we throughout this discussion, implying that we — you and I — are prone to fall prey to all of the same psychological traps. But let's admit it, we aren't as cuckoo as others. Right?

You may want to refill that drink before you proceed.

Designing for Designers

A few years ago I co-founded a little community website for Web designers and developers. Our community published articles by invited guests (not unlike Smashing Magazine) about everything from UX strategy and the Web design process to management and philosophy. We also built open source software and shared it on a section of our community site.

Over time, the website gained some popularity with the Web community. The incoming traffic was enough for our team to consider redesigning the website to better handle our future plans. The original website was something I'd designed and coded over a couple of weekends. It wasn't very maintainable, and in the first year of running the website, we'd learned much more about our own brand, goals and identity. So, we set a deadline for ourselves, and I agreed to lead the redesign project. We shall dub it Project Redo.

I determined pretty quickly that I needed some help for this project. I had many other responsibilities at my job; the website redesign was simply one of them. But, I wasn't about to hand over my baby to just anyone. I needed someone I could trust, someone who'd give their life before letting my baby get hurt.

I reached out to a friend and local designer who fit the bill. Let's call him Dave. I called him on the phone and we chatted about the goals of the project. The stakes were high, I told him. "You have an incredible amount of freedom on this project. I am, after all, the only stakeholder. I want you to pretend like you're redesigning your own personal website. I want that care and energy. You game?" Dave signed up. In that moment, I became not only a friend and peer designer, but also a client.

We split the work between ourselves. I would be responsible for the information architecture. He would be responsible for visual design and front-end markup. We agreed to collaborate through it all. With that, I went to the drawing board to work on the information architecture. A week or so later I posted the wireframes to Basecamp. Dave reviewed them, we had a quick phone call, and he set out to turn the skeleton into a full-color being. A few days later he posted a color composition of one of the pages to our Basecamp project to give me a quick peek at the art direction. Needless to say, he really liked what he'd created. It's only natural, right?[9] Unfortunately, I could not see what he saw. Where he saw beauty, I saw the opposite. It was almost as if he was functioning in a reality entirely different from mine.

And, as the ingenious Sally–Anne test illustrates, he was.

THE SALLY–ANNE TEST

I first came across this gem in Kathryn Schulz's excellent book, *Being Wrong*. The Sally–Anne test is taken by children between the ages of three and four. It involves staging a simple puppet show involving two characters, Sally and Anne (figure a on the next page). Sally places a marble in a basket, closes its lid and leaves the room (figure b). Shortly thereafter, the very naughty Anne flips open the lid of the basket, pulls out the marble (c) and places it in a box sitting in the corner (d). Now, the child who has witnessed all of this is asked a simple question: when Sally returns, where will she look for the marble (e)?

Almost every child in this age group exclaims with confidence, "In the box!" This answer is baffling to adults for the obvious reason:

---

9 The tendency to fall in love with our own work is quintessentially human. It's beyond the scope of this chapter to deconstruct all the factors that go into this behavior, but a significant contributor is something known as the Ikea Effect.

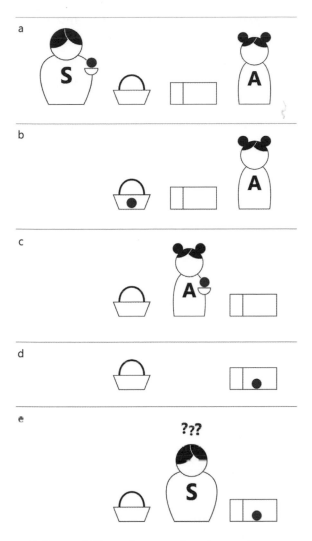

there's no way Sally could have known that the marble was mischievously displaced by Anne because Sally wasn't around to witness that. But the children don't care about this detail. To them, reality and their minds' representations of reality are one and the same. Sally thinks the marble is in the box because, well, it is in the box.[10]

10   Kathryn Schulz, "Our Minds, Part Two: Belief", Being Wrong: Adventures in the Margin of Error, 4 Jan 2011, pp. 87-111.

The children provide an incorrect answer because they have yet to develop what is known as the *theory of mind (ToM)*, a differentiating feature of human beings when compared to most other mammals. We develop ToM by the time we're five years old. In fact, if you were to administer the test to five-year-olds, you would be greeted with sheer bewilderment for having wasted their time before they gave you the right answer.

Theory of mind bestows on us two critical pieces of knowledge that, when wielded properly, have the ability to bring out the best in us:

1. Our mind's version of reality isn't true reality: it's just one interpretation of reality.
2. Everybody has their own mind and, thus, their own interpretation of reality.

But as David Eagleman, author of *Incognito: The Secret Lives of Brains* writes, "There can be a large gap between knowledge and awareness".[11] Back on Project Redo, I was completely unaware of the vicious cycle of irrationality I was about to enter. I called Dave.

IT'S MY PARTY AND I'LL CRY IF I WANT TO

I gave Dave my honest feedback. "I don't think this is the right direction, Dave. I don't know what else to say other than, it's too expected. The design is not bold." My Dan Ariely bobble-head was staring at me, and I admitted to Dave that I could be under some irrational spell. It was his call on how to proceed (but I had my fingers crossed behind my back). Seasoned as he was dealing with clients like me, he didn't flinch. "Let's try a completely new direction. It'll be fun." He went back to the drawing board, but his first design had already done the necessary damage in the form of setting a very negative anchor for me.

---

11 David Eagleman, Incognito, 15 May 2012, p. 58.

I just couldn't shake the fear that Dave was in over his head on this project. And by the time he posted the next color comp, a beautiful and entirely fresh direction for Project Redo, I was well into a psychological tailspin. What's worse was that I was completely unaware of it.

When I first opened the newly posted design, I was pleasantly surprised. It was definitely different. But after a few minutes, my limbic system — responsible for emotions such as fear and anger, and also the home of the amygdala that I mentioned earlier — took over. I concluded that this new design, while better, was simply a cousin of the first one, which, I was convinced, was truly horrible. Knowing well that I may have been under the spell of irrational biases, I decided to sleep on it. The next day, I pulled the design up on my monitor and nothing had changed. In fact, it'd gotten worse. I showed it to my wife, a teammate and a few others. Nobody shared my reaction. Most people said, "It's nice. But I'm not a designer."

I reasoned with myself, "OK, I'm a designer. I'm someone who's very aware of irrational behavior. I know how it works. I've read so much about the brain and psychology. I've followed the advice of many of my favorite authors: everything from getting a devil's advocate to letting my initial reactions simmer. But I still feel that this is the wrong direction. I must be right. Right?" Of course, I concurred with myself.

I then quickly decided that I had to save the day, and committed the ultimate designer faux pas: I started working on a color comp myself.

Eagleman was twitching somewhere in the distance as, in one swift moment, all of my knowledge escaped my awareness. But what's truly frightening is that this occurs far more often than most of us know, and this is by design. It is quintessentially human.

And nothing exposes this elegant flaw better than a seemingly unrelated fact about ourselves: most of us can't draw.

IN ORDER TO LEARN TO DRAW, YOU MUST LEARN TO SEE

"I can't draw," said my wife plainly. "Well, I can draw stick figures, but that's about it. But sure, I'll give it a try." I had suggested that we work our way through the world's most widely used drawing instruction book, Betty Edwards' modern classic, *Drawing on the Right Side of the Brain*. Most of us can relate to my wife's words because most of us can't draw any better than the neighbor's kid. And the prevailing belief around why we can't draw is that the ability to draw is an innate gift: something we're born with. But Edwards vehemently disagrees with this theory.

Instead, she believes that anyone can learn to draw realistically with a little instruction. She's proven this an infinite number of times through her books and courses. Edwards writes, "A beginning drawing student asked to draw a frontal view of a chair often distorts the retinal image of the chair seat into a fully round or square shape, even through the retinal image of the seat is a narrow, horizontal shape." She identifies the culprit behind this phenomenon as a core neural process known as size constancy: a process that ensures that our perceptions of objects are relatively constant irrespective of their true distance from the retina. Without size constancy we wouldn't be able to identify an elephant on the horizon from its tiny silhouette. "Size constancy can muddle perception by actually overriding direct information that hits the retina, causing us to 'see' images that fit pre-existing knowledge," continues Edwards[12].

A chair drawn with proper perspective (left); a chair drawn under the influence of size constancy (right).

---

12 Betty Edwards, "The Constancies: Seeing and Believing", Color: A Course in Mastering the Art of Mixing Colors, 23 Sep 2004, p. 8.

In fact, when we attempt to draw the chair, it is our pre-existing knowledge deliberately sabotaging our hand. Edwards continues, "The left hemisphere (of the brain) has no patience with this detailed perception and says, in effect, it's a chair, I tell you. That's enough to know. In fact, don't bother to look at it, because I've got a ready-made symbol for you. Here it is; add a few details if you want, but don't bother me with this looking business."

The key to Edwards' drawing instruction method is that she focuses on teaching her students how to temporarily turn off visual processes like size constancy. Put another way, Edwards teaches her students how to see what is rather than what their brain thinks is. There's a subtle, but profound difference between the two, one that some individuals often stumble upon naturally. For the rest of us, there's Edwards' method. It is so effective that my wife was able to dramatically improve her self-portrait after following just a few pieces of advice in Edwards' book.

My wife's first attempt at a self-portrait (left); my wife's attempt at a self-portrait after 15 minutes of instruction from Edwards' book (right).

Now consider that size constancy is just one of thousands of silent neurological and physiological processes that are involved in the proper functioning of the human being. And, unlike size constancy, we don't have the ability to access them or turn them off. In fact, our proper functioning relies on these processes working non-stop behind the scenes. When combined with our own personal experiences, these processes play a major role in shaping our reality: a reality that, even if we pass the Sally–Anne test by the time we're five, often remains unfathomably distorted and, more importantly, uniquely our own.

Unfortunately, Project Redo was a runaway train at this point, and there was nobody around to help my brain make the cognitive shift it needed to see reality for what it truly was.

SAVING THE DAY

In *The Honest Truth About Dishonesty: How We Lie to Everyone—Especially Ourselves*, Ariely writes about the prevailing economic model for cheating and lying known as SMORC: simple model of rational crime. He writes, "We all seek our own advantage as we make our way through the world. Whether we do this by robbing banks or writing books is inconsequential to our rational calculations of costs and benefits." But this doesn't quite paint the entire picture. "How can we secure the benefits of cheating and at the same time still view ourselves as honest, wonderful people?" he challenges. "This is where our amazing cognitive flexibility comes into play. Thanks to this human skill, as long as we cheat only a little bit, we can benefit from cheating and still view ourselves as marvelous human beings. This balancing act is the process of rationalization, and it is the basis of what we'll call the fudge factor theory."[13]

Along these lines, when I posted my own design to the Project Redo Basecamp a few hours after I started working on it, I titled the message with the auspicious and rather obnoxious, "A Fresh Direction." In it I waxed poetic about the strengths of this new design and why it was the right way forward (acknowledging, of course, that I could be completely wrong with my assessment).

By now, my brain had constructed an elaborate story about the entire situation, and thanks to the fudge factor I had given myself the part of the

---

13 Dan Ariely, "Testing the Simple Model of Rational Crime (SMORC)", The Honest Truth About Dishonesty: How We Lie to Everyone—Especially Ourselves, 18 June 2013, p. 17.

protagonist. I was the hero who, after much contemplation and tribulation, was going to save this project. I had to do what I had to do, but it was for a good cause, I reasoned.

In hindsight, the six hours I spent working on my concept didn't hold a candle to Dave's entire week of hard work. Dave must have seen that immediately when he held my design up next to his, but decided to remain silent. Instead, he did what we often do when faced with confrontation in the design process: he tried to salvage the situation by suggesting that he take a crack at combining our designs. I didn't particularly like the idea, but didn't quite respond with that. I avoided confrontation as well. The neocortex had stepped in for us both, but it was a little too late. I said, "OK, let's give it a shot."

We didn't make it past two Frankenstein versions of the design. By then, there was a tinge of undeniable awkwardness in the air, and we both knew that the project had gone off the rails. We decided to chat on the phone. I finally admitted, "Dave, I don't think this is working out. No hard feelings, but I think I'd like to take over the visual design." But this time Dave surprised me by pushing back. "Nishant, I think my second concept was the best one. I even showed another designer the two designs side-by-side, and he agreed," he said. He shared the name of the other designer, a well-known veteran whom I respected.

I felt like the wind had been knocked out of me. In an accidental moment of clarity, I responded, "I think I should take myself out of the decision-making process." Dave, shocked, agreed. We hung up. Dave had stuck his neck out, and I respected that. But I still couldn't see what he could see. I could even admit that maybe my design wasn't the right one. But I couldn't see how his was.

As it turns out, willing ourselves to *see* the world differently has some unfortunate hard limits. And it provides the final clue to the source of our woes.

SEEING IS BELIEVING ISN'T SEEING

Optical illusions provide a great example of our limitations.[14] My personal favorite is the checkershadow illusion first developed by MIT researcher Edward Adelson.[15] The illusion here involves deciphering the colors of the squares marked A and B in the left image of figure 7. When asked, participants (including you) will indicate that A is dark gray, while B is light gray. The squares, in fact, are the same shade of gray. And this becomes clear as day when you connect the two squares with a solid gray rectangle as shown in the right image. But the best part of this illusion is yet to come.

If you take the gray rectangle away (look back at the left figure), it's as if we're stupid again. No matter how hard we try, we see the two squares as entirely different shades of gray.

Despite the fact that our visual system — more than thirty different parts of the brain dedicated to helping us see — is about the most anatomically sophisticated part of the human body, we are predictably fooled over and over again by optical illusions like Adelson's checkershadow. In *Predictably Irrational*, Ariely wonders how often, then,

---

14   Dan Ariely at EG '08 Podcast, FORA.tv.
15   Edward Adelson, Checkershadow Illusion.

must we be predictably fooled in areas where the brain provides no specialized help? Like making financial decisions? Or, a little closer to home, recognizing a great design as *great*?

Ariely's research deals with discovering and documenting these so-called *illusions of the mind*, more formally known as *cognitive biases*. Anchoring is but one of hundreds of cognitive biases that exist in human beings. Once you've read these findings, it becomes virtually impossible to view the world, and yourself, the same way again. In one sense, it's a relief to have scientific explanations for some of life's troubles. But in a different sense, you are confronted with how much you don't know about the world, how much you take for granted, and how fallible we are as human beings.

Back on Project Redo, I was starting to get convinced of my own fallibility in the situation. I sent the two designs for a blind vote to the rest of my team adding no context other than, "Here are two options for the design. Pick the one you like the most." All five of my team members voted for Dave's design. The decision was clear to me even if I couldn't understand it. I was Adelson's smirking revenge. I couldn't see the squares as the same color no matter how hard I tried, yet I knew they were the same color. So, I made the call.

"We're going to move forward with yours, Dave. Thanks for sticking your neck out there," I posted on Basecamp. Dave was elated. Three weeks later we finished the website and it received much fanfare. It was a hit with the community, was featured on several design showcases, and even won a few prestigious awards. Dave maintains that it remains one of his best portfolio pieces even today.

And for me, it remains an undying reminder of my own irrationality.

And... Scene

As I look back to my first true encounter with workplace dysfunction — my episode with Prakash and team — I can't help but wonder what I would have done differently then had I the knowledge I have now.

Over the past few years, I've had the pleasure (and pain) of discovering a whole new side of humans. By applying the work of folks like the Brafman brothers, Ramachandran, Eagleman, Gigerenzer, Edwards, Ariely and many others to the world of design collaboration, I've been able to navigate through many tricky situations, and have also been able to develop a whole new set of seemingly counter-intuitive rules of thumb to help me along the way. To list a few (and most of these are from experiences that I haven't specifically mentioned in this chapter):

- Don't try to educate clients and stakeholders about design. Rather, spend time priming them to realize that it's not their domain.
- Never conduct a design review in a conference room with all stake-holders present together. Social conformity studies have firmly established that this approach is destined for failure. When you succeed, it's simply because statistics can be forgiving.
- If your client demands multiple versions of a design, you will improve your chances of a quick sign-off by creating three versions: two that are similar (the one you would like the client to pick needs to be better), and another that's obviously the worst and dissimilar to the pair. That said, you might be better off firing the client.
- Getting even great designers to collaborate will generally produce a design that isn't as good as that produced by an individual great designer (unless, those designers can really function as one; rare, but certainly possible). This is because you are attempting to converge independent realities and average independently great visions.
- Trying to convince someone of something that's contrary to his or her existing belief generally worsens the situation. You have to look for a subtler solution to deal with the individual.
- In most circumstances at work, praise and positive reinforcement are far better motivators than monetary or other in-kind payments.

- Stakeholders generally want to be upstanding citizens of the design process even if their behavior may seem to indicate otherwise. Learn to read between the lines to influence the natural propensity of humans to want to do good.
- The worst goal you can set for yourself is to be the best. The best goal you can set for yourself is to (always) be better. There's a subtle, but profound difference.
- Nobody is immune to irrational behavior. And no matter how much you try, you will never eliminate it in yourself or others. The best approach to dealing with irrationality is to set checks and balances in place to detect and manage it (especially for yourself). Learn to self-monitor and along the way ask yourself questions like, "Am I unknowingly in my own optical illusion right now?"
- People discount the future. That is, we are wired to be short-term thinkers. This is why promises of the long-term benefits of a design generally never serve as convincing arguments.

I have many more heuristics that I haven't listed. And it's worth pointing out that my intention for listing the above is certainly not to make you feel cheated; after all, I haven't provided relevant experiences and arguments for over half of these. Rather, my intention is to make a critical point: *while the above heuristics have served me well, they are not hard and fast rules, and I often need to break them.*

In the past few years I've become particularly passionate about spreading what I've learned. In my own little way, I've written about certain perspectives on my blog, and presented some of these concepts at conferences. During this time, I've been approached by a number of people, including a few publishers, urging me to write articles, even books about the topic. But most of these conversations quickly converge on one question: what are the best practices that can resolve these problems once and for all?

My answer has consistently been, "There aren't any." Admittedly, it's an answer that disappoints. And it may disappoint you as well. It certainly disappointed me the first time I found myself uttering those words in a Q&A after one of my talks. But this disappointment — particularly in light of what we've learned about ourselves in this chapter — is as ironic as it is paradoxical.

We don't have static best practices that always work in creating a perfect design or writing perfect code. Instead, we take all of our knowledge, skills and experiences, and apply them creatively on our projects. Each situation is different from the next. The reality is that our field — really, our world — is grossly imperfect and nothing, not the combined intellect of all its experts or the power of a thousand fire-breathing dragons, will ever change that. We are constantly updating our best practices, from those dealing with structuring markup to designing for a seemingly infinite number of devices — often finding ourselves exactly where we started. As frustrating as this is at times, we've all come to appreciate it as one of the things that make our work interesting.

In fact, it may even be the source of our happiness. As Mihaly Csikszentmihalyi suggests in his book, *Flow: The Psychology of Optimal Experience*, setting goals that are just out of reach and working towards them is the true secret to happiness. Or as Gandhi put it, "Glory lies in the attempt to reach one's goal and not in reaching it."

All that remains between you and glory is a goal.

NEXT STEPS

I believe our need to find a silver bullet for people problems stems from the very cognition that paints forgiving self-images and constructs elaborate theories about the world. But if we've learned anything in this chapter, it's that our theories and ideologies are often built on shaky foundations, informed by very little real information, and choreographed by biology beyond our conscious control. The sooner we can accept that people are like our technologies and systems — irreversibly imperfect — the sooner we can start dealing with people problems the way we deal with all our problems in life: by acquiring knowledge, practicing, analyzing and repeating.

Here are some next steps to help you on your journey:

1. *Acquire knowledge*
   I maintain a list of books and articles that have helped (and continue to help) me. This is a good place to start: http://rainypixels.com/thereadinglist.

2. *Practice*
   Aggressively look for opportunities to apply your acquired knowledge in situations at work and at play. Push yourself to step outside of your comfort zone.

3. *Analyze*
   Make a note of what worked and what didn't and thoughtfully analyze why. Look at the situation from all angles, including your own behaviors and motivations.

4. *Repeat*
   Make this a habit and an integral part of your life.

ABOUT THE AUTHOR

Nishant Kothary (@rainypixels) is a cofounder of *Minky*, a design and technology company based in Seattle. After cutting his teeth as a Program Manager at Amazon.com on projects like Instant Video & the original Kindle, Nishant honed his multidisciplinary skills at Microsoft as a Web Strategist. His writings and work have been featured in UXMag, Smashing Magazine and A List Apart.

ABOUT THE REVIEWER

Kristen Berman is a co-founder of *Irrational Labs*. Kristen founded the largest behavioral economics conference, StartupOnomics, and currently consults at Google, Intuit and a variety of Startups that are trying to change the world for the better.

ABOUT THE REVIEWER

Before starting *Minky* with her husband, *Kalpita Kothary* spent close to a decade at Microsoft where she managed the team responsible for one of the top 50 web sites in the world and helped oversee the responsive redesign of Microsoft's home page.

ABOUT THE REVIEWER

Joshua Allen has been addicted to the quirky collection of hacks known as "the web". Over his career, he's served as developer lead and program manager for XML APIs and MSN, helped co-found *MIX Online*, and more. He takes pride in using a wide variety of industrial-strength tools to clean up messes.

Chapter

13

On Creative Spirit

Written by Christopher Murphy

CHAPTER THIRTEEN · BY CHRISTOPHER MURPHY

ON CREATIVE SPIRIT

W HEN EMBARKING ON NEW PROJECTS we often find ourselves confronted by intense pressure to deliver something – *anything!* – in as short a time frame as possible. All too often the client needs it tomorrow, or better still yesterday, certainly by the end of the week! (And, guess what, today's Thursday.)

Faced with unyielding, unrealistic deadlines we buckle under the weight of expectation and find ourselves looking for shortcuts. Before we know it, we're taking the path of least resistance to new ideas, which, as a consequence, often aren't new ideas at all, merely recycled ones from the folder of abandoned past projects.

When time is short and budgets are tight we turn immediately to our computers in an effort to realize an idea as quickly as possible. The computer, however, is the last place we should look. History shows us that ideas are all around us and if we choose to widen our frame of reference and expand our field of vision, even just a little, we'll find them quite quickly.

STOP! Take a deep breath. Let's rediscover what an ideas culture is really all about and, along the way, remind ourselves that it's about stepping back from the digital world of ones and zeros and, instead, looking towards the analogue world of dusty libraries and aroma-filled coffee shops.

So, how do you establish an idea generation culture? How do you open the proverbial floodgates and unleash an endless supply of new and original ideas? Is it possible to adopt strategies that allow us to reliably generate meaningful ideas, which we can then execute skillfully? I believe, by adopting a simple mental framework and embracing a core set of strategies, it is.

I believe the process involves three factors: first, priming the brain; second, empowering a conductor or orchestrator of ideas; and third, considering space as a facilitator.

The first part of the idea-generation equation lies in ensuring the brain is sustained and regularly nurtured with knowledge, keeping it well stocked with fuel. The second part of the equation lies in finding a conductor to enable primed brains to work well in harmony. The third part of the equation lies in encouraging chance collisions, facilitating the regular collision of primed brains with one another. When these parts of the equation come together, ideas flow in abundance.

PUTTING THEORY INTO PRACTICE

Don't take my word for it, however — many successful companies adopt much the same process. As we'll see through a series of examples later in this chapter, world-class companies like Apple, Pixar and Google employ similar strategies to ensure that their companies are overflowing with great ideas. Let's take a look at one example in a little more detail.

You may or may not have heard of 3M, but you'll most certainly have heard of its many innovative products. Post-it notes and Scotch Tape are just two of a seemingly endless series of ideas which grew out of 3M's creative approach to building an ideas culture and allowing innovation to flourish.

We've all heard of Google's "20 percent time" — it's lead to a wealth of interesting ideas. When Google was just a star in the sky, however, 3M was embracing the benefits of flexible working that its very own 15 percent time offered. Believing that "creativity needs freedom", 3M has offered this "dream day[1]" as time to explore and space to reflect, since 1948 — a remarkably open-minded approach if you stop to consider it. Encouraging employees to spend 15% of their working time on their own projects, the company also offers resources to staff and grants them licence to self-organize and build their own teams. This approach enables 3M's people "to follow their own insights in pursuit of problem-solving."

As the company puts it:[2]

In today's fast-paced, pressure-packed business climate, many companies take a very short-term approach to the new product development pipeline. Because innovation does not occur on a set timeline, 3M takes a different path — thanks in large part to the principles that former CEO, William L. McKnight instilled in the company. McKnight believed in the imperatives of hiring the right people, tolerating mistakes and giving employees freedom to explore in order to foster a culture of innovation. 3M has put the McKnight Principles into practice by encouraging employees to dedicate a significant portion of their time to projects and research that go beyond their core responsibilities. Although it may take years for such innovative "tinkering" to bear fruit, the results of 3M's storied 15 Percent Time are truly remarkable. Examples include Scotch® Brand Tapes, Post-it® Notes, Scotchgard™ Fabric Protector[...]

If you break the McKnight Principles down into their constituent parts, you might notice the same three factors outlined earlier, factors that lead towards ideas and innovation: allow people to tinker and learn new things (in short, give them the space to prime their brains); allow people

---

1   http://solutions.3m.com/innovation/en_US/stories/time-to-think
2   http://smashed.by/3m

to self-organise and manage themselves, enabling them to form ad hoc teams that bring together the pieces of the jigsaw (in short, allow conductors to orchestrate teams to create wonderful things); and finally, allow for serendipitous meetings that potentially lead to new discoveries (in short, encourage chance collisions).

As we can see from this example (and as you probably know from your own experience), ideas, contrary to popular opinion, are relatively easy to come by; it's the *execution* of ideas through a meaningful and thorough implementation that's the hard part. Set aside time for idea generation and you should find an endless supply of ideas flowing, far too many to implement; the hard part really lies in deciding where to apply resources to develop these ideas. Let's get started and take a look at the three aspects of idea generation, outlined above, in a little more detail.

Priming the Brain

To foster a culture of idea generation, we need to promote a hunger for information. Such a process shouldn't just happen at the start of a project, it should occur all the time. A naturally inquisitive mind will be forever overflowing with ideas. The primary task we have to accomplish, then, is to get the brain in the right place.

One simple strategy to encourage more ideas? Read more, and read widely.

There are a number of excellent books on ideas and where they come from. Two that should be at the top of any self-respecting designer's list are Scott Berkun's *The Myths of Innovation* and James Webb Young's *A Technique for Producing Ideas*. Both are worth their proverbial weight in gold and will pay for themselves many times over. Perhaps unsurprisingly, both follow similar pathways, proposing models which — if adhered to — lead inevitably to an endless supply of ideas.

THE MYTHS OF INNOVATION

Berkun's *The Myths of Innovation* from 2007 demystifies the myths often
conjured up to explain innovation. As Berkun puts it, "Ideas never stand
alone"; the ideas we remember are always the product of other ideas and
inventions. Break any idea down (let's say, Twitter and Instagram) and
you'll find other ideas (SMS text messaging and Polaroid photography,
respectively). The accepted wisdom that these ideas are the result of divine
inspiration, appearing fully formed from nowhere, is a million miles from
reality. In fact, they're the result of inquisitive minds that see new connections or see old patterns repeating themselves in new ways.

Berkun uses the idea of a jigsaw to explain the moment of epiphany,
which, rather than a result of divine intervention, is really the moment at
which you see all the pieces of the jigsaw fall into place clearly. As he puts it:

> One way to think about epiphany is to imagine working on a jigsaw puzzle.
> When you put the last piece into place, is there anything special about that
> last piece...? The only reason that last piece is significant is because of the other
> pieces you already put into place. If you jumbled up the pieces a second time, any
> one of them could turn out to be the last, magical piece.

So, where do the pieces of the jigsaw come from?

In short, you develop some of the pieces of the jigsaw yourself (through
experimentation and prototyping), but other critical pieces of the jigsaw
are already out there. You learn to see those other pieces of the jigsaw by
reading widely, exploring unfamiliar and challenging themes, and maintaining a curious mind. Constantly interrogating the world, offline and
online, is critical. The jigsaw pieces are everywhere, they're all around you;
you just need to learn to see them.

Let's take a jigsaw and break it apart.

The iPhone. A beautiful jigsaw that has been through a lengthy and ever-inventive series of iterations, at every turn revealing imaginative and exciting new ideas. When Steve Jobs unveiled it for the first time on June 29, 2007, we were mesmerized. We marvelled, not only at Jobs's charismatic showmanship – "There's just one more thing...." – but also at the magical device he held in his hand. Jobs, ever the impresario, stated:

> *Every once in a while a revolutionary product comes along that changes everything.*

It was, of course, revolutionary and it certainly changed everything. Had it really appeared, however, fully formed from nowhere? A moment of divine inspiration? Of course not. It was the product of other ideas, themselves the product of other ideas, themselves the product of other ideas...

If we interpret the iPhone as a jigsaw using Berkun's metaphor, we see a huge number of technologies coming together. What was remarkable about Jobs's "revolutionary product" was the way it took so many existing ideas, each one a myriad of complexity, and wove them together seemingly effortlessly to create a product we had never seen before — and yet we had seen, in its constituent parts many times before.

Here lies the allure of invention. We see a radically new product and it seems at once unimaginable, and yet so right and so obvious.

Let's examine the pieces of the iPhone jigsaw in a little more detail, exploring how each one of the ideas that came together to form the iPhone is itself the product of other ideas. At the most abstract level, the iPhone weaves together a core set of ideas: the original iPod, itself the product of many other ideas, not least Sony's Walkman; the telephone, stemming from mobile devices of the time (which themselves follow a long line of ideas right back to Alexander Graham Bell — who would, I'm sure, have loved an iPhone, perhaps in return for his earlier ideas which helped bring it into being); the camera, with its own long line of precursors; and the list goes on. Everything, in short, is made from other things.

A TECHNIQUE FOR PRODUCING IDEAS

Funnily enough, Berkun's *The Myths of Innovation* is also the product of other ideas. In the true spirit of academia, which stands on the shoulders of giants more often than you would imagine, Berkun's 2007 book echoes many of the themes of a much slimmer volume published some four decades earlier, James Webb Young's *A Technique for Producing Ideas* from 1965. (A personal recommendation: if you buy just one book to improve your ability to generate ideas, make it Young's.)

Honored as 'Advertising Man of the Year' in 1946, Young (1886–1973) was an award-winning advertising executive who wrote perhaps one of the most influential books on generating ideas; certainly one of the most concise and no-nonsense in approach. Drawn from his own wealth of experience and voracious appetite for knowledge, *A Technique for Producing Ideas* is a short, sharp and extremely valuable treatise on the process of generating ideas.

Young's process is a simple one, centering on "training the mind" by filling it with an ever-ready supply of raw material. From this fuel, as he puts it, ideas form, which are, unsurprisingly, "combinations of old ideas." Young cites noted sociologist, economist and philosopher Vilfredo Pareto (1848–1923) as an influence in his thinking (you may have heard of him via the Pareto Principle, also known as the 80–20 rule). In a chapter called "The Pareto Theory", Young refers to Pareto's thinking, writing:

Pareto thought that all the world could be divided into two main types of people. These types he called, in the French in which he wrote, the "Speculator" and the "Rentier".

In this classification speculator is a term used somewhat in the sense of our word 'speculative.' The speculator is the speculative type of person and the distinguishing characteristic of this type, according to Pareto, is that he is constantly preoccupied with the possibilities of new combinations.

Young summarises this thinking through two principles, as follows: first, "an idea is nothing more nor less than a *new combination* of old elements." Second, "the capacity to bring old elements into new combinations depends largely on the ability to see relationships."

Astute readers will clearly see that one of Berkun's central premises, that ideas never stand alone, echoes one of Young's central principles, that all ideas are combinations of old ideas. This, in turn, echoes one of Pareto's central arguments, that those who have the ability to conjure up ideas are "constantly preoccupied with the possibilities of new combinations."

Three astute thinkers, whose ideas are all, appropriately, an amalgam of other ideas. Coincidence? Highly unlikely. Although Berkun, Young and Pareto share a common language in their articulation of this central thesis — that all ideas are made of other ideas — it is, for me, Young who most clearly articulates the clearest model for applying this thinking in a creative context in the service of reliable idea discovery.

Let's look in a little more detail at Young's core technique, which forms the backbone of a five stage process that can be used to generate ideas. As Young puts it:

> *This technique of the mind follows five steps. I am sure you will recognise them individually, but the important thing is to recognise their relationship and to grasp the fact that the mind follows these five steps in definite order — that by no possibility can one of them be taken before the preceding one is completed, if an idea is to be produced.*

Young's five stages can be essentially labelled as follows:

1. Gather raw material.
2. Masticate.
3. Drop everything and walk away.
4. Marvel as, out of nowhere, an idea materializes.
5. Weigh the idea up the morning after.

The first stage — *gathering raw material* — is easy; and yet, as Young points out in his book, it's so easy it's hard. Sagely, he states: "Gathering raw material is not as simple as it sounds. It's such a terrible chore that we are constantly trying to dodge it." In my experience, this stage is by far the most difficult; it requires the discipline to take time out of work and exercise the mind. Sadly, far too few enjoy exercise, and even fewer enjoy exercising the mind. Why not buck the trend, take the plunge and give your mind a workout?

Believe me, it will thank you for it.

All too often we bypass stage one, the raw material phase, because we're in a headlong rush to complete all manner of tasks at hand. Failing to realize the importance of priming our brains with an ever-ready supply of fuel, we leave our brains undernourished and unable to conjure up new connections (no new fuel, no mastication). In short, we have too few jigsaw pieces to hand, and with the same short supply of jigsaw pieces, we end up creating the same jigsaws. Primed with a rich supply of raw material, the process of mastication can begin.

The second stage — *masticate* — is an important one. Turning ideas over in your mind, looking at them from different angles and seeking relation-ships between them, helps you see the world and its possible connections in new and exciting ways. As Young puts it: "What you are seeking now is the relationship, a synthesis where everything will come together in a neat combination like a jigsaw puzzle."

As Young points out, the second stage can often be confused for absent-mindedness as, lost in thought, ideas churning in your mind, you drift off. At this point you'll find that fragments or, as Young puts it, "partial ideas" begin to surface. Get these down on paper, no matter how inconsequential or absurd they may seem. The act of writing them down rewires your brain and subtly sows the seeds for the next important phase.

The third stage — *dropping everything and walking away* — is often the hardest. Pressed by deadlines, we hurriedly reach for solutions too early; a far better approach is to allow our thoughts to gestate, to ferment a little, like a fine wine or a well-aged whiskey. To stress the importance of this stage, Young uses the example of Sherlock Holmes who understands more deeply than his assistant Dr Watson that for an idea or a solution to appear, you must walk away, take a break and let the unconscious take over. Where Watson would rather work the case night and day, Holmes knows that a trip to the theatre will almost certainly lead to the answers that are eluding you.

The fourth stage — *marvel as, out of nowhere, an idea materializes* – is, one would hope, an experience all creative people have had. By giving ourselves some breathing room we find solutions bubble naturally to the surface, as stage three (the trip to the theatre) works its magic. This is why we often hear of creative people having a "Eureka!" moment in the shower (or, so I've heard, in the bath).

The fifth and final stage — *critically assessing the idea* after the rush of imagining — is the moment of truth, or what Linds Redding calls *The Overnight Test*[3], the point in the cold, gray dawn of the morning at which you take your new idea out and test it against reality. As Young wisely puts it: "In this stage you have to take your little newborn idea out into the world of reality. When you do, you usually find that it is not quite the marvelous child it seemed when you first gave birth to it."

It's critical, in this final phase, to share your idea widely. Don't hold back — put it up for scrutiny and encourage constructive criticism. If the idea doesn't survive, better to repeat the process (back to stage one) in the quest for a newer and more robust concept. I'll leave the last word to Young, who states:

> Do not make the mistake of holding your idea close to your chest at this stage. Submit it to the criticism of the judicious. When you do, a suprising thing will happen. You will find that a good idea has, as it were, self-expanding qualities. It stimulates those who see it to add to it. Thus possibilities in it which you have overlooked will come to light.

3   http://j.mp/ashortlessoninperspective

This is the process: it's easy, but like every seemingly simple thing, it's really quite difficult. Learn the process. Apply it. Repeat it. Practice it. It will, I believe, serve you well; it has so served me.

With the weight of evidence (gathered by Pareto, Young and Berkun) revealing that raw material is where new ideas emerge from, it becomes self-evident that we need to put in place strategies and techniques to gather ideas. You'll not be surprised to discover that there are a number of tried-and-tested approaches, not least the scrapbook or sketchbook (and their digital equivalents) to do just this. Press them into service and all will be well.

STRATEGIES

I'd like to suggest three techniques you can adopt to prime the brain with raw material.

1. Libraries
2. Sketchbooks and scrapbooks
3. A digital toolbelt

Libraries... Who Knew?

Use them! Libraries contain a wealth of knowledge — much, much more than we have available at our fingertips through search engines. Libraries encourage chance discovery, serendipitous unearthings when you happen on a bookshelf rich with potential. Search engines, on the other hand, are self-selecting: a predictable world filtered by Google. Search for a term and find an algorithmically ranked selection merely; there's very little luck involved at all. (And luck, in this case, sets you apart.)

Learn to love dusty, musty libraries. There you'll find ideas aplenty, setting you apart from your peers who remain reliant on the same old digital sources. If you're in the unfortunate situation of lacking a neighborhood library, fear not — book shops make a good susbtitute and if they're secondhand bookshops, all the better!

Keep a Sketchbook or Scrapbook to Hand

Sketchbooks and scrapbooks promise an endless supply of inspiration; you simply have to fill them. Always — always! — carry a sketchbook and a pen. Although it seems that the very best ideas are scribbled on the back of a beermat or a napkin, carrying your thinking utensils should be second nature.

The more you use your sketchbook, the less precious you'll find yourself becoming. Sketching isn't about being an excellent draughtsman, it's about synthesizing and processing your thoughts and ideas, as Jason Santa Maria summarises nicely in his article "Pretty Sketchy[4]": "Sketchbooks are not about being a good artist, they're about being a good thinker."

Wear a Digital Toolbelt

The last maneuvre to make (*after* you've embraced the offline tools) is to fit yourself with a bespoke digital toolbelt. We're blessed with a cornucopia of tools at our disposal, like Gimme Bar[5], Instapaper[6], Instagram[7], and even our old friend RSS, which offer us ready methods of gathering and saving raw material. Equipping your digital toolbelt will fill those moments on the go and enable you to repurpose downtime (bus queues, short trips, dull or never-ending meetings), enabling you to add yet more jigsaw pieces to your EndlessJigsawPuzzleBox™. Remember, more raw material equals more new combinations.

Choose a Conductor

With a collection of primed brains in place we can begin to orchestrate them, coaxing even greater ideas from their collective consciousness. When we embrace the opportunities that arise when harnessing a hive

---

4 http://j.mp/jasonisprettysketchy
5 https://gimmebar.com
6 http://www.instapaper.com/
7 http://instagram.com

mind, we begin to generate ideas that are greater than the sum of their parts. It's simple Gestalt where 1 + 1 + 1 = 5.

In order to avoid cacophony, it helps to have a conductor to hand to orchestrate everything, ensuring everyone works together in harmony. Your conductor might be a figure cast in the Steve Jobs mould, manipulating the action according to a grand, singular vision; or they could be a low- to mid-level team leader, or series of leaders occupying a leadership role that passes between them, designed to encourage new reactions between your primed brains. Think of the conductor as a catalyst, bringing disparate elements into contact with one another and facilitating a reaction between them to create something new.

The conductor doesn't have to be the most senior person to hand. Indeed, turning the organizational hierarchy upside down on occasion can lead to radical new thinking. Put the secretaries in charge for a day and you'll be surprised at the wisdom they can share through their own unique worldview (a worldview you might have forgotten in your relentless rise to the top).

History provides many examples of great conductors, most recently Steve Jobs at Apple (and NeXT); John Lasseter at Pixar; David Kelley at IDEO; and many, many more. Two that bear exploring in a little more detail, for different reasons, are Tony Fadell and Thomas Edison, known as 'The Podfather' and 'The Wizard of Menlo Park', respectively. Both tell us stories about the various roles the conductor can play in helping to organize and shape teams, to extract the maximum value from the creative spirit on hand. In Fadell's case, we learn that sometimes the right conductor for the task at hand is an outside hire, someone beyond the existing team. From Edison we learn that sometimes the conductor's skill lies in simply stepping back and acting as the guiding hand for others, getting the right teams in place and allowing them to discover (and marvelling as you witness, and patent, what they do).

Under the guidance of a conductor, we can end up with wonderful music. Without one there may just be sound and fury, signifying nothing.

THE PODFATHER

You may or may not have heard of Tony Fadell, but you'll certainly have heard of the iconic product he championed and helped to shape: the iPod. A virtuoso conductor, and a true gentleman too, he was the ideal candidate to manage Apple's iPod development team.

In his biography of Steve Jobs, Walter Isaacson underlines the importance the iPod had for Jobs in late 2000. Frustrated with existing portable music players (he thought they all "truly sucked"), Jobs was keen for Apple to create the portable music player others just couldn't. Working with Jon Rubinstein, Jobs set about finding the right person to lead the development team.

Fadell, just 21 years old at the time, had the perfect track record. Having started three companies while still at the University of Michigan, he had spent time working at the handheld device maker General Magic before spending some time at Philips. Fadell had a number of ideas for creating a better digital music player, but had been unsuccessful pitching these to RealNetworks, Sony and Philips.

One day, while skiing, he got the call. As Isaacson puts it:

> Rubinstein told him that Apple was looking for someone who could work on a 'small electronic device'. Fadell, not lacking in confidence, boasted that he was a wizard at making such devices.

A wizard *and* a conductor... the rest is history.

Fadell's story centers around getting the right brains in place — bringing together the right people. It serves to demonstrate that priming the brain is only the first part of the equation.

Fadell's story is an interesting one. (If you get the chance to hear him speak, clear your diary as he's a deeply engaging presenter.) During his initial period working on the development of the iPod, Fadell was an independent contractor; only later, under pressure, did he join Apple permanently. This underlines the fact that a conductor need not always be a CEO; nor do they even need to be a full-time employee to shape a vision and coordinate a team. Under intense pressure from Jobs to deliver an iPod in time for Christmas, Fadell looked beyond Apple's internal teams to identify external talent. This ability, to identify the best team members — the right primed brains — and bring them in to assist on the task at hand is what a great conductor possesses. Need a new drummer to add another dimension to your sound? There are talented session musicians aplenty; use them.

It's Fadell's lateral thinking — recasting the team members — that's interesting. Lateral thinking, a phrase coined by Edward de Bono in 1967, is another term the idea-hunter should understand:

> With logic you start out with certain ingredients, just as in playing chess you start out with given pieces [...] Lateral thinking is concerned not with playing with the existing pieces but with seeking to change those very pieces.

Fadell arguably took this a stage further, changing not only the pieces, but the players in the game playing with those pieces.

Pulling together a carefully selected range of players from different teams and then using their hive mind to conjure up ideas can prove incredibly powerful and it lies at the heart of companies like Apple, Google and many other giants of innovation. Drawing from a rich gene pool of talent and seeking new combinations of assembled ideas can very quickly result in an abundance of riches.

Get a number of people together in a room, equipped with Sharpies and flip charts, give yourself a limited amount of time (half an hour should prove more than enough), and you'll be surprised at the results a few well-chosen people can generate. The key is to work fast, pursue divergent thinking and not inhibit anyone's creativity. With a conductor in control guiding the process, ideas will be flowing in no time.

Of course, your choice of conductor will influence matters immensely, so how do you select the right conductor? I believe it's important to let go a little and explore. The conductor needn't always be the most senior member present, indeed, if that member is worthy of their seniority, they'll understand that empowering others and letting them take the baton can have surprising and often game-changing results.

Try rotating the baton and let every member of the team conduct a passage, for short, sharp periods of differing inputs. You'll soon find that in most of your team members – if you offer them encouragement – lies the ability to stir a rousing number.

Let go, listen to the conductor, and just start playing.

THE WIZARD OF MENLO PARK

An inventor, businessman and school dropout, Thomas Edison (1847–1931), is perhaps best known for his prodigious inventions, including: the phonograph (a little similar to an iPod, only older and – well – different); the motion picture camera; and, of course, the electric light bulb.

But it is Edison's approach to team management and coordination that remains perhaps his most interesting, if often overlooked, achievement.

Nicknamed 'The Wizard of Menlo Park', Edison was one of the first businessmen to apply the principles of mass production and large-scale teamwork to the process of invention. He is perhaps one of the first true conductors, leading a team of scientists and researchers at his "invention factory" at Menlo Park Laboratory, widely considered to be the world's first industrial research laboratory. As Edison's long-standing assistant, Francis Jehl, put it: "Edison is in reality a collective noun and means the work of many men."

By creating a laboratory that was filled with all the materials necessary — as Edison put it: "a stock of almost every conceivable material" —

to spark new ideas, Edison was able to amass a huge portfolio of patents. According to Rutgers, The State University of New Jersey, Edison held 1,093 successful US patents and well in excess of a thousand patents beyond the US. The sheer number of patents Edison registered is striking, and proof that his applied research laboratory had no shortage of ideas. His patents are available to peruse at Rutgers' fascinating archive[8] and they individually represent facets of the process of invention and are a window into a world filled with fascinating ideas. Collectively they comprise Edison's true calling, as a leader and orchestrator of extremely intelligent individuals.

Edison's talent lay in surrounding himself with highly primed minds, with whom he could have interesting and wide-ranging discussions, which sparked new ideas by virtue of dialogue and exchange. Edison filed numerous patents for separate, exploratory ideas that cumulatively lead to the light bulb he is credited for. In each case, teams of researchers worked to create and refine, orchestrated by him. Edison showed that successful ideas are collaborative in nature and a good conductor can deliver greatness simply by understanding and harnessing that.

In fact, and contrary to popular opinion, Edison did not invent the first electric light bulb, but instead invented the first commercially practical incandescent light. (The words "commercially practical" are guaranteed to appeal to any self-respecting business person.) Numerous earlier inventors had devised incandescent lamps, including Alessandro Volta's demonstration of a glowing wire in 1800 (over eight decades before Edison's patent).

These early bulbs suffered from varying flaws — extremely short life spans, high production costs, and a need for high electric currents — making them difficult to apply on a large scale commercially. After many experiments with platinum and other metal filaments, Edison returned to a carbon filament. It was not until several months after the patent was granted that Edison and his team discovered a carbonized bamboo filament that could last over 1,200 hours.

---

8   http://edison.rutgers.edu/patents.htm

What prompted Edison to consider bamboo?

The idea of using bamboo originated from Edison's recollection of examining a few threads from a bamboo fishing pole, while relaxing on a trip. Astute readers will, of course, see in this a clear resonance of the importance of priming the brain. The bamboo was the missing piece of the jigsaw and, as always seems to be the case in such discoveries, wasn't a piece of the jigsaw supplied in the 'Create a Light Bulb' puzzle box.

STRATEGIES

Here are three techniques you can adopt to maximize idea returns by exploring ways of shaping and rethinking teams on the fly.

1. Find square pegs for round holes
2. Reverse the hierarchy
3. Ban the culture of "They"

Find Square Pegs for Round Holes

Sometimes it helps to find someone who doesn't quite fit neatly into place. An outsider can offer new ways of seeing things within a discipline. If you've been trained to always do something in a particular way, it can be difficult, if not impossible, to see things from a different perspective.

One way to circumvent such behavior is to actively hire team members who don't fit. Sometimes the most valuable employee can be the one who, on the surface, appears highly unproductive, but who acts as a valuable catalyst for change. It's easy to find people who can follow instructions and get the job done on time and within budget. Creative catalysts who can disrupt innovation, however, are harder to find. If you find a perfect square peg, hang on to them — they'll more than repay you through their unique insight and perspective.

Reverse the Hierarchy

The CEO tells the CFO who queries the COO who consults the CAO...
seriously, who invents these titles? While this conversation cycles perpetu-
ally, like a scene in Dilbert's office[9], the PA shrugs and gets the job done.

If you're stuck at a creative impasse, one idea to force change is to reverse the hierarchy. Give control to those further down the pecking order.
Ask them how they would approach the task at hand — you just might be
surprised at the insight you receive. Wisdom does not always flow from
the top down and truly great leaders understand that. Switch roles from
time to time and experience life in another's shoes. You'll find the change
of perspective leads to new understanding.

Ban the Culture of "They"

If you've adopted fluid approaches to reconfiguring your team members,
embraced a culture of chance collisions and your team is working well,
the word "they" shouldn't exist. Ban phrases like, "Oh, 'they' do that job." If
everyone's pulling together, there's no reason for a "they" to exist. Who are
they anyway?

In his book *The Art of Innovation*, IDEO's Tom Kelley describes a major
transportation company that had decided to "loosen up". He writes:

> 'They' suggested there had been a lot of confusion and anxiety about what to
> wear on 'casual Fridays'. So 'they' formed a task force. 'They' issued a memo
> saying, among other things, that if you were unsure about whether something
> was appropriate [to wear] or not, it's probably not.

And so it went on... Banish "they" and, whatever you do, don't be like
them.

---

9 http://www.dilbert.com

485

Brief Encounter

We've all experienced that moment when bumping into someone in the corridor, or running into them in a coffee shop, sparks a conversation that brings together the different pieces that lead to something new. These chance collisions — when, before you know it, you're having a two-hour conversation, conjuring up plans for world domination — are where magic happens.

Companies like Google, Pixar and IDEO understand this all too well and arrange their spaces to encourage these fortuitous interactions. Power outlets in the stairwells, beanbags in open-plan spaces, seemingly un-owned desks dotted around... these are all facilitators. Good ideas need creative, chaotic environments; surroundings which aren't based on strict hierarchies; settings which embrace flexible and spontaneous workflows.

Getting the physical environment in which a team works right is a challenge. It's one that can, however, when approached intelligently, lead to a multiplication and amplification of ideas. While different people will hold different pieces of the jigsaw, truly insightful thinkers realize that only when they come together is the picture formed. The best way to do this is through shaping space to encourage brief encounters.

By designing workspaces to harness chance meetings and facilitate new patterns of work, we can ensure our primed brains collide to create unexpected ideas with potential. You don't need to have the budget of Google to put these pieces in place; you can instead foster a more freeform office culture or perhaps — heaven forfend — permit your employees to occasionally work off-campus.

It's no surprise that we're beginning to understand the creative potential of spaces to excite idea generation. After all, we now have no shortage of companies to draw inspiration from. Whether it's the giant atrium of Pixar, which Steve Jobs insisted on to encourage chance collisions, or Google's ladder chutes in its New York City offices, designed to encourage Googlers to "casually collide" throughout the working day (presumably on the way down), we have a wealth of spaces to learn from.

486

Two smaller but no less potent spaces are the d.school at the Institute of Design at Stanford, and Erik Spiekermann's innovative model for a perfect studio, the "Centralized Office", which channels all its staff purposefully past each other every day. The d.school comprises a kind of flexible space design that is slowly but surely influencing creative office designs the world over. The Centralized Office is currently just a concept, Spiekermann's idea of a perfect workspace — let's hope that he puts his enthusiasm and passion into making it a reality. I, for one, would like to visit it.

THE D.SCHOOL

The d.school[10] at the Institute of Design at Stanford has a simple manifesto, which fits neatly on the back of a napkin[11]. It reads, simply:

> *Our intent:*
> - *Create the best design school. Period.*
> - Prepare *future innovators* to be breakthrough thinkers & doers
> - Use *design thinking* to inspire multidisciplinary teams
> - Foster *radical collaboration* between students, faculty & industry
> - Tackle *big projects* and use prototyping to discover new solutions

Founded in 2004 by David Kelley, (chairman and managing partner of internationally respected multidisciplinary design firm IDEO) the d.school's approach to creative space design has informed creative spaces the world over. The d.school started in a "decrepit one-room trailer on the outskirts of Stanford's campus." Within a year it had to move to larger and larger spaces as demand for its projects and classes grew.

The school's attitude towards space as a fluid tool, designed to reshape and mould collaborative working is summarized neatly in the school's thoughts on how to "Make a Space for Innovation"[12]:

---

10 http://j.mp/thedschool
11 http://j.mp/napkinmanifesto
12 http://dschool.stanford.edu/make-a-space-for-innovation/

The d.school[...] approaches space as a tool to affect student behavior in biasing toward action[...] when manipulated intentionally, space can be used as a tool to fuel the creative process by encouraging and discouraging specific behaviors/ actions and by creating venues for emotional expression and physical nego- tiation. With this disposition, the d.school[...] explore[s] the use of artifacts, arrangements and the actual physical space of a designed environment, to support the role of space as a teacher.

Read that last phrase again: "to support the role of space as a teacher." At the d.school, space is now, rightly, a participant.

A space intended to ignite creativity, the d.school's approach (which was informed by its founder David Kelley's previous experiments with spatial design at IDEO) has filtered into other, larger creative business environments, where space is seen increasingly as a critical tool in the pro- cess of shaping ideas. Generous in spirit, the school has created a series of guides that enable you to build your own tools to shape space. Encouraging others to follow in their footsteps and create spaces that encourage open exploration and facilitate chance collisions, the d.school offers the follow- ing advice:

We think the most important factor in creating a space for innovation is to start: start small, and start now. What we learned from a year in the trailer formed the foundation of our approach to space; if we'd waited until we had a big, new building, it would have been five years before the learning process would have begun. Make your space!

The d.school's open-minded and inventive approach to space, and how it can be used as another tool in the ideas culture toolbox, manifests itself through its students' projects and their ongoing success. With its open- source DIY guides and the book *Make Space*[13] by Scott Doorley and Scott

---

13 http://dschool.stanford.edu/makespace/

488

Witthoft, its secrets aren't, in fact, secrets. You have no excuses not to pick up a copy and start to understand and unleash the creative potential of space when used well. As the d.schoolers put it: "Make your space!"

THE CENTRALIZED OFFICE

If you've ever had the pleasure of hearing Erik Spiekermann speak, you'll know that not only is he an extremely engaging and hugely knowledgeable speaker (entertainer is a far better term), but that he also has a vision for the perfect studio.

Writing in *Studio Culture: The Secret Life of the Graphic Design Studio*, design critic Adrian Shaughnessy states:

> *Unusually among contemporary designers, Spiekermann has a sophisticated set of theories relating to the layout, structure and management of design studios. His theories have been extensively roadtested in the various creative enterprises he has founded and run during a long career.*

> *During the 1970s Spiekermann worked as a freelance designer in London before returning to Berlin in 1979 where, with two partners, he founded MetaDesign. In 2001 he left MetaDesign and started UDN (United Designers Network), with offices in Berlin, London and San Francisco. Since January 2009 he has been a director of Edenspiekermann, which employs over 100 people and has offices in Berlin and Amsterdam.*

Spiekermann's Centralized Office collects his lifetime of experience running design agencies both large and small, and proposes a design for the perfect studio. The design solves numerous problems that offices routinely present, namely: different teams are all too often separated; chance collisions rarely occur; management hierarchies often (intentionally or unintentionally) lead to physical separation by rank; and many, many more.

FormFiftyFive has a wonderful video "Erik Spiekermann on the Centralised Office"[14] in which Spiekermann, in typically robust manner, follows the train of thought that lead him to his studio vision, while sketching his ideas, giving his vision form. I urge you to take ten minutes to watch it.

So, what does the office look like?

The Centralized Office is round, made up of three or four concentric circles. At its center lies a reception area, where all employees and visitors enter. By channeling everyone — employees at all levels as well as clients — through this central area, chance collisions are encouraged. Further prompting these collisions, the center of the office, its beating heart, is where "all the machinery is," as Spiekermann puts it. Chief among this machinery are the computer printers and the espresso machine. (The espresso machine is something Spiekermann feels strongly about — "Always invest in the most expensive espresso machine you can buy!". Good coffee will always get you up from your desk.)

Siting printers and coffee at the heart of the Centralized Office is a careful piece of strategic thinking, encouraging flow from the periphery of the office to its center and back again. Like Pixar's studio was creatively envisioned to "promote encounters and unplanned collaborations," the core of Spiekermann's vision serves a similar purpose, to drive everyone together.

Walter Isaacson's biography of Jobs echoes this vision. Isaacson states:

> Jobs believed that, "If a building doesn't encourage [collaboration], you'll lose a lot of innovation and the magic that's sparked by serendipity. So we designed the building to make people get out of their offices and mingle in the central atrium with people they might not otherwise see."

Brad Bird, director of "The Incredibles", says:

---

14 http://j.mp/thecentralisedoffice

The atrium initially might seem like a waste of space, but Steve realized that when people run into each other, when they make eye contact, things happen.

This understanding of facilitating brief encounters is further enhanced in the Centralized Office through the careful construction of its walls. Despite its concentric structure, the office's walls do not extend up to the ceiling. As Spiekermann puts it: "The walls are only shoulder height. If a secretary wants to see if I'm in the outer ring, she can get up and look across and see if I'm actually there."

It can't be a coincidence that these spaces, from the smaller spaces of the d.school and the Centralized Office, to the larger spaces of Apple and Pixar, encourage idea generation and idea exchange in the very fabric of their design. These are true idea factories, intended to nurture that most magical of elusive elements, the creative spark. By building spaces which encourage chance collisions we can finally pull together the three facets of the idea-generation process, nourishing and feeding the creative spirit, unlocking the ideas that lie dormant inside us. Opening the floodgates, if you will.

STRATEGIES
I'd like to suggest three techniques you can adopt to rethink how spaces are organized to contribute to an ideas culture.

1. Café culture
2. The Lego office
3. Free space

Café Culture
Break away, get out a little more and lose those punch cards. Marissa Mayer may have banned teleworking at Yahoo! (while single-handedly re-designing the company's branding), but that doesn't mean you can't loosen the ties of the workplace a little.

By arranging the occasional off-campus meeting with co-workers, you get away from your desk and unbuckle your thinking a little. Not only is this often a much-needed exercise, but it allows you to talk away from your space and break free a little. It's no surprise that we hear of startups that germinated in coffee shops; café culture not only provides free Wi-Fi, but also provides an environment away from the ever-present micro-managers who stifle creativity.

The Lego Office

Why limit yourself to the office that came off-plan, with it's off-white walls and generic carpet, when you can build your own office, large or small, as you see fit? Google understands that employees aren't one-size-fits-all by providing the building blocks — or *Bloxes* — to create the perfect office or ad hoc team-working spaces.

Bloxes[15], interlocking cardboard boxes designed to build flexible work-spaces, are the invention of Jef Raskin (who started the Macintosh project at Apple). They might not keep out the rain, but they doubtless keep out boredom.

Free Space

Resist the urge to plan every square inch of your office. Allow corners, or other open-plan spaces, to remain unfilled, with easily movable screens or whiteboards, where ad hoc teams can escape from their desks and col-laborate. No one likes a cubicle farm and you're doing your employees no favours if you build one. Free up office space and use it more flexibly; your ideas culture will improve and your team will thank you.

---

15 http://j.mp/cardboardcreativity

Conclusion

Ideas don't materialize in a vacuum. Without constant input, your outputs will inevitably remain the same. As such, it's essential to maintain an inquisitive mind, ensuring a steady flow of new triggers and stimuli that enable your thinking to evolve. Widen the idea gene pool and you'll deepen the well of ideas you are capable of creating.

Similarly, the best ideas are more often than not the result of teams that aren't afraid to reconfigure periodically (either from project to project or, if a creative dead end has been reached, mid-project, to help shake things up). Consider the role of conductors to orchestrate teams, ensuring they deliver more than the sum of their parts. If it works for companies like IDEO, which routinely reshape teams to keep inputs varied, it can work for you.

Finally, consider workspaces. You don't need to have the multi-billion dollar budget pouring in to Apple's new Cupertino campus, but that doesn't mean you can't put a little thought into how your spaces facilitate chance collisions. At the simplest level, it can just be a change of scenery, working from a coffee shop, or even the park. A change is as good as a rest and sometimes just looking at things from a different perspective — literally — can make all the difference.

Generating ideas isn't difficult, and if you follow the strategies outlined above it's very easy to stimulate a culture of ideas. All you need to do is place the pieces in an intelligent manner. Idea factories and creative idea spaces are easy to build if approached strategically. The fact that they work has been demonstrated over and over: Thomas Edison proved it at his Menlo Park Laboratory in the late 19th century; and Steve Jobs amply underscored that thinking in the early 21st century.

Allow yourself the latitude to:

1. Step away from the computer from time to time to prime the brain.
2. Choose a conductor to orchestrate everything (and don't be afraid to mix this role up from time to time).
3. Encourage chance collisions between fertile minds, by creating spaces that allow for serendipitous meetings.

Adopt these three strategies and interweave them and you'll find the rest of the pieces fall into place. It's easy — all it takes is a little hard work.

ABOUT THE AUTHOR

Christopher Murphy is a writer, designer and educator based in Belfast. Creative Review described him as, "a William Morris for the digital age," an epithet he aspires to fulfil, daily. He writes for Five Simple Steps, 8 Faces, The Manual and the typography journal *Glyph*. An internationally respected speaker, he is regularly invited to talk on a range of topics, including: *Design Education*; *Exploring How Design is Changing*; and *Growing Idea Cultures*. He has spoken at conferences worldwide, including: *Build*, *New Adventures* and at *Brooklyn Beta*.